# Introduction to Ethnic Studies

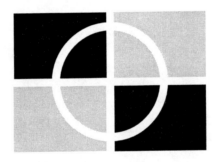

EDITED BY

Brian Baker ■ Boatamo Mosupyoe ■ Robert Muñoz, Jr. ■
Wayne Maeda ■ Eric Vega ■ Gregory Mark

*California State University—Sacramento*

KENDALL/HUNT PUBLISHING COMPANY
4050 Westmark Drive    Dubuque, Iowa 52002

# Table of Contents

## RESPONSE AND RESPONSIBILITY

## RACE, CLASS AND GENDER

# Introduction to Ethnic Studies

*Brian Baker*

Between December 15 and 28, 2003, a group of 72 Lakota people traveled more than 300 miles on horseback in the cold South Dakota winter weather.[1] Why did they do this at this time of year? These *Future Generations Riders* of Lakota traversed the same path taken by Chief Bigfoot whose goal was to find refuge among relatives on the Pine Ridge Indian Reservation. On foot, and carrying only what they could take with them, Chief Bigfoot and over 350 Lakota, mostly women, children and elders, made this journey in 1890. Many of the Lakota were weak due to illness and hunger, Chief Bigfoot himself was ill with pneumonia. Despite this, they continued walking through the winter snow because they had fled and were in search of safety.

Eventually, the U.S. Calvary caught up with this so-called band of *renegade Indians* at Wounded Knee Creek on the Pine Ridge Reservation. Completely surrounded by American troops, without weapons, and exhausted from their 300 mile trek on foot, the Indians wondered what would happen next on the morning of December 28. When a single gun shot was heard, the soldiers commenced shooting indiscriminately. The Lakota dispersed and ran in every direction. Unarmed, they were chased by soldiers on horseback. When the shooting stopped, more than a few hundred Lakota people were on the ground in an area that stretched nearly four square miles. Following this tragedy a blizzard set in and the Lakota who were not already dead were left there to die by the American military. For the Lakota who survived as witnesses to this act of terror, they had no choice but to follow a life defined by the laws and policies dictated by the American government towards American Indians.

In 2003, the descendants of those who survived the Wounded Knee massacre followed in the footsteps left by their relatives under the leadership of Chief Bigfoot in 1890. Along the way, the Lakota riders on horseback could feel the presence of their ancestors who lost their lives. The *Future Generations Riders* has become an annual journey of discovery and healing for many contemporary Lakota since 1986, an important event that includes many children. This event not only reflects the relevance of historical memory and grief to contemporary identity, it is also an example of how an ethnic group asserts identity and culture.[2]

According to Ron His Horse is Thunder, president of Sitting Bull College and one of the event organizers:

> *For 100 years, our young people have been taught that they needed to forget about being Indian in order to succeed. Today we're trying to reverse that by letting them know that our culture is important and that being Indian is a great thing. The ride is part of that process.[3]*

For the Lakota, the massacre continues to be an important memory and marker of their history and identity, and it has come to symbolize ethnic persistence and cultural pride.

Beyond holidays and other significant events that define our culture and national identity as Americans, a number of unique and culturally specific ethnic events are held around the country. In fact, it would be impossible to list all of the cultural events that acknowledge and/or celebrate various aspects of the history, culture and identity of all ethnic groups in America. Once subject to more extreme discrimination at the institutional and individual level in American history, contemporary African Americans, Asian Americans, Latino Americans and Native Americans continue to assert their ethnic identities and play an important role in the remaking of contemporary American identity and culture. While America has always been a nation marked by racial and ethnic diversity, the difference in the contemporary world is that this diversity is now recognized and sanctioned as a vital and vibrant dimension of American society. America's future seems to be one that will become even more multicultural and multilingual.

## The Dynamics of Ethnicity, Ethnocentrism and Racism

The 1960s and 1970s were important for many reasons, particularly due to the politics around race, class and gender. Before the 1960s, *institutionalized racism* supported by law and politics defined and structured race relations in America. For example, it was *politically correct* for African Americans to sit in the back of the bus or eat at separate lunch counters before the civil right movement in the American south. Americans of Asian, Latino and Native (indigenous) descent were also the targets of such racism that shaped and limited their life opportunities in terms of education, housing, and occupation, among other things. In fact, dominant ethnocentric justifications played a key role in explaining and perpetuating racial and ethnic inequality. Dominant sentiments expressed in American culture defined Native Americans as ignorant and lazy people in need of protection, a powerful idea that was sanctioned in the historical development of Federal Indian law and policy under the guise of a *guardian* to *ward* relationship. Through the Bureau of Indian Affairs, Americans presumed that dominant society was burdened with the responsibility to care for American Indians because they could not do so on their own. In fact, the *white man's burden* and *manifest destiny* were the basic tenets of American political culture that also adversely impacted the daily lives of African

Americans, Asian Americans and Latinos. However, in the face of exclusion and oppression, and even under conditions of powerlessness, ethnic minorities survived and have successfully continued to define and assert their ethnic identity.

In a society where income and occupation continue to be important factors in how Americans gain access to health, housing, and education, to name but a few, socioeconomic status plays a central role in determining quality of life. Despite positive changes in recent decades, such as the implementation of Affirmative Action law and policy, to reconfigure race and ethnic relations in the U.S., the fact is that racial socioeconomic inequality based on race remains the reality. For example, the median family income for Hispanic ($26,502) and African American ($32,180) men was far below that for white men ($44,525) in 2001.[4] Do these income differences reflect something about the continuing role of race and ethnicity in the United States? How can we explain these differences? Further, while the median family income for white women ($31,575) is above that for Hispanic ($26,502) and African American women ($27,335), comparatively, women overall still earned less when compared to men in 2001. Do the differences in median family income between men and women reflect something about the continuing significance of gender inequality in the United States? How can we account for the differences? To what extent have the dynamics of ethnic and gender inequality been altered?

## Culture, Experience and Contributions

The historical experience of African, Asian, Latino and Native Americans relative to U.S. society is necessary to sufficiently understand current events and circumstances in the dynamics of ethnic relations. Due to their own unique historical circumstances and contributions to the making of America, each group possesses its own unique culture and historical memory. At the same time, we must take note of the fact that these groups are pan-ethnic identities. For example, the Asian American population as a group reflects something about dominant ideas regarding a race while simultaneously including distinct groups. Asian American as a category of ethnicity encompasses groups that have their own culture and identity, as in the case of people of Asian Indian, Japanese, Filipino, Korean or Chinese descent. While this is not an exhaustive representation of all the distinct ethnic groups that come under the category of Asian American, there is something about American society that brings them together on some level *as* Asian American. While there is an element of experience and culture that brings a people together as Asian American on some level, it is also important to pay attention to the fact that there is a diversity in the identities of the various groups that make up Asian Americans in the U.S. This is also true for African Americans, Latino Americans, and Native Americans.

Through an understanding of their historical experience, we can also highlight the contributions that African Americans, Asian Americans, Latino Americans and Native Americans have made to America. For example, although Japanese Americans were ousted from their homes and pushed out of their businesses to live in *Evacuation Camps,* and while Filipinos in America had the status of non-citizens, adult males from both groups joined the military and fought for the United States during World War II. Thus, while subject to conditions of oppression in the United States, Filipino and Japanese Americans made a positive contribution to the American war effort. In fact, a closer and more inclusive examination of American history reveals that Asian Americans, African Americans, Latino Americans and Native Americans have all made a number of important contributions to the United States in addition to their own ethnic communities.

## What Are Ethnic Studies?

The *National Ethnic Studies Association* defines Ethnic Studies as an "interdisciplinary forum for scholars and activists concerned with the national and international dimensions of ethnicity."[5] Given the politics of the 1960s and 1970s, coupled with the emergence of a vocal and visible population of African American, Asian American, Latino American and Native Americans students attending colleges and universities, Ethnic Studies came into existence as an outcome of activism during this time period. As a discipline, Ethnic Studies has consciously cut across traditional academic disciplines as a necessary strategy to highlight the unique experiences of ethnic communities, and to build and strengthen connections with those communities outside of the academic institution. As a result, the voices and ideas of ethnic peoples, scholars and non-scholars alike, have changed academic institutions and affected the production of knowledge and ideas.

This volume, *Introduction to Ethnic Studies,* is designed to reflect the interdisciplinary nature of Ethnic Studies—the readings are drawn from academic fields in the humanities and social sciences. A few first person narratives are also included, so we can get a sense of how individuals experience their ethnic group status. Overall, the readings in this book are meant to provide students with a foundation in ethnic studies.

This book is divided into four sections. The first section, *History,* is intended to provide students with a basic understanding of the distinct histories of Asian Americans, African Americans, Latino Americans and Native Americans. Comparatively, how are these histories similar on the one hand and dissimilar on the other? What can we learn from these histories?

The purpose of the second section, *Identity,* is to demonstrate the various circumstances under which ethnic groups not only define themselves on their own terms, but also show how external conditions affect this process. This section is based on the perspective of *racial formation* first articulated by Omi and Winant. Racial formation places an emphasis on the sociohistorical processes that give rise to racial categories, and how those categories are transformed and redefined over time.[6] In order to fully understand the significance of ethnic identity, we need to pay attention to the fact that ethnic identity is fluid and dynamic, subject to external and internal ethnic group pressures. This section also highlights the significant role of culture in the creation and protection of identity. What role does culture play in shaping and sustaining ethnicity?

Section three touches on the issue of *Response and Responsibility*. Given that American society continues to manage and deal with the politics relating to ethnic identity, what are the responsibilities of Americans as citizens? To what extent do Americans contribute to problems relating to ethnicity by participating in and accepting popularized images and stereotypes? For example, one issue that is introduced in this section has to do with the use of Native Americans as mascots in sports. Why is this a problem and what should be the appropriate response by society? Another example has to with the problem of gender inequality within social movement organizations during the Civil Rights Movement of the 1960s. Why was gender inequality a problem in a movement that emphasized racial equality?

The last section of this book addresses the intersection of *Race, Class and Gender* as the primary dimensions of stratification in the United States. The purpose of this section is not only to provide students with an understanding of how individuals and groups gain access to valued resources in society, but also to demonstrate that race, class and gender play a key role in that process. In what ways do race, class and gender continue to be important dimensions of inequality in the United States? In what ways do race, class and gender intersect and why are those intersections important?

## Notes

[1]See *This Ride is About Our Future*, by Kevin Fedarko, pages 4–6, in **Parade** (The Sacramento Bee, Sunday, May 16, 2004).

[2]See *The American Indian Holocaust: Healing Historical Unresolved Grief*, by Mara Yellow Horse Brave Hear and Lemyra DeBruyn. American Indian and Alaska Native Mental Health Research, Volume 8(2), pages 60–82 (2000).

[3]Fedarko, page 5.

[4]Richard Schaefer, page 82 in **Racial and Ethnic Groups.** New York: Prentice Hall, 2003.

[5]National Ethnic Studies Association <http://www.ethnicstudies.org>.

[6]Michal Omi and Howard Winant, **Racial Formations in the United States.** New York: Routeledge. 1994.

# History

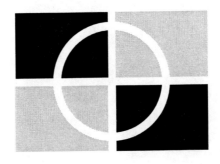

# Introduction

*Wayne Maeda*

Ethnic Studies as a program and field of study was born during the Third World Liberation strikes at San Francisco State College from November 1968 to March 1969 and University of California, Berkeley from January 1969 to March 1969.[1] African American, Chicano, Asian American, Native American and other students demanded, among other things, that institutions of higher learning provide access to poor and minority students, hiring minority faculty, administrators, and provide relevant curriculum. For those in the burgeoning field of ethnic studies, relevant curriculum broadly meant developing new perspectives, different methods of analysis, reconsidering what constituted "facts" and "interpretations" that shaped social realities for America's racial groups.

Thus, one of the most important functions envisioned over three decades ago in the field of ethnic studies was to provide a scholarly critique of the methods, theories, and practices of framing "the minority" experience by mainstream disciplines. This new breed and generation of historians challenged the notion that interpretation of history merely rested on dates, great men, and that "facts" speak for themselves in the grand narrative that passed as "the" definitive national history of America. In reality, the actual interpretation of history is affected by which facts are used, omitted, falsified, distorted, and known by the historian. More importantly, historical interpretation depends as much on the historian's own assumptions, biases, and agendas as it does on "facts." Because student activists of the late 1960s realized that the facts in the histories of African, Asian, Chicano and Native Americans were distorted, buried, or was simply "MIH" (*missing in history*), they argued that it was necessary to recover, re-interpret, and revise those histories. Thirty-five years later ethnic studies still commits itself to these goals of recovering, re-interpreting, and revising our past so that we can make better sense of the present in order to prepare for a future that will become even more diverse.

"The problem of the twentieth century is the problem of the color line." Although this prophetic statement was made by W. E. B. DuBois in 1903 reflected the concerns and ideas of student activists in the 1960s, it still remains one of the most salient and intractable issues facing America at the dawn of the twenty-first century. For DuBois, the color line went beyond the more traditional racial paradigm that has placed a focus on "black and white." When he published *The Souls of Black Folks* in 1903, DuBois was well aware of the Chinese who journeyed to "Gold

Mountain" in the 1850s were denied naturalization rights, prevented from inter-marrying with whites. In fact, the Chinese held the distinction of being the first ethnic group in the United States to be persecuted and excluded from immigration based on race in 1882. The Japanese, who followed the Chinese immigration beginning in 1880s, not only inherited the anti-Asiatic sentiment but faced the same fate of denial of citizenship and ownership of land, as well as ultimate exclusion in 1924. Moreover, by the time DuBois's book was published, America was on the verge of concluding its first imperialistic venture into Asia with the military conquest and occupation of the Philipines. Under the guise of "benign assimilation," American imperialistic policy brought civilization to the "brown monkeys," "savages," and Filipino "niggers" in the Philippines. DuBois recognized the depth, complexities and nuances of navigating the issue of the "color line" across the color spectrum: the challenge for all of us in the twenty-first century remains. . . *the problem of the color line – the relationship of the darker to the lighter races of men in Asia and Africa, in America and the islands of the sea.*[2]

In ethnic studies like in any other fields of study, there are terms, concepts, theories, and explanatory models that are used to help us understand the phenomena of race, class, and gender relations. The first article in this section, *Ethnicity in American Life,* John Franklin challenges us to rethink the widely held notion that the path to becoming an American had to with the "melting pot." According to this myth, it was believed that the assimilation process required immigrants as newcomers to shed their old world languages, customs, and cultures. Upon doing this, they would become a part of America. According to Franklin, the acceptance into this melting pot was limited to those who could construct themselves as white or Anglo-Saxon. For African Americans and other people of color, the problem of the color line reared its ugly head and prevented acceptance into the melting pot of America. Moreover, for those who could not re-invent themselves as "Americans," their consolation prize for not being accepted was, cynically stated by Franklin "cultural pluralism."

In *Ethnic Diversity,* Cruz Reynoso examines religious, linguistic, and historical diversity through his own personal reflections on being Mexican American. Reynoso also incorporates his legal expertise and reflects on his role as a justice on the California Supreme Court. With his legal knowledge and insight Reynoso helps shed light on divisive "hot button" issues from segregation in public schools, what language can we use in the public, and who is an American. In reference to the law and politics that structure and organize race relations, recent public discourse has celebrated the accomplishments of the 50 years that followed the landmark ruling made by the Supreme Court *Brown v. Board of Education of Topeka, Kansas.* Political pundits have pontificated that "we have come a long way" from the era of disenfranchisement, segregated schools, lunch counters, drinking fountains, telephone booths, bus stations, "race music and movies," as well as segregated neighborhoods. Otis Scott, however, moves beyond the self-congratulatory waxing of "progress" to provide a searing critical assessment, not only of the real progress but also how integration or lack of integration has shaped the realities for African Americans and, indeed, America itself.

In *History of Asians in America* Timothy Fong highlights the diversity that makes up this group labeled "Asian Americans" and divides this history into four general time periods. In doing so Fong situates various Asian American groups throughout American history beginning in 1840s, through War World II, Southeast Asian refugee groups fleeing the effects of Vietnam War, to the "new immigrants" who have invigorated the pre-1965 Asian American communities. Asian Americans, with changes in immigration laws and growth of globalization, are now posed to become, in more urban and suburban cities in California, the majority population.

This history section is only an introduction, and it should not be viewed as a complete or definitive history on African, Asian, Chicano and Native Americans. There are many more areas that need to be studied, explored, recovered, re-interpreted, and even continually re-written. It is hoped that the seeds of curiosity and a desire to question approach have been sown, for there is much more work to be done in Ethnic Studies by future generations of historians, researchers, and writers.

## Notes

[1]William Wei, *The Asian American Movement* (Philadelphia: Temple University Press, 1993), 15.
[2]DuBois, 23.

# Ethnicity in American Life: The Historical Perspective

*John Hope Franklin*

The United States is unique in the ethnic composition of its population. No other country in the world can point to such a variety of cultural, racial, religious, and national backgrounds in its population. It was one of the salient features in the early history of this country; and it would continue to be so down into the twentieth century. From virtually every corner of the globe they came—some enthusiastically and some quite reluctantly. Britain and every part of the continent of Europe provided prospective Americans by the millions. Africa and Asia gave up great throngs. Other areas of the New World saw inhabitants desert their own lands to seek their fortunes in the colossus to the North. Those who came voluntarily were attracted by the prospect of freedom of religion, freedom from want, and freedom from various forms of oppression. Those who were forced to come were offered the consolation that if they were white they would some day inherit the earth, and if they were black they would some day gather their reward in the Christian heaven.

One of the interesting and significant features of this coming together of peoples of many tongues and races and cultures was that the backgrounds out of which they came would soon be minimized and that the process by which they evolved into Americans would be of paramount importance. Hector St. Jean de Crevecoeur sought to describe this process in 1782 when he answered his own question, "What, then, is the American, this new man?" He said, "He is either an European, or the descendant of an European, hence that strange mixture of blood, which you will find in no other country. . . . He is an American, who, leaving behind him all his ancient prejudices and manners, receives new ones from the new mode of the life he has embraced, the new government he obeys, and the new rank he holds. He becomes an American by being received in the broad lap of our great *Alma Mater.* Here individuals of all nations are melted into a new race of men, whose labours and posterity will one day cause great changes in the world."

This was one of the earliest expressions of the notion that the process of Americanization involved the creation of an entirely new mode of life that would replace the ethnic backgrounds of those who were a part of the process. It contained some imprecisions and inaccuracies that would, in time, become a part of the lore or myth of the vaunted melting pot and would grossly misrepresent the crucial factor of ethnicity in American life. It ignored the tenacity with which the Pennsylvania Dutch held onto their language, religion, and way of life. It overlooked the way in which the Swedes of New Jersey remained Swedes and the manner in which the French Huguenots of New York and Charleston held onto their own past as though it was the source of all light and life. It described a process that in a distant day would gag at the notion that Irish Catholics could be assimilated on the broad lap of Alma Mater or that Asians could be seated on the basis of equality at the table of the Great American Feast.

By suggesting that only Europeans were involved in the process of becoming Americans, Crevecoeur pointedly ruled out three quarters of a million blacks already in the country who, along with their progeny, would be regarded as ineligible to become Americans for at least another two centuries. To be sure, the number of persons of African descent would increase enormously, but the view of their ineligibility for Americanization would be very slow to change. And when such a change occurred, even if it merely granted freedom from bondage, the change would be made most reluctantly and without any suggestion that freedom qualified one for equality on the broad lap of Alma Mater. It was beyond the conception of Crevecoeur, as it was indeed beyond the conception of the founding fathers, that Negroes, slave or free, could become true Americans, enjoying that fellowship in a common enterprise about which Crevecoeur spoke so warmly. It was as though Crevecoeur was arguing that ethnicity, where persons of African descent were concerned, was either so powerful or so unattractive as to make their assimilation entirely impossible or so insignificant as to make it entirely undesirable. In any case Americanization in the late eighteenth century was a precious commodity to be cherished and enjoyed only by a select group of persons of European descent.

One must admit, therefore, that at the time of the birth of the new nation there was no clear-cut disposition to welcome into the American family persons of any and all ethnic backgrounds. Only Europeans were invited to fight for independence. And when the patriots at long last relented and gave persons of African descent a chance to fight, the concession was made with great reluctance and after much equivocation and soul-searching. Only Europeans were regarded as full citizens in the new states and in the new nation. And when the founding fathers wrote the Constitution of the United States, they did not seem troubled by the distinctions on the basis of ethnic differences that the Constitution implied.

If the principle of ethnic exclusiveness was propounded so early and so successfully in the history of the United States, it is not surprising that it would, in time, become the basis for questioning the ethnic backgrounds of large numbers of prospective Americans, even Europeans. Thus, in 1819, a Jewish immigrant was chilled to hear a bystander refer to him and his companion as "more damned emigrants." A decade later there began a most scathing and multifaceted attack on the Catholic church. On two counts the church was a bad influence. First, its principal recruits were the Irish, the "very dregs" of the Old World social order; and secondly, its doctrine of papal supremacy ran counter to the idea of the political and religious independence of the United States. Roman Catholics, Protestant Americans warned, were engaged in a widespread conspiracy to subvert American institutions, through parochial schools, the Catholic press, immoral convents, and a sinister design to control the West by flooding it with Catholic settlers. The burning of convents and churches and the killing of Catholics themselves were indications of how deeply many Americans felt about religious and cultural differences for which they had a distaste and suspicion that bordered on paranoia.

Soon the distaste for the foreign-born became almost universal, with Roman Catholics themselves sharing in the hostility to those who followed them to the new Republic. Some expressed fear of the poverty and criminality that accompanied each wave of immigrants. Some felt that those newly arrived from abroad were a threat to republican freedom. Some saw in the ethnic differences of the newcomers an immediate danger to the moral standards of Puritan America. Some feared the competition that newcomers posed in the labor market. Some became convinced that the ideal of a national homogeneity would disappear with the influx of so many unassimilable elements. Soon, nativist societies sprang up all across the land, and they found national expression in 1850 in a new organization called the Order of the Star Spangled Banner. With its slogan, "America for Americans," the order, which became the organizational basis for the Know-Nothing party, engendered a fear through its preachments that caused many an American to conclude that his country was being hopelessly subverted by the radical un-Americanism of the great variety of ethnic strains that were present in the United States.

If there was some ambivalence regarding the ethnic diversity of white immigrants before the Civil War, it was dispelled by the view that prevailed regarding immigrants in the post–Civil War years. The "old" immigrants, so the argument went, were at least assimilable and had "entered practically every line of activity in nearly every part of the country." Even those who had been non-English speaking had mingled freely with native Americans and had therefore been quickly assimilated. Not so with the "new" immigrants who came after 1880. They "congregated together in sections apart from native Americans and the older immigrants to such an extent that assimilation had been slow." Small wonder that they were different. Small wonder that they were barely assimilable. They came from Austro-Hungary, Italy, Russia, Greece, Rumania, and Turkey. They dressed differently, spoke in unfamiliar tongues, and clung to strange, if not exotic customs. It did not matter that Bohemians, Moravians, and Finns had lower percentages of illiteracy than had the Irish and Germans or that Jews had a higher percentage of skilled laborers than any group except the Scots. Nor did it matter that, in fact, the process of assimilation for the so-called "new" group was about as rapid as that of the so-called "old" group.

What did matter was that the new nativism was stronger and more virulent than any anti-immigration forces or groups of the early nineteenth century and that these groups were determined either to drive from the shores those who were different or to isolate them so that they could not contaminate American society. Old-stock

Americans began to organize to preserve American institutions and the American way of life. Those who had been here for five years or a decade designated themselves as old-stock Americans and joined in the attack of those recently arrived. If the cult of Anglo-Saxon superiority was all but pervasive, those who were not born into the cult regarded themselves as honorary members. Thus, they could celebrate with as much feeling as any the virtues of Anglo-Saxon institutions and could condemn as vehemently as any those ideas and practices that were not strictly Anglo-Saxon. Whenever possible they joined the American Protective Association and the Immigrant Restriction League; and in so doing they sold their own ethnicity for the obscurity that a pseudoassimilation brought. But in the end, they would be less than successful. The arrogance and presumption of the Anglo-Saxon complex was not broad enough to embrace the Jews of eastern Europe or the Bohemians of central Europe or the Turks of the Middle East. The power and drive of the Anglo-Saxon forces would prevail; and those who did not belong would be compelled to console themselves by extolling the virtues of cultural pluralism.

By that time—near the end of the nineteenth century—the United States had articulated quite clearly its exalted standards of ethnicity. They were standards that accepted Anglo-Saxons as the norm, placed other whites on what may be called "ethnic probation," and excluded from serious consideration the Japanese, Chinese, and Negroes. It was not difficult to deal harshly with the Chinese and Japanese when they began to enter the United States in considerable numbers in the post–Civil War years. They simply did not meet the standards that the arbiters of American ethnicity had promulgated. They were different in race, religion, language, and public and private morality. They had to be excluded; and eventually they were.

The presence of persons of African descent, almost from the beginning, had helped whites to define ethnicity and to establish and maintain the conditions by which it could be controlled. If their color and race, their condition of servitude, and their generally degraded position did not set them apart, the laws and customs surrounding them more than accomplished that feat. Whether in Puritan Massachusetts or cosmopolitan New York or Anglican South Carolina, the colonists declared that Negroes, slave or free, did not and could not belong to the society of equal human beings. Thus, the newly arrived Crevecoeur could be as blind to the essential humanity of Negroes as the patriots who tried to keep them out of the Continental Army. They were not a part of America, these new men. And in succeeding years their presence would do more to define ethnicity than the advent of several scores of millions of Europeans.

It was not enough for Americans, already somewhat guilt-ridden for maintaining slavery in a free society, to exclude blacks from American society on the basis of race and condition of servitude. They proceeded from that point to argue that Negroes were inferior morally, intellectually, and physically. Even as he reviewed the remarkable accomplishments of Benjamin Banneker, surveyor, almanacker, mathematician, and clockmaker, Thomas Jefferson had serious doubts about the mental capabilities of Africans, and he expressed these doubts to his European friends. What Jefferson speculated about at the end of the eighteenth century became indisputable dogma within a decade after his death.

In the South every intellectual, legal, and religious resource was employed in the task of describing the condition of Negroes in such a way as to make them the least attractive human beings on the face of the earth. Slavery was not only the natural lot of blacks, the slaveowners argued, but it was in accordance with God's will that they should be kept in slavery. As one sanctimonious divine put it, "We feel that the souls of our slaves are a solemn trust and we shall strive to present them faultless and complete before the presence of God. . . . However the world may judge us in connection with our institution of slavery, we conscientiously believe it to be a great missionary institution—one arranged by God, as He arranges all moral and religious influences of the world so that the good may be brought out of seeming evil, and a blessing wrung out of every form of the curse." It was a difficult task that the owners of slaves set for themselves. Slaves had brought with them only heathenism, immorality, profligacy, and irresponsibility. They possessed neither the mental capacity nor the moral impulse to improve themselves. Only if their sponsors—those to whom were entrusted not only their souls but their bodies— were fully committed to their improvement could they take even the slightest, halting steps toward civilization.

What began as a relatively moderate justification for slavery soon became a vigorous, aggressive defense of the institution. Slavery, to the latter-day defenders, was the cornerstone of the republican edifice. To a governor of South Carolina, it was the greatest of all the great blessings which a kind Providence had bestowed upon the glorious region of the South. It was, indeed, one of the remarkable coincidences of history that such a favored institution had found such a favored creature as the African to give slavery the high value that was placed on it. A childlike race, prone to docility and manageable in every respect, the African was the ideal subject for the slave role. Slaveholders had to work hard to be worthy of this great Providential blessing.

Nothing that Negroes could do or say could change or seriously affect this view. They might graduate from college, as John Russwurm did in 1826, or they might write a most scathing attack against slavery, as David Walker did in 1829. It made no difference. They might teach in an all-white college, as Charles B. Reason did in New York in the 1850s, or publish a newspaper, as Frederick Douglass did during that same decade. Their racial and cultural backgrounds disqualified them from becoming American citizens. They could even argue in favor of their capacities and potentialities, as Henry Highland Garnet did, or they might argue their right to fight for union and freedom, as 186,000 did in the Civil War. Still, it made no sense for white Americans to give serious consideration to their arguments and their actions. They were beyond the veil, as the Jews had been beyond the veil in the barbaric and bigoted communities of eastern Europe.

The views regarding Negroes that had been so carefully developed to justify and defend slavery would not disappear with emancipation. To those who had developed such views and to the vast numbers who subscribed to them, they were much too valid to be discarded simply because the institution of slavery had collapsed. In fact, if Negroes were heathens and barbarians and intellectual imbeciles in slavery, they were hardly qualified to function as equals in a free society. And any effort to impose them on a free society should be vigorously and relentlessly resisted, even if it meant that a new and subordinate place for them had to be created.

When Americans set out to create such a place for the four million freedmen after the Civil War, they found that it was convenient to put their formulation in the context of the ethnic factors that militated against complete assimilation. To do it this way seemed more fitting, perhaps even more palatable, for the white members of a so-called free society. And they had some experience on which to rely. In an earlier day it had been the Irish or the Germans or the free Negroes who presented problems of assimilation. They were different in various ways and did not seem to make desirable citizens. In time the Irish, Germans, and other Europeans made it and were accepted on the broad lap of Alma Mater. But not the free Negroes, who continued to suffer disabilities even in the North in the years just before the Civil War. Was this the key to the solution of the postwar problems? Perhaps it was. After all, Negroes had always been a group apart in Boston, New York, Philadelphia, and other northern cities. They all lived together in one part of the city—especially if they could find no other place to live. They had their own churches—after the whites drove them out of theirs. They had their own schools—after they were excluded from the schools attended by whites. They had their own social organizations—after the whites barred them from theirs.

If Negroes possessed so many ethnic characteristics such as living in the same community, having their own churches, schools, and social clubs, and perhaps other agencies of cohesion, that was all very well. They even seemed "happier with their own kind," some patronizing observers remarked. They were like the Germans or the Irish or the Italians or the Jews. They had so much in common and so much to preserve. There was one significant difference, however. For Europeans, the ethnic factors that brought a particular group together actually eased the task of assimilation and, in many ways, facilitated the process of assimilation, particularly as hostile elements sought to disorient them in their drive toward full citizenship. And, in time, they achieved it.

For Negroes, however, such was not the case. They had been huddled together in northern ghettoes since the eighteenth century. They had had their own churches since 1792 and their own schools since 1800. And this separateness, this ostracism, was supported and enforced by the full majesty of the law, state and federal, just to make certain that Negroes did, indeed, preserve their ethnicity! And as they preserved their ethnicity—all too frequently as they looked down the barrel of a policeman's pistol or a militiaman's shotgun—full citizenship seemed many light years away. They saw other ethnic groups pass them by, one by one, and take their places in the sacred Order of the Star Spangled Banner, the American Protective Association, the Knights of the Ku Klux Klan—not always fully assimilated but vehemently opposed to the assimilation of Negroes. The ethnic grouping that was a way station, a temporary resting place for Europeans as they became Americans, proved to be a terminal point for blacks who found it virtually impossible to become Americans in any real sense.

There was an explanation or at least a justification for this. The federal government and the state governments had tried to force Negroes into full citizenship and had tried to legislate them into equality with the whites. This was not natural and could not possibly succeed. Negroes had not made it because they were not fit, the social Darwinists[1] said. Negroes were beasts, Charles Carroll declared somewhat inelegantly. "Stateways cannot change folkways," William Graham Sumner, the distinguished scholar, philosophized. The first forty years of Negro freedom had been a failure, said John R. Commons, one of the nation's leading economists. This so-called failure was widely acknowledged in the country as northerners of every rank and description acquiesced, virtually without a murmur of objection, to the southern settlement of the race problem characterized by disfranchisement, segregation, and discrimination.

Here was a new and exotic form of ethnicity. It was to be seen in the badges of inferiority and the symbols of racial degradation that sprang up in every sector of American life—in the exclusion from the polling places with its specious justification that Negroes were unfit to participate in the sacred rite of voting; the back stairway or the freight elevator to public places; the separate, miserable railway car; the separate and hopelessly inferior school; and even the Jim Crow[2] cemetery. Ethnic considerations had never been so important in the shaping of public policy. They had never before been used by the American government to define the role and place of other groups in American society. The United States had labored hard to create order out of its chaotic and diverse ethnic backgrounds. Having begun by meekly suggesting the difficulty in assimilating all groups into one great society, it had acknowledged failure by ruling out one group altogether, quite categorically, and frequently by law, solely on the basis of race.

It could not achieve this without doing irreparable harm to the early notions of the essential unity of America and Americans. The sentiments that promoted the disfranchisement and segregation of Negroes also encouraged the infinite varieties of discrimination against Jews, Armenians, Turks, Japanese, and Chinese. The conscious effort to degrade a particular ethnic group reflects a corrosive quality that dulls the sensitivities of both the perpetrators and the victims. It calls forth venomous hatreds and crude distinctions in high places as well as low places. It can affect the quality of mind of even the most cultivated scholar and place him in a position scarcely distinguishable from the Klansman or worse. It was nothing out of the ordinary, therefore, that at a dinner in honor of the winner of one of Harvard's most coveted prizes, Professor Barrett Wendell warned that if a Negro or a Jew ever won the prize the dinner would have to be canceled.

By the time that the Statue of Liberty was dedicated in 1886 the words of Emma Lazarus on the base of it had a somewhat hollow ring. Could anyone seriously believe that the poor, tired, huddled masses "yearning to breathe free," were really welcome here? This was a land where millions of black human beings whose ancestors had been here for centuries were consistently treated as pariahs and untouchables! What interpretation could anyone place on the sentiments expressed on the statue except that the country had no real interest in or sympathy for the downtrodden unless they were white and preferably Anglo-Saxon? It was a disillusioning experience for some newcomers to discover that their own ethnic background was a barrier to success in their adopted land. It was a searing and shattering experience for Negroes to discover over and over again that three centuries of toil and loyalty were nullified by the misfortune of their own degraded ethnic background.

In the fullness of time—in the twentieth century—the nation would confront the moment of truth regarding ethnicity as a factor in its own historical development. Crevecoeur's words would have no real significance. The words of the Declaration of Independence would have no real meaning. The words of Emma Lazarus would not ring true. All such sentiments would be put to the severe test of public policy and private deeds and would be found wanting. The Ku Klux Klan would challenge the moral and human dignity of Jews, Catholics, and Negroes. The quotas of the new immigration laws would define ethnic values in terms of race and national origin. The restrictive covenants[3] would arrogate to a select group of bigots the power of determining what races or ethnic groups should live in certain houses or whether, indeed, they should have any houses at all in which to live. If some groups finally made it through the escape hatch and arrived at the point of acceptance, it was on the basis of race, now defined with sufficient breadth to include all or most peoples who were not of African descent.

By that time ethnicity in American life would come to have a special, clearly definable meaning. Its meaning would be descriptive of that group of people vaguely defined in the federal census returns as "others" or "non-whites." It would have something in common with that magnificent term "cultural pluralism," the consolation prize for those who were not and could not be assimilated. It would signify the same groping for respectability that describes that group of people who live in what is euphemistically called "the inner city." It would represent a rather earnest search for a hidden meaning that would make it seem a bit more palatable and surely more sophisticated than something merely racial. But in 1969 even a little child would know what ethnicity had come to mean.

In its history, ethnicity, in its true sense, has extended and continues to extend beyond race. At times it has meant language, customs, religion, national origin. It has also meant race; and, to some, it has always meant only race. It had already begun to have a racial connotation in the eighteenth century. In the nineteenth century, it had a larger racial component, even as other factors continued to loom large. In the present century, as these other factors have receded in importance, racial considerations have come to have even greater significance. If the history of ethnicity has meant anything at all during the last three centuries, it has meant the gradual but steady retreat from the broad and healthy regard for cultural and racial differences to a narrow, counter-productive concept of differences in terms of whim, intolerance, and racial prejudice. We have come full circle. The really acceptable American is still that person whom Crevecoeur described almost two hundred years ago. But the true American, acceptable or not, is that person who seeks to act out his role in terms of his regard for human qualities irrespective of race. One of the great tragedies of American life at the beginning was that ethnicity was defined too narrowly. One of the great tragedies of today is that this continues to be the case. One can only hope that the nation and its people will all some day soon come to reassess ethnicity in terms of the integrity of the man rather than in terms of the integrity of the race.                                                                    [1989]

## Notes

¹SOCIAL DARWINISM: The theory that applied Darwin's theory of evolution, "survival of the fittest," to society; it assumed that upper classes were naturally superior, and the failure of the lower classes was the result of their natural inferiority, not of social policies and practices.

²JIM CROW: Laws and practices, especially in the South, that separated Blacks and Whites and enforced the subordination of Blacks.

³RESTRICTIVE COVENANTS: Codes prohibiting members of some groups—often Blacks, Jews, and Asians—from buying real estate in certain areas.

# Brown et al. v. Board of Education of Topeka et al. 347 U.S. 483 (1954)

Mr. Chief Justice Warren delivered the opinion of the Court.

These cases come to us from the States of Kansas, South Carolina, Virginia, and Delaware. They are premised on different facts and different local conditions, but a common legal question justifies their consideration together in this consolidated opinion.[1]

In each of the cases, minors of the Negro race, through their legal representatives, seek the aid of the courts in obtaining admission to the public schools of their community on a nonsegregated basis. In each instance, they had been denied admission to schools attended by white children under laws requiring or permitting segregation according to race. This segregation was alleged to deprive the plaintiffs of the equal protection of the laws under the Fourteenth Amendment. In each of the cases other than the Delaware case, a three-judge federal district court denied relief to the plaintiffs on the so-called "separate but equal" doctrine announced by this Court in *Plessy v. Ferguson,* 163 U.S. 537. Under that doctrine, equality of treatment is accorded when the races are provided substantially equal facilities, even though these facilities be separate. In the Delaware case, the Supreme Court of Delaware adhered to that doctrine, but ordered that the plaintiffs be admitted to the white schools because of their superiority to the Negro schools.

The plaintiffs contend that segregated public schools are not "equal" and cannot be made "equal," and that hence they are deprived of the equal protection of the laws. Because of the obvious importance of the question presented, the Court took jurisdiction.[2] Argument was heard in the 1952 Term, and reargument was heard this Term on certain questions propounded by the Court.[3]

Reargument was largely devoted to the circumstances surrounding the adoption of the Fourteenth Amendment in 1868. It covered exhaustively consideration of the Amendment in Congress, ratification by the states, then existing practices in racial segregation, and the views of proponents and opponents of the Amendment. This discussion and our own investigation convince us that, although these sources cast some light, it is not enough to resolve the problem with which we are faced. At best, they are inconclusive. The most avid proponents of the post–War Amendments undoubtedly intended them to remove all legal distinctions among "all persons born or naturalized in the United States." Their opponents, just as certainly, were antagonistic to both the letter and the spirit of the Amendments and wished them to have the most limited effect. What others in Congress and the state legislatures had in mind cannot be determined with an degree of certainty.

An additional reason for the inconclusive nature of the Amendment's history, with respect to segregated schools, is the status of public education at that time.[4] In the South, the movement toward free common schools, supported by general taxation, had not yet taken hold. Education of white children was largely in the hands of private groups. Education of Negroes was almost nonexistent, and practically all of the race were illiterate. In fact, any education of Negroes was forbidden by law in some states. Today in contrast, many Negroes have achieved outstanding success in the arts and sciences as well as in the business and professional world. It is true that public school education at the time of the Amendment had advanced further in the North, but the effect of the Amendment on northern States was generally ignored in the congressional debates. Even in the North, the conditions of public education did not approximate those existing today. The curriculum was usually rudimentary; ungraded schools were common in rural areas; the school term was but three months a year in many states; and compulsory school attendance was virtually unknown. As a consequence, it is not surprising that there should be so little in the history of the Fourteenth Amendment relating to its intended effect on public education.

In the first cases in this Court construing the Fourteenth Amendment, decided shortly after its adoption, the Court interpreted it as prescribing all state-imposed discriminations against the Negro race.[5] The doctrine of "separate but equal" did not make its appearance in this Court until 1896 in the case of *Plessy v. Ferguson, supra*, involving not education but transportation.[6] American courts have since labored with the doctrine for over half a century. In this Court, there have been six cases involving the "separate but equal" doctrine in the field of public education.[7] In *Cumming v. County Board of Education*, 175 U.S. 528, and *Gong Luin v Rice*, 275 U.S. 78, the validity of the doctrine itself was not challenged.[8] In more recent cases, all on the graduate school level, inequality was found in that specific benefits enjoyed by white students were denied to Negro students of the same educational qualifications. *Missouri ex rel. Gaines v. Canada*, 305 U.S. 337; *Sipuel v. Oklahoma*, 332 U.S. 631; *Sweatt v. Painter*, 339 U.S. 629; *McLaurin v. Oklahoma State Regents*, 339 U.S. 637. In none of these cases was it necessary to reexamine the doctrine to grant relief to the Negro plaintiff. And in *Sweatt v. Painter, supra*, the Court expressly reserved decision on the question whether *Plessy v. Ferguson* should be held inapplicable to public education.

In the Instant cases, that question is directly presented. Here, unlike *Sweatt v. Painter*, there are findings below that the Negro and white schools involved have been equalized, or are being equalized, with respect to buildings, curricula, qualifications and salaries of teachers, and other "tangible" factors.[9] Our decision, therefore, cannot turn on merely a comparison of these tangible factors in the Negro and white schools involved in each of the cases. We must look instead to the effect of segregation itself on public education.

In approaching this problem, we cannot turn the clock back to 1868 when the Amendment was adopted, or even to 1896 when *Plessy v. Ferguson* was written. We must consider public education in the light of its full development and its present place in American life throughout the Nation. Only in this way can it be determined if segregation in public schools deprives these plaintiffs of the equal protection of the laws.

Today education is perhaps the most important function of state and local governments. Compulsory school attendance laws and the great expenditures for education both demonstrate our recognition of the importance of education to our democratic society. It is required in the performance of our most basic public responsibilities, even service in the armed forces. It is the very foundation of good citizenship. Today it is a principal instrument in awakening the child to cultural values, in preparing him for later professional training, and in helping him to adjust normally to his environment. In these days, it is doubtful that any child may reasonably be expected to succeed in life if he is denied the opportunity of an education. Such an opportunity, where the state has undertaken to provide it, is a right which must be made available to all on equal terms.

We come then to the question presented: Does segregation of children in public schools solely on the basis of race, even though the physical facilities and other "tangible" factors may be equal, deprive the children of the minority group of equal educational opportunities? We believe that it does.

In *Sweatt v. Painter, supra,* in finding that a segregated law school for Negroes could not provide them equal educational opportunities, this Court relied in large part on "those qualities which are incapable of objective measurement but which make for greatness in a law school." In *McLaurin v. Oklahoma State Regents, supra,* the Court, in requiring that a Negro admitted to a white graduate school be treated like all other students, again resorted to intangible considerations; ". . . his ability to study, to engage in discussions and exchange views with other students, and, in general, to learn his profession." Such considerations apply with added force to children in grade and high schools. To separate them from others of similar age and qualifications solely because of their race generates a feeling of inferiority as to their status in the community that may affect their hearts and minds in a way unlikely ever to be undone. The effect of this separation on their educational opportunities was well stated by a finding in the Kansas case by a court which nevertheless felt compelled to rule against the Negro plaintiffs:

> "*Segregation of white and colored children in public schools has a detrimental effect upon the colored children. The impact is greater when it has the sanction of the law; for the policy of separating the races is usually interpreted as denoting the inferiority of the negro group. A sense of inferiority affects the motivation of a child to learn. Segregation with the sanction of law, therefore, has a*

*tendency to retard the educational and mental development of negro children and to deprive them of some of the benefits they would receive in a racially integrated school system."[10]*

Whatever may have been the extent of psychological knowledge at the time of *Plessy v. Ferguson,* this finding is amply supported by modern authority.[11] Any language in *Plessy v. Ferguson* contrary to this finding is rejected.

We conclude that in the field of public education the doctrine of "separate but equal" has no place. Separate educational facilities are inherently unequal. Therefore, we hold that the plaintiffs and other similarly situated for whom the actions have been brought are, by reason of the segregation complained of, deprived of the equal protection of the laws guaranteed by the Fourteenth Amendment. This disposition makes unnecessary any discussion whether such segregation also violates the Due Process Clause of the Fourteenth Amendment.[12]

Because these are class actions, because of the wide applicability of this decision, and because of the great variety of local conditions, the formulation of decrees in these cases presents problems of considerable complexity. On reargument, the consideration of appropriate relief was necessarily subordinated to the primary question—the constitutionality of segregation in public education. We have now announced that such segregation is a denial of the equal protection of the laws. In order that we may have the full assistance of the parties in formulating decrees, the cases will be restored to the docket, and the parties are requested to present further argument on Questions 4 and 5 previously propounded by the Court for the reargument this Term.[13] The Attorney General of the United States is again invited to participate. The Attorneys General of the states requiring or permitting segregation in public education will also be permitted to appear as *amici curiae* upon request to do so by September 15, 1954, and submission of briefs by October 1, 1954.[14]

*It is so ordered.*

## Notes

[1]In the Kansas case, *Brown v. Board of Education,* the plaintiffs are Negro children of elementary school age residing in Topeka. They brought this action in the United States District Court for the District of Kansas to enjoin enforcement of a Kansas statute which permits, but does not require, cities of more than 15,000 population to maintain separate school facilities for Negro and white students. Kan. Gen. Stat. § 72-1724 (1949). Pursuant to that authority, the Topeka Board of Education elected to establish segregated elementary schools. Other public schools in the community, however, are operated on a nonsegregated basis. . . .

In the South Carolina case, *Briggs v. Elliott,* the plaintiffs are Negro children of both elementary and high school age residing in Clarendon County. They brought this action in the United States District Court for the Eastern District of South Carolina to enjoin enforcement of provisions in the state constitution and statutory code which require the segregation of Negroes and whites in public schools. . . .

In the Virginia case, *Davis v. County School Board,* the plaintiffs are Negro children of high school age residing in Prince Edward County. They brought this action in the United States District

Court for the Eastern District of Virginia to enjoin enforcement of provisions in the state constitution and statutory code which require the segregation of Negroes and whites in public schools. . . .

In the Delaware case, *Gebhart v. Belton,* the plaintiffs are Negro children of both elementary and high school age residing in New Castle county. They brought this action in the Delaware Court of Chancery to enjoin enforcement of provisions in the state constitution and statutory code which require the segregation of Negroes and whites in public schools. . . .

[2]technical footnote deleted.

[3]technical footnote deleted.

[4]technical footnote deleted.

[5]technical footnote deleted.

[6]technical footnote deleted.

[7]technical footnote deleted.

[8]technical footnote deleted.

[9]technical footnote deleted.

[10]technical footnote deleted.

[11]K. B. Clark, Effect of Prejudice and Discrimination on Personality Development (Midcentury White House Conference on Children and Youth, 1950); Witmer and Kotinsky, Personality in the Making (1952), c. VI; Deutscher and Chein, The Psychological Effects of Enforced Segregation: A Survey of Social Science Opinion, 26 J. Psychol. 259 (1948); Chein, What Are the Psychological Effects of Segregation Under Conditions of Equal Facilities?, 3 Int. J. Opinion and Attitude Res. 229 (1949); Brameld, Educational Costs, in Discrimination and National Welfare (MacIver, ed., 1949), 44–48; Frazier, The Negro in the United States (1949), 674–681. And see generally Myrdal, An American Dilemma (1944).

[12]technical footnote deleted.

[13]technical footnote deleted.

[14]technical footnote deleted.

# Brown v. Topeka Board of Education: Fifty Years Later

*Otis L. Scott*

## Introduction

May of 2004 marked the fiftieth anniversary of the landmark Supreme Court decision, *Brown vs. Topeka Board of Education.* Across the nation countless events have been carried out in commemoration of the 1954 decision. It is safe to assert that most of these events hailed the significant role *Brown* played in dismantling the walls of Jim Crow segregation surrounding public schools in southern and border states of the United States.

This article is a general examination of the pre and post *Brown* eras with critical attention given to the extent to which the decision fulfilled the dreams of the proponents of public school desegregation. I contend that the effects of *Brown* must be examined within a heuristic model that demands we critically examine the responses of American society-especially its formal governing institutions-and secondly, its citizenry, to policies and practices of desegregation. In raising these concerns I also raise up the need for a critical examination of the concept of integration which has, and to a diminishing extent today, serves as the norm driving the discourse around public school desegregation.

## Historical Context

The United States prior to the *Brown v. Board* decision of 1954 was for all intents and purposes an apartheid society. Policies and practices separating African Americans from white Americans was a defining feature of this nation beginning in the seventeenth century. Segregation practices became engrained by habits of custom and heart. These practices were subsequently canonized into the ethos and processes of the nation's social systems at both the national and state levels simultaneously with the framing of a new governing experiment. An experiment resting on the bedrock proposition touting political equality. In fact, the United States was created with what the historian W. E. B. DuBois called the color line. This line has historically divided Black and whites into two distinct societies; separate and unequal. The metaphorical line is as much an issue today as it was at the dawn of the

20th century following the 1896 Supreme Court decision in *Plessy v Ferguson*. This decision established in legal concrete, that the races-meaning particularly African descended people and white people-must be kept separate in public spaces. This decision also had negative implications for other people racialized as a *minority* in the United States. Following habits of heart and mind in matters of race long in force in this nation, *Plessy* articulated this nation's policy on race. Namely, the separation of African people from whites was right, just and proper in order to maintain domestic tranquility and most importantly, white supremacy.

There were few spaces in public life in the United States where the operation of what became known as the "Jim Crow" doctrine of racial separation was more pronounced and more destructive than in public education. And no where were the practices of the pronouncement more destructive than when used to deny African American children living in border and southern states a quality education and the life enhancing opportunities derived from being educated.

## Jim Crow's Children

This nation's dereliction in providing any form of a meaningful education for African Americans long predates the 1896 *Plessy* decision. The Virginia legislature as early as 1680 passed a law prohibiting Africans from gathering together for any reason. Doing so was punishable by "Twenty Lashes on the Bare Back well laid on" (Irons 2002). The intent of such severe legislation was seemingly to discourage slaves from forming their own schools and from meeting to conjure up plans to overthrow their masters. If Africans in colonial America received any form of education it was one heavily doused with biblical teachings counseling the virtues of obedience, supplication, faith in the deliverance of God and the benevolence of white people. Within the antebellum south any efforts at educating African men, women and children were typically clandestine. Throughout the south such efforts were almost always illegal. Slave owners feared that any form of literacy would lead to insurrection. One defender of this position asked in 1895, "Is there any great moral reason why we should incur the tremendous risk of having our wives and children slaughtered in consequence of our slaves being taught to read incendiary publications?" (Irons 2002).

The first institutionalized efforts to educate African Americans were made after the Civil War by the Reconstruction Congress. There is clear evidence that African Americans took advantage of the opportunity to learn to read and write (Bullock 1967). If one reviews the policy positions taken by African Americans elected and appointed to office during the brief period of Reconstruction, it will be revealed the extent to which newly freed African Americans expressed an unflagging desire for an education for both adults and especially for children. Reconstruction efforts were brought to a screeching halt after 1876 by virtue of the grand betrayal brokered between the political forces supporting the Republican, Rutherford B. Hayes and those supporting Democrat, Samuel B. Tilden. After receiving sufficient electoral votes to be declared president of the United States in 1877, Hayes began dismantling the fledgling political–legal infrastructure being crafted by African Americans and their white allies for their inclusion into the civic culture of this nation. In effect, he sabotaged efforts by African Americans to become citizens by re-creating the ante bellum conditions for racists in both the north and the south to again get the upper hand in determining the racial etiquette of the south and the nation as a whole. For African Americans this meant a return to the abject status of racial pariah.

Typical of the educational environment for African Americans living in the post *Plessy* south is described by James T. Patterson (2001),

> *Schools for black people were especially bad-indeed primitive. . . . Sunflower County, Mississippi, a cotton plantation region, had no high schools for Blacks. In the elementary grades of the county's Black schools, many of the teachers worked primarily as cooks or domestics on the plantations. Most had no more than a fourth grade education (10).*

Continuing, he notes that,

> *In the 1948–49 school year, the average investment per pupil in Atlanta public school facilities was $228.05 for Blacks and $570.00 for whites. In 1949–50 there was an average of 36.2 Black children per classroom, compared to an average of 22.6 among whites (11).*

By the early 1950s just as in the preceding decades after the civil war, racial segregation was the hallmark of American apartheid. Public schools in the south and border states were the parade ground where Jim Crow marched and drummed out his message of separation, inequality and inferiority. Schools for African American children were the by products of systematic and institutionalized racism.

Chinks in the armor of Jim Crow began to appear in the decades of the 1940s primarily due to the activism of the National Association for the Advancement of Colored People (NAACP). The NAACP had won some important cases before the U.S. Supreme Court in controversies involving all white primary elections (*Smith v. Allwright* 1944) and segregated law schools (*Sweatt v. Painter,* 1950). The belated initiatives by presidents Franklin D. Roosevelt to open the nation's war industries to African American workers and Harry Truman's Executive Order desegregating the armed forces as the decade of the 1940s closed, at least gave notice that the Executive Branch was willing to address America's race dilemma.

## The Brown Case

When the 1950s began Linda Brown had just turned six years old. In many respects she typified the thousands of African American children attending segregated public schools. She lived within walking distance, or a short car ride, of a white school in or near their neighborhood. In Linda's case there was a bit of an irony. She lived in an integrated neighborhood and regularly played with white school children. On occasion her white playmates even stayed overnight in her parent's home. Yet, she could not attend the white elementary school just a few blocks from her house. Instead she had to rise early each school morning, walk through a dangerous train switch yard, which was usually a hang out place for some of the town's derelicts and transients, catch a bus which took her to an all Black elementary school some two miles from her house.

Fed up with the color line and the indignities of public school segregation, Oliver Brown, Linda's father, challenged Topeka, Kansas' Jim Crow school system. The challenge came after his being unable to register his daughter in the white school near his house. Typically a mild mannered man-not having a record of activism-Oliver Brown sought out the assistance of the local branch of the NAACP headed by McKinley Burnett (Kluger 1976). Burnett is often times acknowledged as the understated and real hero of the Brown saga. It was he who developed the strategy, organized parents, pulled together the resources necessary to challenge the Topeka School Board's segregation policies (Irons 2002). It was McKinley Burnett who convinced the national NAACP to take on the Topeka case as part of a growing number of school segregation cases the national office was seriously considering.

The Brown case was initially heard before the District Court for the District of Kansas on February 28th, 1951. Robert L. Carter, an able and respected attorney with the NAACP Legal and Defense Fund argued for an injunction forbidding Topeka's public schools from segregating African American elementary school children from white children. By all accounts Carter's presentation was masterfully structured and convincingly presented to the District judges. Indeed, the judges of the District Court were moved to register their empathy for African American children deprived of the higher quality education typically provided to white children. On this point the Court noted, "Segregation of white and colored children in public schools has a detrimental effect on colored children" (Kluger 2002). But the judges refused to issue an injunction, resting their decision instead on the fact that the provisions of the 1896 *Plessy* decision which decreed that public schools were to be "separate but equal" was still the law of the land.

On October first of the same year, the Brown case was joined with other law suits from South Carolina, Delaware, Virginia, and the District of Columbia challenging public school segregation. While the end results of the case are well known and certainly represent a sea change in the application of the 14th amendment's equal protection clause to African American children, it was not the first challenge to segregated public schools. In 1849 a similar challenge in the Sarah Roberts case (*Roberts v. City of Boston*) was filed in Boston, Massachusetts. In 1947, seven years before the Brown decision, The California State Supreme Court declared that the segregated public school system in Orange County, in southern California, was discriminatory towards Mexican American elementary school children (*Mendez v. Westminster School District*). In Kansas between 1881 and 1949 some eleven cases were filed challenging segregated schools. At the time Brown was argued before the U.S. Supreme Court, the racially segregated public school system was the norm in a good part of the nation. It was legally sanctioned or permitted in twenty four states.

The legal strategy leading to the cases comprising *Brown* deserves more attention than is the subject of this article. It is important to point out that the assault against public school segregation was well planned for in advance by some of the best legal minds both African American and white associated with the NAACP. The plans were underway earnestly in the 1930s with legal challenges being considered against segregation in graduate and professional schools, voting rights and housing (Greenberg 1994).

The chief architect of the desegregation strategy was Charles H. Houston, who was the dean of the Howard University Law School at the time he was also taking the lead in orchestrating a response to public school segregation. The core of the strategy was its focus on graduate and professional education institutions rather than elementary education. Houston's thinking was that by drawing on the equal provisions of *Plessy* and forcing states to build professional and graduate schools *equal* in all aspects to the white graduate and professional schools, he would overwhelm their ability to support two separate systems of graduate and professional education. Thus, making it impossible for states to maintain expensive dual systems of post secondary education and graduate systems. Using this strategy he won a landmark decision in 1936 when the Maryland Supreme Court ordered the University of Maryland's law school to admit Donald Murray, a Black student, rather than send him to an out of state law school. (*Murray v. Maryland*). He won a similar case before the U.S. Supreme Court in 1938 (*Missouri ex rel Gaines v. Canada*). The Supreme Court in this case found that the University of Missouri, though it did create a separate law school for Black students, the facility-in a building shared with a hotel and a movie theatre-provided a "privilege . . . for white students" which it did not provide for Black students.

In 1939 Houston's prize student, Thurgood Marshall, took over as the chief counsel for the NAACP and established the NAACP Legal Defense and Education Fund. By the late 1940s Marshall was of a mind that the "validity" of the segregation statutes which the NAACP had left unchallenged with its "equalization" strategy was insufficient as a strategy for dismantling segregation laws. At the time the elementary school cases were accepted by the NAACP, the organization's strategy was focused on proving that public school segregation imposed restrictions on African American school children which denied them equal protection of the laws as prescribed by the 14th amendment to the U.S. Constitution. Interestingly, Marshall and his brilliant team of colleagues drew from the research studies by social and behavioral scientists in making their case. In particular the doll studies by Professors Kenneth Clarke and his wife, Mamie were instrumental. Using black and white dolls the Clarkes' demonstrated that the actions of African American children in choosing white dolls in a testing situation and attributing to the dolls positive characteristics displayed the extent to which segregation had diminished their sense of identity and self esteem. Their studies, while controversial were sufficient to convincing the Justices of the destructive effects racial segregation can have on children.

## Significance of *Brown*

To assert that the unanimous decision rendered by the Court on May 17, 1954 was of landmark proportions is now well supported. Given its message and the times the decision was tantamount to the earth tilting a few degrees off its normal axis. The Court's pronouncement that "separate educational facilities are inherently unequal," and thus constituting a denial of the equal protection clause of the 14th amendment was for its day a profound rebuke of the long standing provisions of the 1896 *Plessy* decision. In effect the Court said that African American children deserved to receive an opportunity for an education which constitutionally should be on par with that provided to most white children living in the South.

Because of many questions and uncertainties as how to implement the provisions of the decision, the Supreme Court delivered a *Brown II* decision a year later. This decision did not provide necessary direction to southern school boards or establish the standards they were to follow in desegregating their public schools. Instead, the Court established the vague principle that desegregation should proceed "with all deliberate speed." This limp edict allowed southern states, their school boards and their public officials, elected and appointed, a huge escape route from implementing fourteenth amendment provisions of the first *Brown* decision.

## Critique of *Brown II*

*Brown II* was a failure. It failed to give sufficient guidance and direction to the federal courts in desegregation cases. As such, it did not hold states or courts accountable for implementing 14th amendment protections for African American public school children in the south. Thus, only the most courageous judges would venture on their own and rule in the favor of fourteenth amendment protections for African American school children. *Brown II* was also a failure in that it, in effect, succumbed to the deeply entrenched belief of white supremacy subscribed to by the great majority of white southerners and no few northerners. The Warren Court, notwithstanding its unanimous decision in *Brown I,* was not about the business of transforming southern racial values and practices. It had spoken loudly in extending the 14th amendment anew to African American children, but it was not about to take on–head to head-the ideology of white supremacy. The court had gone as far as it cared on the issue of state sponsored school desegregation.

And because of this the "with all deliberate speed" clause allowed southern politicians, policy makers of various stripes and the ordinary white citizens to dodge school desegregation. As noted above, the Supreme Court should have stepped in and ordered compliance with its order. It took no such action. As a result racial segregation in southern school districts changed very little between 1955 and 1964 (Patterson 2001). Regarding the glacial movement of desegregation in the south, James T. Patterson notes, "By early 1964, only 1.2 percent of black children in the eleven southern states attended school with whites" (Patterson, 2001). Similarly, northern schools were virtually untouched by desegregation until the mid 1970s. The major point here is that the adherents of *Brown* were unable to muster the political or moral might necessary to transform the decision into a national social/political strategy the object of which would have been to desegregate this nation's public schools.

The fact that this was not done is more of a comment on the unwillingness of this nation's leadership communities to advance desegregation than it is a negative comment on the failings of the U.S. Supreme Court. It is more a critical comment on the lack of a national will; a will undergirded by the moral premise that it is fundamentally wrong, intolerable and unacceptable for any of this nation's children to have to attend schools-especially those segregated by race-where they will predictably receive an inferior education. An education which will predictably-cause doors of opportunity to be closed in their faces.

While there were many millions of Americans of all ethnicities and social economic classes in agreement that African American children and children of color should have an opportunity for a quality education, there was never a national consensus of commitment to bringing about the radical changes in how this nation conducted the business of public school education. To wit, there was never a national will to make *Brown* other than the symbolization of an education norm. That this is the case is disturbingly illustrated by the strident and racist oppositional voices generated by both *Brown* decisions.

## Resistance to the *Brown* Decisions

To state that the Supreme Court's desegregation decision caused severe undulations in the social, political and legal fabric of the south is to speak to the obvious. This was not a decision that most southerners were expecting although there were for decades growing signs of African American impatience with Jim Crow.

In the main, resistance to the *Brown* decisions was the order of the day in the south. While there was some reluctant compliance in states, e.g., Arkansas and Tennessee, in the main, resistance was fierce and unrelenting. Typically such resistance took three forms: litigation, privatization and terror. Most southern states challenged desegregation orders through the courts; thus, dragging out implementation. Privatization of public schools was a second form of resistance. White parents, with the aid of school officials and politicians, formed private academies and other institutions, often times using public funds as a way of evading desegregation. The third form of resistance was well known. Use of terror. White segregationists formed hate groups like the White Citizen's Councils which became vehicles for the transport of hate speech and acts of violence against African Americans and any one or anything presumed to be a threat to segregation.

The most effective assault against the idealistic, albeit vague, mandates of the Supreme Court was launched by Presidents Richard Nixon, Ronald Reagan and George Bush, the elder. All three presidents were hostile to desegregation and especially when the federal courts ordered bussing as the device to accomplish the fact. The three, beginning with Nixon, sought to change what they felt was an overly active federal judiciary (with particular criticism aimed at the decisions by the Warren Court) by appointing conservative judges to the federal judiciary and to the Supreme Court. Appointees to the federal judiciary in the decades of the 70s and 80s were made by presidents committed to shaping a more conservative federal judiciary with judges having no zeal for enforcing civil rights laws. It is perversely ironical to note that during this era of redemption, President Ronald Reagan, with mean spirited intentions, nominated Clarence Thomas, the second African American to serve on the U.S. Supreme Court and no friend of civil rights causes, to replace Thurgood Marshall.

In a series of Supreme Court decisions beginning in 1974 and extending into the mid-nineties, the conservative voices on the Court and elsewhere in the federal judiciary essentially rendered a moribund *Brown,* dead. Examples of key decisions during this period were *Milliken v Bradley* (1974); *Board of Education of Oklahoma City v. Dowell* (1991); *Freeman v. Pitts* (1992); *Missouri v. Jenkins* (1995).

In *Milliken,* a Detroit, Michigan case, the Court made *Brown* all but irrelevant for most northern cities by not approving desegregation plans combining city and suburban schools. In the *Board of Education of Oklahoma City v. Dowell* the Court ruled that school districts could be released from desegregation orders if they created "unitary"–meaning racially mixed-schools. In the *Freeman* case the Court provided that a school district could dismantle its desegregation plans without having to desegregate its faculty and provide students equal access to its programs. And finally, in *Missouri v. Jenkins,* the Court prohibited efforts to attract white suburban and private school students voluntarily into city schools by using strong academic programs.

Today for all intents and purposes the idealistic, albeit toothless, provisions of *Brown* are memories of a failed future. This is because of the factors previously mentioned: a combination of a weak commitment by policy makers at all levels to enforce desegregation; a Supreme Court's unwillingness to pursue enforcement of its mandates; an intense backlash by both southerners and northerners against court ordered desegregation; no national will to undo segregated schools; the general inability of the African American civil rights community to mount an effective response to the "with all deliberate speed" clause which was used as subterfuge to desegregation.

## Post *Brown* and Public School Resegregation

In a 2002 report, "Race in American Public Schools: Rapidly Resegregating School Districts," authored by Erika Frankenberg and Chungmei Lee, we are given a fresh and disturbing look at the nation's rush back to resegregation. A telling conclusion of their study is that,

*"Virtually all public school districts . . . are showing lower levels of inter-racial exposure since 1986, suggesting a trend towards resegregation, and in some districts, these declines are sharp" (4).*

These two scholars, as have several before them, note that since the mid 1980s African American and Latino students have become increasingly more segregated in public schools (Orwell and Eaton 1996). Again, the significant problematic here is-not that increasing racial isolation is underway, but the fact that the schools attended by African American and Latino students are more closely associated with "low parental involvement, lack of resources, less experienced and credentialed teachers, and higher teacher turnover all of which in combination exacerbate educational inequality for mostly minority student" (Frankenberg and Lee).

There is much good to say about having children of diverse backgrounds learning in the same classroom setting; attending the same schools. Indeed, if this nations is to become truly a democratic society, one which accepts multiculturalism as a fundamental characteristic of its being, we-children and their parents and other adults-must learn about each other with each other; children (and we) must learn to collaborate across gender, sexual orientation, social class, religious, ethnic and other lines, borders, and margins which function as social lines of demarcation. They must learn to see themselves in others. Which is to say that the struggle is to identify those aspects of who we are as distinct cultural beings which can be tapped for collaborative purposes, rather than placing emphasis on changing or muting our defining cultural attributes. But this is the ideal.

The reality of social formation in this nation is that its history of discrimination, the *minoritizing* and marginalizing of cultural groups is deeply institutionalized in habits of both heart and mind. We cannot escape who we are. No matter the feel good fluffy escapist attempts by popular culture outlets to portray contemporary America society as only challenged by the need for more sun blocker and the proliferation of trendy unproven weight loss schemes. The color line remains as a defining feature of who we are. Yet, as a nation we remain hopelessly deluded, believing that the sins of the past are in the past.

This is clearly evident when one look at the state of public school education for African American children. These are children attending urban schools enter where they are not being prepared to take advantage of opportunities for social, economic, and education mobility. The education issue for the African American community is not one framed by who the child sits next to in a classroom, but whether or not the child is receiving a quality education at the school she/he is attending. The compelling social/education/political challenge for the African American community is not desegregation, but access to *quality education*. There is compelling and disturbing evidence that African Americans in too many of this nation's urban public schools are being drastically shortchanged.

It is clear to this writer that this nation has turned its back on issues relating to the civil rights of citizens. Such issues have always focused this nation on how some groups of citizens have fared at the hands of other citizens and the government. Especially condemning have been those recurrences of longstanding discrimination and acts of brutality carried out against people of color and especially African Americans. Too many people now believe that the civil rights legislation, namely, the 1964 Civil Rights and the 1965 Voting Rights Act and subsequent equal opportunity legislation have significantly addressed race and other forms of discrimination. As a result, so this line of thinking goes, the once existing barriers to opportunity have fallen. And as a result, no such impediments stand in the way of anyone's entry into or progress within America's institutional formations. Or so it is widely believed.

This is to say different strategies for addressing longstanding institutional practices which remain as barriers must be considered and adopted. This is especially the case given the fact that this nation has also turned its back on the normative provisions of the first *Brown* decision. In effect saying "we don't care if African American school children receive low quality education experiences."

## What Is to Be Done?

The central question at this point concerns the responses to the fact that the promises of *Brown* have not been realized. In the main, I believe the responses should be framed, or at least influenced, by what have been the responses to efforts to effect public school desegregation. Indeed, there are salient lessons to be learned from this history. For example, one of the important lessons learned from *Brown* is that, at least for the foreseeable future, there is neither the national will nor leadership structures to reshape public schools. That is, to reshape them around value laden resource allocation practices designed to insure that all children have an opportunity to receive a high quality education experience. Another clearly delivered lesson is that the parents of children attending quality public schools in suburbs and exurbs are adamantly against any desegregation schemes which will take their children from neighborhood schools. And are only luke warm to any in-bussing efforts bringing urban children into suburban schools and neighborhoods. Another lesson learned and which must be heeded is that the African American civil rights and the broader civil rights communities and the progressive elements of the education communities were unable to develop the political education strategies needed to translate the promise of *Brown* I into policy directives and statutes compelling desegregation. Seemingly the thinking was that the Supreme Court decision in and of itself would prompt a transformation of racist attitudes and practices.

Given these and other lessons gained from the era of *Brown* and the predictable lack of appetite for more substantive approaches to institutional change in this nation, this writer is not surprised that the typical small "l" liberal approaches to addressing the shortcomings of the nation's response to public school desegregation. Contemporarily the strategies offered and righteously defended include the following in various iterations:

- Mounting a national campaign to educate Americans regarding the inequalities of education provided to urban dwelling African Americans and other people of color and the dire implications of this.
- Energizing civil rights organizations to take more aggressive lobbying tactics on behalf of access to quality education for all public school students.
- Filing law suits on behalf of aggrieved students of color.
- Energizing and holding public policy makers accountable for passing legislation designed to close education gaps and holding school officials accountable for implementing the expectations.

These strategies are in and of themselves are reasonable. They intend to lay claim on this nation's advocacy organizations, policy making and education structures for doing the right thing on behalf public school children. Indeed, noble intentions. But, unfortunately, these strategies fail to take into account the history of responses this nation has made to the social justice claims by people of color. If the past is prologue, this writer simply does not put much faith in the likelihood that these approaches-even if adopted-would have the desired effect. The strategies place too much stock in normalistic and gradualistic approaches to social change which historically have not met the needs or social objectives of people of color. These approaches rest on the presumptive belief that decision making processes are fair, equally accessible to prince and pauper alike, and are fundamentally committed to the concept and practices of a quality education for all children. The evidence supporting these beliefs is thin.

Given the gravity of the challenges facing African American children and given the responses by this nation to desegregation efforts along with the lessons learned from *Brown*, it is time for African Americans to give serious attention to other strategies. The social and cultural costs for not doing so are too horrifying to disregard. Simply stated, consider the life chances for a young person graduating from high school without the critical thinking skills, numeracy skills, reading skills and experiences with information technology today. Consider the life chances of someone who has dropped out of school before graduating.

I am recommending that African American parents, community members and leaders develop education strategies based on a fundamental proposition emanating from the social history of African people in this nation. The proposition is this. African Americans and any allies gained along the way must first and foremost take the responsibility for educating African American children. This proposition arises out of lessons from the social history of Africans in this land. The proposition is neither defeatist (likely to be a charge) nor cynical. Its truth is based in the truth of the social experiences of African Americans. This truth demonstrates that there have been only two instances in nearly four centuries of the African presence in this part of the diaspora where the federal government has willfully committed resources to educate African people.

The first was during the Reconstruction Era after the Civil War with the formation of the Freedmen's Bureau. According to historian, John Hope Franklin, the Bureau's most significant impact was providing education opportunities for newly freed slaves. The Bureau established and helped to administer an array of educational institutions from day schools to colleges (1966). The second instance of a federal commitment to addressing and repairing social damage done to African Americans due to institutionalized and individual discrimination was during the administration of President Lyndon B. Johnson. The Johnson administration's advocacy of civil rights and equal opportunity legislation set the tone for improvements in education programs benefiting African American and poor children and for opening access to colleges and universities. Unfortunately, both of these instances were short lived and existed within the maelstrom of challenge and resistance, especially from white southerners.

Against this backdrop and given what we know about the nation's responses to the concept and practice of desegregation and given the grave consequences now facing African American students in too many inner city schools, I strongly recommend that another course of action be considered. African American must reorganize institutional resources, e.g., families, churches, civic and social organizations, etc., around a fundamental proposition. Namely, educating children is the primary responsibility of African Americans. Any one wishing to assist in this effort should be considered, but the primary responsibility rests with African Americans. Institutionalizing this proposition can take several delivery forms, among these are:

● Private schools-secular or sectarian

● Charter schools

● Gendered schools-all male or all female

● Charter magnet schools

These institutions would be open to all students, but the emphasis would be on providing African American students a high quality education experience that is culturally relevant. The considerable wealth (approximately 800 billion dollars in annual spending power) and talent from such sectors in the African American community such as: education, business, entertainment, churches, professional athletics and ordinary citizens must be marshaled and focused on providing education alternatives to African Americans. The capacity to do this is present. The will to do so must be bolstered and redirected. In short, African Americans must themselves take on this imperative project.

This is a much needed and long overdue approach to addressing the fact that this nation has not taken the education interests of African American and most children of color seriously. Again, this step towards education independence and self reliance is dictated by the African American's social history. As pointed out above, this history is replete with incidences of betrayal and subterfuge by the institutions charged with protecting the rights of African Americans (Bell 2002). It seems foolhardy, and in fact, is culturally suicidal, to continue to depend on institution of education to prepare African American children to compete on equal footing with others in this nation. Lessons from African American history speak to the need for a drastically different education paradigm. The stakes for not doing so are much too high. A people simply cannot advance socially, economically, politically or culturally, if their children and subsequently, their adults, are miseducated at worst, and poorly educated at best.

In its final analysis, the need for an independent course of action rests on another critically important proposition. History is not kind to a people who deliver up their children to a society's institutions of education when these institutions like the others comprising the social order have been implicated in the historical oppression of the people.

## Sources

1. Bullock, H. (1967). *A History of Negro Education in the South.* Cambridge, Massachusettes: Harvard University Press.
2. Bell, D. (2004). *Silent Covenants.* New York, New York: Oxford University Press.
3. Frankenberg, E. and Lee, C. (2002). *Race in American Public Schools: Rapidly Resegregating School Districts.* Cambridge, Massachusetts: The Civil Rights Project Harvard University.
4. Franklin, J. H. (1966). *From Slavery to Freedom.* New York, New York: Vintage Books.
5. Greenberg, J. (1994). *Crusaders in the Courts: How a Dedicated Band of Lawyers Fought for the Civil Rights Revolution.* New York, New York: Basic Books.
6. Hochschild, J. (1984). *The New American Dilemma: Liberal Democracy and School Desegregation.* New Haven, Connecticut: Yale University.
7. Irons, P. (2002). *Jim Crow's Children.* New York, New York: Penguin Books.
8. Kluger, R. (1976). *Simple Justice: The History of Brown v. Board of Education and Black Americans' Struggle for Equality.* New York, New York: Alfred P. Knopf.
9. Orfield, G. and Eaton, S. (1996). *Dismantling Desegregation: The Quiet Reversal of Brown v. Board of Education.* New York, New York: The New Press.
10. Patterson, J. (2001). *Brown v. Board of Education: A Civil Rights Milestone and its Troubled Legacy.* New York, New York: Oxford University Press.

### Court Cases Cited in Article

[1]*Roberts v. City of Boston,* 59 Massachusetts. 198 (1849)
[2]*Plessy v. Ferguson,* 163 U.S. 537 (1896)
[3]*University v. Murray,* 169 Maryland 478 (1936)

[4]*Missouri ex.rel. Gaines v. Canada*, 305 U.S. 337 (1938)

[5]*Mendez v. Westminster*, S.D. California (1946)

[6]*Sweatt v. Painter*, 339 U.S. 629 (1950)

[7]*Brown v. Board of Education of Topeka*, 349 U.S. 294 (1954)

[8]*Brown v. Board of Education of Topeka*, 349 U.S. 294 (1955)

[9]*Milliken v. Bradley*, 418 U.S. 717 (1974)

[10]*Board of Education of Oklahoma City v. Dowell*, 489 U.S. 265 (1991)

[11]*Freeman v. Pitts*, 503 U.S. 467 (1992)

[12]*Missouri v. Jenkins*, 515 U.S. 1139 (1995)

# Ethnic Diversity: Its Historical and Constitutional Roots

*Cruz Reynoso*

I want to talk with you about the law and ethnic diversity in our country. Since the birth of our nation, we Americans have been in an evolutionary process of defining who we are as Americans, what the American community is, and who belongs to it. In that regard, the American experience has been a great historical experiment, successful sometimes, but not successful other times. The experience we have had as a people is intertwined with out Constitution and the principles that the Constitution has established. The basic question we have to ask ourselves is the following: How can we as a people, or as peoples of diverse religions, races and ethnicities live together and prosper together?

Before the birth of our nation, and sadly it continues today, some of the great wars in this world have come about due to the hatred toward those who are different—by religion, race or ethnicity. We see what is happening in the former Soviet Union, Eastern Europe, the Middle East, Africa and even such places as South America. These hatreds are live issues, traumatic issues that have brought a great deal of suffering to the human family. When we as Americans came together to form our nation, I think we asked the same basic question: Can we have a nation, can we have a people, who can live together and consider themselves as one, and yet be as different as the peoples of this world?

One of America's experiments was in religion. Even though the Constitution declares that the federal government shall not establish religion, we understood early that the essence of that constitutional mandate was a concern about our right, as individual Americans, to practice our own religion. Those who penned the Constitution had in mind the great wars of Europe and the Middle East which had killed so many and had brought so much suffering. So they concluded that the new country had to be one in which folk of different religions could live together. The living together by those who practice different religions has not been all that easy. Books have been written about the "other Americans," Americans who were not of European,

From *Villanova Law Review,* 1992 by Cruz Reynoso. Copyright © 1992 Villanova Law Review. Reprinted by permission of the Law Review.

Protestant ancestry. Fred Hart, former Dean of the University of New Mexico, and still a professor there, tells that his dad remembers when they were growing up in Boston. Signs in some establishments that hired workers would read something like, "Help wanted: Irish and Dogs need not apply." That reaction of prejudice and hatred by some of the owners of those plants was based on religion as well as ethnicity. Indeed, it was not until John Kennedy's presidential campaign that the nation said, "We have matured enough that we can see a Catholic in the White House." That is a long time—from the inception of our country until 1960.

We have succeeded in creating an American culture wherein folk of different religions can live together and consider themselves one people. We appear to have reached a relatively satisfactory solution, at least for a while, because the issue of religion does not come up all the time. There is a fellow you may have heard of by the name Pat Buchanan. He is described by some as a conservative, a right winger, a racist, and by others as a great American. Never is he described as "the Catholic candidate." Yet he is a Catholic, and he often cites his Catholicism to reject the accusation that he is a racist. To me, it is an evolution in the public life of our country that we have a person running for president whose Catholicism hardly gets mentioned.

Others have also suffered. Non-Christians, particularly Jewish people, as well as Hindus and Native Americans have suffered from exclusion. A few years ago, the Alaska Supreme Court issued, I thought, a moving opinion about the rights of a Native American to kill a moose because it was part of the religion of that particular tribe.[1] The Alaska Supreme Court was balancing the right of the state to protect the environment with the right of that particular tribe to exercise its own religion, and, in a sensitive opinion, tried to balance those interests. Thus, the historic process continues.

Issues of religion will always be with us, because who we are religiously is so important to each of us. Yet, we have made so much progress. That is our success story. In America we have been able to live together and consider ourselves as one people, though a people of great religious diversity.

The next area in which we as a nation have worked so hard has been that of race, particularly pertaining to African-Americans. We succeeded so poorly that we experienced here what had happened in other countries—a great war, a great civil war. A larger percentage of Americans were killed and maimed during that war than any other war, over something called race. The Civil War is just a reminder of how important and divisive issues of diversity can be. But from the suffering of this nation in that great war, which pitted brother against brother and sister against sister, came an important amendment to the Constitution—the Fourteenth Amendment. Some post-Civil War amendments, like the Thirteenth, are easily understood. The more difficult Fourteenth Amendment provided the source for a redefinition of who we are as Americans. The constitutional notions of equality and due process found within the pre-Civil War Fifth Amendment were incorporated into the post-Civil War amendments. With the Fourteenth Amendment our country was saying, "We meant what we said in the original Ten Amendments." We redefined ourselves as a people to include African-Americans, including former slaves. While many African-Americans had lived as freed men and women before the Civil War we had not previously succeeded in dealing with the issue of race.

You recall that in the Lincoln-Douglas debates Abraham Lincoln argued that the Constitution set forth the ideal of equality. Those who signed the Constitution understood that we would not meet that ideal immediately, but that we as Americans had a duty to work day in and day out to get the reality of our country a little bit closer to that ideal. To me, and this may sound strange to you, we reached a new public understanding of the reality that we as Americans are of many races, when we built the Vietnam Veterans Memorial in Washington, D.C., and included a black soldier among the soldiers represented. I think we recognized publicly that all races have sacrificed to make this nation great.

Native Americans, like African-Americans, have suffered because of race. Our country originally dealt with Native Americans through the War Department. We viewed Native Americans as the enemy—they were to be killed or captured. Since then American history has evolved to a better understanding between the Indian and non-Indian.

In recent years, the issue of ethnicity and language has come into the forefront. Ethnicity and language, like religion and race, define us. Are we as Americans, or should we be, a people of one language and one ethnicity? In many states there is what is called the English-only movement. A friend of mine from New England, with whom I have served on several committees of the American Bar Association, came up to me one day and said, "Cruz, I know an elderly couple, friends of mine, who went from New England to Florida, and when they came back they said that they were taken aback. They found portions of Miami where everybody spoke Spanish. Only when the couple explained that they did not speak Spanish was English spoken." My friend said, "Cruz, we must do something about this; we must have one language for all of us." I responded: "You are absolutely right. When are you learning Spanish?"

We have struggled with the issue of language and ethnicity throughout our national life. I do not think that we have yet decided what our national ideal is in that regard. My own view is that we Americans are now, and have historically always been, a people of many languages and many ethnic groups. I mentioned the Native Americans, who were here before the European-Americans, and who enjoyed great civilizations and who created marvelous works of art. Somehow we look at the Native Americans of Mexico and the Latin Americans as being those who created great civilizations and great art. The reality is that Native Americans who have lived in what we now call the United States also had that great creativity. We can look to the great irrigation system constructed in New Mexico, or we can look to the political organization of the Navajo nation. Other ethnic groups, such as the Spanish-speaking, came to this land over a hundred years before the English-speaking. Travel in New Orleans or Florida, certainly in Puerto Rico and the Southwest, demonstrates their influence. Sante Fe, New Mexico claims to be the longest standing city that has been a seat of government in what is now the United States. It goes back to the mid-sixteenth century. So folk of different languages and different ethnics groups have been here for a long time.

In the seventeenth century, when the English-speaking Europeans came to the eastern shores of the United States, so did those who spoke French and German and other languages. Indeed, in his autobiography, Benjamin Franklin spoke about how the United States Constitution was translated into the German language during the political debates about whether or not the Constitution should be approved by the people of this country. It seems to me that we have always recognized the importance of people who are of different ethnic groups and tongues.

Take a look at the history of my own state of California. While I spent four years in New Mexico, and I tell folks that I consider myself part manito (a New Mexican is a manito), I was born in California. First came the Native Americans, then the Mexicans and Spaniards who came and settled that land well before the Americans got there. Then came groups from South America, particularly the Chilean community in San Francisco, in large parts because they were fishermen and traders who sailed up and down the Pacific coast. In the middle of the last century, the Americans came to California, and about the same time came many Chinese, followed by Japanese and Filipinos. Currently we have great influxes of people from Southeast Asia and Central America. In Los Angeles, I see whole communities change in a matter of few years. I used to stay in a certain part of Los Angeles which a few years ago was mostly Mexican-American (Chicano) and Anglo-Americans. Now it is mostly Central Americans.

We have seen these great historical changes in our country. It seems to me that we have the political foundation and the ideals of our Constitution to help us meet those realities. Those ideals will help us craft a country in which we consider ourselves as one people, while continuing to enjoy the strength which comes from different religions, races, languages and ethnicities.

We start with basics. The Constitution states that all of us, all the "persons" in this country, enjoy constitutional protections; it is not "citizens," the "English-speaking" or the "Spanish-speaking," who are protected, but all of us as "persons." The United States Supreme Court had occasion to deal with the issue of ethnicity and language in a case that came before it in 1923. You may have read about it in your Constitutional Law classes, *Meyer v. Nebraska.*[2] You may remember that it is a case that dealt with a state statute enacted around 1919 during the First World War.[3] There was a strong anti-German feeling during that time in America. I recall older persons I knew, who were adults during that war, telling me that in their schools, German books and music were destroyed. If they were German, they could not be good. At the time, the Nebraska legislature enacted a criminal statute that prohibited the teaching of German to youngsters before they had graduated from the eighth grade.[4] There was a parochial school in Nebraska called the Zion Parochial School where youngsters were taught in English and in German.[5] A young teacher by the name of Meyer, despite the law, continued to teach in German. He was arrested and convicted.[6] Here is what the statute said:

> No person individually or as a teacher, shall, in any private, denominational, parochial or public school, teach any subject to any person in any language other than the English language. . . . Languages, other than the English language, may be taught as languages only after a pupil shall have attained and successfully passed the eighth grade as evidenced by a certificate of graduation issued by the county superintendent of the county in which the child resides.[7]

Meyer appealed his conviction, but the courts in Nebraska upheld the constitutionality of the statute.[8] Interestingly, court decisions in Nebraska excluded the "dead languages,"—Latin, Greek and Hebrew—from this statute.[9] The legislature, according to the state supreme court, did not mean that students could not study dead languages, only that they could not study certain "live" languages.[10] Eventually the case reached the United States Supreme Court, and the Court looked at the facts and asked itself whether the statute could be constitutional. The Court tried to define what "liberty" meant under the Fourteenth Amendment.[11]

Although the Justices did not talk about it, I think they were also concerned about the Ninth Amendment. When the first Ten Amendments were introduced, an important political debate took place regarding the question of whether those protections that we receive from the first ten amendments were exclusive. In many states, many people said, "No, we want to make clear that those protections are by way of description, for there are many other rights that we have as Americans that government does not have the right to take away." That conclusion was echoed in the *Meyer* case:

> While this Court has not attempted to define with exactness the liberty thus guaranteed [by the Fourteenth Amendment], the term has received much consideration and some of the included things have been definitely stated. Without a doubt, it denotes not merely freedom from bodily restraint but also the right of the individual to contract, to engage in any of the common occupations of life, to acquire useful knowledge, to marry, to establish a home and bring up children, to worship God according to the dictates of his own conscience, and generally to enjoy those privileges long recognized at common law as essential to the orderly pursuit of happiness by free men.[12]

Notice that none of these protections mentioned are found in the Constitution. The Court was saying that surely the right to marry, the right to have children, the right to bring up your family have to be so fundamental that Congress and the states cannot monkey around, if you will, with those rights. Those unstated rights include the right to worship God according to the dictates of a person's own conscience, and generally to enjoy those privileges long recognized at common law as essential to the orderly pursuit of happiness by free men and women. The Court then went on to discuss the importance of language to an individual.[13] The Court ruled that the Nebraska statute was unconstitutional, and that the state had to have an overwhelmingly important reason to prohibit a youngster from learning German, or a teacher from teaching German.[14] The state, the Court wrote, clearly may go very far in order to improve the quality of its citizens, physically, mentally and morally.[15] The individual, however, has certain fundamental rights which must be respected and that includes the right of languages.[16] It seems to me that such a right includes the right of ethnicity. The right to one's own language was recognized as fundamental within our constitution.

The Court had another occasion to look at the issue of ethnicity in a case from the state of California. We produce a great deal of constitutional law from the state of California. A case came up in 1947, if I remember correctly, called *Oyama v. California*.[17] California had passed a statute that prohibited aliens from owning land in California.[18] The breadth of the statute had been narrowed by court decisions; by the 1940s the statute had been interpreted to mean that Japanese could not own land in California. A Japanese immigrant had bought and paid for some land and then put the title in the name of his son, so the son was the legal owner.[19] The father then filed in court to become the guardian, and, in fact, was the child's actual guardian.[20] The statute declared that if a person, who could not legally become a citizen, paid for the land, it would be presumed that such payment was an effort to get around the statute.[21] In that event, the land would escheat to the state.[22] Interestingly, it was the Attorney General of California who brought the action against Mr. Oyama. The only person who testified was the person in charge of the land.[23] The Oyamas did not testify because the hearing took place during the Second World War, when the Oyamas were confined in a concentration camp.[24]

The trial court decided against the Oyamas, and the case was appealed in the California courts.[25] The courts found that the father had paid for the land, and that the Oyamas were clearly trying to get around the statute, and, therefore, the land properly escheated to the state.[26]

The United States Supreme Court looked at the case from the point of view of the little boy, Fred Oyama, and said, "Wait a minute. We are looking at the rights of a citizen, Fred Oyama."[27] Another contemporaneous statute in California permitted parents to make a gift of land to a child by paying for the land.[28] The Court underscored that an American citizen, the child, was being treated differently because of who his parents were.[29] This case presented a conflict between a state's right to formulate a policy in land holding within its boundaries and the right of American citizens to own land anywhere in the United States.[30] The Court concluded that when these two rights clash, the rights of a citizen may not be subordinated merely because of his father's country of origin (that is, the ethnicity of the citizen).[31]

So we start to see a constitutional pattern which protects persons from discrimination on the basis of ethnicity. And I just want to remind us that the Constitution so often deals in the negative, that is, "You can't do A, B, and C," but what it really means is that people have certain rights. While the Court ruled that the Constitution provided protection from discrimination, it really was defining the right of Americans to their own language and ethnicity.

When I was a youngster in Orange County, California, we still had segregated schools. For several years I was sent to a public grammar school referred to as "The Mexican School." There were other schools called "The American Schools." I was born in the then-little town of Brea; Orange County was rural in those pre-Disneyland days. I had gone to school in Brea for a couple years and then my family moved to the nearby community of La Habra. There were a lot of folks in La Habra of Mexican ancestry. When September came, we looked for a school and found a place that looked like a school we were used too—it was built with bricks, it was two stories and had a playground in the back. My brothers and I went there to sign up, and the school officials said, "No, you don't go to this school, you go to another, the Wilson School." So we went to Wilson School. We noticed that all the youngsters there were Latinos and Chicanos, and we asked why we were being sent to this school. We were told that we were being sent to this school to learn English. Since my brothers and I already knew English, we were a little bit suspicious that maybe that was not the reason. After a few months a black family with two youngsters moved into our barrio. They did not speak a word of Spanish; they only spoke English. Nonetheless, they were sent to our school. So we got doubly suspicious. Incidentally, educationally-speaking, it was not a lost cause at all. You may have heard of the "immersion system" of learning a language other than your own; those black youngsters were speaking Spanish as well as we in about six months. Meanwhile, we noticed that there were Anglo-American families whose houses literally abutted on Wilson School, and they were being sent to distant schools. After a while we recognized that, in fact, ours was a segregated school.

A few years after I "graduated" from Wilson (grades kindergarten through sixth), the school was integrated. A lawsuit was filed challenging the segregation of Mexican-American school children in a nearby school district. A federal judge ruled that under California law, school segregation was unlawful.

Related issues reached the United States Supreme Court. It was in a different context that the case of *Hernandez v. Texas*[32] came before the high Court in 1954. A Texan who was Mexican-American had been convicted of murder and appealed.[33] He was unhappy that there had been no Latinos, Chicanos or Mexican-Americans on the jury.[34] The county in Texas where he was tried was fourteen percent Mexican-American, yet for twenty-five years there had not been one Latino on a jury commission, a grand jury or a petit jury.[35] During that time apparently 6,000 persons had been called to serve on one of those commissions or juries and not one had a Spanish surname.[36] Indeed, the Court also pointed out that there were some suspicious matters in that community. In the courthouse, there were two bathrooms, one unmarked, and the other with a sign that read "Colored Men" and then below it "Hombres Aqui" (Men Here). That made the Court a little bit suspicious.[37] There was at least one restaurant in town, the Court said, that had a sign in front that read, "No Mexicans Served." Until very recently the public schools had been segregated.[38] There was extensive testimony in the record by the authorities arguing that they had never discriminated against Latinos; all they tried to do was to find the best possible people to serve.[39] The Supreme Court concluded that despite the generalized denial, it was very difficult to believe that out of 6,000 people, they had not been able to find one qualified Latino.[40] The Court noted that "[t]he state of Texas would have us hold that there are only two classes—white and Negro—within the contemplation of the Fourteenth Amendment,"[41] even as late as 1954. Incidentally, you will find *Hernandez v. Texas* reported just before a case that may sound familiar to you, *Brown v. Board of Education of Topeka.*[42] The Court was busy in those days. The Court rejected the Texas notion out of hand. "The Fourteenth Amendment," the Court said, "is not directed solely against the discrimination due to a 'two-class theory'—that is, based upon differences between 'white' and Negro."[43] The Court went on to say that the Constitution indeed protects everybody:

> *The exclusion of otherwise eligible persons from jury service solely because of their ancestry or national origin is discrimination prohibited by the Fourteenth Amendment. The Texas statute makes no such discrimination, but the petitioner alleges that those administering the law do.*[44]

And, in fact, the Court was convinced that that is exactly what had happened. So again we have a confirmation by the Court that ethnicity is protected.

For those of you who might be concerned about the current Supreme Court, I just want to tell you that the following is written by a distinguished observer of the court:

> *Even Justice Rehnquist, the modern Justice who takes the least interventionist view of equal protection and who is the strongest opponent of the expansion of "suspect classification" jurisprudence, acknowledged in Trimble v. Gordon . . . that classifications based on "national origin, the first cousin of race" . . . were areas where "the Framers obviously meant [equal protection] to apply."*[45]

So apparently even those who take lightly the post-Civil War amendments are convinced that in this area, in the area of ethnicity, there is no question that it is protected by the Constitution.

Finally, I want to mention a case decided by the California Supreme Court called *Castro v. California.*[46] It is one of my favorite cases, maybe because I was the director of a legal services group called California Rule Legal Assistance (CRLA) which filed this action on the behalf of its clients. The challenged California constitutional provision read: "[N]o person who shall not be able to read the Constitution in the English language, and write his or her name, shall ever exercise the privileges of an elector in this State."[47] That constitutional provision was passed in 1891, and I will come back to that fact in a few minutes.[48]

Our clients were able to show that in Los Angeles County where they lived, there were seventeen newspapers published in Spanish, eleven magazines, many radio and television stations, and through these, they were able to know exactly what the public issues of the day were and were able to cast a vote that was educated.[49] The California Supreme Court, analyzing the state constitutional provision by the standards of the federal Constitution, said, in essence, "It cannot stand. We consider the right of citizens. The right to vote is very important." The court determined that the state could not take away the right to vote unless there was a very important reason to do so, and here the court simply did not find that reason. These voters, by reading and hearing, could, in fact, educate themselves.[50] Then, at the end of the opinion, the court added one of my favorite paragraphs in American jurisprudence. Writing for the court, Justice Raymond Sullivan said:

> We add one final word. We cannot refrain from observing that if a contrary conclusion were compelled it would indeed be ironic that petitioners, who are the heirs of a great and gracious culture, identified with the birth of California and contributing in no small measure to its growth, should be disenfranchised in their ancestral land, despite their capacity to cast an informed vote.[51]

So we have come a long way—in California and in the nation.

In *Castro*, the court reviewed the history of constitutional and statutory changes in California, and in one of the footnotes it cited to a case called *People v. Hall*.[52] It is one of my favorite cases in California jurisprudence for a reason opposite that of *Castro v. California*. Let me tell you about the *Hall* case. When California was first formed into a state, the English-speaking and the Spanish-speaking worked cooperatively. They got together in the constitutional convention of 1849 and agreed upon a constitution, even though some who were at that convention spoke no English, and others spoke no Spanish. Yet they got together and created a constitution that was published in both English and Spanish.

But then, sadly, the atmosphere started changing in California, and the case of *People v. Hall*,[53] decided in 1854, gives you a sense of how much change had come about. The legislature had passed a statute that prohibited any testimony against a white person in court if the testimony came from a black, mulatto or an American Indian.[54] A white man was convicted of murder by the testimony of a Chinese man.[55] At that time we had no intermediate court, so the lawyers for the convicted appealed directly to the California Supreme Court.

The California Supreme Court was composed of three members at that time, and it wrote an opinion that is great fun to read in its historical context. The court pointed out that the Native Americans are part of the Mongoloid races and that eons ago, the Mongoloid races from Asia had travelled over the Bering Straits and through Alaska. In the course of many thousands of years these migrants ended up in the lands we now call the United States. The Indians and the Chinese were of the Mongoloid race. When the legislature said Indians could not testify, it obviously meant to include anybody of the Mongoloid race.[56] Since Chinese belong to the Mongoloid race, the court reasoned, they obviously cannot testify against a white man, and so the court reversed the murder conviction.

The *Hall* court described the Chinese people as a "distinct people . . . whose mendacity is proverbial; a race of people whom nature has marked as inferior, and who are incapable of progress or intellectual development beyond a certain a point, as their history has shown. . . ."[57] This quote does not include another discussion in which the court noted that if allowed to testify against a white person, the Chinese would soon want to vote, want to be lawyers, and would even want to sit on the bench.[58] The court ruled on the basis of clear statutory construction. The court seemingly asked, "How could anybody disagree that Indian means Chinese." Indeed, the court wrote: "[E]ven in a doubtful case we would be impelled to this decision on the grounds of public policy."[59]

Sadly, just a few years thereafter, Manuel Dominguez, who had been at the California constitutional convention, and had signed the constitution, was not permitted to testify in a court of law in San Francisco in 1857 because he was of Indian ancestry. That is part of the history of California. To look at the *Castro* decision and see how the law has evolved is a matter of great satisfaction to me.

Incidentally, I have always been interested in Los Angeles. If you visit Los Angeles, go down to the area where Los Angeles was first founded, La Placita (the little plaza). There is a plaque there which has the names of all of the people who helped found Los Angeles. The Spaniards were great record keepers. The records identify people by race and by occupation as well as other characteristics. That plaque identifies the race of the original settlers. I have a book here[60] which published a census taken about the time Los Angeles was founded. Let me just go down the line; you will see the great variety of people that founded California. The reality contrasts with the early romanticized movies that came out of Hollywood portraying Spanish vaqueros as typical. Here are the real Californios: Josef de Lara, Spaniard; his wife Maria, india sabina; Josef Navarro, mestizo; his wife Maria, mulata; Basil Rosas, indian; a husband, indian; his wife, indian; another husband Alejandro Rosas, indian; his wife Juana, coyote indian—mixture of pure Indian and mestizo; Pablo Rodriguez, indian; wife Maria Rosalia, indian; Manuel Camero, mulato; his wife Maria Tomasa, mulata; Luis Quintera, negro; his wife Maria Petmulata; Jose Moreno, mulato; Antonio Rodriguez, chino (Chino—a person who has negroid features, but was born of white parents).[61] That is the real mixture of Los Angeles from whence many of us come.

Let me just read you a passage from that same book. A very distinguished early Californio, Pablo de la Guerra, who was late as state senator, is quoted. The title of the book was FOREIGNERS IN THEIR NATIVE LAND, taken from a speech he delivered in the California legislature in 1856:

> It is the conquered who are humble before the conqueror asking for his protection, while enjoying what little their misfortune has left them. It is those who have been sold like sheep—it is those who were abandoned by Mexico. They do not understand the prevalent language of their native soil. They are foreigners in their own land. I have seen seventy and sixty year olds cry like children because they have been uprooted from the lands of their fathers. They have been humiliated and insulted. They have been refused the privilege of taking water from their own wells. They have been denied the privilege of cutting their own firewood.[62]

This is our history.

Yet we have struggled. As the cases from the California and the United States Supreme Courts indicate, we have indeed made a great deal of progress. The struggles continue. Issues like education and political empowerment create conflict. As we all know, progress does not come overnight. My hope is that as we struggle with these issues, we will also struggle with that notion of how can we be diverse and yet be one people.

For myself, I have enjoyed that diversity. I have a friend by the name of Bill Ong Hing, a professor at Stanford. He invited my family and me to go to his church where a Chinese play was presented. We enjoyed tremendously seeing a culture that my family and I had not seen before. I remember walking down the streets of San Francisco and a gentleman coming up to Bill. The two of them chatted for a couple of minutes in Chinese and then spoke in English. I did not feel that they were talking about me during that time. So often we reject folk who speak a language other than our own, because we think, "Well, they must be talking about me." I never thought that any one person was that important. I would hope that we learn to enjoy the reality that other people are different and that they have a language, a cultural richness, if you will, that we can enjoy. Indeed, I really do give thanks for the fact that we have people in this country who speak different languages and come from different cultures who will make our country far stronger economically and far stronger politically.

I always think of the advertising that we as Americans do. I am told that there was a time when General Motors was advertising in Latin America for their then-new car called the Nova. Apparently nobody had told them that "Nova" in Spanish is "Nova," which means "It won't go." It was not a successful advertising campaign. Or another time when my former colleague, Justice Joseph Groden of the California Supreme Court, came back from a long trip in China, and he told me there were Coca-Cola signs all over China. I asked about Pepsi-Cola because I had read that Pepsi had a contract with the Chinese government. At that time Pepsi-Cola had a little ditty, you may remember many years ago, that went something like, "Pepsi, come alive with Pepsi." Unfortunately, it had been mistranslated in Chinese, to read, "Pepsi brings your ancestors back to life," and the Chinese, with their respect for their ancestors, were not amused. Pepsi apparently lost its contract.

I also remember reading an article by a German industrialist who said basically, "You know, I speak English, and I go to all of these gatherings where folk come from all over the world selling their high-tech equipment. I go and look at all that and I see that the Americans make very good equipment, and the Japanese have very good equipment, as do other nationals. They all look very good. Then afterwards, though I speak English, I socialize with folks generally in the German language, because I feel more comfortable in German. All I can tell you is that in Germany, you'll sell in the German language."

I think that our diversity will indeed bring strength to us, and I think that we can profit from it. But more importantly, we need to continue working with the reality that we are a very diverse people, ethnically and linguistically. Despite those differences, as with differences of race and religion, we ought to look at what unites us, what makes us all Americans. We need to look at our history, at the land, at the suffering we have been through as a people. We need to examine the ideals that we find in the Constitution, those very ideals that have brought the California and the United States Supreme Courts to declare that there are those rights so important that government can not take them away from us. If nobody can take those rights away from us, we need to rejoice in those rights, to rejoice in our differences, to appreciate those differences, and to profit one from another.

## Notes

[1] Frank v. State of Alaska, 604 P.2d 1068 (Ala. 1979).

[2] 262 U.S. 390 (1923).

[3] *Id.* at 397 (citing Neb Laws 1919, ch. 249 (entitled "An act relating to the teaching of foreign languages in the State of Nebraska" (approved April 9, 1919))).

[4] *Id.* (citing Neb. Laws 1919, ch. 249, § 2).

[5] *Id.* at 396–97.

[6] *Id.* at 396.

[7] *Id.* at 397 (quoting Neb Laws 1919, ch. 24, §§ 1–2).

[8] *Id.*

[9] *Id.* at 400–01.

[10] *Id.* at 401.

[11] The Fourteenth Amendment states, in pertinent part: "No State shall . . . deprive any person of life, liberty, or property, without due process of law; nor deny to any person within its jurisdiction the equal protection of the laws." U.S. Const. amend. XIV, § 1.

[12] *Meyer,* 262 U.S. at 399.

[13] *Id.* at 400–03.

[14] *Id.* at 402–03.

[15] *Id.* at 402.

[16] *Id.* at 400–01.

[17] 332 U.S. 633 (1948).

[18] *Id.* at 635–36 & nn. 1 & 3 (citing Alien Land Law, 1 Cal. Gen. Laws, Act 261 (Deering 1944 & Supp. 1945)).

[19] *Id.* at 636–37.

[20] *Id.*

[21] *See id.* at 636 (citing Alien Land Law, 1 Cal. Gen. Laws, Act 261, § 9(a)).

[22] *Id.*

[23] *Id.* at 638. The witness, John Kurfurst, had been left in charge of the Oyama property when the Oyama family was evacuated in 1942 as part of the evacuation of persons of Japanese descent during World War II. *Id.* at 637–38.

[24] *See id.* at 638.

[25] *See id.* at 639.

[26]*Id.* at 639–40.

[27]*See id.* at 640.

[28]*Id.* at 640 & n. 16 (citing CAL., PROB. CODE ANN. § 1407).

[29]*Id.* at 640–41.

[30]*Id.* at 647.

[31]*See id.* at 646–47.

[32]347 U.S. 475 (1954).

[33]*Id.* at 476.

[34]*Id.* at 476–77.

[35]*Id.* at 480–81 & n. 12.

[36]*Id.* at 482.

[37]*Id.* at 479–80.

[38]*Id.* at 479.

[39]*Id.* at 481.

[40]*Id.* at 482.

[41]*Id.* at 477.

[42]347 U.S. 483 (1954).

[43]*Hernandez,* 347 U.S. at 478.

[44]*Id.* at 479.

[45]CONSTITUTIONAL LAW 624 n.3 (Gerald Gunther ed., 11th ed. 1985) (citing Trimble v. Gordon, 430 U.S. 762, 777 (1977) (Rehnquist, J., dissenting)).

[46]466 P. 2d 244 (Cal. 1970).

[47]*Id.* at 245 (quoting CAL. CONST. art. 2, § 1).

[48]*Id.* The English literacy requirement was proposed in 1891 by a California state assembly-man, A. J. Bledsoe, who in 1886 had been part of a committee that expelled all persons of Chinese ancestry from Humboldt County, California. *Id.*

[49]*Id.* at 254–55.

[50]*See, e.g., id.* at 254–57.

[51]*Id.* at 259.

[52]*Id.* at 248 n.11 (citing People v. Hall, 4 Cal. 399 (1854)).

[53]4 Cal. 399 (1854).

[54]*Id.* at 399 (quoting Act of April 16, 1850 (regulating California criminal proceedings)).

[55]*Id.*

[56]*Id.* at 400–04.

[57]*Castro,* 466 P.2d at 248 n.11 (quoting *Hall,* 4 Cal. at 404–05.

[58]*Hall,* 4 Cal. at 404–05.

[59]*Id.* at 404.

[60]FOREIGNERS IN THEIR NATIVE LAND 33 (David J. Weber ed., 1st ed. 1973).

[61]*Id.* at 34–35.

[62]*Id.* at vi (quoting Pablo de la Guerra, Speech to the California Senate (1856)).

# Native Americans and the United States, 1830–2000 Action and Response

*Steven J. Crum*

## Introduction

In this chapter, I will focus on federal government policies toward Native American people from the early nineteenth century forward. Although this story has been told numerous times, and scholars have called it an old-fashioned historical approach to the writing of Indian history–an assessment I agree with–I will work hard not to repeat the same examples others have given over the years. Instead, I will provide some new examples as much as possible. My main argument is that the history of federal government policy toward Indian people is one of action on one side and response and reaction on the other. More often than not, the federal government initiated the action and the Indians responded or reacted to it. At times, however, the Indians served as actors and persuaded the federal government what to include in its interactions with tribal people, including treaty provisions of the nineteenth century.

## Indian Removal

In 1830, Congress passed the Indian Removal Act, which paved the way for the mass-scale physical removal of thousands of Native Americans who lived east of the Mississippi River. In the southeast alone, the federal government moved roughly 60,000 tribal people to the area we now call eastern Oklahoma (Indian Territory up to 1907). Those of us who study Native American history know the historical accounts of the removed Cherokee, Choctaw, Creek, Chickasaw, and Seminole. We are fully aware of the Trail of Tears of 1838 in which thousands of Cherokee died en route from their former homeland.[1]

Although Indian removal was a case of the American government having its way, at the same time, some of the tribes made certain that favorable provisions ended up in the removal treaties. In the Treaty of Dancing Rabbit Creek of 1830, negotiated with the Choctaw of Mississippi, the Choctaw leadership persuaded the government to include a provision for the education of Choctaw people. The tribe viewed education as a means of "survival" and a way of dealing with the white Americans. With the funds coming from the treaty, the tribe eventually created the Forty Youth Fund, which helped several Choctaws pursue a higher education. Some earned college and university degrees from eastern postsecondary institutions and returned home to help maintain their Choctaw Nation. Concerning the educational provision of the 1930 treaty, it was a case of the Choctaw leadership calling the action and the treaty negotiators responding.[2]

When we read about Indian removal of the nineteenth century, we typically think about eastern Indians being removed west of the Mississippi River. What we seldom read about are the number of far western tribes who were also subjected to the same policy. In the state of California alone, the government applied its removal policy to the tribes of this state, especially in the 1860s. In 1863, California state troops gathered up roughly 400 Concow Maidu of Butte County (about 100 miles north of Sacramento) and marched them across the Sacramento Valley, over the coastal range, and placed them on the Round Valley Reservation in Mendocino County. The descendants of the Maidu still live at Round Valley.[3] In another case, the military gathered up 800 Owens Valley Paiute from eastern California and placed them at Fort Tejon in the mountains overlooking the San Joaquin Valley. Because the military did not have the strength to manage the Paiutes, every one of them eventually escaped and most returned to Owens Valley. A few ended up on the Tule River Reservation between Fresno and Bakersfield.[4]

Along with these actual removal cases in California, there were also removal proposals made by federal officials. In 1862, Senator Milton Latham of the state submitted a bill into Congress which, if passed, would have paved the way for the tribes of the state to be removed over the Sierra Nevada Mountains and placed in Owens Valley. This bill never made it out of Congress. There was also a removal proposal to colonize the tribes of California on some of the off-shore islands near Santa Barbara.[5]

## The Reservation Policy

Around the mid-nineteenth century, the government created a new policy called the reservation policy. Its objective was to gather up the tribes of the North American continent and place them on reserves where they could be managed and controlled. Under the supervision of federal agents, the tribes could slowly be subjected to so-called American "civilization" since the white Americans viewed Indians as savages. The new reservation policy did not replace the earlier removal policy entirely. Instead, the federal sector carried out both simultaneously, with the tribes being removed to reservations. The only noticeable difference was that the government did not move the eastern tribes farther west.[6]

Some tribal individuals showed their extreme dislike of the reservation policy by eventually rejecting reservation life. The Office of Indian Affairs (today's BIA), the federal agency given the responsibility to run Indian affairs, required the Modoc of extreme northern California to move across the state line and settle on the newly established Klamath reservation of southern Oregon in the 1860s. At first the tribe went along with the plan. However, the Modoc felt uncomfortable living in a foreign area. Not willing to face confined reservation life, the Modoc left and returned to their ancestral homeland in northern California. The government branded the Modoc as lawbreakers and declared war against them. This led to the well-known Modoc War of 1873 in which the American military finally won.[7]

To punish the Modoc, the government carried out three forms of punishment. In the first instance, it hung the major leaders and sent their skulls to Washington, D.C., for so-called scientific study. Next, it confined two leaders on Alcatraz Island as prisoners. Third, it removed the larger number of Modoc to eastern Indian Territory, where they remained as prisoners of war of the government until 1909. Removal thus became a form of punishment for tribes that did not accept the reservation policy.[8]

Other Native Americans refused to move to newly established reservations when asked. For example, in 1877, the government created the Duck Valley Reservation, which straddles the Idaho-Nevada border. The plan was to induce all the Western Shoshones of the Great Basin region to move there in the years immediately thereafter. But this effort was largely a failure, for only one-third of the tribe moved, those tribal groups and bands that lived closest to Duck Valley. The other two-thirds publicly refused to move and used the aboriginal argument of their deep attachment to particular valleys and mountain ranges where their ancestors had lived "since time immemorial." Their form of punishment was deliberate indifference; that is, the government largely pretended that nonreservation Indians did not exist in the Basin area. Thus they received little or no services from the Indian bureau. Not until the 1930s would the BIA give these Shoshones consistent federal attention.[9]

## Assimilation

Around 1880, the American government came up with a third generalized Indian policy called assimilation with the objective to Americanize those Indians living on reservation land. The assimilation campaign had several components. The Indian bureau created on-reservation police forces and tribal courts to make adult Indians give up their native ways. The police forces consisted of tribal members who were bought off by BIA agents. Agents provided them various benefits and services, which included wood-frame houses, firewood, and extra food provisions. Under the supervision of the agent, the police tried to make their own kind surrender their Indian ways and become good Americans.[10]

Many tribal individuals outsmarted the assimilation plan by pretending to become responsible Americans. They joined Christian churches, learned rudimentary

English, and displayed different forms of American patriotism. Some reservation Indians organized Fourth of July Grounds where they camped out for days to celebrate American independence and democracy. But in reality these encampments were a way for the Indians to create underground cultures that allowed the participants to perpetuate native dances and social practices, including indigenous forms of gambling. To this day, the descendants of the nineteenth-century reservation Indians still remain native to varying degrees.[11]

One of the most visible forms of assimilation for young Indians was formal schooling. The government developed three kinds of schools in the last quarter of the nineteenth century: reservation day schools, reservation boarding schools, and off-reservation boarding schools. Typically, the youngest children started their schooling in the reservation schools. As they became older, the bureau removed them from their families, kinship groups, and tribes and sent them to large off-reservation schools located hundreds or even thousands of miles away from home. In other instances, very young children spent all their schooling in distant off-reservation boarding schools.[12]

In the government schools, the government subjected the students to a detribalization process. It stripped them of their native dress and issued military uniforms for young boys and Victorian dresses for the girls. It suppressed tribal languages and required the students to speak and read English. It made the students follow American values and practices, which included the puritanical work ethic, Christian values, and die-hard individualism.[13]

As for the students, they reacted to forced schooling by expressing various forms of resistance, which can be classified as "overt" and "covert." Perhaps the most popular form of overt resistance was running away. Unable to cope with institutionalized schooling, an unspecified number of students ran away with the objective of returning home. Most were captured, but some succeeded in returning to their families and tribes. Covert forms of resistance included "work slow down," talking tribal languages behind the scenes, and stealing food from the cafeteria.[14]

Although the vast majority of students ended up learning English and wearing American clothing, they still remained native to varying degrees, and most returned home to their Indian communities. There they lived out their lives by being both American and native. They built wood-frame houses and acquired horses and cattle. Yet, at the same time, they continued to speak their native languages and relied on indigenous medicinal remedies. In short, their schooling was only a partial success.[15]

Another form of assimilation was the breaking apart of Indian reservation land. To carry out this initiative, Congress passed the Dawes Act (General Allotment Act) of 1887, which allowed the federal sector to subdivide reservation land and issue individual allotments to the tribal members. For the most part, adult heads of households received 160 acres of land since this specific acreage represented the size of a nineteenth-century American homestead. The BIA expected the Indian allottees to farm the land and become American-style homesteaders. Once the government surveyed and allotted a reservation, it sold any remaining surplus land. By carrying out these initiatives, it hoped to destroy the tribal way of life and make Indians think and act individualistically rather than communally or tribally.[16]

Many tribal people did not passively accept the allotment process. They expressed their dislike in a number of ways. One person, Lone Wolf of the Kiowa tribe in Indian Territory, took the American government to court because of his opposition to the 1887 act. In the Supreme Court decision *Lone Wolf v. Hitchcock* (1903), Lonewolf argued that the Dawes Act could not be applied to the Kiowa because of prior treaty rights. He was correct, for some years earlier, under the Medicine Lodge Treaty of 1867 made with the Kiowa and other tribes of the southern Great Plains area, the treaty specified that the only way the government could alter the landbase of the reservation given to the Kiowa was if the majority of adults agreed to any form of alteration. But years later, the Kiowa never agreed in the majority to have their reservation subdivided by the Dawes act. Thus the act violated Kiowa treaty rights. However, the Supreme Court disregarded treaty rights and argued that the federal government had superior power over Indian tribes.[17] Therefore, Congress could apply an act to Native Americans, regardless of prior treaty rights.

To show their anger over the Dawes Act, which of course led to substantial land loss, other Native Americans considered leaving the United States completely in the late nineteenth and early twentieth centuries and moving to Mexico. Several tribal individuals from Indian Territory made trips to Mexico between 1890 and 1938 to look for a new homeland where Indian tribes could be free from negative governmental laws and policies. In the opening decade of the twentieth century, Crazy Snake and his followers of Creek Indians of eastern Oklahoma talked about moving to Mexico. As late as the 1930s, some Seminoles of Oklahoma met with the president of Mexico to discuss Mexico as a future home. In the end, these delegations chose to remain in the U.S.[18]

Other aspects of the overall assimilation policy surfaced after the turn of the century. One was the BIA's in-house regulation called Circular 1665 of 1921 and 1923. This BIA regulation either suppressed or prohibited Native American religious practices. It allowed Indians to have only one monthly traditional dance, which could be held from September to February. No dances could be held from March to August. Moreover, the monthly dance could take place only during the day time. No nighttime dance could take place. Only those fifty years and older could participate in the monthly daytime dance. Lastly, Indians could no longer carry out their traditional giveaways.[19]

Most Native American people rejected Circular 1665 and found ways to maneuver around the regulation. Some tribal individuals held dances in remote areas where BIA agents could not find them. Some joined the dances of other tribes held in outlying areas where agents would not or could not visit. Others practiced public exhibition dancing for white audiences, thus enabling them to practice traditional dances throughout the year. The BIA did not prohibit exhibition dances because these dances were nonthreatening and pleased the white crowds that wanted to observe what it labeled "exotic" Indians. Some Indians performed popular forms of white dances and entertainment during early evening hours to convince watchful agents that they were becoming good Americans. Once the officials left, and late at night, the Indians resorted to their traditional dances. All these tactics allowed tribal individuals to outwit the BIA in the early years of the twentieth century.[20]

## Cultural Pluralism and the Indian New Deal

As time moved forward in the twentieth century, some white people realized that the government's campaign to assimilate the Indians had largely failed. Native Americans simply could not be completely transformed because of their deep-rooted cultures and traditional beliefs. White reformists advanced the argument that because the U.S. was a democracy where people are given choices, then Indian people must be given the choice to remain native if they wanted. One of the noted reformers was non-Indian John Collier who created the American Indian Defense Association in 1923 with a two-fold purpose: that Indians must be given their religious freedom and that the Indian landbase must be preserved. Besides private individuals such as Collier, even some federal officials concluded that the BIA needed to change some of its policies toward Indian people. In response, Hubert Work, the Secretary of the Interior in 1926, authorized the establishment of a ten-member team to study the "so-called Indian problem" and make recommendations in a published report of how the BIA could be improved.[21]

In 1928, the Meriam team released its lengthy study called *The Problem of Indian Administration,* or popularly known as the Meriam report. The report pointed out the serious problems within Indian affairs, including the substantial land loss of Indian people since the passage of the Dawes Act in 1887, poor health care, and the poor quality of education and life students had received in the BIA boarding schools. At the same time, the report team made positive recommendations of how life could be improved for Native Americans. The federal government needed to provide improved health care for Indians, Indian students needed to be given a quality education in the Indian schools, and the Indian students needed to be taught native subject matter. Here was a case of reformists rejecting the half-century assimilationist policy.[22]

One of the ten members of the Meriam team was Henry Roe Cloud of the Winnebago tribe in Nebraska. After experiencing the boarding school process as a youngster, Cloud made the decision to go to college. He earned more than one college degree, including the bachelor's degree from Yale in 1910. Aware that the BIA did not give Indian students a full high school education in the early twentieth century, he established the American Indian Institute, an all-Indian high school in Wichita, Kansas, for those students who aspired to a full secondary education. Cloud encouraged his students to appreciate their Indianness, and it became obvious why the Meriam report favored the teaching of native subject matter in the Indian schools.[23]

One important end result of the reform sentiment of the 1920s and early 1930s was the Indian Reorganization Act (IRA) of 1934. The provisions of this congressional act were largely the work of John Collier, who became the new commissioner of the BIA in 1933. As a federal official, Collier put his reformist ideas into action by making sure Congress passed the IRA. Some of the provisions of the act were as follows: it ended any further allotment of Indian reservations; it returned to reservation status any remaining surplus land; it allowed tribes to organize politically with tribal constitutions and charters, or it gave tribes a kind of quasi-sovereign status; it provided loans so that tribal individuals could create business enterprises and become better off economically; it provided loans so that Indian students could pursue a college or university education; and it introduced "Indian preference," which was a measure to employ qualified Indians to work in the BIA.[24]

The majority of Indian tribes voted to become IRA tribes since they liked the provisions of the act. Specifically, 181 of them voted in favor of the act. However, 77 tribes voted against it for their own reasons.[25] As a case in point, the Paiutes of Owens Valley voted against the act in large numbers, not because they disliked the act, but because of the BIA's recent rhetoric of Indian removal. Both before and at the time of the act's passage, the BIA had considered removing the Owens Valley Paiutes completely from their ancestral valley in eastern California. The bureau used the argument that the Indians could not really make a living there because the city of Los Angeles had taken much of the water from the Owens River for its California Aquaduct, channeling the river water across the desert to Los Angeles. Thus the BIA wanted the Paiutes to move either to the Walker River Reservation in western Nevada or to move over the Sierra Nevada Mountains and settle down near Merced in the San Joaquin Valley. Insecure about possible removal, the Paiutes voted against the act. In the end, the bureau backed away from removal, allowed the Paiutes to remain, and even created three small reservations for them in the second half of the 1930s: Bishop, Big Pine, and Lone Pine.[26]

The Hupa of northern California also voted against the IRA. Unlike the Paiutes of Owens Valley, the Hupa voted against the act for completely different reasons. First, the tribal leaders favored land allotment, which the IRA ended. Secondly, the Hupa already had a tribal council in operation for some years before Congress passed the act. Thus, there was no need to create a new one under the IRA. Lastly, the Hupa, as well as other tribes of California, had impending claims against the American government. This claims matter was rooted in the eighteen treaties that the Senate did not ratify in the mid-nineteenth century, which would have set aside over seven million acres of land for California Indians. Six years before Congress passed the IRA, it had approved the California Indian Jurisdiction Act of 1928 to allow the California tribes to file suit for past injustices, including the unratified treaties. The Hupa in the mid-1930s felt that the IRA might somehow disrupt the current claims case even though the act itself specified that cases would not be affected.[27] Here was a case of government action and tribal reaction.

Since the passage of the IRA in 1934, tribal individuals have expressed a wide range of views about the act. Some leaders pointed out that despite the act's limitations, it still had some good outcomes. Tim Giago (Lakota), former editor of *Indian Country Today,* stressed that "there wouldn't be any reservations left today if it wasn't for the IRA."[28] Another Lakota, Pat Spears, leader of the Lower Brule Sioux, stated.: "It's better than what it replaced. . . . I don't think we're better off by the IRA. . . . It's been the only vehicle we had, but I think it's time we trade it in."[29] Webster Two Hawk, chairperson of the Rosebud Sioux Tribe, expressed a similar view: "I have mixed opinions regarding the IRA. I have to support it because I work for an IRA government. . . . The IRA was a child of the federal government and did not really contain Indian ideas. . . . In redoing it, I would remove many of the restrictions."[30] Some Lakota leaders were much more critical of the IRA. Robert Fast Horse, tribal judge from Pine Ridge, stressed that the IRA "wouldn't recognize our traditional form of government."[31] Bertha Chasing Hawk of Cheyenne River argued that "the tribal court is useless to us because the [IRA] tribal council can overrule the tribal court's decisions."[32] All of the above individuals are from reservations in North and South Dakota.

Regardless of the IRA's shortcomings, it did create some new directions. The Indian preference clause made it possible for more Indians to be employed by the BIA, especially those who were college educated. By the mid-1940s, the following individuals were superintendents of BIA agencies and reservations: Henry Roe Cloud (Winnebago), Kenneth Marmon (Laguna Pueblo), George LaVatta (Shoshone), Archie Phinney (Nez Perce), Frel Owl (Cherokee), and Gabe Parker (Choctaw).[33]

# Termination

In the late 1940s and early 1950s. the BIA inaugurated a new Indian policy called Termination. Its basic purpose was the end of the "long-term historic relationship" the Indian tribes had with the American government. The government wanted Indians to assimilate into the larger dominant society. To carry out the new policy, the BIA and other branches of the government came out with several components of termination. The first was the congressional Indian Claims Commission Act of 1946. Under it, the government wanted to compensate the Indian tribes for all unjust acts committed against Indian people. The tribes would be given the opportunity to develop shopping lists and submit documented examples of injustices before the Indian Claims Commission. If a tribe won suit, it was awarded a monetary settlement or claims money. The BIA distributed this money in the form of per capita payments.[34]

Another component was House Concurrent Resolution (HCR) 108 in 1953, which paved the way for the elimination of various Indian reservations across the country. Under HCR 108, the Indians lost 1.3 million acres of land in the postwar period. The BIA wanted the more successful tribes to be terminated first, including the Menominee of Wisconsin and the Klamath of Oregon. But in the end, most of the tribes terminated were small and defenseless. This included forty small Indian rancherias of California and four Southern Paiute bands of southwestern Utah.[35]

Another component of termination was Operation Relocation (1952) in which the BIA induced reservation people to leave their respective reservations and move to urban areas. The BIA provided incentives, including paid transportation; rent money for the first few months; short-term educational training that included auto mechanics, welding, licensed practical nursing, and dental assistant training; and the overall promise of a better way of life, which included jobs, education, and recreation.[36]

From a statistical standpoint, relocation was extremely successful, for thousands of Indians across the nation moved to various big cities that had BIA-run relocation centers. Some of the cities included Chicago, Dallas-Fort Worth, Denver, Detroit, Los Angeles, Oakland, San Francisco, and San Jose. As a result of relocation, Native Americans became markedly urbanized from the 1950s forward. In 1950, only 13.4 percent of the Indian population lived in cities, whereas by 1980, fifty percent of them were urbanites. The Indian population of California alone skyrocketed after 1950. In 1950, only 19,000 Indians lived in the state. By 1960, it was 39,000. By 1980, it stood at 200,000 with relocation being the huge factor.[37]

The relocation component was both a success and a failure. On the success side, if the BIA's plan was to amalgamate Indians into the overall population in urban America, this effort led to urban Indians having one of the highest out-marriage rates in the nation. Those in the cities have a 50/50 chance of marrying non-Indians. On the failure side, many urban Indians did not melt into urban white America. Instead, they looked for ways to remain native. Some worked hard to live in certain neighborhoods so that families could visit one another. Christian Indians established all-Indian churches in the inner city. Those who were more traditional held sweat ceremonies in their backyards and carried out Peyote ceremonies.

Most attended intertribal pow wows. Others sponsored all-Indian sports, which included basketball and softball tournaments. Others gathered at intertribal urban Indian centers that provided various services, including job referral and social gatherings. In short, urban Indians reacted and created ways to remain native and never surrendered their identities, both tribal and intertribal.[38]

## Self-Determination

After 1960, the American government came up with still another Indian policy called self-determination. This policy in certain ways was the opposite of termination. The government encouraged Indians to remain on reservations if they chose. The BIA wanted the tribes to become involved in running their own affairs with federal financial support. Like termination, self-determination had a number of components. The Department of Housing and Urban Development (HUD) helped tribal families build "self-help" houses to replace the older substandard houses that lacked indoor running water and other basic necessities. These new houses of the 1960s forward eventually became known as HUD houses, named after the federal department.[39]

Reservation Indians also benefitted from aspects of the Office of Economic Opportunity (OEO) which was intended for poor people in general, regardless of race. Young Indian students entered preschool programs called Headstart, and high school students lived on college campuses during summer months under Upward Bound. This latter program sought to encourage the high school students to consider higher education after graduating from high school.[40]

The BIA also encouraged the teaching of Indian languages and culture in reservation-based schools run by the tribes themselves. The Rough Rock Demonstration School of the Navajo reservation in Arizona was an example of the Navajos creating their own school to emphasize native culture. The school received financial support from the BIA. Several other tribes would also build their own tribally run schools to provide elementary and secondary education. These schools received support from the congressional Indian Self-Determination and Education Assistance Act of 1975.[41]

Self-determination also encouraged tribal people to develop reservation-based higher education programs because of the shortcomings of mainstream higher education. The Navajo Nation established its Navajo Community College in 1968 (renamed Dine College in 1997). This tribally controlled college inspired dozens of other tribes also to establish tribal colleges.[42] As of 2000, thirty-three tribally run colleges existed throughout the U.S. They are run largely by college-educated tribal people, and they offer Indian courses to the students. The colleges receive funding from a number of sources, including the congressional Tribally Controlled Community College Act of 1978.

Congress supported the notion of self-determination in the late 1960s and 1970s by passing more than one act. The Indian Civil Rights Act of 1968 applied certain aspects of the U.S. Bill of Rights to Indian reservations. This meant that reservation-based Indian people possessed certain constitutional guarantees, including the freedom of religion, the freedom of the press, and the right to assemble. The Indian Child Welfare Act of 1978 provided a preference of who could adopt Indian children. First preference is given to the child's extended family, second to other members of the child's tribe, third to members of other tribes, and fourth to non-Indians if no one adopted from the three higher categories. Congress passed this law to make sure an adopted Indian child would remain connected to his native culture. In the same year, Congress passed the American Indian Religious Freedom Act which allowed Indian people to possess sacred objects (e.g., eagle feathers), overall freedom to practice traditional religions both on and off reservation, and the right to practice ceremonies at traditional places.[43]

# Self-Governance

The most recent federal Indian policy is self-governance, which emerged in the late 1980s. For the most part, self-governance is an extension of self-determination but with some big differences. Under it, the BIA wants to shift its long-term functions over to the tribes themselves. One example of this action is higher education, which has been a BIA function since the early 1930s. From the 1950s forward, the BIA's regional area offices administered higher education grants and loans to Indian students pursuing a postsecondary education. But under self-governance, the tribes themselves receive BIA funds to run their own higher education programs. The BIA is no longer involved except to channel funds.[44]

# Conclusion

In this brief account of the history of Indian policy, we have looked at the pattern of government action and native responses and reactions. Although this has been the prevalent pattern for almost two centuries, there are also times when the process is reversed with the Indians as actors and the government as the reactor. For example, in 1916, the BIA began to add the higher high school grades to its off-reservation boarding schools, which went only to the eighth grade. This BIA action was in response to the Indian members of the intertribal organization Society of American Indians, which asserted that Indians should be given more education instead of being educated as simple laborers in the Indian schools.[45] More recently, in 1988, Congress passed the Indian Gaming Regulatory Act, which determines what tribal nations can do in the domain of gaming. The act designates three classes of gaming: (1) traditional gaming, which tribes can carry out without restriction; (2) gaming such as bingo and card games, which Indian tribes can have in their casinos but would be regulated by a national Indian gaming commission; and (3) Nevada-styled gaming, which the tribes can carry out but only if these forms are legal within a given state where the Indian casino is located. Congress passed the law because it wanted to regulate the rising tide of Indian gaming that started in 1979 with the Seminole tribe in Florida. As of the late 1990s, 148 tribal groups had casinos with class three gaming. They introduced them for two reasons in the 1980s. The first was to move away from the state of poverty that many tribes had lived in for decades. Second, in the early 1980s, President Reagan's administration reduced substantially federal funds for poverty programs. The tribes sought new sources of funding for tribal survival, and one means was the revenue from new casinos. But when casinos started to become too numerous, the government stepped in with its regulations.[46] Here was a case of Indian action and government reaction.

# ◼️ Notes

[1]Philip Weeks, *Farewell My Nation: The American Indian and the United States, 1820–1890* (Arlington Heights, IL: Harlan Davidson, Inc., 1990), 22–23; Francis Paul Prucha, *The Great Father: The United States Government and the American Indians,* abridged edition (Lincoln: University of Nebraska Press, 1984), 64–93.

[2]7 Stat. 315; Grayson B. Noley, "The History of Education in the Choctaw Nation from Precolonial Times to 1830," (Ph.D. dissertation, Pennsylvania State University, 1976), 172; Clara Sue Kidwell, *Choctaws and Missionaries in Mississippi, 1818–1918* (Norman: University of Oklahoma Press, 1995), 96; 136; James D. Morrison, *Schools for the Choctaws* (Durant, OK: Choctaw Bilingual Education Program, 1978), 240.

[3]Dorothy Hill, *The Indians of Chico Rancheria* (Sacramento, CA: Department of Parks and Recreation, 1978), 39–42.

[4]Steven Crum, "Deeply Attached to the Land: The Owens Valley Paiutes and Their Rejection of Indian Removal, 1863 to 1937," *News From Native California,* 14 (summer 2001): 18.

[5]"A bill . . ." *The Visalia (Weekly) Delta,* 5 June 1862, p. 2; "About Indian Affairs," *The Visalia (Weekly).Delta,* 17 December 1983, p. 2; James J. Rawls, *Indians of California: The Changing Image* (University of Oklahoma, 1984), 169.

[6]Prucha, *The Great Father,* 116, 129–132, 181–197; Weeks, *Farewell My Nation,* 60, 159, 170, 178, 208.

[7]Lucille J. Martin, "A History of the Modoc Indians: An Acculturation Study," *The Chronicles of Oklahoma,* 47 (winter 1969–70): 398–417.

[8]Ibid., 420–421, 441.

[9]Steven Crum, *The Road on Which We Came* (Salt Lake City: University of Utah Press, 1994), 43–84.

[10]Prucha, *The Great Father,* 195–197, 218–219; Weeks, *Farewell My Nation,* 217–232.

[11]Crum, *The Road,* 52.

[12]David Wallace Adams, *Education for Extinction: American Indians and the Boarding School Experience, 1875–1928* (Lawrence: University Press of Kansas, 1995), 21–24, 28–59.

[13]Ibid., 97–163.

[14]Ibid., 232–238; K. Tsianina Lomawaima, *They Called It Prairie Light: The Story of Chilocco Indian School* (University of Nebraska Press, 1994), 115–126.

[15]Adams, *Education for Extinction,* 273–306.

[16]Prucha, *The Great Father,* 224–228.

[17]Blue Clark, *Lone Wolf v. Hitchcock: Treaty Rights and Indian Law at the End of the Nineteenth Century* (University of Nebraska, 1994).

[18]Steven Crum, " 'America, Love It or Leave It': Some Native American Initiatives to move to Mexico, 1890–1940," *The Chronicles of Oklahoma,* 79 (winter 2001–02): 408–429.

[19]Peggy V. Beck and Anna L. Walters, *The Sacred: Ways of Knowledge, Sources of Life* (Tsaile: Navajo Community College Press, 1977), 158–161.

[20]Annette Louise Reed, "Rooted in the Land of Our Ancestors, We Are Strong: A Tolowa History," (Ph.D. dissertation, University of California, Berkeley, 1999), 155–163.

[21]Kenneth R. Philp, *John Collier's Crusade for Indian Reform, 1920–1954* (Tucson: University of Arizona Press, 1977), 55–91; Peter Iverson, *'We Are Still Here,' American Indians in the Twentieth Century* (Wheeling, IL: Harlan Davidson, Inc., 1998), 58–76.

[22]Prucha, *The Great Father,* 277–279; Iverson, *'We Are Still Here,'* 75.

[23]Steven Crum, "Henry Roe Cloud: A Winnebago Indian Reformer: His Quest for American Indian Higher Education," *Kansas History*, 11 (autumn 1988): 171–184.

[24]Prucha, *The Great Father*, 311–339; Philp, *John Collier's Crusade*, 135–186; Iverson, '*We Are Still Here*,' 77–102.

[25]Philp, *John Collier's Crusade*, 163; Prucha, *The Great Father*, 324.

[26]Crum, "Deeply Attached to the Land," 19.

[27]Joachim Roschmann, "No 'Red Atlantis' on the Trinity: Why the Hupa Rejected the Indian Reorganization Act," paper presented at the Sixth Annual California Indian Conference, 27 October 1990; George H. Phillips, *The Enduring Struggle: Indians in California History* (San Francisco: Boyd & Fraser Publishing Company, 1981), 50, 69.

[28]Quoted in "Lakotas Have Different Views on Indian Reorganization Act," *Lakota Times*, 28 November 1984, 7.

[29]Ibid.

[30]Quoted in "Fifty Years of IRA–Working or Not?" *Lakota Times*, 4 July 1984, 1.

[31]"Lakotas Have Different Views," 7.

[32]Ibid.

[33]*Interior Department Appropriation Bill for 1947*, 97th Congress, 2nd session, Part I (Washington, D.C.: Government Printing Office, 1946), 822.

[34]Donald L. Fixico, *Termination and Relocation: Federal Indian Policy, 1945–1960* (Albuquerque: University of New Mexico Press, 1986), 3–21; Larry W. Burt, *Tribalism in Crisis: Federal Indian Policy, 1953–1961* (UNM, 1982); Prucha, *the Great Father*, 340–356; Iverson, '*We Are Still Here*,' 103–138.

[35]Fixico, *Termination and Relocation*, 91–110; Prucha, *The Great Father*, 340–356.

[36]Ibid., 137–157; Donald L. Fixico, *The Urban Indian Experience in America* (University of New Mexico, 2000), 8–25.

[37]Prucha, *The Great Father*, 394; Francis Paul Prucha, *Atlas of American Indian Affairs* (University of Nebraska Press, 1990), 142; Russell Thornton, *American Indian Holocaust and Survival: A Population History Since 1492* (University of Oklahoma, 1987), 227.

[38]Thornton, *American Indian Holocaust*, 236; Fixico, *The Urban Indian Experience*, 74, 80, 125, 127, 133.

[39]George Pierre Castile, *To Show Heart: Native American Self-Determination and Federal Indian Policy, 1960–1975* (University of Arizona Press, 1998), 23–42.

[40]Ibid, 35–42.

[41]Margaret Connell Szasz, *Education and the American Indian: The Road to Self-Determination*, 3rd ed. (University of New Mexico, 1999), 169–187.

[42]Wayne J. Stein, *Tribally Controlled Colleges: Making Good Medicine* (New York: Peter Lang, 1992).

[43]Iverson, '*We Are Still Here*,' 170–171; Prucha, *The Great Father*, 379.

[44]David E. Wilkins, *American Indian Politics and the American Political System* (New York: Rowman & Littlefield Publishers, Inc., 2002), 105, 117–118.

[45]"Editorial Comment," *Quarterly Journal of the Society of American Indians*, 2 (April–June 1914): 99; *Annual Report of the Department of the Interior, 1915, Vol. II: Indian Affairs and Territories* (Washington, D.C.: GPO, 1916), 7.

[46]W. Dale Mason, *Indian Gaming: Tribal Sovereignty and American Politics* (University of Oklahoma, 2000), 44, 47, 64–65; Wilkins, *American Indian Politics*, 164–172.

# The History of Asians in America

*Timothy Fong*

## Visibility and Invisibility

On October 14, 2000, Miss Hawaii, Angela Perez Baraquio, was crowned Miss America 2001, becoming the first Filipino American and Asian American ever to hold the title. Miss California, Rita Ng, the first Asian American to hold that state's beauty title, was selected as the second runner-up. This seemingly innocent historical event was not lost to many Asian Americans, especially Filipino Americans. "After years of invisibility in the mainstream and being seen as inferior to accepted standards of beauty, we now have a sudden validation of the multicultural in America," beamed *Asian Week* columnist Emil Guillermo. Despite his celebratory mood, Guillermo also touched on an important irony. Baraquio was never referred to as Filipino American or Asian American. Instead, she was referred to as Hawaiian. On the surface, this would seem to make sense because she is from Honolulu. "So what explains Miss Louisiana being reported as 'black' . . . and Baraquio's Hawaiian?" Guillermo asked incredulously. "The significance is that since their arrival on the scene in America at the turn of the century, Filipinos have toiled quietly and invisibly. It seems when they get face time, they don't get the credit they deserve."[1]

Guillermo's observation speaks loudly to the fact that Asian Americans are at once visible, yet invisible. This is particularly true with regards to the history of Asians in the United States. The historical experience of Asian Americans is not at all atypical of other minority groups. As a distinct racial minority group, and as immigrants, Asian Americans faced enormous individual prejudice, frequent mob violence, and extreme forms of institutional discrimination. But Asian Americans have not merely been victims of hostility and oppression; indeed, they have also shown remarkable strength and perseverance, which is a testimony to their desire to make the United States their home.

Fong, Timothy P., *Contemporary Asian American Experience, The: Beyond The Model Minority*, 1st Edition, © 1998. Reprinted by permission of Pearson Education, Inc., Upper Saddle River, NJ.

# Immigration

Between 1848 and 1924, hundreds of thousands of immigrants from China, Japan, the Philippines, Korea, and India came to the United States in search of a better life and livelihood. Although this period represents the first significant wave, these immigrants were by no means the very first Asians to come to America. Recent archaeological finds off the coast of Southern California have led to speculation that the West Coast may have been visited by Buddhist missionaries from China in the fifth century. Direct evidence of this claim is still being debated, but it is known that the Spanish brought Chinese ship-builders to Baja California as early as 1571, and later Filipino seamen were brought by Spanish galleons from Manila and settled along the coast of Louisiana. Chinese merchants and sailors were also present in the United States prior to the discovery of gold in California in 1848. Most people are unaware that Asian Indians were brought to America during the late eighteenth century as indentured servants and slaves.[2]

The California gold rush did not immediately ignite a mass rush of Chinese immigrants to America. In fact, only a few hundred Chinese arrived in California during the first years of the gold rush, and most of them were merchants. However, large-scale immigration did begin in earnest in 1852 when 52,000 Chinese arrived that year alone. Many Chinese came to the United States not only to seek their fortunes but also to escape political and economic turmoil in China. As gold ran out, thousands of Chinese were recruited in the mid-1860s to help work on the transcontinental railroad. Eventually more than 300,000 Chinese entered the United States in the nineteenth century, engaging in a variety of occupations. During this same period Chinese also immigrated to Hawaii, but in far fewer numbers than to the continental United States.[3]

Large capitalist and financial interests welcomed the Chinese as cheap labor and lobbied for the 1868 Burlingame Treaty, which recognized "free migration and emigration" of Chinese to the United States in exchange for American trade privileges in China. As early as 1870 Chinese were 9 percent of California's population and 25 percent of the state's work force.[4] The majority of these Chinese were young single men who intended to work a few years and then return to China. Those who stayed seldom married because of laws severely limiting the immigration of Chinese women and prohibiting inter-marriage with white women. The result was the Chinese were forced to live a harsh and lonely bachelor life that often featured vice and prostitution. In 1890, for example, there were roughly 102,620 Chinese men and only 3,868 Chinese women in the United States, a male to female ratio of 26:1.[5] Despite these conditions, Chinese workers continued to come to the United States.

Following the completion of the transcontinental railroad in 1869, large numbers of unemployed Chinese workers had to find new sources of employment. Many found work in agriculture where they cleared land, dug canals, planted orchards, harvested crops, and were the foundation for successful commercial production of many California crops. Others settled in San Francisco and other cities to manufacture shoes, cigars, and clothing. Still others started small businesses such as restaurants, laundries, and general stores. Domestic service such as house boys, cooks, and gardeners were also other areas of employment for the Chinese. In short, the Chinese were involved in many occupations that were crucial to the economic development and domestication of the western region of the United States.[6] Unfortunately, intense hostility against the Chinese reached its peak in 1882 when Congress passed the Chinese Exclusion Act intended to "suspend" the entry of Chinese laborers for ten years. Other laws were eventually passed that barred Chinese laborers and their wives permanently.[7]

The historical experience of Japanese in the United States is both different yet similar to that of the Chinese. One major difference is that the Japanese immigrated in large numbers to Hawaii, and they did not come in large numbers to the United States until the 1890s. In 1880 only 148 Japanese were living in the U.S. mainland. In 1890 this number increased to 2,000, mostly merchants and students. However, the population increased dramatically when an influx of 38,000 Japanese workers from Hawaii arrived in the U.S. mainland between 1902 and 1907.[8] The second difference was the fact the Japanese were able to fully exploit an economic niche in agriculture that the Chinese had only started. The completion of several national railroad lines and the invention of the refrigerator car were two advancements that brought tremendous expansion in the California produce industry. The early Japanese were fortunate to arrive at an opportune time, and about two thirds of them found work as agricultural laborers. Within a short time the Japanese were starting their own farms in direct competition with non-Japanese farms. By 1919 the Japanese controlled over 450,000 acres of agricultural land. Although this figure represents only 1 percent of active California agricultural land at the time, the Japanese were so efficient in their farming practices that they captured 10 percent of the dollar volume of the state's crops.[9]

The third major difference was the emergence of Japan as a international military power at the turn of the century. Japan's victory in the Russo-Japanese War (1904–1905) impressed President Theodore Roosevelt, and he believed a strategy of cooperation with the Japanese government was in the best interest of the United States. Roosevelt blocked calls for complete Japanese exclusion and instead worked a compromise with the Japanese government in 1907 known as the "Gentleman's Agreement." This agreement halted the immigration of Japanese laborers but allowed Japanese women into the United States. With this in mind, the fourth difference was the fact that the Japanese in the United States were able to actually increase in population, start families, and establish a rather stable community life.[10]

Filipino immigration began after the United States gained possession of the Philippines following the Spanish-American War in 1898. The first Filipinos to arrive were a few hundred *pensionados,* or students supported by government scholarships. Similar to the Japanese experience, a large number of Filipinos went directly to Hawaii before coming to the U.S. mainland. Between 1907 and 1919 over 28,000 Filipinos were actively recruited to work on sugar plantations in

Hawaii. Filipinos began to emigrate to the United States following the passage of the 1924 Immigration Act, which prohibited all Asian immigration to this country, and there was a need for agricultural and service labor.[11]

Because Filipinos lived on American territory, they were "nationals" who were free to travel in the United States without restriction. In the 1920s over 45,000 Filipinos arrived in Pacific Coast ports, and a 1930 study found 30,000 Filipinos working in California. These Filipinos were overwhelmingly young, single males. Their ages ranged between 16 and 29, and there were 14 Filipino men for every Filipina. Sixty percent of these Filipinos worked as migratory agricultural laborers, and 25 percent worked in domestic service in Los Angeles and San Francisco. The rest found work in manufacturing and as railroad porters. Unlike the Japanese, Filipinos did not make their mark in agriculture as farmers, but as labor union organizers.[12] Both Filipino farm worker activism and Japanese farm competition created a great deal of resentment among white farmers and laborers.

Koreans and Asian Indians slightly predated the Filipinos, but arrived in much smaller numbers. Between 1903 and 1905 over 7,000 Koreans were recruited for plantation labor work in Hawaii, but after Japan established a protectorate over Korea in 1905, all emigration was halted.[13] In the next five years, Japan increased its economic and political power and formally annexed Korea in 1910. Relatively few Koreans lived in the United States between 1905 and 1940. Among those included about 1,000 workers who migrated from Hawaii, about 100 Korean "picture brides," and a small number of American-born Koreans. The Korean population in the United States during that time was also bolstered by roughly 900 students, many of whom fled their home country because of their opposition to Japanese rule. Like other Asian immigrant groups, Koreans found themselves concentrated in California agriculture working primarily as laborers, although a small number did become quite successful farmers.[14]

The first significant flow of Asian Indians occurred between 1904 and 1911, when just over 6,000 arrived in the United States. Unlike the other Asian groups, Asian Indians did not work in Hawaii prior to entering the American mainland, but they worked primarily in California agriculture. Similar to the Chinese, Filipinos, and Koreans, they had an extremely high male to female ratio. Of the Asian Indians who immigrated to the United States between 1904 and 1911, there were only three or four women, all of whom were married.[15] Eighty to ninety percent of the first Asian Indian settlers in the United States were Sikhs, a distinct ethnoreligious minority group in India. Despite this fact, these Sikhs were often called Hindus, which they are not. Sikhs were easily recognizable from all other Asian immigrant groups because of their huskier build, their turbans, and their beards. But like other Asians in the United States at the time, they also worked primarily in California's agricultural industry. Asian Indians worked first as farm workers, and like the Japanese, they also formed cooperatives, pooled their resources, and began independent farming.[16] Immigration restrictions, their relatively small numbers, and an exaggerated male to female ratio prevented Asian Indians from developing a lasting farm presence. One major exception can be found in the Marysville/Yuba City area of Northern California, where Asian Indian Sikhs are still quite active in producing cling peaches.[17]

## Anti-Asian Laws and Sentiment

The United States is a nation that claims to welcome and assimilate all newcomers. But the history of immigration, naturalization, and equal treatment under the law for Asian Americans has been an extremely difficult one. In 1790 Congress passed the first naturalization law limiting citizenship rights to only a "free white person."[18] During the period of reconstruction in the 1870s following the end of the Civil War, Congress amended the law and allowed citizenship for "aliens of African nativity and persons of African descent."[19] For a while there was some discussion on expanding naturalization rights to Chinese immigrants, but that idea was rejected by politicians from western states.[20] This rejection is exemplary of the intense anti-Chinese sentiment at the time.

As early as 1850 California imposed the Foreign Miners Tax, which required the payment of $20 a month from all foreign miners.[21] The California Supreme Court ruled in *People v. Hall* (1854) that Chinese could not testify in court against a white person. This case threw out the testimony of three Chinese witnesses and reversed the murder conviction of George W. Hall, who was sentenced to hang for the murder of a Chinese man one year earlier.[22] In 1855 a local San Francisco ordinance levied a $50 tax on all aliens ineligible for citizenship. Because Chinese were ineligible for citizenship under the Naturalization Act of 1790, they were the primary targets for this law.[23]

The racially distinct Chinese were the primary scapegoats for the depressed economy in the 1870s, and mob violence erupted on several occasions through to the 1880s. The massacre of 21 Chinese in Los Angeles in 1871 and 28 Chinese in Rock Springs, Wyoming, in 1885 are examples of the worst incidents. It is within this environment that Congress passed the 1882 Chinese Exclusion Act. The act suspended immigration of Chinese laborers for only ten years, but it was extended in 1892 and 1902. The act was eventually extended indefinitely in 1904.[24] The intense institutional discrimination achieved the desired result: The Chinese population declined from 105,465 in 1880 to 61,639 in 1920.[25]

Anti-Chinese sentiment easily grew into large-scale anti-Asian sentiment as immigrants from Asia continued to enter the United States. During the same period that the Chinese population declined, the Japanese population grew and became highly visible. As early as 1910 there were 72,157 Japanese Americans compared to 71,531 Chinese Americans in the United States.[26] Japanese farmers in California were particularly vulnerable targets for animosity. One of the most sweeping anti-Asian laws was aimed at the Japanese Americans but affected all other Asian American groups as well. The 1913 Alien Land Law prohibited "aliens ineligible to citizenship" from owning or leasing land for more than three years. Initially the

Japanese Americans were able to bypass the law primarily because they could buy or lease land under the names of their American-born offspring (the Nisei), who were U.S. citizens by birth. The law was strengthened in 1920, however, and the purchase of land under the names of American-born offspring was prohibited.[27]

Several sweeping anti-immigration laws were passed in the first quarter of the twentieth century that served to eliminate Asian immigration to the United States. A provision in the 1917 Immigration Act banned immigration from the so-called "Asian barred zone," except for the Philippines and Japan. A more severe anti-Asian restriction was further imposed by the 1924 National Origins Act, which placed a ceiling of 150,000 new immigrants per year. The 1924 act was intended to limit eastern and southern European immigration, but a provision was added that ended any immigration by aliens ineligible for citizenship.[28]

Asian Americans did not sit back passively in the face of discriminatory laws; they hired lawyers and went to court to fight for their livelihoods, naturalization rights, and personal liberties. Sometimes they were successful, but oftentimes they were not. In the case of *Yick Wo v. Hopkins* (1886), Chinese successfully challenged an 1880 San Francisco Laundry Ordinance, which regulated commercial laundry service in a way that clearly discriminated against the Chinese. Plaintiff Yick Wo had operated a laundry service for 22 years, but when he tried to renew his business license in 1885 he was turned down because his storefront was made out of wood. Two hundred other Chinese laundries were also denied business licenses on similar grounds, although 80 non-Chinese laundries in wooden buildings were approved. The Supreme Court ruled in favor of Yick Wo, concluding there was "no reason" for the denial of the business license "except to the face and nationality" of the petitioner.[29]

The inability to gain citizenship was a defining factor throughout the early history of Asian Americans. The constitutionality of naturalization based on race was first challenged in the Supreme Court case of *Ozawa v. United States* (1922). Takao Ozawa was born in Japan but immigrated to the United States at an early age. He graduated from Berkeley High School in California and attended the University of California for three years. Ozawa was a model immigrant who did not smoke or drink, he attended a predominantly white church, his children attended public school, and English was the language spoken at home. When Ozawa was rejected in his initial attempt for naturalization, he appealed and argued that the provisions for citizenship in the 1790 and 1870 acts did not specifically exclude Japanese. In addition, Ozawa also tried to argue that Japanese should be considered "white."

The Court unanimously ruled against Ozawa on both grounds. First, the Court decided that initial framers of the law and its amendment did not intend to *exclude* people from naturalization but, instead, only determine who would be *included*. Ozawa was denied citizenship because the existing law simply didn't include Japanese. Second, the Court also ruled against Ozawa's argument that Japanese were actually more "white" than other darker skinned "white" people such as some Italians, Spanish, and Portuguese. The Court clarified the matter by defining a "white person" to be synonymous with a "person of the Caucasian race." In short, Ozawa was not Caucasian (although he thought himself "white") and, thus, was ineligible for citizenship.[30]

Prior to the *Ozawa* case, Asian Indians already enjoyed the right of naturalization. In *United States v. Balsara* (1910), the Supreme Court determined that Asian Indians were Caucasian and approximately 70 became naturalized citizens. But the Immigration and Naturalization Service (INS) challenged this decision, and it was taken up again in the case of *United States v. Thind* (1923). This time the Supreme Court reversed its earlier decision and ruled that Bhagat Singh Thind could not be a citizen because he was not "white." Even though Asian Indians were classified as Caucasian, this was a scientific term that was inconsistent with the popular understanding. The Court's decision stated, "It may be true that the blond Scandinavian and the brown Hindu have a common ancestor in the dim reaches of antiquity, but the average man knows perfectly well that there are unmistakable differences between them today."[31] In other words, only "white" Caucasians were considered eligible for U.S. citizenship. In the wake of the *Thind* decision, the INS was able to cancel retroactively the citizenship of Asian Indians between 1923 and 1926.

Asian Americans also received disparate treatment compared to other immigrants in their most private affairs, such as marriage. In the nineteenth century, antimiscegenation laws prohibiting marriage between blacks and whites were common throughout the United States. In 1880 the California legislature extended restrictive antimiscegenation categories to prohibit any marriage between a white person and a "negro, mulatto, or Mongolian." This law, targeted at the Chinese, was not challenged until Salvador Roldan won a California Court of Appeals decision in 1933. Roldan, a Filipino American, argued that he was Malay, not Mongolian, and he should be allowed to marry his white fiancee. The Court conceded that the state's antimiscegenation law was created in an atmosphere of intense anti-Chinese sentiment, and agreed Filipinos were not in mind when the initial legislation was approved. Unfortunately, this victory was short-lived. The California state legislature amended the antimiscegenation law to include the "Malay race" shortly after the Roldan decision was announced.[32]

## World War II and the Cold War Era

For Asian Americans, World War II was an epoch, but the profound impact was distinct for different Asian American groups. For over 110,000 Japanese Americans, World War II was an agonizing ordeal soon after Japan's attack of Pearl Harbor on December 7, 1941. The FBI arrested thousands of Japanese Americans who were considered potential security threats immediately after the Pearl Harbor bombing raid. Arrested without evidence of disloyalty were the most visible Japanese American community leaders, including businessmen, Shinto and Buddhist priests, teachers in Japanese-language schools, and editors of Japanese-language newspapers. Wartime hysteria rose to a fever pitch, and on February 19, 1942, President Franklin

Roosevelt issued Executive Order 9066. This order established various military zones and authorized the removal of anyone who was a potential threat. Although a small number of German and Italian aliens were detained and relocated, this did not compare to the mass relocation of Japanese Americans on the West Coast of the United States.[33]

The order to relocate Japanese Americans because of military necessity and the threat they posed to security, was a fabrication. Even military leaders debated the genuine need for mass relocation, and the government's own intelligence reports found no evidence of Japanese American disloyalty. "For the most part the local Japanese are loyal to the United States or, at worst, hope that by remaining quiet they can avoid concentration camps or irresponsible mobs," one report stated. "We do not believe that they would be at least any more disloyal than any other racial group in the United States with whom we went to war."[34] This helps explain why 160,000 Japanese Americans living in Hawaii were not interned. More telling was the fact that Japanese Americans in the continental United States were a small but much resented minority. Despite government reports to the contrary, business leaders, local politicians, and the media fueled antagonism against the Japanese Americans and agitated for their abrupt removal.[35]

With only seven days notice to prepare once the internment order was issued, and no way of knowing how long the war would last, many Japanese Americans were forced to sell their homes and property at a mere fraction of their genuine value. Japanese Americans suffered estimated economic losses alone of at least $400 million. By August 1942 all the Japanese on the West Coast were interned in ten camps located in rural regions of California, Arizona, Utah, Idaho, Wyoming, and Arkansas. Two thirds of the interned Japanese American men, women, and children were U.S. citizens, whose only crime was their ancestry; even those with as little as one-eighth Japanese blood were interned. The camps themselves were crude, mass facilities surrounded by barbed wire and guarded by armed sentries. People were housed in large barracks with each family living in small cramped quarters dubbed "apartments." Food was served in large mess halls, and toilet and shower facilities were communal. Many of the camps were extremely cold in the winter, hot in the summer, and dusty all year round. The camps remained open for the duration of the war.[36]

After the first year of the camps, the government began recruiting young Japanese American men to help in the war effort. The military desperately needed Japanese Americans to serve as interpreters for Japanese prisoners of war and translators of captured documents. But to the military's incredulity, most American-born Japanese had only modest Japanese-language skills and needed intense training in the Military Intelligence Service Language School before they could perform their duties.[37] It was, however, the heroic actions of the 100th Infantry Battalion, which later merged with the 442nd Regimental Combat Team, that stand out the most among historians. The two segregated units engaged in numerous campaigns and served with distinction throughout Europe. By the end of the war in Europe, for example, the Nisei soldiers of the 442nd suffered over 9,000 casualties, and earned over 18,000 individual decorations of honor. The 442nd was the most decorated unit of its size during all of World War II.[38]

Compared to the Japanese American experience, other Asian American groups fared far better during and after World War II. Changes for Chinese Americans were particularly dramatic. Prior to the war, the image of the Chinese was clearly negative compared to the Japanese. A survey of Princeton undergraduates in 1931 thought the top three traits of the Chinese were the fact they were "superstitious, sly, and conservative," whereas Japanese were considered "intelligent, industrious, and progressive."[39] Immediately after the bombing of Pearl Harbor, Chinese store owners put up signs indicating they were not Japanese, and in some cases Chinese Americans wore buttons stating, "I am Chinese." To alleviate any further identification problems, *Time* magazine published an article on December 22, 1941, explaining how to tell the difference between Chinese and "Japs." The article compared photographs of a Chinese man and a Japanese man, highlighting the distinguishing facial features of each.[40] Just months later, a 1942 Gallup Poll characterized the Chinese as "hardworking, honest, and brave," and Japanese were seen as "treacherous, sly, and cruel."[41]

Employment opportunities outside of the segregated Chinatown community became available to Chinese Americans for the first time during the war and continued even after the war ended. Chinese Americans trained in various professions and skilled crafts were able to find work in war-related industries that had never been open to them before. In addition, the employment of Chinese American women increased threefold during the 1940s. Leading the way were clerical positions, which increased from just 750 in 1940 to 3,200 in 1950. In 1940 women represented just one in five Chinese American professionals, but by 1950 this increased to one in three. On another level, Chinese actors suddenly found they were in demand for film roles—usually playing evil Japanese characters. Shortly after the war, writers such as Jade Snow Wong and Pardee Lowe discovered the newfound interest and appreciation of Chinese Americans could be turned into commercial success through the publication of their memoirs.[42]

On the military front, Asian Americans also distinguished themselves. Over 15,000 Chinese Americans served in all branches of the military, unlike the Japanese Americans who were placed only in segregated infantry units and in the Military Intelligence Service. Similarly, over 7,000 Filipino Americans volunteered for the army and formed the First and Second Filipino Infantry Regiments. About 1,000 other Filipino Americans were sent to the Philippines to perform reconnaissance and intelligence activities for Gen. Douglas MacArthur.[43] Equally significant was the War Bride's Act of 1945, which allowed war veterans to bring wives from China and the Philippines as non-quota immigrants. This resulted in a rapid and dramatic shift in the historic gender imbalance of both groups. For example, between 1945 and 1952, nine out of ten (89.9 percent) Chinese immigrants were female, and 20,000 Chinese American babies were born by the mid-1950s.

Similarly, between 1951 and 1960 seven out of ten (71 percent) Filipino immigrants were female.[44]

On the broad international front, alliances with China, the Philippines, and India eventually began the process of changing the overtly discriminatory immigration laws against Asians. The Chinese Exclusion Law was repealed in 1943, and an annual quota of 105 immigrants from China was allotted. In 1946 Congress approved legislation that extended citizenship to Filipino immigrants and permitted the entry of 100 Filipino immigrants annually. Also in 1946, the Luce-Cellar Act ended the 1917 "Asian barred zone," allowed an immigration quota of 100 from India, and for the first time permitted Asian Indians to apply for citizenship since the *United States v. Thind* case of 1923. Although these changes were extremely modest, they carried important symbolic weight by helping create a favorable international opinion of the United States during and immediately after the war.[45]

Geopolitical events during the Cold War era of the 1950s and 1960s immediately following World War II continued to have important ramifications for Asian Americans. After the 1949 Communist Revolution in China, about 5,000 Chinese students and young professionals were living in the United States. These "stranded" individuals were generally from China's most elite and educated families and not necessarily anxious to return to China because their property had already been confiscated and their livelihoods threatened. They were eventually allowed to stay in the United States.[46] Several other refugee acts in the late 1950s and early 1960s allowed some 18,000 other Chinese to enter and also stay in the United States. Many of these refugees were well-trained scientists and engineers who easily found jobs in private industry and in research universities. These educated professionals were quite distinct from the vast majority of earlier Chinese immigrants because they usually were able to integrate into the American mainstream quickly, becoming the basis of an emerging Chinese American middle class.[47]

The Cold War affected immigration from Asian countries as well, but in a very different fashion. During and after the Korean War (1950–1953), American soldiers often met and married Korean women and brought them home to the United States. Between 1952 and 1960 over 1,000 Korean women a year immigrated to the United States as brides of U.S. servicemen. At the same time, orphaned Korean children, especially girls, also arrived in the United States in significant numbers. Throughout the 1950s and up to the mid-1960s, some 70 percent of all Korean immigrants were either women or young girls. Korea was the site of the actual conflict, but large numbers of troops were also stationed in nearby Japan. Even higher numbers of Japanese women married American soldiers, left their home country, and started a new life in the United States. Roughly 6,000 Japanese wives of U.S. servicemen annually immigrated to the United States between 1952 and 1960, which was over 80 percent of all immigrants from Japan. These Korean and Japanese war brides and Korean orphans were spread throughout the United States and, as a result, had very little interaction with other Asian Americans already living in this country.[48] These war bride families were, however, a significant part of the biracial Asian American baby boom that is discussed in greater detail in Chapter 7.

# Post-1965 Asian Immigrants and Refugees

A number of factors have clearly influenced Asian immigration and refugee policies, including public sentiment toward immigrants, demands of foreign policy, and the needs of the American economy. World War II and the Cold War years were epochal for Asian Americans, but the period since the mid-1960s has proven to be even more significant. An overview of U.S. immigration statistics shows just how important recent immigration reforms and refugee policies have affected Asian Americans.

Official records on immigrants entering the United States did not exist before 1820, but since that time it is quite obvious that the largest number of immigrants come from European countries. Between 1820 and 1998 over 38.2 million Europeans immigrated to the United States (see Table 1-1). In contrast, only 8.3 million immigrants came from Asia during the same period of time. Looking at this figure more closely, however, we find over 6.6 million immigrants from Asia arrived in the United States in the period between 1971 and 1998. Although the Chinese and Japanese have the longest histories in the United States, the largest group of Asian immigrants since 1971 has come from the Philippines. Over 1.4 million Filipino immigrants entered the United States between 1971 and 1998. It is also significant to note that over 90 percent of Filipino, Asian Indian, Korean, and Vietnamese have entered the United States since 1971.

This next section focuses on three broad events that have directly influenced both the numbers and diversity of Asians entering the United States since 1965: (1) the passage of the 1965 Immigration Reform Act, (2) global economic restructuring, and (3) the Vietnam War.

## The 1965 Immigration Reform Act

Why did the dramatic increase in Asian immigration take place? What changes in the law or public attitudes facilitated such a rapid influx of immigrants from Asia? One important reason was the civil rights movement of the 1960s, which brought international attention to racial and economic inequality in the United States—including its biased immigration policies. This attention is the background for the passage of the 1965 Immigration Reform Act, the most important immigration reform legislation. This act, along with its amendments, significantly increased the token quotas established after World War II to allow the Eastern Hemisphere a maximum of 20,000 per country, and set a ceiling of 170,000.

This act created the following seven-point preference system that serves as a general guideline for immigration officials when issuing visas: (1) unmarried children of

| Region | Total 1820–1998 | 1971–1998 | % of Immigrants Since 1971 |
|---|---|---|---|
| All countries | 64,599,082 | 18,836,444 | 29.2 |
| Europe | 38,233,062 | 2,693,920 | 7.0 |
| Asia | 8,365,931 | 6,673,085 | 79.7 |
| China* | 1,262,050 | 818,747 | 64.9 |
| Hong Kong† | 398,277 | 298,129 | 74.9 |
| India | 751,349 | 710,553 | 94.6 |
| Japan | 517,686 | 152,302 | 29.4 |
| Korea | 778,899 | 738,305 | 94.8 |
| Phillippines | 1,460,421 | 1,337,519 | 91.6 |
| Vietnam | 699,918 | 692,243 | 98.9 |
| North America | | | |
| Canada and Newfoundland | 4,453,149 | 484,441 | 10.9 |
| Mexico | 5,819,966 | 4,115,959 | 70.7 |
| Caribbean | 3,525,703 | 1,435,703 | 40.7 |
| Central America | 1,242,394 | 985,240 | 79.3 |
| South America | 1,693,441 | 1,200,740 | 70.9 |
| Africa | 614,375 | 537,902 | 87.6 |
| Oceana | 250,206 | 132,031 | 52.8 |
| Not specified | 290,679 | 24,264 | .8 |

*Beginning in 1957, China includes Taiwan.
†Data not reported separately until 1952.
Source: U.S. Immigration and Naturalization Service, 1998 Statistical Yearbook of the Immigration and Naturalization Service (Washington, DC: U.S. Government Printing Office, 2000), Table, pp. 8–10.

U.S. citizens who are at least 21 years of age; (2) spouses and unmarried children of permanent resident aliens; (3) members of the professions, scientists, and artists of exceptional ability; (4) married children of U.S. citizens; (5) brothers and sisters of U.S. citizens who are at least 21 years of age; (6) skilled or unskilled workers who are in short supply; and (7) non-preference applicants.

U.S. immigration policy also allowed virtually unrestricted immigration to certain categories of people including spouses, children under 21, and parents of U.S. citizens. These provisions served to accelerate immigration from Asia to the United States. The primary goal of the 1965 Immigration Reform Act was to encourage family reunification, however, a much higher percentage of Asian immigrants initially began entering the United States under the established occupational and non-preference investment categories. In 1969, for example, 62 percent of Asian Indians, 43 percent of Filipinos, and 34.8 percent of Koreans entered the United States un-

| Decade | Europe | Asia | North America | South America | Africa |
|--------|--------|------|---------------|---------------|--------|
| 1901–10 | 91.6 | 3.7 | 3.2 | .2 | .1 |
| 1911–20 | 75.3 | 4.3 | 19.2 | .7 | .1 |
| 1921–30 | 60.0 | 2.7 | 35.9 | 1.0 | .2 |
| 1931–40 | 65.8 | 3.1 | 28.8 | 1.5 | .3 |
| 1941–50 | 60.0 | 3.6 | 32.2 | 2.1 | .7 |
| 1951–60 | 52.7 | 6.1 | 36.0 | 3.6 | .6 |
| 1961–70 | 33.8 | 12.9 | 43.9 | 7.8 | .9 |
| 1971–80 | 17.8 | 35.3 | 37.5 | 6.6 | 1.8 |
| 1981–90 | 10.4 | 37.3 | 43.0 | 6.3 | 2.4 |
| 1991–98 | 14.9 | 30.9 | 43.8 | 5.8 | 3.7 |

Source: U.S. Immigration and Naturalization Service, *Naturalizations, Fiscal Year 1998* (Washington, DC: U.S. Government Printing Office, 2000), Chart B, p. 4.

Note: Figures may not add to 100 due to rounding. Oceana and unspecified regions represent no more than 1 percent of legal immigration each decade.

der the occupational and investor categories. By the mid-1970s, however, 80 to 90 percent of all Asian immigrants entered the United States through one of the family categories.[49] Studies clearly show that most post-1965 Asian immigrants tend to be more middle-class, educated, urbanized, and they arrive in the United States in family units rather than as individuals, compared to their pre-1965 counterparts.[50]

The framers of the 1965 law did not anticipate any dramatic changes in the historical pattern of immigration, but it is clear Asian immigrants have taken advantage of almost every aspect of the 1965 Immigration Reform Act. Asians were just 6.1 percent of all immigrants to the United States between 1951 and 1960; this rose to 12.9 percent between 1961 and 1970, and increased to 35.3 percent between 1971 and 1980. The percentage of Asian immigrants peaked at 37.3 percent between 1981 and 1990 but declined to 30.9 percent by the 1990s (see Table 1-2). This decline was due to the sudden increase of mostly Mexicans who were able to apply for legal status following the passage of the Immigration Reform and Control Act of 1986 (IRCA). By the late 1990s, about 3 million aliens received permanent residence status under IRCA.[51]

This "amnesty" provision was only a part of IRCA, which was fully intended to control illegal immigration into the United States. IRCA also required that all employers verify the legal status of all new employees, and it imposed civil and criminal penalties against employers who knowingly hire undocumented workers.[52] While IRCA closed the "back door" of illegal immigration, another reform, the Immigration Act of 1990, was enacted to keep open the "front door" of legal immigration. Indeed, this law actually authorizes an *increase* in legal immigration to the United States. In response to uncertain economic stability at home, growing global economic competition abroad, and the dramatically changed face of immigration, the 1990 law sent a mixed message to Asian immigrants.

First of all, the law actually authorized an increase in legal immigration, but at the same time placed a yearly cap on total immigration for the first time since the 1920s. For 1992 to 1995, the limit was 700,000 and 675,000 thereafter. This appears to be an arbitrary limit, but it still allows for an unlimited number of visas for immediate relatives of U.S. citizens. This may not have a negative effect on Asian immigration because, as a group, Asians have the highest rate of naturalization compared to other immigrants.[53] Second, the law encourages immigration of more skilled workers to help meet the needs of the U.S. economy. The number of visas for skilled workers and their families increased from 58,000 to 140,000, and the number for unskilled workers was cut in half to just 10,000. This may prove to be a benefit to Asians who, since 1965, have been among the best educated and best trained immigrants the United States has ever seen. Third, the 1990 immigration law also seeks to "diversify" the new immigrants by giving more visas to countries who have sent relatively few people to the United States in recent years. This program has been popular with lawmakers who want to assist those from Western European countries at the expense of Asians. For example, up to 40 percent of the initial visas allocated for the diversity category were for Ireland. Noted immigration attorney Bill Ong Hing found sections of the Immigration Act of 1990 "provide extra independent and transition visas that are unavailable to Asians."[54]

The lasting legacy of the civil rights movement on immigration policy was the emphasis on fairness, equality, and family reunification. But the increased emphasis on highly skilled immigrants found in the 1990 immigration law indicates some loosening of those ideals and priorities. It is clear from the descriptions of Asian American history here that the conditions for the post-1965 Asian migrants are quite distinct from pre-1965 migrants. This seemingly obvious observation reflects the fact that international migration is not a simple, stable, or homogeneous process. Even with this in mind, the most popular frame of reference for all movement to the United States continues to be the European immigrant experience throughout the nineteenth and early twentieth centuries. The popular European immigrant analogy is highlighted in the words of welcome written on the Statue of Liberty:

> *Give me your tired, your poor*
> *Your huddled masses yearning to breathe free*
> *The wretched refuse of your teeming shore.*
> *Send these, the homeless, tempest-tost to me,*
> *I lift my lamp beside the golden door!*

The European immigrant experience, however, is by no means universal, and it is only part of what scholars today see as a much broader picture of the international movement of people and capital. Understanding the broader dynamics of global economic restructuring is useful in comparing and contrasting post-1965 Asian immigrants with other immigrants and minority groups in the United States.

## Global Economic Restructuring

What makes people want to leave their home country and migrate to another country? The most commonly accepted answer is found within what is known as the push-pull theory. This theory generally asserts that difficult economic, social, and political conditions in the home country force, or push, people away. At the same time, these people are attracted, or pulled, to another country where conditions are seen as more favorable. On closer examination, however, this theoretical viewpoint does run into some problems. Most significantly, the push-pull theory tends to see immigration flows as a natural, open, and spontaneous process, but it does not adequately take into account the structural factors and policy changes that directly affect immigration flows. This is because earlier migration studies based on European immigration limited their focus on poor countries that sent low-skilled labor to affluent countries with growing economies that put newcomers to work. The push-pull theory is not incorrect, but is considered to be incomplete and historically static. Recent studies have taken a much broader approach to international migration and insist that in order to understand post-1965 immigration from Asia, it is necessary to understand the recent restructuring of the global economy.[55]

Since the end of World War II, global restructuring has involved the gradual movement of industrial manufacturing away from developed nations such as the United States to less developed nations in Asia and Latin America where labor costs are cheaper. This process was best seen in Japan in the 1950s through 1970s, and accelerated rapidly in the 1980s to newly industrialized Asian countries, namely Taiwan, Hong Kong, Singapore, and South Korea. Other Asian countries such as India, Thailand, Indonesia, Malaysia, and the Philippines also followed the same economic course with varying degrees of success. In the 1990s mainland China increased its manufacturing and export capacity dramatically and was steering on the same economic path of other Asian nations.

Among the effects of global restructuring on the United States is the declining need to import low-skilled labor because manufacturing jobs are moving abroad. At the same time, there is an inclining need to import individuals with advanced specialized skills that are in great demand. According to research by Paul Ong and Evelyn Blumenberg (1994), this phenomena is evidenced in part by the increasing number of foreign-born students studying at U.S. colleges.[56] In the 1954–1955 academic year the United States was host to just 34,232 foreign exchange students; this number increased to over 440,000 in 1994.[57] Today over half of all foreign students in the United States are from Asian countries, and most major in either engineering, science, or business. In 1997 foreign students earned 53 percent of the doctorates in engineering, 50 percent of doctorates in mathematics, and 49 percent of doctorates in computer science.[58] Many of these foreign graduate students planned to work in the United States and eventually gained permanent immigrant status. Companies in the United States have, of course, been eager to hire foreign-born scientists and engineers. Not only are highly skilled immigrants valuable to employers as workers, but many also start their own high-tech businesses. For example, Vinod Khosla is the co-founder of Sun-Microsystems, and Gururaj Deshpande is co-founder of a number of high-tech businesses worth around $6 billion.[59]

The medical profession is another broad area where Asian immigrants have made a noticeable impact. Researchers Paul Ong and Tania Azores (1994) found that Asian Americans represented 4.4 percent of the registered nurses and 10.8 percent of the physicians in the United States in 1990. Ong and Azores estimate that only a third of Asian American physicians and a quarter of Asian American nurses were educated in the United States. Graduates of overseas medical and nursing schools have been coming to the United States since the passage of the 1946 Smith-Mundt Act, which created an exchange program for specialized training. Although this exchange was intended to be temporary, many medical professionals were able to become permanent immigrants. A physician shortage in the United States during the late 1960s and early 1970s, coupled with the elimination of racial immigration quotas in 1965, brought forth a steady flow of foreign-trained medical doctors from Asian countries. A 1975 U.S. Commission on Civil Rights report found 5,000 Asian medical school graduates entered the United States annually during the early 1970s. But, under pressure from the medical industry, Congress passed the 1976 Health Professions Educational Act, which restricted the number of foreign-trained physicians who could enter the United States. Despite the passage of this law, almost 30,000 physicians from Asia immigrated to the United States between 1972 and 1985, and data up to 1990 show roughly half of all foreign-trained physicians entering the United States have come from Asia.[60]

Asia is also the largest source for foreign nurses. In particular, over half of all foreign-trained nurses come from the Philippines. One 1988 study conservatively estimated 50,000 Filipino nurses were working in the United States at the time. Filipino nurses find work in the United States attractive because they can earn up to 20 times the salary they can make in the Philippines, and their English-speaking abilities make them highly desired by employers. Filipino nurses are also attracted to the United States because of liberal policies that eventually allow them to stay permanently. Most foreign-trained nurses are brought to work initially on a temporary basis, but the passage of the Immigration Nursing Relief Act of 1989 allows nurses to adjust to permanent status after three years of service.[61]

The general explanations for the origins of migration found that the push-pull theory continues to have some value today. Opportunities for large numbers of professionals in Asian countries are still difficult and limited, and opportunities and relatively high salaries are available in the United States. Political instability throughout Asia also continues to be an important push factor for Asian immigrants and refugees. At the same time, this immigration process is not totally natural or spontaneous, as witnessed by foreign student and immigration policies encouraging well-trained individuals to come to the United States. Overall, the changing character of the push and pull in terms of the types of immigrants entering the United States and the new skills they bring are very much a result of dynamic global economic restructuring. Global economic restructuring is an important context for understanding not only why Asian immigrants have come to the United States but also how well they have adjusted and been accepted socially, economically, and politically. Note that not all Asian immigrants are middle-class and successful professionals; a sizable number of other Asian immigrants, especially refugees, have also found their lives in America extremely difficult. The extreme diversity among Asian Americans is due in large part to the third major event affecting migration from Asia—the Vietnam War.

## The Vietnam War and Southeast Asian Refugees

Since 1975 large numbers of Southeast Asian refugees have entered the United States, and today California is the home for most of them (see Table 1-3). Roughly three quarters of all Southeast Asian refugees are from Vietnam, with the rest from Laos and Cambodia. Unlike most other post-1965 Asian immigrants who came to the United States in a rather orderly fashion seeking family reunification and economic opportunities, Southeast Asian refugees arrived as part of an international resettlement effort of people who faced genuine political persecution and bodily harm in their home countries. Southeast Asian refugees to the United States can be easily divided into three distinct waves: the first arrived in the United States in 1975 shortly after the fall of Saigon; the second arrived between 1978 and 1980; and the third entered the United States after 1980 and continues to this day. The United States has accepted these refugees not only for humanitarian reasons but also in

**TABLE 1-3** States with the Largest Southeast Asian Populations, 1990

| State | Vietnamese | Cambodian | Laotian | Hmong | Total |
|---|---|---|---|---|---|
| Washington | 18,696 | 11,096 | 6,191 | 741 | 36,724 |
| California | 280,223 | 68,190 | 58,058 | 46,892 | 453,363 |
| Texas | 69,634 | 5,887 | 9,332 | 176 | 85,029 |
| Minnesota | 9,387 | 3,858 | 6,381 | 16,833 | 36,459 |
| Massachusetts | 15,449 | 14,050 | 3,985 | 248 | 33,732 |
| Virginia | 20,693 | 3,889 | 25,899 | 7 | 27,178 |
| Pennsylvania | 15,887 | 5,495 | 2,048 | 358 | 23,788 |
| Wisconsin | 2,494 | 521 | 3,622 | 16,373 | 23,010 |
| New York | 15,555 | 3,646 | 3,253 | 165 | 22,619 |
| Florida | 16,346 | 1,617 | 242 | 7 | 20,379 |

Source: U.S. Bureau of the Census, *1990 Census of the Population, General Population Characteristics, United States Summary* (Washington, DC: U.S. Government Printing Office, 1993), CP-1-1, Table 262.

recognition that U.S. foreign policy and military actions in Southeast Asia had a hand in creating much of the calamity that has befallen the entire region.

U.S. political interests in Southeast Asia actually began during World War II, although for years efforts were limited to foreign aid and military advisers. Direct military intervention rapidly escalated in 1965 when President Lyndon B. Johnson stepped up bombing raids in Southeast Asia and authorized the use of the first U.S. combat troops in order to contain increasing communist insurgency. The undeclared war continued until U.S. troops withdrew in 1973 at the cost of 57,000 American and 1 million Vietnamese lives. The conflict also caused great environmental destruction throughout Southeast Asia and created tremendous domestic antiwar protests in the United States.[62]

As soon as the U.S. troops left, however, communist forces in Vietnam regrouped and quickly began sweeping across the countryside. By March 1975 it was clear that the capital of South Vietnam, Saigon, would soon fall to communist forces. As a result, President Gerald Ford authorized the attorney general to admit 130,000 refugees into the United States.[63] In the last chaotic days prior to the fall of Saigon on April 30, 1975, "high-risk" individuals in Vietnam, namely high-ranking government and military personnel, were hurriedly air-lifted away to safety at temporary receiving centers in Guam, Thailand, and the Philippines. This group marked the first wave of Southeast Asian refugees, who would eventually resettle in the United States. The first wave is distinct in that they were generally the educated urban elite and middle class from Vietnam. Because many of them had worked closely with the U.S. military, they tended to be more westernized (40 percent were Catholics), and a good portion of them were able to speak English (30 percent spoke English well). Another significant feature is the fact that roughly 95 percent of the first wave of Southeast Asian refugees were Vietnamese, even though the capitals of Laos and Cambodia also fell to communist forces in 1975.[64]

Once these first-wave refugees came to the United States, they were flown to one of four military base/reception centers in California, Arkansas, Pennsylvania, and Florida. From these bases they registered with a voluntary agency that would eventually help resettle them with a sponsor. About 60 percent of the sponsors were families, while the other 40 percent were usually churches and individuals. Sponsors were responsible for day-to-day needs of the refugees until they were able to find jobs and become independent. The resettlement of the first wave of refugees was funded by the 1975 Indochinese Resettlement Assistance Act and was seen as a quick and temporary process. Indeed, all the reception centers closed by the end of 1975, and the Resettlement Act expired in 1977.

The second wave of Southeast Asian refugees was larger, more heterogeneous, and many believe even more devastated by their relocation experience than the first wave. The second wave of refugees were generally less educated, urbanized, and westernized (only 7 percent spoke English and only about 7 percent were Catholic) compared to their predecessors; at the same time they were much more ethnically diverse than the first wave. According to statistics, between 1978 and 1980, about

55.5 percent of Southeast Asian refugees were from Vietnam (including many ethnic Chinese), 36.6 percent from Laos, and 7.8 percent from Cambodia. The second wave consisted of people who suffered under the communist regimes and were unable to leave their countries immediately before or after the new governments took power.[65]

In Vietnam, the ethnic Chinese merchant class was very much the target of resentment by the new communist government. Many of the Chinese businesses in Vietnam were nationalized, Chinese language schools and newspapers were closed, education and employment rights were denied, and food rations were reduced. Under these conditions, about 250,000 escaped North Vietnam, seeking refuge in China. Roughly 70 percent of the estimated 500,000 boat people who tried to escape Vietnam by sea were ethnic Chinese. The treacherous journey usually took place on ill-equipped crowded boats that were unable to withstand the rigors of the ocean or outrun marauding Thai pirates. The U.S. Committee for Refugees estimates at least 100,000 people lost their lives trying to escape Vietnam by boat.[66] Along with the Chinese, others in Vietnam, particularly those who had supported the U.S.-backed South Vietnamese government and their families, were also subject to especially harsh treatment by the new communist leadership. Many were sent to "reeducation camps" and banished to work in rural regions clearing land devastated by 30 years of war.

The holocaust in Cambodia began immediately after the Khmer Rouge (Red Khmer) marched into the capital city of Phnom Penh on April 17, 1975. That same day the entire population of the capital was ordered to the countryside. After three years it has been broadly estimated between 1 and 3 million Cambodians died from starvation, disease, and execution out of a population of less than 7 million. In 1978 Vietnam (with support from the Soviet Union) invaded Cambodia, drove the Khmer Rouge out of power, and established a new government under its own control. Famine and warfare continued under Vietnamese occupation, and by 1979 over 600,000 refugees from Cambodia fled the country, mostly to neighboring Thailand. In Laos, the transition from one government to another was initially rather smooth compared to Vietnam following the fall of Saigon. After over a decade of civil war, a coalition government was formed in April 1974 that included Laotian communists, the Pathet Lao. But shortly after communists took power in Vietnam and Cambodia, the Pathet Lao moved to solidify its full control of the country. It was at this time that troops from both Laos and Vietnam began a military campaign against the Hmong hill people, a preliterate ethnic minority group that lived in the mountains of Laos who were recruited by the U.S. government to serve as mercenaries against communist forces in the region. The Hmong were seen as traitors to the communist revolution, and massive bombing raids were ordered against them that included the dropping of napalm and poisonous chemicals. Thousands of Hmong were killed in these fierce assaults, and those who remained had little choice but to seek refuge in neighboring Thailand. The Hmong were not the only people in Laos who were persecuted. By 1979 roughly 3,000 Hmong were entering Thailand every month, and as late as 1983 an estimated 75 percent of the 76,000 Laotians in Thai refugee camps were Hmong people.[67]

The world could not ignore this massive outpouring of refugees from Southeast Asia, and in 1979 President Jimmy Carter allowed 14,000 refugees a month to enter the United States. In addition, Congress passed the Refugee Act of 1980, which set an annual quota of 50,000 refugees per year, funded resettlement programs, and allowed refugees to become eligible for the same welfare benefits as U.S. citizens after 36 months of refugee assistance (this was changed to 18 months in 1982).

Many of the Southeast Asians who came in the third wave are technically not considered refugees, but are in actuality immigrants. This has been facilitated by the 1980 Orderly Departure Program (ODP), an agreement with Vietnam that allows individuals and families to enter the United States. ODP was a benefit for three groups: relatives of permanently settled refugees in the United States, Amerasians, and former reeducation camp internees. By the end of 1992, over 300,000 Vietnamese immigrated to the United States, including 80,000 Amerasians and their relatives, as well as 60,000 former camp internees and their families.[68] The resettlement experience, the development of Southeast Asian communities, as well as the influx of Amerasians to the United States are respectively discussed in greater detail in Chapters 2 and 7.

It is obvious that Southeast Asian refugees/immigrants have been a rapidly growing and extremely diverse group. According to the 1990 census, there were 1,001,054 Southeast Asians in the United States, or 13 percent of the total population of Asian Americans. Individually, the census counted 614,547 Vietnamese, 149,014 Laotians, 147,411 Cambodians, and 90,082 Hmong. Some have argued that these census figures are an undercount of the actual numbers of people from Southeast Asian countries. Researchers point to the fact that the total number of arrivals to the United States from Southeast Asia is roughly the same as census figures. This is an anomaly because the census figure should be about 20 percent larger to reflect the number of American-born Southeast Asians. There are, however, several reasons for this disparity. First of all, new arrivals from Southeast Asia who have little knowledge of the English language may simply not have responded to census questionnaires. This certainly is a general concern for all Asian American groups. Second, and probably most important, an estimated 15 to 25 percent of those from Vietnam, Cambodia, and Laos are actually ethnic Chinese. It is quite possible that many ethnic Chinese from Southeast Asia answered the appropriate census question of ethnicity without regard to their nationality. Third, no one is exactly sure how Amerasians identified themselves on the 1990 census or if they even participated at all. Although a factor, note that most of the Amerasians from Vietnam did not actually enter the United States until after the 1990 census was taken. In all references to the Southeast Asian population, keep these considerations in mind.[69]

# Conclusion

This chapter briefly describes the history and recent growth of the Asian population in the United States. It also highlights the significance of the 1965 Immigration Reform Act, global economic restructuring, and the Vietnam War as three broad events that profoundly impacted both the number and type of migrants who have come to the United States from Asian countries. In order to examine post-1965 Asian Americans comprehensively, it is particularly important to look at the rapid growth of the population, personal history, nativity, length of time in the United States, premigration experiences and traumas, education, socioeconomic class background, and gender. Chapter 2 details the social and economic diversity of immigrant and American-born Asians, as well as their settlement patterns and impact on various communities across the United States.

# Notes

[1] Emil Guillermo, "From Miss America to Mr. President," *Asian Week,* October 19, 2000.

[2] Shih-shan Henry Tsai, *The Chinese Experience in America* (Bloomington: Indiana University Press, 1986), p. 1; also see Stan Steiner, *Fusahang: The Chinese Who Built America* (New York: Harper & Row, 1979), pp. 24–35; Elena S. H. Yu, "Filipino Migration and Community Organization in the United States," *California Sociologist 3:2* (1980): 76–102; and Joan M. Jensen, *Passage from India: Asian Indian Immigrants in North America* (New Haven: Yale University Press, 1988), pp. 12–13.

[3] Sucheng Chan, *Asian Californians* (San Francisco: MTL/Boyd & Fraser, 1991), pp. 5–6.

[4] Ronald Takaki, *Strangers from a Different Shore* (Boston: Little, Brown, 1989), pp. 79, 114.

[5] Stanford Lyman, *Chinese Americans* (New York: Random House, 1974), pp. 86–88.

[6] Chan, *Asian Californians,* pp. 27–33.

[7] Lyman, *Chinese Americans,* pp. 63–69.

[8] Yuji Ichioka, *The Issei: The World of the First Generation Japanese Immigrant's, 1885–1924* (New York: Free Press, 1988), pp. 64–65.

[9] Roger Daniels, *Concentration Camps: North American Japanese in the United States and Canada During World War II* (Malabar, FL: Robert A. Kreiger, 1981), p. 7.

[10] Bill Ong Hing, *Making and Remaking Asian America Through Immigration Policy, 1850–1990* (Stanford, CA: Stanford University Press, 1993), pp. 28–30.

[11] Chan, *Asian Californians,* p. 7.

[12] Edwin B. Almirol, *Ethnic Identity and Social Negotiation: A Study of a Filipino Community in California* (New York: AMS Press, 1985), pp. 52–59; and H. Brett Melendy, "Filipinos in the United States," in Norris Hundley, Jr. (ed.), *The Asian American: The Historical Experience* (Santa Barbara: Cleo, 1977), pp. 101–128.

[13] Takaki, *Strangers from a Different Shore,* pp. 53–57.

[14] Chan, *Asian Californians,* pp. 7, 17–19, 37; and Warren Y. Kim, *Koreans in America* (Seoul: Po Chin Chai, 1971), pp. 22–27.

[15] Joan M. Jensen, *Passage from India: Asian Indian Immigrants in North America* (New Haven: Yale University Press, 1988), pp. 24–41; and Rajanki K. Das, *Hindustani Workers on the Pacific Coast* (Berlin and Leipzig: Walter De Gruyter, 1923), p. 77.

[16]Das, *Hindustani Workers*, pp. 66–67.

[17]Bruce La Brack, "Occupational Specialization Among Rural California Sikhs: The Interplay of Culture and Economics," *Amerasia Journal* 9:2 (1982): 29–56.

[18]Naturalization Act of 1790, I Stat. 103 (1790).

[19]Act of 14 July 1870, 16 Stat. 256.

[20]Roger Daniels, *Asian Americans: Chinese and Japanese in the United States* (Seattle: University of Washington Press, 1988), p. 43.

[21]Chan, *Asian Californians*, p. 42.

[22]Robert F. Heizer and Alan F. Almquist, *The Other Californians: Prejudice and Discrimination Under Spain, Mexico, and the United States to 1920* (Berkeley: University of California Press, 1971), p. 129.

[23]Takaki, *Strangers from a Different Shore*, p. 82.

[24]Lyman, *Chinese Americans*, pp. 55–85.

[25]Takaki, *Strangers from a Different Shore*, pp. 111–112.

[26]Juan L. Gonzales, *Racial and Ethnic Groups in America*, 2nd ed. (Dubuque, IA: Kendall/Hunt, 1993), p. 136; and Juan L. Gonzales, *Racial and Ethnic Families in America*, 2nd ed. (Dubuque, IA: Kendall/Hunt Publishing Co., 1993), p. 3.

[27]Chan, *Asian Californians*, pp. 44–45.

[28]Hing, *Making and Remaking Asian America*, pp. 32–39.

[29]*Yick Wo v. Hopkins*, 118 U.S. 356 (1886); and Lyman, *Chinese Americans*, p. 79.

[30]*Takao Ozawa v. United States*, 260 U.S. 178 (1922); Heizer and Alquist, *The Other Californians*, pp. 192–193; and Ichioka, *The Issei*, pp. 210–226.

[31]*United States v. Bhagat Singh Thind*, 261 U.S. 204 (1923); Jensen, *Passage from India*, pp. 255–260; and Gurdial Singh, "East Indians in the United States," *Sociology and Social Research* 30:3 (1946): 208–216.

[32]Megumi Dick Osumi, "Asians and California's Anti–Miscegenation Laws," in Nobuya Tsuchida (ed.), *Asian and Pacific American Experiences: Women's Perspectives* (Minneapolis: Asian/Pacific American Learning Resource Center, University of Minnesota, 1982), pp. 1–37; and Takaki, *Strangers from a Different Shore*, pp. 330–331.

[33]William Petersen, *Japanese Americans* (New York: Random House, 1971), pp. 66–100; Roger Daniels, *Concentration Camps, U.S.A.* (New York: Holt, Rinehart & Winston, 1971), pp. 75, 81–82; and Jacobus tenBroek, Edward N. Barnhart and Floyd W. Matson, *Prejudice, War, and the Constitution* (Berkeley: University of California Press), pp. 118–120.

[34]Cited in Commission on Wartime Relocation and Internment of Civilians, *Personal Justice Denied* (Washington, DC: U.S. Government Printing Office, 1982), pp. 52–53.

[35]Takaki, *Strangers from a Different Shore*, pp. 379–392.

[36]Commission on Wartime Relocation and Internment of Civilians, *Personal Justice Denied*, p. 217; tenBroek, Barnhart, and Matson, *Prejudice, War, and the Constitution*, pp. 155–177, 180–181; and Daniels, *Concentration Camps: North America*.

[37]Chan, *Asian Californians*, p. 101.

[38]Petersen, *Japanese Americans*, p. 87.

[39]Cited in Marvin Karlins, Thomas L. Coffman, and Gary Walters, "On the Fading of Social Stereotypes: Studies of Three Generations of College Students," *Journal of Personality and Psychology* 13 (1990): 4–5.

[40]*Time*, December 22, 1941, p. 33.

[41]Cited in Harold Isaacs, *Images of Asia: American Views of China and India* (New York: Harper & Row, 1972), pp. xviii–xix.

[42]Chan, *Asian Californians*, pp. 103–104; and Lyman, *Chinese Americans*, pp. 127, 134.

[43]Takaki, *Strangers from a Different Shore*, pp. 357–363, 370–378; Manuel Buaken, "Life in the Armed Forces," *New Republic* 109 (1943): 279–280; and Bienvenido Santos, "Filipinos in War," *Far Eastern Survey* 11 (1942): 249–250.

[44]Harry H. L. Kitano and Roger Daniels, *Asian Americans: Emerging Minorities*, 2nd ed. (Upper Saddle River, NJ: Prentice Hall, 1995), p. 42, Table 4–2; and Monica Boyd, "Oriental Immigration: The Experience of Chinese, Japanese, and Filipino Populations in the United States," *International Migration Review* 10 (1976): 48–60, Table 1.

[45]Chan, *Asian Californians*, pp. 105–106.

[46]Diane Mark and Ginger Chih, *A Place Called Chinese America* (San Francisco: The Organization of Chinese Americans, 1982), pp. 105–107.

[47]Chan, *Asian Californians*, pp. 108–109.

[48]Ibid., pp. 109–110.

[49]Hing, *Making and Remaking Asian America*, Appendix B, pp. 189–200; Table 9, p. 82.

[50]Hing, *Making and Remaking Asian America*, pp. 79–120; Luciano Mangiafico, *Contemporary American Immigrants: Patterns of Filipino, Korean, and Chinese Settlement in the United States* (New York: Praeger, 1988), pp. 1–26; James T. Fawcett and Benjamin V. Carino (eds.), *Pacific Bridges: The New Immigration from Asia and the Pacific Islands* (Staten Island, NY: Center for Migration Studies, 1987); and Herbert R. Barringer, Robert W. Gardner, and Michael J. Levine (eds.), *Asian and Pacific Islanders in the United States* (New York: Russell Sage Foundation, 1993).

[51]U.S. Immigration and Naturalization Service, *Statistical Yearbook of the Immigration and Naturalization Service, 1993* (Washington DC: U.S. Government Printing Office, 1994), p. 20.

[52]Roger Daniels, *Coming to America* (New York: HarperCollins, 1990), pp. 391–397.

[53]U.S. Immigration and Naturalization Service, *Statistical Yearbook of the Immigration and Naturalization Service, 1994* (Washington, DC: U.S. Government Printing Office, 1996), p. 126, Chart O.

[54]Hing, *Making and Remaking Asian America*, pp. 7–8.

[55]Paul Ong, Edna Bonacich, and Lucie Cheng (eds.), *The New Asian Immigration in Los Angeles and Global Restructuring* (Philadelphia: Temple University Press, 1994), pp. 3–100; and Edna Bonacich, Lucie Cheng, Norma Chinchilla, Nora Hamilton, and Paul Ong (eds.), *Global Production: The Apparel Industry in the Pacific Rim* (Philadelphia: Temple University Press, 1994), pp. 3–20.

[56]Paul Ong and Evelyn Blumenberg, "Scientists and Engineers," in Paul Ong (ed.), *The State of Asian Pacific America: Economic Diversity, Issues & Policies* (Los Angeles: LEAP Asian Pacific American Public Policy Institute and UCLA Asian American Studies Center, 1994), pp. 113–138. Note that I am distinguishing between foreign exchange students who are overseas nationals from Asian American students who happen to be foreign born.

[57]Ibid., p. 173; and U.S. Department of Commerce, *Statistical Abstract of the United States, 1995* (Washington, DC: U.S. Government Printing Office, 1995), p. 188, Table 295.

[58]U.S. Department of Commerce, *Statistical Abstract of the United States, 1999* (Washington, DC: U.S. Government Printing Office, 2000), p. 625, Table 1004.

[59]"The Golden Diaspora: Indian Immigrants to the U.S. Are One of the Newest Elements of the American Melting Pot—and the Most Spectacular Success Story," *Time Select/Global Business*, June 19, 2000, pp. B26–27.

[60]Paul Ong and Tania Azores, "Health Professionals on the Front-Line," in Paul Ong (ed.), *The State of Asian Pacific America: Economic Diversity, Issues & Policies*, pp. 139–164.

[61] Paul Ong and Tania Azores, "The Migration and Incorporation of Filipino Nurses," in Ong et al. (eds.), *The New Asian Immigration in Los Angeles and Global Restructuring,* pp. 166–195; and Mangiafico, *Contemporary American Immigrants,* pp. 42–43.

[62] Literature on the Vietnam conflict is voluminous. For an excellent and readable overview, see Stanley Karnow, *Vietnam: A History* (New York: Penguin, 1991).

[63] The quota for refugees under the 1965 Immigration Reform Act was only 17,400, so President Gerald Ford instructed the attorney general to use his "parole" power to admit the 130,000 refugees. The use of parole power was also used to bring European refugees to the United States during the 1950s. For more detail, see Hing, *Making and Remaking Asian America,* pp. 123–128; and Paul J. Strand and Woodrow Jones, Jr., *Indochinese Refugees in America: Problems of Adaptation and Assimilation* (Durham, NC: Duke University Press, 1985).

[64] Chan, *Asian Californians,* p. 128; and Chor-Swan Ngin, "The Acculturation Pattern of Orange County's Southeast Asian Refugees," *Journal of Orange County Studies* 3:4 (Fall 1989–Spring 1990): 46–53.

[65] Ngin, "The Acculturation Pattern of Orange County's Southeast Asian Refugees," p. 49; and Ngoan Le, "The Case of the Southeast Asian Refugees: Policy for a Community 'At-Risk,' " in *The State of Asian Pacific America: Policy Issues to the Year 2020* (Los Angeles: LEAP Asian Pacific American Public Policy Institute and UCLA Asian American Studies Center, 1993), pp. 167–188.

[66] For more details, see Strand and Jones, *Indochinese Refugees in America;* Barry L. Wain, *The Refused: The Agony of Indochina Refugees* (New York: Simon & Schuster, 1981); and U.S. Committee for Refugees, *Uncertain Harbors: The Plight of Vietnamese Boat People* (Washington, DC: U.S. Government Printing Office, 1987).

[67] Chan, *Asian Californians,* pp. 121–138; Kitano and Daniels, *Asian Americans: Emerging Minorities,* pp. 170–191; U.S. Committee for Refugees, *Cambodians in Thailand: People on the Edge* (Washington, DC: U.S. Government Printing Office, 1985); and U.S. Committee for Refugees, *Refugees from Laos: In Harm's Way* (Washington, DC: U.S. Government Printing Office, 1986).

[68] U.S. Committee for Refugees, *Uncertain Harbors,* pp. 19–20; and Ruben Rumbaut, "Vietnamese, Laotian, and Cambodian Americans," in Pyong Gap Min (ed.), *Asian Americans: Contemporary Trends and Issues* (Thousand Oaks, CA: Sage, 1995), p. 240.

[69] Ruben Rumbaut and J. R. Weeks, "Fertility and Adaptation: Indochinese Refugees in the United States," *International Migration Review* 20:2 (1986): 428–466; and Rumbaut, "Vietnamese, Laotian, and Cambodian Americans," pp. 239–242.

# Beyond Internal Colonialism: Class, Gender, and Culture as Challenges to Chicano Identity

María E. Montoya[1]

I have a confession to make: I was born in 1964. I was not alive when Oswald shot President John F. Kennedy. I was one year old when Cesar Chavez led his first strike. I was two years old when Reis Tijerina occupied Echo Amphitheatre in New Mexico. And I was five years old when Neil Armstrong walked on the moon. What difference do these events make to my particular life? And more importantly, what do these historical milestones and personal history have to do with the future of Chicana/o history? For me, every one of those events is history—I have no direct memory or relationship to any of them. Take, for example, events that occurred in my own hometown of Denver. The only memory I have of Corky Gonzales and the Crusade for Justice is attending an event sponsored by the crusade (I have no direct memory of him) when I was about five years old. We went with my "radical" (radical because he wore a Nehru jacket) uncle, who was younger than my parents and who had become involved with the crusade while attending the University of Denver Law School. That evening remained a clear and powerful memory, and in the end shaped much about how I think and live my life today. Yet, it is a memory that made sense only after I had left home and *read* about the crusade and Corky Gonzales while in college.

I suspect that for many of the scholars in the field of Chicano/a history who are older than I am, the shooting of JFK, Armstrong's walk on the moon, and, more particularly, the movements led by Cesar Chavez, Corky Gonzalez, and Reis Tijerina are not merely historical events. For most, they are part of a personal history and, in many cases, part of a personal memory. I, however, lived my childhood, received my education, and became politically aware in the early years of

From *Voices of a New Chicana/o History,* edited by Rochin and Valdes. Copyright © 2000 by Julian Samora Research Institute. Reprinted by permission.

the Reagan era and the Republican revolution. The rhetoric of "equality" espoused by the far Right, who were eager to eliminate affirmative action programs, and not the liberal radicalism of the previous decade, shaped by youth. My role models were not liberals like Dolores Huerta and Corky Gonzalez, but conservatives like Linda Chavez and Manuel Lujan.

I came from a family that was far from radical and embraced the American Dream as we made our home in the very white and quietly hostile world of suburban Denver. During their childhood and education my parents had been criticized by well-meaning Presbyterian missionaries for speaking Spanish and practicing anything that vaguely resembled Catholicism. So I grew up without learning my parents' native language and rarely setting foot into the Catholic Church. I suspect that this is a very different experience from most scholars writing in the field to date. Yet, I doubt that my experience is that unique among the Chicana/os of my age cohort or among the graduates and under-graduates I currently teach. It is not an experience that we have written about, and it is one we have rarely discussed publicly.[2] In fact, it is a very unromantic, apolitical coming-of-age tale that cannot compare, in terms of drama and hardship, with the radical youth of the 1960s and 1970s, or even with the struggles of my parents in the 1950s, or my grandparents' experiences during the Depression. I do think, however, that my experience reflects the diversity of people and points of view that are beginning and will continue to shape this field we call Chicana/o history.

For those who fought the battles to establish Chicano studies in the early 1970s, this changing demography among scholars may not come as welcome news. Many older scholars do not trust a new generation to carry on the vision that guided them in the creation of the Chicano Movement. Today, Chicana/o history stands at a crossroads. For the first time, this "new," but really remade, Chicano history will be told and retold by people who were not there at the inception of the field and who will barely be able to muster up a historical memory to go along with the history they write. Moreover, this "new" history will come from a diverse set of scholars trained in a variety of disciplines and schools across the country. This difference will have a profound effect on the field.

As more scholars enter the field, there will be such diversity of thought that it may become difficult to define exactly what we mean by Chicana/o history. The new generation of scholars will create their own methodology, voice, and even definition of the field, and will continue to borrow from other forms of academic discourse, such as postmodernism, postcolonial studies, and transnationalism. Rather than looking for methodologies that separate Chicano history from the fields of U.S., Mexican, and Latin American historiographies, the trend will be for scholars to look for ways to connect Chicana/o history to other methodologies and theoretical frameworks. The political urgency that marked so many of the early writings and the revisionist spirit in which those texts were written will begin to fade away as younger scholars search for a more academic voice in which to place their work. As the field stands at this crossroads it is appropriate to ask: Is it possible to combine the earlier political agenda of writing Chicano history with what will be a very lucid and constantly redefined field of Chicana/o history in the coming decade?

I want to challenge the very notion of "Chicano" and ask what use the term and historiography hold for us as scholars in academia and activists in the world in which we live. In preparing this paper, I was surprised at the relatively small amount of self-critical examination of Chicano history that has been written.[3] I was trained in the history of the American West, where people make their writing careers by doing nothing else but critiquing the field and others in it.[4] It is my sense, however, that Chicana/o historians have been too busy producing actual knowledge. Since relatively few monographs and textbooks about Chicanos and Mexican Americans exist, we have consequently spent the better portion of our time digging through archives, taking oral interviews, and poring over government documents in order to tell the stories of people who have never had their stories told, much less had their lives reexamined by revisionist historians. Chicana/o historians have not had the luxury of the longevity in the field that allows for the kind of self-reflection inherent in a field like western history, which originated over one hundred years ago with an essay by Frederick Jackson Turner.

What troubles me most as I continue to do research and teach in the field of Chicana/o history is that I find it difficult to define the field as a discipline. I have become even more overwhelmed in the last few years because of my move from Colorado to Michigan. At least in Colorado I could delude myself into thinking that geographical boundaries defined Chicana/os and their history—particularly the southwestern states of California, New Mexico, Texas, Arizona, and portions of Colorado and Utah. Now, I come to find out that Chicanos have spread out across the entire Midwest.[5] Speaking with students at both Michigan State University and the University of Michigan, I have been constantly amazed and comforted by the many similarities we share, despite the vast differences in geography, landscape, and economic bases. Nevertheless, there is something unique to the midwestern Chicano experience that defies complete categorization with Chicanos of the American Southwest. Not only do Chicano scholars need to contend with the diversity within the Chicano community, but as the field moves toward a pan-ethnic identity of Latino we will need to look for ways to incorporate the experiences of Cubans, Puerto Ricans, and other Latin American immigrants. Although this is a topic for another paper, it is a concern we should keep within our sights as we move into a twenty-first century that will bring more immigrants and link us all through technology and mass media. Nevertheless, several factors, other than geographical diversity, separate and distinguish the myriad of Chicano experiences. I would like to discuss three issues that I think challenge our community of interest, in terms of both academia and our activism. They are issues centering around class, gender, and what I will broadly label as culture.

In terms of class, diversity among the Mexican-American population has always marked the Chicano experience, but this is becoming even more prevalent as more Chicanos slowly make their way into the middle and even upper classes of

American society. I will limit my remarks, as this is already fairly well traveled territory in the historiography.[6] Internal colonialism, the early model prevalent in Chicano history, tended to subordinate class divisions and differences between Mexican Americans to the common ethnicity, which marked Chicanos as the "other" in U.S. society. Internal colonialism sets up an "us versus them" model of Anglos against Chicanos. In this model there was little room for examining how income, neighborhood, or class divisions affect the unity of Chicanos as a group. Early scholarship in the field focussed primarily on the working-class and economically struggling Mexican Americans, and studies tended to dismiss those persons and experiences that did not fit into that model. For example, among scholars of the Chicano generation it fell out of fashion to study the Spanish conquest of the New World. Part of this was a periodization choice, as most Chicano histories began with the U.S. conquest of Mexican territory in 1848. Nevertheless, the conquest certainly offers spectacular examples of domination and conquest when we think about the how the Spanish government, soldiers, and priests subordinated native peoples. Including the Spanish conquest, however, complicates the internal colonial model significantly. The prospect of thinking about Spanish-speaking men dominating Native Americans simply muddies the picture of Anglo-Mexicano relations too much for the internal colonial model to embrace. Internal colonialism, in fact, has never been able to satisfactorily explain how to deal with the complex problem of *mestizaje* between Spaniards and Native Mexicanos. By picking up the story in 1848, internal colonialism avoids the problem and can simply label all the inhabitants of the recently conquered territory as Mexicans.[7]

Yet, class has been one of the most divisive issues in the community and in scholarship. In particular, those who have moved into the middle class, and seemingly have forgotten their roots, have been singled out for criticism by Chicano scholars.[8] Only with Mario Garcia's work, *Mexican Americans,* has the middle class become a viable and acceptable research topic.[9] Yet, while Garcia's work has been well received and much appreciated, few have followed his lead and pursued other middle-class-based analysis of Mexican Americans: there is virtually no study of post-1960s middle-class Mexican Americans. It is as if there were no conservative, middle-class Mexican Americans during or after the Chicano Movement.

Certainly this is not considered a "hot," or even a viable, topic within the canon of Chicano history, which has preoccupied itself with telling stories that are not based on assimilation or acceptance of the dominant society. Chicano historians' monographic replies to the assimilationist stories of an earlier generation have led the discipline to focus narrowly on tales of resistance and victimization. Consequently, those historical actors who did not particularly interest Chicano historians in the early years have been lost in our historical memory. As a profession and a discipline, we have to cast our net more broadly and look at Mexican Americans of all classes and working backgrounds if we are to truly understand the total Chicana/o experience. It is not enough to label members of our own community as "other" or "Hispanics," implying that the middle class were sellouts to the Chicano

Movement. Instead, we need research that examines forces that lead to assimilation and asks why people make the choices they do about identity, citizenship, and political affiliation.

Even more divisive than class, however, has been the failure of the majority of Chicano (not Chicana) historians to incorporate gender as a meaningful category of analysis in their work.[10] Very little of the early historiography even marginally integrates women into the stories male scholars have told about conquest, resistance, and adaptation.[11] As a community of scholars, the field has readily accepted the one-paragraph excuses of scholars like Mario Garcia in *Mexican Americans* who exempt themselves from writing about women because it takes them too far afield from their main interest of study or because there is seemingly not enough primary source material. Garcia writes, "Finally, although I considered writing a separate chapter on women within the Mexican American Generation, I decided that such a chapter might be construed as patronizing and incorrectly suggest the women did not participate in the larger movement such as those of the Left."[12] In the book, however, there is relatively little of discussion of women as actors within the roles that Garcia defines as "leadership." Perhaps a more fruitful way of examining the experiences of women in this generation would have been for Garcia to critique the idea of "leadership" using gender analysis in the same way that he critiqued the category of "leadership" by looking through the lens of ethnicity. Furthermore, Garcia merely accepts the patriarchal system that kept women out of nationally prominent leadership positions without examining the ideological underpinnings of the men in these groups. I do not mean to single out Professor Garcia; there were many scholars before him and even after his book appeared who simply never examined the role of women or the construction of patriarchy within their work.

Scholars in Chicano studies, unintentionally and subconsciously, have created a gendered division of labor that assigns the telling of women's tales to women, while men get to study and write about everything else. Despite this gendered division, some of the most interesting work in Chicano history has been done by women and in the study of women, particularly the work of Vicki Ruiz, who has been a mentor to a lucky handful of graduate students.[13] Moreover, when women complained (whether in the Chicano Movement, in academia, or even in today's local MECHA organizations) about the inequality of treatment within the community or within the existing scholarship they were told to stop causing division in the field and to go along with the main movement: racial over gender loyalty is always preferred.[14]

Chicana historians find themselves in a precarious and often lonely position. Mainstream (white) women's historians are often blind to the class, racial, or ethnic diversity that marks the experiences of women of color as different from their own experience. Consequently, Chicana historians have found an uneasy home in the world of women's history.[15] To make matters worse, the field of Chicano history, with less than twenty (and here I suspect I am being generous) women Ph.D. historians, has not been an inviting or nurturing place for women and their work. Men should not be so surprised or hurt when these scholars reject the male-dominated paradigms in favor of finding their own voice apart from the often chauvinistic world of Chicano scholarship as well as from the ethnocentric views of women's historiography. Only when women of color scholars are accepted on an equal footing within the Chicano academic community can a bridge be built to cover this gap that threatens to divide our discipline. We simply must cease to have this gendered division of academic labor: women should be encouraged to pursue topics outside of Chicana history and men should naturally reach for gender as a viable and enlightening category of analysis in their work. Just imagine what the work of David Montejano would have looked like if he had looked at women's work and their place in the world economy. How would Mario Garcia's book have changed had he challenged and refined the idea of leadership?

In the final analysis, what and who defines Chicano culture may help us to define what Chicano history is and what it will be in the future. The problem for Chicano historians, however, is how to come to terms with the diversity of interests, both academically and personally, within the Chicano community. If historians want to study and analyze Chicano ethnicity and the role it plays in American society, then we must treat it simply as one category of analysis. Ethnicity is only one of the myriad of ways that people define themselves and their community of interest. We have got to break away from the idea that there is a monolithic, hegemonic ideal that we label "Chicano." More importantly, we must be aware of excluding those, whether scholars, neighbors, or historical figures, who do not fall completely under a strident and unyielding definition of "Chicano."

Let me explain my point by using one example. My own particular confrontation with how diversity of interests affects our definition of Chicano came while looking at the difference between urban and rural Chicanos in the state of Colorado. I am particularly interested in comparing the people of the San Luis Valley, an extremely rural and poor section of the state, with those of the city of Pueblo, a union town that historically has found its economic base in the steel industry, which today struggles to revive its economy. The Chicanos who live in these two places, divided by 150 miles and a mountain range, share the same ethnicity, same familial backgrounds, same religion, and same social customs.[16] Yet, because of where they live, either rural or urban, they often have very different interests that put them at odds with one another and have them allying with other ethnicities and classes in their own region. One particular issue that they differ over is the issue of water. The San Luis Valley sits on possibly one of the largest untapped aquifers in the American Southwest. Cities like Denver, Albuquerque, Pueblo, and even Los Angeles have been eyeing the water for years. The litigation within the state of Colorado over the last five years about who "owns," needs, and ultimately gets to use the water, however, has the possibility of pitting rural and urban Chicanos against each other as both strive to preserve their jobs, community, and homes.

The discipline, and particular models such as internal colonialism, give us few tools with which to analyze this problem. How do we decide which group is more "Chicano" and consequently more deserving of the water and our historical understanding? Is it the traditional Hispano farmers who maintain their own farms in the valley? Is it the recent immigrant farmworkers from Mexico who work for the agribusinesses and larger farm owners in the valley? Or is it the urbanized, out-of-work steelworkers who need the water to help their fledgling community survive and expand? I would argue that all three groups have a viable claim to the resource and to the political power embedded in the term Chicano? As "new" Chicano historians, our job should be to create a paradigm and a discipline that incorporates all of these groups and explains their conflict, as well as their cooperation, with one another. This rural/urban diversity is just one area that needs exploration. Chicano historians should also find a way to accommodate and explain the differences in region, migration patterns, and countries of origins, and determine how these diverse influences shape the Chicana/o experience.[17]

Despite my previous comments, I would like to suggest that in fact there is something we can define as Chicano History and that there is a community that somehow, despite all of our differences, we manage to see as Chicanos. Most of the criticism of the recent Chicano history by scholars of a previous generation focuses on how the younger generation has forgotten the past—forgotten the Chicano Movement of the 1960s and 1970s and, more specifically, the goals set forth by the Plan de Santa Barbara. The plan, written by young scholars in the field at the time, outlined a program for scholarship, scholars and their relationship to the community, and activism.[18] The critique by the older generation of Chicano scholars is that: young scholars are so concerned with the rules of academia, their careers, and their own personal attainment that they have forgotten about their past and their community. The problem with this critique, however, is that it is based on a static notion of what Chicano history is, or should be. The critique harkens back to the past, when it might be more productive to look to the future.

The first and second generations of Chicano scholars may have done their job too well. They opened the doors and allowed younger scholars access into the best schools of California and into Ivy League institutions. They said that Chicanos were equal to the task and could succeed in this white-dominated environment, if only given the chance through affirmative action programs. And, in fact, young scholars thrived. My generation of scholars is a product and a result of the radicalism of the 1970s and we are the beneficiaries of all that hard work. These results are not only evident in academia. Undergraduates who came into contact with Chicano professors, MECHA, and other organizations designed to help them survive the difficult world of university life graduated and took their place in America's middle class. So rather than complaining about how unradical this most recent generation has become, we should examine their experiences and understand why they seem to have no need to embrace radicalism. In fact, I suspect that fewer and fewer of our undergraduates want to fight the old battles of the 1960s and 1970s. They, moreover, face new and difficult challenges posed by the anti-immigrant movement and the affirmative action backlash.

Instead, in this new world of multiculturalism and race and ethnicity requirements in college curriculums, it seems to me that our task as teachers goes way beyond the goals outlined by the Plan de Santa Barbara. I agree wholeheartedly that part of our obligation as scholars in the Academy is to provide a safe, inviting, and nurturing environment in which Chicano and Chicana students can learn and thrive. I, however, see a second obligation to the wider community, which I address through my own teaching. By placing myself in a mainstream department and by teaching such mainstream courses as history of the American West, environmental history, and particularly the U.S. history surveys, I have access to many students that I would not if I were to teach only courses in Chicano history. By reconceptualizing how the U.S. history courses are taught I am able to put the history of women, Chicanos, and all people of color in their correct and proper context. I believe that not only do we have an obligation to teach young Chicana/os about their own history, but we have an even greater obligation to enlighten other students with whom we come into contact about the history of other people—people with whom they will work and live for the rest of their adult lives.

In fact, it may be time for us to reconsider what our goals are as Chicana/o historians who want to live in the community and work within the confines of academia. We may have to abandon documents like the Plan De Santa Barbara and other manifestos written in that unique and radical time period. Instead, I think the time has come to step back and marvel at the numbers we have in our field and the diversity of those scholars. Only then can the field honestly evaluate the political and academic climate in which we live and work, and determine how we can make the best contribution to the field, our students, and to ourselves as scholars and activists.

# Notes

[1] María E. Montoya is an assistant professor at the University of Michigan in the Department of History and the Program in American Culture. Her book, *Translating Property: The Maxwell Land Grant and the Conflict over Land in the American West, 1840–1920* is forthcoming. She would like to thank Natalia Molina, Estevan Rael y Galvez, Tom I. Romero II, and Sonya Smith for their comments.

[2] As an example of this middle-class narrative, see Ruben Navarette Jr., *A Darker Shade of Crimson: Odyssey of a Harvard Chicano* (New York: Bantam Books, 1993). Probably the best known set of these coming-of-age biographies from a middle-class perspective are Richard Rodriquez's *Hunger of Memory* (New York: Bantam Books, 1982) and *Days of Obligation: An Argument with my Mexican Father* (New York: Penguin Books, 1992).

[3] The notable exceptions are Tomas Almaguer, "Ideological Distortions in Recent Chicano Historiography: The Internal Colonial Model and Chicano Historical Interpretation," *Aztlán* 18 (1989): 7; Ignacio M. Garcia, "Juncture in the Road: Chicano Studies since 'El Plan de Santa Barbara,'" in *Chicanas/Chicanos at the Grossroads: Social, Economic, and Political Change* David R. Maciel and Isidro R. Ortiz, eds. (Tucson: University of Arizona Press, 1996), 181; Richard Griswold del Castillo, "Southern California Chicano History: Regional Origins and

National Critique," *Aztlán* 19 (spring 1988–90): 109; David G. Gutiérrez, "The Third Generation: Reflections on Recent Chicano Historiography," *Mexican Studies/Estudios Mexicanos* 5 (summer 1989): 281; David G. Gutiérrez, "Significant to Whom?: Mexican Americans and the History of the American West," *Western Historical Quarterly* 24 (November 1993): 519–39; Alex M. Saragoza, "Recent Chicano Historiography: An Interpretive Essay," *Aztlán* 19 (spring 1988–90): 1.

[4]As an example of this self-reflection of a field see the critiques of Patricia Nelson Limerick's *Legacy of Conquest* (New York: W. W. Norton, 1988), who, herself, was critiquing Frederick Jackson Turner and his frontier thesis. See, for example, Larry McMurtry, "How the West Was Won or Lost," *New Republic* 22 (October 1990): 32–38. See also the most recent reflections of the field in the collection edited by Clyde Milner, ed., *A New Significance: Re-envisioning the History of the American West* (New York: Oxford University Press, 1996).

[5]See the work of Dennis Nodin Valdés, *Al Norte: Agricultural Workers in the Great Lakes Region, 1917–1970* (Austin: University of Texas Press, 1991); and Zaragosa Vargas, *Proletarians of the North: Mexican Industrial Workers in Detroit and the Midwest, 1917–1933* (Berkeley: University of California Press, 1993). The work of the Julian Samora Center at Michigan State University also has provided valuable documentation about Mexican migrants and Mexican Americans in the Midwest.

[6]See, for example, Almaguer, "Ideological Distortions," 11; and Garcia, "Juncture in the Road," 192. One of the best monographs that does use class as a basis of analysis is David Montejano's *Anglos and Mexicans in the Making of Texas, 1836–1986* (Austin: University of Texas Press, 1987). Richard Garcia in *Rise of the Mexican-American Middle Class: San Antonio, 1929–1941* (College Station: Texas A&M Press, 1991) also looks at the Mexican-American community through the lens of class. Certainly the works of David Gutiérrez, *Walls and Mirrors: Mexican-Americans, Mexican Immigrants, and the Politics of Ethnicity* (Berkeley: University of California Press, 1995); and George J. Sanchez, *Becoming Mexican American: Ethnicity, Culture, and Identity in Chicano Los Angeles, 1900–1945* (New York: Oxford University Press, 1993) take into account how class influences issues of identity.

[7]Early Chicano scholars dismissed, rather than revised, the work of earlier scholars like Carlos Casteñeda, who wrote about the Spanish experience in North America in rather glorious terms. See, for example, Carlos Castañeda, *Our Catholic Heritage: The Finding of Texas,* vol 1: Austin University of Texas Press, 1936).

[8]In particular, see Rodolfo Acuña, *Occupied America: A History of Chicanos* 3d ed. (New York: Harper and Row, 1988), chapters on the post-Chicano generation years. For a particularly, and needlessly, harsh critique Garcia, "Juncture in the Road," 192.

[9]Mario T. Garcia, *Mexican Americans: Leadership, Ideology, and Identity 1930–1960* (New Haven: Yale University Press, 1989). Younger scholars like Cynthia Orozco and her work on women in LULAC, however, offer new and gendered interpretations of the middle class.

[10]I mark the exceptions of more recent scholarship like Ramon Gutiéruez *When Jesus Came the Corn Mothers Went Away,* (Palo Alto Stanford University Press, 1989); Sanchez, *Becoming Mexican-American,* and Neil Foley, *The White Scourge* (Berkeley: University of California Press, 1997). While Chicana feminists may not agree with their methods and intervention, nevertheless, these three scholars have sought to incorporate the history of women, and particularly Chicanas, on an equal footing with their male historical subjects.

[11]For a particularly good critique of the field and its lack of gender analysis see Cynthia Orozco, "Chicano Labor History: a Critique of Male Consequences in Historical Writing," *La Red/The Net* 77 (February 1984): 2.

[12]Garcia, *Mexican Americans,* 3.

[13]In particular, articles by Antonia Casteñeda and Deena Gonzales have been important influences in the field. See also Vicki Ruiz, *Cannery Women Cannery Lives: Mexican Women, Unionization,*

*and the California and Processing Industry, 1930–1950* (Albuquerque: University of New Mexico Press, 1987) and *From Out of the Shadow: A History of Mexican Women in the United States, 1900–1995* (New York: Oxford University Press, 1997).

[14] See Garcia, "Juncture in the Road," 190–92; Vicki L. Ruiz, "Texture, Text and Context: New Approaches in Chicano Historiography," *Mexican Studies/Estudios Mexicanos* 1 (winter 1986): 145; Denise A. Segurs and Beatriz M. Pesquera, "Beyond Indifference and Antipathy: The Chicano Movement and Chicana Feminist Discourse," *Aztlán* 19 (fall 1988–90): 69; Ramón Gutiérrez, "Community, Patriarchy and Individualism: The Politics of Chicano History and the Dream of Equality," *American Quartely* (March 1993): 44.

[15] Antonia Castañeda, "Women of Color and the Rewriting of Women History: The Discourse, Politics, and Decolonization of History," *Pacific Historical Review* 61: 4 (November 1992): 501. Recent collections of essays have also been extremely helpful in filling the gaps of Chicana history. See, for example, Cherrie Moraga and Gloria Anzaldúa, eds., *This Bridge Called Mr Back: Writings by Radical Women of Color* (New York: Kitchen Table Women of Color Press, 1983); and Adela de la Torre and Beatriz M. Pesquera, eds., *Building with Our Hands: New Directions in Chicana Studies,* Berkeley: University of California Press, 1993).

[16] See Richard L. Nostrand, *Hispano Homeland* (Norman: University of Oklahoma Press, 1992).

[17] The recent work of David G. Gutiérrez, *Walls and Mirrors,* looks at the diversity of communities within the Chicano community and how those differences have played themselves out in politics and the immigration debate.

[18] For a rather strident critique see Garcia, "Juncture in the Road"; Acuña, *Occupied America,* 363–412. Regarding the *Plan de Santa Barbara* see Carlos Munoz Jr., *Youth, Identity, and Power: The Chicano Movement* (London: Verso, 1989), 84–90.

# Identity

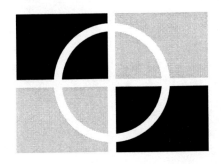

# Introduction

*Robert Muñoz, Jr.*

The history and the meaning of racial identity, racial meanings, and status of racial groups is complex, uneven, and constantly changing. It is clear that dominant beliefs about race and "racial" membership have had powerful and extensive consequences. Omi and Winant developed the perspective of "racial formation" to explain how meanings and ideas about race have changed over time.

Racial identity plays an important role in the allocation of social goods and ideas about who is deserving of public goods, of citizenship and even rights we consider to be universal. As the essays in this section will demonstrate, racial identities and racial meanings are part of racial hierarchy in which racial subordination of people of color, and their resistance, is a signature and enduring feature.

The essays in this section document the relation between identity and several areas of American life. It is not simply a matter of racial identity, in terms of how we see ourselves, but equally the result of a process of racial identification, how others identify us—especially those who have the power and authority over other people's lives, particularly people of color, in the realm of law, politics, public policy, criminal justice, and educational institutions. The essay on Native American children in boarding schools is a sad and powerful example of the ways that the power of others to identify others in a certain way, and specify certain policies on that basis of racial identification, can be brutally injurious, destructive, and even genocidal. The policies here are not just about how Native American cultures were identified by white society but also an attempt to control the ability of Native American children to identify with their indigenous culture. Other examples of the power relative to racial matters and identification include the notion of separate but equal, of classifying blacks as only a certain fraction of human being, or more recently the refusal of the U.S. Congress to remedy disparities in sentencing for possession of cocaine and crack. In this section on identity, the authors demonstrate the way that matters of racial identity have been constructed throughout the history of the formation of this country, particularly in the arena of law, public policy, and the economy and the way that matters of racial identity concern all levels of social life, including psychology, culture, aesthetics (what we consider beautiful and attractive), personal relationships, marriage, family, parenting, and several other areas described and illustrated by the authors involving both historical and contemporary matters.

As some of the authors will demonstrate (particular those writing on Asian Americans), there are several reasons why a black-white dichotomy can not even begin to describe or explain the nature, character, and dynamics of these different groups of people. Some of the relevant factors in their experiences involve matters of immigration, language, nativism, patriotism, and associations regarding race that are quite distinct and varied in comparison to the experience of African Americans. For example, the ways mainstream society has recently racially identified Arab Americans often takes on a patriotic racism based on a perceived negative and foreign identity, one assumed to be essentially evil, uncivilized, or an enemy. There is also a great degree of difference within these groups, depending on when they came to the U.S., the nature of their immigration experience (e.g., reception by larger society), and the level of economic integration. There are also other factors that play important roles in racial identification and racial meanings such as the views of race in the country of origin. Moreover, research is limited on the ways some groups understand or relate to their racial identity, as in the case of South Asian Americans.

The complexity of identity in matters of race is also evident in the difference perspectives and positions present between and within a particular racial or ethnic group. Examining the history of racial and ethnic groups reveals important differences in the experiences and identities of specific racial and ethnic groups. Although a people's identity and practices along the lines of race incorporate views and patterns of racial identification in the larger society, the racial dynamics outcomes are not always the same, as illustrated by the experience of Asian Americans compared to African Americans.

Another factor overlooked in a black-white dichotomy is the level of negative racial identification and behavior between minority groups. As you read this section, be mindful of the dynamics present in the experience of Asian Americans as they tried to distinguish themselves from African Americans. The choices made by all these groups involve strategic choices based in a racial hierarchy. In trying to distinguish themselves from African Americans, some Asian American groups invoked the same negative ways of racially identifying African Americans. In other words, they engaged in the similar processes of negative racial identification and associations employed against them.

This process of racialization also occurs at the individual level. That is, people internalize the racial identification or views of the larger society within their own views of their racial identity. Or stated differently, how people are racialized affects their identity and how they see themselves. To complicate matters even more, or rather to demonstrate the complexity of racial identity, people identify and respond in many different ways. Some people choose to assimilate, to suppress their racial identity or thinking about their racial thinking. Of course, despite what approach people decide to take, there is the reality of how this society and its citizens has gone about accepting or excluding them on the basis of racial forms of identification. Racial identity is not only about the different experiences and stances surrounding racial identity, but also of others, particularly of the majority or dominant social group, and how they see and think about people of color.

Some essays here give a first person account of their struggle to come to terms with conflicting views of the, more liberatory ways they see or wish to see themselves, while at the same time having incorporated some of the problematic and negatively racialized views of the larger society of themselves or others like them. For people who are biracial or multiracial, their views represent conflicting views of the different groups they have grown up with. Furthermore, the intricacy of identity with respect to race is revealed in the different ways this identity is also shaped by matters of gender, class, nationality, and sexuality. The essays in the first person represent a way of articulating their experience, of fighting back, of telling their stories to make better sense of the different dynamics of identity that shape their lives and social being.

Finally racialization is based on power dynamics. One definition of power is the ability to define other people and also the ability to define their experience. It is not simply a matter of what one person thinks about another person's skin. It is a matter of a group having the power to enforce those views, to make them into law and public policy; to be able to broadcast those ways of racially identifying people via television, radio, and newsprint; and, to include those views—and, exclude the group's own views, history, and contributions—from the educational curriculum. However, power does not occur in a vacuum. People respond and resist and form their alternative historical accounts, personal narratives, and oral traditions.

Hence—and this is the point I want to emphasize—racial identity, racial identification, and racial meanings the result of cultural, political, and economic processes. Racial identity has also been a source of collective identity and experiences, on the basis of which people have developed viable identities, coping mechanisms, and resistance strategies. Ultimately, racial identities and meanings contantly changing as various groups struggle to construct and contest the way they are defined. Demographic changes inform and push issues of identity. As a group becomes more visible in our society, they become increasingly subject to the processes of racial identity and construction of racial meanings, and consequently, as some essays note, more aware of their collective experiences in the U.S. These essays on identity reflect and extend ideas about "racial formation," as well as the dynamics of racial matters in the United States. Hopefully, these essays will also shed light on the responses and strategies people can employ in different arenas of their lives to make this reality possible.

# Race and Ethnicity

*Michael Omi and Howard Winant*

## Racial Formations

In 1982–83, Susie Guillory Phipps unsuccessfully sued the Louisiana Bureau of Vital Records to change her racial classification from black to white. The descendant of an eighteenth-century white planter and a black slave, Phipps was designated "black" in her birth certificate in accordance with a 1970 state law which declared anyone with at least one-thirty-second "Negro blood" to be black. The legal battle raised intriguing questions about the concept of race, its meaning in contemporary society, and its use (and abuse) in public policy. Assistant Attorney General Ron Davis defended the law by pointing out that some type of racial classification was necessary to comply with federal record-keeping requirements and to facilitate programs for the prevention of genetic diseases. Phipps's attorney, Brian Begue, argued that the assignment of racial categories on birth certificates was unconstitutional and that the one-thirty-second designation was inaccurate. He called on a retired Tulane University professor who cited research indicating that most whites have one-twentieth "Negro" ancestry. In the end, Phipps lost. The court upheld a state law which quantified racial identity, and in so doing affirmed the legality of assigning individuals to specific racial groupings.[1]

The Phipps case illustrates the continuing dilemma of defining race and establishing its meaning in institutional life. Today, to assert that variations in human physiognomy are racially based is to enter a constant and intense debate. *Scientific* interpretations of race have not been alone in sparking heated controversy; *religious* perspectives have done so as well.[2] Most centrally, of course, race has been a matter of *political* contention. This has been particularly true in the United States, where the concept of race has varied enormously over time without ever leaving the center stage of US history.

From *Racial Formations in the United States: From the 1960s to the 1980s* by Michael Omi and Howard Winant. Reprinted by permission of Taylor and Francis.

# What Is Race?

Race consciousness, and its articulation in theories of race, is largely a modern phenomenon. When European explorers in the New World "discovered" people who looked different than themselves, these "natives" challenged then existing conceptions of the origins of the human species, and raised disturbing questions as to whether *all* could be considered in the same "family of man."[3] Religious debates flared over the attempt to reconcile the Bible with the existence of "racially distinct" people. Arguments took place over creation itself, as theories of polygenesis questioned whether God had made only one species of humanity ("monogenesis"). Europeans wondered if the natives of the New World were indeed human beings with redeemable souls. At stake were not only the prospects for conversion, but the types of treatment to be accorded them. The expropriation of property, the denial of political rights, the introduction of slavery and other forms of coercive labor, as well as outright extermination, all presupposed a worldview which distinguished Europeans—children of God, human beings, etc.—from "others." Such a worldview was needed to explain why some should be "free" and others enslaved, why some had rights to land and property while others did not. Race, and the interpretation of racial differences, was a central factor in that worldview.

In the colonial epoch science was no less a field of controversy than religion in attempts to comprehend the concept of race and its meaning. Spurred on by the classificatory scheme of living organisms devised by Linnaeus in *Systema Naturae,* many scholars in the eighteenth and nineteenth centuries dedicated themselves to the identification and ranking of variations in humankind. Race was thought of as a *biological* concept, yet its precise definition was the subject of debates which, as we have noted, continue to rage today. Despite efforts ranging from Dr. Samuel Morton's studies of cranial capacity[4] to contemporary attempts to base racial classification on shared gene pools,[5] the concept of race has defied biological definition. . . .

Attempts to discern the *scientific meaning* of race continue to the present day. Although most physical anthropologists and biologists have abandoned the quest for a scientific basis to determine racial categories, controversies have recently flared in the area of genetics and educational psychology. For instance, an essay by Arthur Jensen which argued that hereditary factors shape intelligence not only revived the "nature or nurture" controversy, but raised highly volatile questions about racial equality itself.[6] Clearly the attempt to establish a *biological* basis of race has not been swept into the dustbin of history, but is being resurrected in various scientific arenas. All such attempts seek to remove the concept of race from fundamental social, political, or economic determination. They suggest instead that the truth of race lies in the terrain of innate characteristics, of which skin color and other physical attributes provide only the most obvious, and in some respects most superficial, indicators.

## Race as a Social Concept

The social sciences have come to reject biologistic notions of race in favor of an approach which regards race as a *social* concept. Beginning in the eighteenth century, this trend has been slow and uneven, but its direction clear. In the nineteenth century Max Weber discounted biological explanations for racial conflict and instead highlighted the social and political factors which engendered such conflict.[7] The work of pioneering cultural anthropologist Franz Boas was crucial in refuting the scientific racism of the early twentieth century by rejecting the connection between race and culture, and the assumption of a continuum of "higher" and "lower" cultural groups. Within the contemporary social science literature, race is assumed to be a variable which is shaped by broader societal forces.

Race is indeed a pre-eminently *sociohistorical* concept. Racial categories and the meaning of race are given concrete expression by the specific social relations and historical context in which they are embedded. Racial meanings have varied tremendously over time and between different societies.

In the United States, the black/white color line has historically been rigidly defined and enforced. White is seen as a "pure" category. Any racial intermixture makes one "nonwhite." In the movie *Raintree County*, Elizabeth Taylor describes the worst of fates to befall whites as "havin' a little Negra blood in ya'—just one little teeny drop and a person's all Negra."[8] This thinking flows from what Marvin Harris has characterized as the principle of *hypo-descent:*

> By what ingenious computation is the genetic tracery of a million years of evolution unraveled and each man [sic] assigned his proper social box? In the United States, the mechanism employed is the rule of hypo-descent. This descent rule requires Americans to believe that anyone who is known to have had a Negro ancestor is a Negro. We admit nothing in between. . . . "Hypo-descent" means affiliation with the subordinate rather than the superordinate group in order to avoid the ambiguity of intermediate identity. . . . The rule of hypo-descent is, therefore, an invention, which we in the United States have made in order to keep biological facts from intruding into our collective racist fantasies.[9]

The Susie Guillory Phipps case merely represents the contemporary expression of this racial logic.

By contrast, a striking feature of race relations in the lowland areas of Latin America since the abolition of slavery has been the relative absence of sharply defined racial groupings. No such rigid descent rule characterizes racial identity in many Latin American societies. Brazil, for example, has historically had less rigid conceptions of race, and thus a variety of "intermediate" racial categories exist. Indeed, as Harris notes, "One of the most striking consequences of the Brazilian system of racial identification is that parents and children and even brothers and sisters are frequently accepted as representatives of quite opposite racial types."[10] Such a possibility is incomprehensible within the logic of racial categories in the US.

To suggest another example: the notion of "passing" takes on new meaning if we compare various American cultures' means of assigning racial identity. In the United States, individuals who are actually "black" by the logic of hypodescent have attempted to skirt the discriminatory barriers imposed by law and custom by attempting to "pass" for white.[11] Ironically, these same individuals would not be able to pass for "black" in many Latin American societies.

Consideration of the term "black" illustrates the diversity of racial meanings which can be found among different societies and historically within a given society. In contemporary British politics the term "black" is used to refer to all non-whites. Interestingly this designation has not arisen through the racist discourse of groups such as the National Front. Rather, in political and cultural movements, Asian as well as Afro-Caribbean youth are adopting the term as an expression of self-identity.[12] The wide-ranging meanings of "black" illustrate the manner in which racial categories are shaped politically.[13]

The meaning of race is defined and congested throughout society, in both collective action and personal practice. In the process, racial categories themselves are formed, transformed, destroyed and reformed. We use the term *racial formation* to refer to the process by which social, economic and political forces determine the content and importance of racial categories, and by which they are in turn shaped by racial meanings. Crucial to this formulation is the treatment of race as a *central axis* of social relations which cannot be subsumed under or reduced to some broader category or conception.

## Racial Ideology and Racial Identity

The seemingly obvious, "natural" and "common sense" qualities which the existing racial order exhibits themselves testify to the effectiveness of the racial formation process in constructing racial meanings and racial identities.

One of the first things we notice about people when we meet them (along with their sex) is their race. We utilize race to provide clues about *who* a person is. This fact is made painfully obvious when we encounter someone whom we cannot conveniently racially categorize—someone who is, for example, racially "mixed" or of an ethnic/racial group with which we are not familiar. Such an encounter becomes a source of discomfort and momentarily a crisis of racial meaning. Without a racial identity, one is in danger of having no identity.

Our compass for navigating race relations depends on preconceived notions of what each specific racial group looks like. Comments such as, "Funny, you don't look black," betray an underlying image of what black should be. We also become disoriented when people do not act "black," "Latino," or indeed "white." The content of such stereotypes reveals a series of unsubstantiated beliefs about who these groups are and what "they" are like.[14]

In US society, then, a kind of "racial etiquette" exists, a set of interpretative codes and racial meanings which operate in the interactions of daily life. Rules shaped by our perception of race in a comprehensively racial society determine the "presentation of self,"[15] distinctions of status, and appropriate modes of conduct. "Etiquette" is not mere universal adherence to the dominant group's rules, but a more dynamic combination of these rules with the values and beliefs of subordinated groupings. This racial "subjection" is quintessentially ideological. Everybody learns some combination, some version, of the rules of racial classification, and of their own racial identity, often without obvious teaching or conscious inculcation. Race becomes "common sense"—a way of comprehending, explaining and acting in the world.

Racial beliefs operate as an "amateur biology," a way of explaining the variations in "human nature." Differences in skin color and other obvious physical characteristics supposedly provide visible clues to differences lurking underneath. Temperament, sexuality, intelligence, athletic ability, aesthetic preferences and so on are presumed to be fixed and discernible from the palpable mark of race. Such diverse questions as our confidence and trust in others (for example, clerks or salespeople, media figures, neighbors), our sexual preferences and romantic images, our tastes in music, films, dance, or sports, and our very ways of talking, walking, eating and dreaming are ineluctably shaped by notions of race. Skin color "differences" are thought to explain perceived differences in intellectual, physical and artistic temperaments, and to justify distinct treatment of racially identified individuals and groups.

The continuing persistence of racial ideology suggests that these racial myths and stereotypes cannot be exposed as such in the popular imagination. They are, we think, too essential, too integral, to the maintenance of the US social order. Of course, particular meanings, stereotypes and myths can change, but the presence of a *system* of racial meanings and stereotypes, of racial ideology, seems to be a permanent feature of US culture.

Film and television, for example, have been notorious in disseminating images of racial minorities which establish for audiences what people from these groups look like, how they behave, and "who they are." The power of the media lies not only in their ability to reflect the dominant racial ideology, but in their capacity to shape that ideology in the first place. D. W. Griffith's epic *Birth of a Nation*, a sympathetic treatment of the rise of the Ku Klux Klan during Reconstruction, helped to generate, consolidate and "nationalize" images of blacks which had been more disparate (more regionally specific, for example) prior to the film's appearance. In US television, the necessity to define characters in the briefest and most condensed manner has led to the perpetuation of racial caricatures, as racial stereotypes serve as shorthand for scriptwriters, directors and actors, in commercials, etc. Television's tendency to address the "lowest common denominator" in order to render programs "familiar" to an enormous and diverse audience leads it regularly to assign and reassign racial characteristics to particular groups, both minority and majority.

These and innumerable other examples show that we tend to view race as something fixed and immutable—something rooted in "nature." Thus we mask the historical construction of racial categories, the shifting meaning of race, and the crucial role of politics and ideology in shaping race relations. Races do not emerge full-blown. They are the results of diverse historical practices and are continually subject to challenge over their definition and meaning.

## Racialization: The Historical Development of Race

In the United States, the racial category of "black" evolved with the consolidation of racial slavery. By the end of the seventeenth century, Africans whose specific identity was Ibo, Yoruba, Fulani, etc., were rendered "black" by an ideology of exploitation based on racial logic—the establishment and maintenance of a "color line." This of course did not occur overnight. A period of indentured servitude which was not rooted in racial logic preceded the consolidation of racial slavery. With slavery, however, a racially based understanding of society was set in motion which resulted in the shaping of a specific *racial* identity not only for the slaves but for the European settlers as well. Winthrop Jordan has observed: "From the initially common term *Christian,* at mid-century there was a marked shift toward the terms *English* and *free.* After about 1680, taking the colonies as a whole, a new term of self-identification appeared—*white.*"

We employ the term *racialization* to signify the extension of racial meaning to a previously racially unclassified relationship, social practice or group. Racialization is an ideological process, an historically specific one. Racial ideology is constructed from pre-existing conceptual (or, if one prefers, "discursive") elements and emerges from the struggles of competing political projects and ideas seeking to articulate similar elements differently. An account of racialization processes that avoids the pitfalls of US ethnic history remains to be written.

Particularly during the nineteenth century, the category of "white" was subject to challenges brought about by the influx of diverse groups who were not of the same Anglo-Saxon stock as the founding immigrants. In the nineteenth century, political and ideological struggles emerged over the classification of Southern Europeans, the Irish and Jews, among other "nonwhite" categories. Nativism was only effectively curbed by the institutionalization of a racial order that drew the color line *around,* rather than *within,* Europe.

By stopping short of racializing immigrants from Europe after the Civil War, and by subsequently allowing their assimilation, the American racial order was reconsolidated in the wake of the tremendous challenge placed before it by the abolition of racial slavery. With the end of Reconstruction in 1877, an effective program for limiting the emergent class struggles of the later nineteenth century was forged: the definition of the working class *in racial terms*—as "white." This was not accomplished by any legislative decree or capitalist maneuvering to divide the working class, but rather by white workers themselves. Many of them were recent immigrants, who organized on racial lines as much as on traditionally defined class lines. The Irish on the West Coast, for example, engaged in vicious anti-Chinese race-baiting and committed many pogrom-type assaults on Chinese in the course of consolidating the trade union movement in California.

Thus the very political organization of the working class was in important ways a racial project. The legacy of racial conflicts and arrangements shaped the definition of interests and in turn led to the consolidation of institutional patterns (e.g., segregated unions, dual labor markets, exclusionary legislation) which perpetuated the color line *within* the working class. Selig Perlman, whose study of the development of the labor movement is fairly sympathetic to this process, notes that:

> The political issue after 1877 was racial, not financial, and the weapon was not merely the ballot, but also "direct action"—violence. The anti-Chinese agitation in California, culminating as it did in the Exclusion Law passed by Congress in 1882, was doubtless the most important single factor in the history of American labor, for without it the entire country might have been overrun by Mongolian [sic] labor and the labor movement might have become a conflict of races instead of one of classes.

More recent economic transformations in the US have also altered interpretations of racial identities and meanings. The automation of southern agriculture and the augmented labor demand of the postwar boom transformed blacks from a largely rural, impoverished labor force to a largely urban, working-class group by 1970. When boom became bust and liberal welfare statism moved rightwards, the majority of blacks came to be seen, increasingly, as part of the "underclass," as state "dependents." Thus the particularly deleterious effects on blacks of global and national economic shifts (generally rising unemployment rates, changes in the employment structure away from reliance on labor intensive work, etc.) were explained once again in the late 1970s and 1980s (as they had been in the 1940s and mid-1960s) as the result of defective black cultural norms, of familial disorganization, etc. In this way new racial attributions, new racial myths, are affixed to "blacks." Similar changes in racial identity are presently affecting Asians and Latinos, as such economic forces as increasing Third World impoverishment and indebtedness fuel immigration and high interest rates, Japanese competition spurs resentments, and US jobs seem to fly away to Korea and Singapore. . . .

Once we understand that race overflows the boundaries of skin color, superexploitation, social stratification, discrimination and prejudice, cultural domination and cultural resistance, state policy (or of any other particular social relationship we list), once we recognize the racial dimension present to some degree in *every* identity, institution and social practice in the United States—once we have done this, it becomes possible to speak of *racial formation*. This recognition is hard-won; there is a continuous temptation to think of race as an *essence*, as something fixed, concrete and objective, as (for example) one of the categories just enumerated. And there is also an opposite temptation: to see it as a mere illusion, which an ideal social order would eliminate.

In our view it is crucial to break with these habits of thought. The effort must be made to understand race as *an unstable and "decentered" complex of social meanings constantly being transformed by political struggle.*

## Notes

[1] *San Francisco Chronicle,* 14 September 1982, 19 May 1983. Ironically, the 1970 Louisiana law was enacted to supersede an old Jim Crow statute which relied on the idea of "common report" in determining an infant's race. Following Phipps's unsuccessful attempt to change her classification and have the law declared unconstitutional, a legislative effort arose which culminated in the repeal of the law. See *San Francisco Chronicle,* 23 June 1983.

[2] The Mormon church, for example, has been heavily criticized for its doctrine of black inferiority.

[3] Thomas F. Gossett notes:

Race theory . . . had up until fairly modern times no firm hold on European thought. On the other hand, race theory and race prejudice were by no means unknown at the time when the English colonists came to North America. Undoubtedly, the age of exploration led many to speculate on race differences at a period when neither Europeans nor Englishmen were prepared to make allowances for vast cultural diversities. Even though race theories had not then secured wide acceptance or even sophisticate formulation, the first contacts of the Spanish with the Indians in the Americas can now be recognized as the beginning of a struggle between conceptions of the nature of primitive peoples which has not yet been wholly settled. (Thomas F. Gossett, Race: The History of an Idea in America (New York: Schocken Books, 1965), p. 16)

Winthrop Jordan provides a detailed account of early European colonialists' attitudes about color and race in *White Over Black: American Attitudes Toward the Negro, 1550–1812* (New York: Norton, 1977 [1968]), pp. 3–43.

[4] Pro-slavery physician Samuel George Morton (1799–1851) compiled a collection of 800 crania from all parts of the world which formed the sample for his studies of race. Assuming that the larger the size of the cranium translated into greater intelligence, Morton established a relationship between race and skull capacity. Gossett reports that:

In 1849, one of his studies included the following results: The English skulls in his collection proved to be the largest, with an average cranial capacity of 96 cubic inches. The Americans and Germans were rather poor seconds, both with cranial capacities of 90 cubic inches. At the bottom of the list were the Negroes with 83 cubic inches, the Chinese with 82, and the Indians with 79. (Ibid., p. 74)

On Morton's methods, see Stephen J. Gould, "The Finagle Factor," *Human Nature* (July 1978).

[5] Definitions of race founded upon a common pool of genes have not held up when confronted by scientific research which suggests that the differences *within* a given human population are greater than those between populations. See L. L. Cavalli-Sforza, "The Genetics of Human Populations," *Scientific American* (September 1974), pp. 81–89.

[6] Arthur Jensen, "How Much Can We Boost IQ and Scholastic Achievement?", *Harvard Educational Review,* vol. 39 (1969), pp. 1–123.

[7] Ernst Moritz Manasse, "Max Weber on Race," *Social Research,* vol. 14 (1947), pp. 191–221.

[8] Quoted in Edward D. C. Campbell, *Jr, The Celluloid South: Hollywood and the Southern Myth* (Knoxville: University of Tennessee Press, 1981), pp. 168–70.

[9] Marvin Harris, *Patterns of Race in the Americas* (New York: Norton, 1964), p. 56.

[10] Ibid., p. 57.

[11]After James Meredith had been admitted as the first black student at the University of Mississippi, Harry S. Murphy announced that he, and not Meredith, was the first black student to attend "Ole Miss." Murphy described himself as black but was able to pass for white and spent nine months at the institution without attracting any notice (ibid., p. 56).

[12]A. Sivanandan, "From Resistance to Rebellion: Asian and Afro-Caribbean Struggles in Britain," *Race and Class*, vol. 23, nos. 2–3 (Autumn–Winter 1981).

[13]Consider the contradictions in racial status which abound in the country with the most rigidly defined racial categories—South Africa. There a race classification agency is employed to adjudicate claims for upgrading of official racial identity. This is particularly necessary for the "coloured" category. The apartheid system considers Chinese as "Asians" while the Japanese are accorded the status of "honorary whites." This logic nearly detaches race from any grounding in skin color and other physical attributes and nakedly exposes race as a juridicial category subject to economic, social and political influences. (We are indebted to Steve Talbot for clarification of some of these points.)

[14]Gordon W. Allport, *The Nature of Prejudice* (Garden City, New York: Doubleday, 1958), pp. 184–200.

[15]We wish to use this phrase loosely, without committing ourselves to a particular position on such social psychological approaches as symbolic interactionism, which are outside the scope of this study. An interesting study on this subject is S. M. Lyman

# Anatomy of Culture

*Alexandre Kimenyi*

Culture is the subject of inquiry of different disciplines such as anthropology, sociology, linguistics, economics, geography, psychology, history, philosophy, and political science. Each discipline has its own definition. This is not a ground-breaking essay on the subject of culture, nor is it reinventing the wheels since culture is the most studied subject in all academic fields. It only offers a new look, perspective and interpretation. The views that are expressed in the present article are based on my own studies but they are also supported by data. Culture is not an abstraction. Thus any assumptions, presuppositions about culture to be valid, have to undergo the scrutiny of empirical investigation. The goal of this article is not only to present a fresh look but also to renew a high level debate on the subject and to show its importance especially in social sciences and more importantly for students of ethnic studies.

## 1. Explaining the Title of the Essay

The two nouns which make up the title of this essay are metaphors. Although anatomy is recognizable as a dead metaphor from biology, very few people are aware of the fact that culture is a metaphor as well. It has been part of the unconscous mind. Etymologically, it comes from Romance languages as a conceptual metaphor from plantation, meaning 'cultivation'. In French, a learned person is called "cultivée" cultivated. The word culture falls thus in the general category of visual metaphors, in which light is used as the embodiment of knowledge and lack of it as ignorance as shown in Kimenyi (2003). A non-cultivated area such as a forest lacks light whereas a cultivated area does. Hence the expression "It is a jungle out there" meaning total darkness, thus ignorance. Synonymous conceptual metaphors are journey metaphors, as "advanced" versus "backward" or "retrograde," food metaphors, such as "seasoned" versus "raw" or tectile metaphors such as "polished" versus "rough." The onomatopeic word "barbarians" which etymologically means people who speak an incomprehensible language was extended to mean people "without culture" because they do things differently. The name Berber which refers to the indigenous people of Northern Africa who waged many wars with both Greeks and Romans is clearly a phonetic variation of "barbare."

Some social scientists equate culture with civilization which implies a people or society that have made a specific and significant contribution to humanity in science, technology, arts, religion and ideas. It is the reason why for instance, the Southeast Native American groups namely Cherokees, Choctaws, Chicasaws, Creeks and Seminoles were labeled the *Five Civilized Nations* by the first European settlers when other groups were called savages and primitive. The new settlers were impressed by this Native American group because they were advanced in agriculture and had everything Europeans wanted namely tobacco, cotton, indigo and corn. This group was, unfortunately the first one to be affected by the 1830 Removal Act which is responsible for the creation of Indian reservations that inspired the building of "bantustans" or "homelands" for blacks in South Africa by the white apartheid regime. The journey to the new territory is referred to, in history books, as the Trail of Tears because thousands of people: children, old people, the sick, pregnant women, who were forced to walk on foot thousands of miles under harsh conditions to the Indian Territory, the present-day Oklahoma, died along the way, before reaching their destination.

This etymological definition of culture is not only eurocentric and elitist but wrong. There is no society without culture. Even today, some scientists continue to reference African, American Indian and Asian languages as "dialects," ethnic groups as "tribesmen," rebel leaders in developing countries as "war lords," and traditional healers, as "witch doctors." These labels are used because of eurocentrism. Those who use these expressions believe that their respective cultures are not as advanced as the Western culture. In the former African Belgian colonies, for instance, Africans who were educated in European schools were called "evolués," evolved in the Darwinian sense and the rest *indigènes,* indigenous, a term which had a negative connotation that time. There is no primitive language, however. All languages have rules and all have dialects, which are either regional, socio-economical or ethnic. The so called high culture and low culture are also found in all hierachical societies of both city-states and nation-states.

The anatomy metaphor is used to illustrate that even though it is abstract, culture like the human body, is indeed biological and can also be dissected and analyzed to study its structure which consists of components with their respective formal and functional properties.

## 2. The Importance of Culture

Culture is a very important driving force. It is the reason why, together with space, it is the major cause of conflict in all pluralistic societies and colonized countries. The dominant group not only removes the minority from the most desirable space and creates spatial segregation but it also always imposes its culture on subordinate groups and occupied territories. The minorities resist the assimilation because they consider their culture not only as their character, personality and identity but mostly as their "soul". It is the reason why even here in the United States, against all odds the Amish culture of Pennsylvania and the black Gullah or Geeche culture of South Carolina have been able to survive. The cultural conflict also exists at the global level. The cold war between the Soviet Union and the United States which have fought in proxy developing countries was largely ideological. The US and European military interventions in Asia and the Middle East as well as the treatment of people in the Middle East in the West have prompted scholars to coin the terms *Orientalism* and *Occidentalism*. Orientalism was created by the late Columbia University Professor Edward Said to refer to the negative stereotypes that Europeans have of Asians and Occidentalism was conceived by Ian Buruma and Margalit Avishal (2004) to refer to the caricatural view that people have of Europe which is seen as materialistic, spiritually wanting and morally bankrupt. Culture is a collective behavior, a code of conduct or societal attitudes.

# 3. Components of Culture

All cultures consist of concepts, values, customs, systems, icons, symbols, rituals, aesthetics and entertainment. What makes cultures distinct from each other is either the maximization or the variation of the properties of these components.

## 3. 1. Concepts

Concepts have to do with how we conceive and perceive both physical and metaphysical phenomena. Depending on our cultural background the same "reality" may be perceived or conceived differently or may not be perceived and conceived at all. For instance, even though death is universal, there are societies in which it is viewed as the end of life but there are others where it is seen as the beginning of life. The concept of beauty not only varies from culture to culture but also shifts from generation to generation. Natural gaps between teeth and black gum are signs of beauty in Rwanda but in the US gaps have to be filled. Fat is seen today as a sign of poverty and bad eating habits and slimmess as a symbol of wealth and aristocracy, but it used to be the opposite. Time also has been found to be conceived differently. Among Anglo-Saxons, time is objective, unidirectional and seen as a commodity, hence the saying "Time is money". It has very much affected their lives. Among the Latins (French, Italians, Portuguese, Spaniards) time can be subjective as demonstrated by their languages: thus morning is either *le matin* or *la matinée*, day is *le jour* or *la journée*, evening *le soir* or *la soirée*, year *l'an* or *l'année*. The masculine form shown by the article *le* is objective whereas the feminine form marked by the article *la* is subjective. Among Rwandans, however, and some other Bantu groups, time is both phenomenological and cyclical. It is phenomenological because it is produced by events and activities. If the events that produce it such as change of seasons, sunset, sunrise, or moonlight, fail to materialize, time doesn't take place either. This is seen in the language use, thus hour is "watch" *isáahá*, month is "moon" *ukwéezi*, year "crop" *umwáaka* and a political regime "drum" *ingoma*. These temporal expressions are metonymically related to the meanings of the primary plane of expression. A watch is used to show the time, a new month is shown by a new moon in the sky, crops are planted once a year and traditionally before colonialism the symbol of authority was the drum during the monarchy. Time is also elastic. It can be short or long depending on the length of the event. Among the Bantu time is also cyclical. It comes back. For instance, "soon" is seen as "recently", "tomorrow" as "yesterday" and "distant future" as "far past." The expression for "soon" and "recently" is the same in Kinyarwanda *vuba*, for "tomorrow" and "yesterday" it is *ejo*, whereas "the distant future" and "the far past" it is *kera*.

That people don't see or understand the same reality the same way even in the same culture is demonstrated by language use. Thus a city may be seen as "sitting," "standing," "lying," "spreading," "stretching," "sprawling," or "rolling." In all cultures, all people also intuitively know that the same reality may be seen and understood differently. This is again shown by linguistic expressions such as "to see through the lens of" or "to see the bottle half-full or half-empty."

The classical example mentioned in anthropological linguistics literature about differences in cultural perceptions and conceptions, although some scientists think it is a hoax, is the concept of snow in Eskimo (Inuit-Aleut). Apparently, the Inuit-Aleut have an analytic view rather than a synthetic view of snow. Twelve terms are used to refer to different types of snow whereas English uses one word to refer to all of them.

## 3. 2. Values

Values are things that matter for the society and play a very important role in its members' behavior. They are not innate and don't have any intrinsic value. Like many other components of culture, they are conventional because what is important for one culture may not have any value whatsoever in other societies.

In the Western culture, for instance, flowers, especially roses, are very much valued. They have inspired great poets and painters. Flowers are appreciated as presents by girls and women from their lovers. Some cultures don't understand why people would be excited by flowers as presents when they can be picked up for free from the bush. In Rwanda, on the other hand, the great present that people give to the ones they love, admire, or are grateful to is a cow. During the monarchy, cows were given as gifts to visiting heads of states, and there were both military and cow parades everywhere in all regions when the king was touring the country. This cow parade called *kubyukurutsa* still takes place at weddings.

It is not flowers that inspire artists but cows. For instance, pastoral poetry (cow praise-poems) called *amazina y'inka* in Kinyarwanda ranks first among the three traditional elite poetic genres. The other two are dynastic poetry (praise-poems for kings) *ibisigo* and panegyric poetry (praise-poems for national heroes and great warriors) *ibyivugo*. Female folk dances imitate the cow's elegance and its beautiful long horns. Not only are cow songs a genre of folk music that are sung by herders when they take them to graze, to drink or in the evening when they return home, but are also motifs in other music folk genres and modern music as well. The popular stone game, called *igisoro,* which some people call the African chess game consists of capturing the adversary's cows (game stones) and children have cow dolls.

The cow is the icon par excellence of the Rwandan society. It is seen as the quintessential paradigm of beauty, elegance and grace. In the Rwandan culture it is thus a great complement to tell a woman that she has cows' eyes or walks like a cow.

The cow has been integrated into the whole culture. It has also affected the language. Many Rwandan names are related to cows, people swear by the name of the person from whom they received cows, greeting expressions are about cows and many metaphors come from cow vocabulary. The cow plays in Rwanda the same role that the buffalo did among Great Plains Indian (Sioux, Cheyenne, Comanche, Kiowa, Apache, Blackfeet, Osage, Arapaho, Crow, Ojibwa, Omaha, Hidatsa, Wichita, Pawnee, etc). There is a symbiotic relationship between cows and Rwandans. It is a gift to them from the country's founding father, Gihanga, who the legend says created both cows and drums (*Gihanga cyahanze inka n'ingoma*). Everything from the cow whether it is its product, waste, body part, has a use and value. Nothing from the cow is wasted.

In the Western culture youth is prized and celebrated and old people feel good when they are told that they look young. In other cultures, however, it would be an insult to call an adult young, since old age is respected as a sign of experience and wisdom.

Individualism and mobility are some of the main characteristics of American culture and are very much idealized. People don't owe any loyalty to any place or institution. Americans can change jobs, religions, political parties any time they want. They can move from one city to another or from one state to another state. A house is not a home but a piece of real estate that can be sold any time when its value has gone up. People here can marry or divorce many times, choose not to marry or have children. In other societies, however, the community comes first. For this reason, the mobility found in the United States is inexistent, because of the loyalty to one's birth of place, employer and other institutions. If I have turned down job offers from other universities with better pay and I have been teaching at the same university for more than a quarter of a century it is because of my culture which has followed me. I would feel guilty if I left.

## 3. 3. Customs and Traditions

Customs are recurrent activities or events in which actions, actors and stages are predictable. Greetings, eatings, naming ceremonies, dating systems, weddings, funerals, rite of passage are examples of customs. Eating habits are part of the customs.

The society decides how many meals are eaten a day and what is eaten at each meal. The naming system differs from culture to culture. In some societies, naming ceremonies take place several days after the baby is born. The Some cultures give only one name. In others, there are two names, the first name and the last name whereas Americans have a first name, a middle name and a last name. Europeans and Americans think that Alexandre is my first name and Kimenyi is my last name. In Rwanda we don't have the concept of first name and last or family name. We just have a name. Everybody has his or her own name. Children have their individual names. Wives don't take their husbands' names. Those who become Christians, however, get a Christian name when they get baptized. It is embarrassing to me when my wife's students and friends call me Mr. Mukantabana. They assume that Mathilde is her first name and Mukantabana is my name. But Mukantabana is clearly a female name for Kinyarwanda speakers because of the onomastic prefix *muka-* found in many female names. There are, of course, some Westernized Rwandans who have adopted the European system but they are still a minority. I got the name Alexandre when I started school, because to be admitted everybody had to get a European name since all the schools belonged to the European missionaries. Since in the American customs names are monosyllabic, such Joe for Joseph, Dick for Richard, Bob for Robert, Fred for Frederick, Greg for Gregory, Ted for Edward, Bill or Will for William, Tom for Thomas . . . those who think that Alexandre is my first call me Alex whereas others call me Kim.

### 3. 4. Systems

Systems, institutions or societal organizations are the pillars on which the society is built. Some of these institutions are the family structure, government system, economy, justice, religion, and education.

*Family Structure*

Families in various societies are either nuclear or extended, patriarchal or matriarchal. For a family to be nuclear or extended seems to be dictated by economics. During the agricultural period and the industrial revolution, America had an extended family system, because of the share of labor for each member of the family. In the computer age, however, any individual can be self-sufficient. Because of this, the size of the family has shrunk and many single families with single mothers or single fathers have increased exponentially.

In patriarchal societies, the father is the head of the family, children receive the last name of the father, boys are the ones who inherit the family property and in case of divorce, the wife goes back to her parents. A matriarchal system is the mirror image of the former, the children get the mother's last name, only girls inherit the family property, in the case of divorce, the husband is sent back to his parents but the head of the family in many cases that have been reported so far is not the mother but one of her brothers.

The family structure in some cultures dictates the rules of exogamy and endogamy. In the Middle East, for instance, people marry parallel cousins (father's brother's child) whereas in others it is cross cousins (father's sister's child or mother's brother's child).

## Economy

Economy has to do with wealth production and distribution and ownership. The society decides who should participate in the work force, what and how much should be produced. These policies are the ones which are responsible for the existence of subsistence economies and consumer economies, capitalist economies like the United States and welfare states like Western Europe and Canada. In some societies, the land belongs to the state or the community like in many African, Asian and American Indian nations before colonialism, in others it belongs to the aristocracy, the landlords, like in Medieval Europe. It is unthinkable and uncomprensible in many societies how an individual can own a river, a lake, a forest or an island. They believe that like the sun, the moon, the sky, and the air, all natural resources, should be public.

The 1887 Indian Allotment Act also known as the Dawes Act was detrimental to Native Americans. Not only did it steal 90 million acres from them from the 138 previously allocated, but did it destroy their culture as well. By giving 164 acres to one family, the extended family structure was destroyed and so was the community because what united them was the communal property, the sharing of space and their traditional leaders.

## Government

All societies, besides hunter-gather and nomadic ones, have a system of government. It can be the council of elders, monarchy, theocracy, plutocracy, gerontocracy, etc. The monarchy can be constitutional or absolute. A government can be a presidential system like the US and France or parliamentary system like the majority of European countries. Democratic governments also differ from one another. They can be ethnic democracies, liberal democracies, consociative democracies. The concept of federal government applied here in the United States and which European countries have started adopting was borrowed from the Iroquois Confederacy also known as the League of Six Nations, namely Seneca, Mohawk, Cayuga, Onondaga, Oneida and Tuscarora. The reason why there is political instability in many developing nations, it is because of the importation or the experimentation of alien systems of government by the Western-educated elite in which the majority of the people especially the traditional wise elders don't have a voice.

A new term, *kleptocracy*, has been recently introduced to refer to some of the regimes of corrupt leaders such as the late dictator of the Democratic Republic of Congo, Mobutu Sese Seko, Sani Abacha of Nigeria, Marcos of the Philippines, Charles Taylor of Liberia, because these leaders are more interested in stealing their countries' resources than managing them for the interest of the people.

## Justice

To service and keep a social balance and harmony, all societies have a system of law and order. Some societies put more emphasis on the protection of community rights than on individual rights. Each society defines what is a crime and implements its own system of handling these crimes. Some African countries are undergoing turmoil because of the conflict between the application of Western law brought in during colonialism, the traditional legal system and Islamic law, called *Shariah.* In the United States, many immigrants find themselves in legal trouble when they try to use the system of their home country to punish their children. "It takes a whole village to raise a child" is not a slogan in Africa. Any adult who is not related to the child can reprimand a child, spank him/her or use any other means if s/he is misbehaving or doing things which are not acceptable.

The Rwandan government is going back to the traditional justice system called *gacaca,* which handled petty crimes, to judge Hutu responsible of genocide. The outcome of this system which, in a sense looks like the American jury system, was always reconciliation. Survivors of genocide, however, see the reintroduction of *gacaca* as a travesty of justice by the government because traditionally it dealt with small problems existing between neighbors whereas murders were handled by the Royal Court, because all Rwandans considered themselves *rubanda rw'umwami,* the king's people.

When the Southwest was taken from Mexico after its defeat in the 1846–48 American-Mexican war by the United States after the signing of the Treaty of Guadalupe Hidalgo in 1848, Mexicans living in those territories lost their properties to the Anglos and the US government because of the Anglo-Saxon law which required titles and property taxes for all owners of businesses, houses, land and ranches. This is how important individuals of that time such Salvador Vallejo of Napa and the Swiss-born immigrant John Augustus Sutter got ruined.

## Religion

All societies have their own religions and spiritual values. Many African religions, for instance, have the same concept of God as Christians do. They are monotheistic. God is conceived as transcendent, omnipresent, omnipotent, and omniscient. The only difference is how they relate to him and the fact they respect other people's religions, practice ancestor worship and don't try to prosetylize. To European missionnaries, however, these religions are not religions but paganism. In many cases, messianic religions in their holy wars, evangilizing and proselytizing, have done more harm than good, by prosecuting those who don't believe in their dogmas or refuse to convert to their religions.

## Education

The educational system is there to maintain the society's values and the status quo. Many European countries practice an elitist education, meaning that many students fail to go to high school or the university. These educational systems are mostly by-products of economics. The governments make sure that those who graduate have jobs. The US has a similar system. Since agriculture is done by Mexicans and migrant workers, children of migrant workers end up becoming migrant workers as well, thus creating a caste system, because they cannot attend regular schools which would allow them both socio-economical vertical and horizontal mobility.

People who rule the US such as senators, CEOs of big companies, university presidents come from the elite universities, mostly private ones such as Stanford, the University of Chicago or Ivy League schools. In France, however, public schools are more prestigious and the majority of important personalities are graduates of *Les Grandes Ecoles.*

Although he meant well, as recounted in the video *In the White Man's Image,* Richard Henry Pratt is also responsible for the destruction of Native Americans' culture by forcibly taking children from their parents to the Carlisle Indian School thus missing their parents' education. The 1934 Indian Reorganization Act was too late since separating children from parents had created a new generation of Indians who were alienated, unable to live either in the White world or the Indian world because they had lost their language and culture.

## 3. 5. Icons

All societies have objects or people that everybody identifies with which become a unifying factor. They can be national heroes, religious leaders, intellectuals, or pop stars such as athletes, musicians, actors, and products. Landmarks such as rivers, mountains, and cities and monuments, even buildings can be icons as well. Examples of rivers which have become icons are for instance, the Mississippi river for Americans, the Seine for French, the Nile for Egyptians, the Yangtze for Chinese, Nyabarongo for Rwandans. Examples of mountains are Mount Shasta for Shasta Indians, Wintu, Tolowa, Karok, Yurok, Hupa, Chilula, Whilikut, Wiyot, Chimariko, and others, Mount Kenya for the Kikuyu and Mount Kilimanjaro for Tanzanians. The Statue of Liberty and Eiffel Tower are examples of monuments which are icons for Americans and French respectively. The Taj Mahal, in Agra, is not only a tourist attraction but the national icon of India. McDonalds, Coca-Cola, etc. are icons of the United States abroad. Not only do these icons inspire artists but they are part of collective heritage.

One of the major sources of conflicts between Native Americans and the U.S. government is that the government is destroying these icons or desecrating important landmarks such burial sites, or sacred areas.

## 3. 6. Symbols

Symbols are objects which have a conventional meaning for a society. In semiotics, however, the science of signs in general, linguistic and non-linguistic, it has a specific meaning. A symbol means a sign whose relationship with the object it stands for has become opaque. There are two semiotic systems depending on how much information they can convey: namely macrosemiotic systems or speech surrogates and microsemiotic systems. Microsemiotic systems such as uniforms, body wear, highway code, . . . give a very much limited information such as profession, gender, religion or age for the uniform, social status for bodywear, and driving information for the latter. Macrosemiotic systems such as language, writing, sign language . . . don't have any constraints on what can be communicated. It is the reason why sign language was the lingua franca of Great Plains Indians, since coming from many different linguistic backgrounds, it was the only way they could communicate.

Semiotics classifies signs defined as "something which stands for something else" into three categories, namely icons, indices and symbols. Icons which are either images, metaphors, and diagrams have a similarity either physical or functional with objects they stand for. Indices namely signals and symptoms have an association with the objects they refer to such as cause and effect, content and container, possession and possessor, part and whole, product and producer, whereas symbols as said earlier fail to show any connection with their referents. Like linguistic signs, the majority of signs in all cultures belong to the last category. The majority of words are symbols. Their etymological history shows, however, that they initially started as either icons or indices. It is the same for non-linguistic communication systems as well. We are born in a society with symbols without any knowledge of their genesis and history.

Whether these signs are icons, indices or symbols, however, they all can be polysemous or homonymous and this shows clearly that they are conventional. Homonymy, the use of signs which look alike but have different meanings or functions occur by accident. Polysemy, the use of the same sign for different meanings or functions is very common because of the asymmetry which exists between symbols and the real world. The real world is infinite but the number of signs is very much limited. Within the same culture, the same object can be assigned different meanings or functions such as the ring in the Western culture but it is also possible for two or many objects which look similar but are not related to function as symbols. This is referred to as homonymy. The cross, for instance, may show that somebody is a Christian but it is also a luxury jewerly for others.

The society thus decides which objects will be used as symbols. Uniforms, headwear, chestwear, bracelets, medals can give information about profession, religion, social status. In Rwanda for instance, before colonization, married women and unmarried women dressed differently and had a different hair style. Mothers also, in formal ceremonies, have to wear a maternity crown called *urugore*. Symbols may be icons of companies or organizations such as logos and mascots for schools and sports teams. There are national symbols as well. Before the late nineteenth century partition of Africa by European powers at the Berlin Conference, many countries had drums with specific names as national emblems instead of flags as in Europe. The capture of these drums was also a national defeat.

Although symbols seem to be arbitrary, anthropologists have found out that totems are not. Clans in all societies are characterized by the existence of totems and taboos. Clans are still found in Africa, Asia and among Native Americans. I belong to the *Abazirankende* clan and our totem is *inyamanza*, a wagtail. The majority of totems happen to be plants and animals. Totems grew out of the necessity to protect the environment, explain the experts. The clan whose totem is a certain plant or animal is assured protection. The animal totem cannot be killed by the clan and the plant cannot be cut down either.

## 3. 7. Rituals

Like symbols, rituals also have conventional meanings. They differ from the former in that symbols are objects sometimes frozen in space and time whereas the latter are actions or activities. They usually accompany customs and ceremonies like greetings, eating, weddings, funerals, the rite passage, the transfer of power, naming ceremonies, farewell, etc. Libation in Africa to thank the ancestors at all important ceremonies, the 21-gun salute for visiting foreign dignataries in the Western culture, the Japanese tea ceremony, the Ethiopian coffee ceremony, the breaking of kola nuts among the Igbos of Nigeria and the Wolof of Senegal in various ceremonies, or in time of war the tying of yellow ribbons in the United States and the wearing of the leaf from the plant *impumbya* by Rwandan women are examples of rituals.

## 3. 8. Entertainment

To survive, members of the society are busy, each, depending on age, gender, or experience assigned a specific task. For a better performance, time for leisure and relaxation is also put aside. For instance, in France, people work 35 hours instead of 40 hours like here in the United States. The society decides the number of work days a week and how many hours people have to work. The American concept of weekend is now being adopted by many countries. In Europe, it used to be half-days. The work would stop at noon on both Wednesdays and Saturdays. In France and Italy, for instance, all activites including banks, schools, and hospitals, stop for lunch and nap from twelve to two in the afternoon. I made a mistake once of going to Paris in the month of August. Many businesses including hotels and restaurants were closed for a month because everybody had gone on vacation!

It is the society which also decides how its members are going to kill the time during this period of relaxation and which games and sports to play. It is the reason why some games and sports such as soccer, cockfighting, bullfighting, cricket, rugby, or hockey, become popular in some countries but not in others. In Japan, sumo wrestlers are treated like Hollywood movie stars, but the late satirist Mike Royko compared sumo wrestler stars with fat babies wearing diapers. When Americans talk about the "world series," non Americans get confused because they are expecting a real world competition and not about U.S. baseball teams.

There is a ranking and hierarchy in sports and games as well. If African-Americans outnumber whites in football, basketball and boxing, it is not because of their ethnicity which makes them superior athletes but because of the deliberate decision of the establishment. Even in Ancient Rome, entertaining sporting events such as the gladiators were performed by slaves. Elite sports and games such as golf, tennis, horse riding, car racing, swimming, pheasant hunting, chess . . . are the monopoly of the elite.

## 3. 9. Aesthetics

All societies express their aesthetic experiences through the same mediums and genres. These are visual (paintings, sculpture, decoration, graphics, photography, ceramics), aural (music, poetry), kinetic (dancing and gymnastics), and multimedia (theater, cinema, opera). Each culture maximizes or selects these genres found in the different mediums. It also ranks which ones are more important. In the visual arts, for instance, calligraphy is very highly valued in both Islamic and Japanese art. In Rwanda it is decoration whereas in West Africa it is masks and figurines. In paintings and decorations, some socities prefer certain colors and certain shapes. The appreciation of musical melodies differs from culture to culture even musical instruments. The piano is the instrument of choice in the Western culture, but in Rwanda it is the cithare *inanga*.

The tastes in rhythm, movement, body parts in dancing performance are also culturally conditioned. The Middle East is the birth place of belly dancing. In Ethiopia, dancing consists of lifting and moving shoulders. Among the Banyankore, women dance while sitting. Among the Maasai dancing consists of jumping rhythmically as high as they can without moving any other parts of the body. Congolese dance moving hips whereas Rwandan women dance with their arms arched like horns of Tutsi cows.

Visual arts of non-Western countries are collectively referred to as craft and other genres such as music, dance, poetry, oral literature . . . as folklore. These artistic objects are not considered as art because they are utilitarian, their creators are not known, and are not housed in museums and galleries. To consider them as craft, however, is a manifestation not only of lack of knowledge of local cultures and history but what true art is as well. In Africa, both high art and folk art existed before colonialism. Individual painters and sculptors were known and their work was sometimes commissioned by the king or the chiefs. Although literature was oral, there was a distinction also between elite literature namely court literature in Rwanda and folk literature. These composers, poets, singers, were also known by everybody in the country. The griots in West Africa in the countries of Mali, Guinea, Senegal and Gambia, who were poets, story tellers, oral historians belonged to this high culture and still do.

Art is an aesthetic experience that the artist tries to share with the community through creation using any of the mediums of expression. The perfect art is the one which is able to bring the three types of pleasure: sensual pleasure, intellectual pleasure and spiritual pleasure. So, whether the object is utilitarian, the author is anonymous, or is not housed in the museum, doesn't matter, as long as the target consumers like it.

Because of other cultural contacts and new experiences aesthetics in all cultures always keeps changing as shown by the influence of raggae and rap on world music today or the history of Western visual arts, which from the 16th century went through the Italian Renaissance, Classism, Baroque, Rococco, Dutch art, Romanticism, Impressionism, Expressionism, Fauvism, Cubism, Surrealism, and Minimalism.

It is interesting to note that these universal cultural components are also found in animals' cultures. All species have their symbols to communicate information, they have their own rituals and their social organization is similar to that of humans. Some animals are monogamous whereas others are polygamous. Some are patriarchal when others like the bonobos of Congo are matriarchal. Some practice endogamy while others practice exogamy. The only difference between the two species is probably the last component. Are they capable of sharing their aesthetic experience through visual, aural, kinetic and multimedia creativity? This is what I think should be the first priority of scientists to find out. Research in further cultural studies should also shed more light on why the Batwa and Pygmies of Central Africa and Gypsies (Bohemians) of Europe are natural born artists.

## 4. Nature and Nurture

The debate as to whether culture is natural, thus innate, being part of our biological make-up or whether it is man-made, manufactured by societies has not been settled yet. The proponents of culture as nurture advance five main arguments to support their view: (a) culture is not connected to language, race or ethnicity; (b) some aspects of culture are arbitrary, (c) there exist societies with evidence of clearly manufactured cultures, (d) some individuals find their culture to be unnatural and exile themselves to societies which have cultures in which they feel less alienated and (e) finally, culture is learned. In Central Africa, for instance, the Pygmies and the Batwa don't have a language of their own but speak languages of the Bantu groups with whom they live. Here in the United States, African Americans are Anglo-Saxon culturally and linguistically. Arbitrariness of culture is used in Saussurian sense to mean conventional. This arbitrariness is not only limited to symbols and rituals but to all components of the society as the section on cultural components shows. The society arbitrarily decides what is important for its members. This is indeed supported by the fact that what is important and meaningful for one culture may not mean anything in other cultures. Even body gestures such as finger pointing, handshaking, head bowing, head shaking, head scratching, shoulder shrugging, throat clearing, and whistling. While these seem to be universal forms of behaviors, they do not have the same meanings in all societies.

Pidgins and creoles found mostly on coasts and islands are also recent phenomena, thus hybrids of languages and cultures of new immigrants who come from different linguistic backgrounds. It is also true that counterculture movements and intergenerational conflicts exist in all societies and migration has been occuring since times immemorial not only to run away from bad economies but also from oppressive regimes and oppressive cultures as well.

That culture is learned from both informal and formal education is also a fact. Abandoned wild children have never acquired neither culture or language. This has pushed behaviorists led by B. E. Skinner to claim that children are born with blank slates, *tabula rasa,* and that both culture and language are learned through the process of stimulus-response.

For a culture to grow it has to have a proper soil the way an infant cannot survive without its mother. The proponents of culture as a social construction miss the point, however, because these phenomena emerge as a result of language death, cultural destruction, cultural contact and forced assimilation. Human behavior is what distinguishes the homo sapiens from other species. All species have strategies which help them to keep the balance and ensure their survival: how they relate to each other, the protection of both private and public space, mating practices, means of communication, social hierachy. This behavior is hard-wired. It is part of the genetic evolution. The human culture is different from that of animals in only that it is more elevated due to the fact that the human brain has more genes than animals.

The studies of language, the existence of cultural universals and current research in evolutionary biology and neuroscience support the biological basis of culture.

Language, a component of culture, through which culture is communicated and transmitted is biological (Chomsky, Kimenyi). It is located in the brain. When this location is damaged language is affected. All children from different linguistic backgrounds are preprogrammed to master it within a specific time. There is a critical stage as well. If the language is not acquired by the age of seven, the child is doomed not to develop it. Linguists have also found out that rules that govern language are so elegantly mathematically formulated that the child and the average native speaker cannot make them themselves. Suprasegments such as stress rules or tone rules are out of control of the conscious mind. Studies also show that native speakers of tone languages are tone deaf. They are unaware of tone rules and cannot tell which syllables have tones and which ones don't. For instance, although I am a professional linguist and Kinyarwanda is my mother tongue, it has taken me years to be able to understand, describe and explain the tone patterns of this language. Cognitive linguists (George Lakoff & Mark Johnson; Alexandre Kimenyi) also have found that speakers of all languages use conceptual metaphors without being aware that they are metaphors. All this suggests that there is a software in the human mind which is responsible for formal linguistic rules of encoding, processing and decoding. Many rules happen also to be universal. Because of their universality, cultures have the same deep structure and differ only on the surface structure in Chomskian sense with their diverse physical manifestations or parametric variations due to societies' individual environmental and experiential factors.

Evolutionary biologists have also found similarities between biological systems and cultural systems such as common ancestry, adaptation and transmission. Death and hybridity are also found in both. Studies of autism, a social learning disorders disease, have found it to be caused by specific genes.

Although culture is biological, it is not genetically connected to race. Cultural diversity is due environmental factors, cultural dynamism and people's different existential experiences. The négritude poets, Léopold Sédar Senghor, the late president of Senegal and the Caribbean poets Aimé Césaire and Léon Damas who were influenced by the Harlem Renaissance, a group of African-American artists, poets and writers such as Langston Hughes, Claude McKay, Richard Wright, Countee Cullen, Irving Miller, Anne Spenser, Jean Turner and James Weldon Johnson, were wrong when they attributed the difference between African culture and European culture to race, a perspective that ignores geography, history and experience.

With their stereotypes and preconceived ideas that all Africans were primitive and savages, European scientists came out also with the so-called Hamitic Hypothesis when they found out that some Africans such as the Tutsi had a very advanced culture. To the Europeans, African societies which impressed them were their distant cousins who came before them to colonize the continent.

# 5. Archetype and Stereotype

Although national character or identity is a reality, it is impossible to find any single individual who is the exemplar, the embodiment of this culture because of the existence of subcultures. Some of these subgroups are regional, ethnic, socio-economic, educational, generational and gender related.

A society is characterized by members occupying the same space, although it can be discontinuous like in the case of Alaska and Hawaii which are distant American territories. All physical cultural spaces have subregions: a north, a south, an east, a west, a center and peripheries. These regions do not only have a physical character they also a subcultural identity in terms of dialect, architecture, food, and customs. People at the periphery have more in common with neighboring cultures than their cultural center. The rural and urban population, the elite and the masses differ everywhere mostly in values, and lifestyles. Although, the US dominant culture is historically Anglo-Saxon, not only have other European ethnicities and racial minority groups namely Native Americans, African Americans, Asian Americans and Latinos, contributed to it but do they still practice their respective ethnic cultures as well. Upper classes, middle classes and lower classes are defined by specific lifestyles and values. Men and women, children and adults are supposed to behave differently in some situations. All these factors make it impossible to find any individual in any society who is a prototype of the culture. Culture is real but abstract. Because of this abstractness and dynamism, it becomes very difficult to find the right metaphor, for instance, which describes ethnic and race relations in the United States. The ones that have been proposed such as melting pot, salad bowl, kaleidoscope, quilt, fabric, grocery bag, or mosaic, all capture some of the defining characteristics of the American culture but fail, unfortunately to account for others.

## 6. The Sapir-Whorf Hypothesis

In cultural anthropology and anthropological linguistics, the Sapir-Whorf hypothesis corresponds to both cultural relativity and cultural determinism. Edward Sapir was the father of American linguistics and Benjamin Whorf his student. They were specialists of American Indian languages. Their research and studies of these languages convinced them that indeed language reflects and affects people's view of the world and their behavior. Cultural relativity entails the fact that there is no superior or inferior culture. It is thus against ethnocentrism, the tendency to judge other cultures using the standard of one's own. In cultural relativity there are no absolutes. There is no one way of looking or evaluating things. This article has given abundant examples from all the components of culture which show this to be the case. Cultural determinism implies that we are products of our culture. The culture shapes our conception of the world. Our tastes, smells, visions, sounds are acquired from it. We are freed from this determinism through cultural dynamism which is caused by environmental changes, cultural contact, and systemic changes.

It is from the Sapir-Wholf hypothesis that the concept *moral relativism* developed. What is considered morally wrong for one culture, may be morally good for another. For instance, polygamy which is condemned in the West was universally practiced in Africa. This practice emerged for both religious and practical reasons: the desire for immortality and to give status to unmarried women with fatherless children. Africans obtain immortality through ancestor worship. This can be achieved only if the deceased has many offspring. In the African mind, people die only when they are not remembered. It also happens that everywhere, not only in Africa, women outnumber men. Studies show that there is a higher male infant mortality than female. Because of gender behavior, more boys die in their teen years than girls. And when there are wars, men are the ones who are sent to the front. Monogamy thus prevents many women from finding husbands. In many African countries single mothers are treated as prostitutes and their children become outcasts. Polygamy gives a status to the women and makes children legitimate. Celibacy for priests, nuns or other individuals might be a virtue in Europe but is incomprehensible to the Africans. Africans believe that all individuals have a responsibility to keep both the family and the community alive through marriage and procreation. It is also common to find bare-breasted women in all African countries and to breast-feed babies in public. This is seen by Westerners as indecency. These opposing views show that morality is indeed in some cases culturally constructed.

When ANC led by Nelson Mandela was fighting against the supremacist regime of South Africa, it was called a terrorist organization by the government and its allies but hailed by the rest of the world as freedom fighters. When the Contras financed by the U.S. government trying to topple the Sandinista's regime, they were called by the Reagan administration freedom fighters but to others they were just criminals.

There are times when moral relativism is misused to condone flagrant violations of universal inalienable human rights, to refuse to condemn them or to remain inactive. In 1959 thousands and thousands of tutsi were massacred and others sent into exile with the blessing of the archbishop André Perraudain and the assistance of the Belgian government, because this was not a genocide but a revolution. The late colonial Belgian governor of Rwanda, Jean-Paul Harroy, stated in his memoirs that he was proud to have "assisted the Hutu Revolution." International organizations stationed in Kigali and churches didn't do anything to plead for mercy for the victims of this pogrom. Apparently killing thousands of innocent civilians is justified if it is done in the name of the Revolution. The non-intervention in 1994 Tutsi in Rwanda although it was broadcast live in people's homes everywhere in the world because according to the pundits, there was a deep-hatred between Hutu and Tutsi and that they had been fighting each other for centuries. This "root cause" explanation is of course both a cliché and a myth.

## Conclusion

Cultures are means by which societies ensure their survival and create societal balance and harmony. Because of the diversity of cultural spaces due to different landscapes, fauna and flora, histories and experiences, each culture obviously has a better way than others of seeing and understanding certain phenomena and reacting in a more appropriate way to them. For instance, some societies which have undergone certain universal experiences before others know how to handle better the same situations when they reoccur. Like academic fields, some societies are experienced and specialized in certain areas. Therefore other cultures have to learn from them. In Rwanda, before colonialism, the only meat that was eaten was beef, although there was plenty of fish, chickens, goats, pigs and sheep. Chickens were used only for divination purposes. Eggs were not eaten. Sheep were sacred animals. Only the Batwa, the pariah of the society like the Burakumin in Japan and the Dalit or Untouchables in India, ate lamb. The only use of sheep was their skins, which were used to carry babies. A Hutu or a Tutsi who ate lamb became automatically an outcast. Pork was eaten for the first time in the late 1950's by the European educated elite. This action caused such a sensation and scandal that a very popular satiric poem by the Rwandan scholar Alexis Kagame, called *Indyohe-shabirayi*, meaning "what makes potatoes taste better" is still the most popular written work among Rwandans inside the country and in the diaspora. It is from Congolese also that Rwandans learned that cassava leaves make a delicious relish called *isombe* and that when pounded these roots produce a flour from which a dough called *ugari* is eaten with all types of sauces. There are certain plants which are found in all parts of the world whose parts such as barks, roots, leaves, and seeve, are used as medicine or food but whose use other cultures are not aware of even if they are found in their ecosystem. For instance, gum arabic, a sap from acacia trees, which is used in soft drinks, beauty products, and pharmaceuticals is the lifeblood of Sudan's economy. Many African countries in the tropics, however, which also have these types of acacia trees, are not aware of this use. It was discovered recently, as reported in the New York Times issue of April 1, 2003, that the !Kung (also known as the San) of the Kalahari desert have a plant called *hoodia* which cures impotency and functions like Viagra and that they have been using it for centuries. This plant was recently bought by the giant pharmaceutical company, Pfizer. These examples support the concept of cultural relativity and cultural complementarity. No culture holds the monopoly on truth, knowledge and wisdom. Cultures need to borrow from each other. It is also evident that what works for one culture may not necessarily be prescribed as the right medicine for another. The attempt, for instance, by the US government to impose the American type of democracy in the Middle East is already dead on arrival because of different respective history and experience. The American type of government was not imported; it was created from the botton up.

Globalization and nationalism are both a threat to cultural pluralism. Globalization is seen by its critics not only as an attempt to prevent developing countries from being able to compete in the world market but mostly as the McDonaldization and Hollywoodization of the world, that is flooding the world with fast food, cheap products and loosened morals. It is viewed as neo-colonialism of developing countries with a different face and a different approach. Not only should the majority group allow minority cultures to exist because of cultural complementarity but members of the majority should also be tolerant of cultural pluralism. Multiculturalism should not be confused or equated with symbolic ethnicity which only allows ethnic groups to celebrate their heritage once a year, as in the case of Cinco de Mayo for Mexicans, or Ockoberfest for Germans. The majority should make a more concerted effort to understand other cultures.

Nationalism is not the best way to protect the culture. Purists, assimilationists and nativist movements can succeed in destroying minority cultures but they cannot prevent the majority culture from changing. The French Academy should serve as a lesson. This institution was created in the 17th Century to protect the purity of the French language but it has not succeeded.

In California navitist movements have been trying to make English the only official language. Although this is against the spirit and the letter of the text of the Treaty of Guadalupe Hidalgo, there is no reason for Anglos to panick. Similarly, assimilationists such as the Harvard professor Samuel P. Huntington should not be afraid that the new immigrants especially Hispanics are going to affect the core of the American culture namely individualism and work ethic as he states. Both "work ethic" for Anglo-Saxons and "the culture of poverty" for Hispanics and African-Americans are myths and clichés that have already been debunked. If the majority of Hispanics live in poverty it is not because they come from "a culture of poverty" background. Their work ethic is also demonstrated by the fact that they work hard to feed their families and contribute to the economy of this country. An effort should be made instead to explain the so-called "Hispanic Paradox". Scientists have found that even though the majority of Hispanics live in poverty, they have less health problems and chronic diseases than middle class whites who have better education and income.

There is no mechanism which will stop the change of the American culture, since all cultures are dynamic. Insular cultures are the ones that die. Even though, for instance, English is an Anglo-Saxon language, its vocabulary in great majority is French not only in the area of superstratum such as administration, justice, army, science, religion, art, but in the substratum as well including even kinship terms such as *family, grandparents, uncle, aunt, cousin*. The borrowing has not affected the English language identity, but it has made it richer. There is anxiety and fear among many European countries right now because countries of East Europe, former states of the Soviet Union are going to be integrated into the European Union. Although many European countries share many cultural elements such as religion, traditions and values, some members of the European Union are afraid that their culture might be affected. These fears are unfounded because the borrowings make the culture stronger and richer without losing its identity. And since today many individuals, organizations and groups with similar interests live in "a world without borders", in virtual spaces, all attempts to protect national cultures will fail.

Multiculturalism and multilingualism make people more complete. Learning other cultures opens our eyes, makes us hear new sounds, helps us develop new tastes and expand our horizons and allows us to have different world views with a magnifying glass. Our knowledge becomes richer, deeper and broader.

Many cultures, unfortunately, have become extinct because of colonialism, invasion, and genocide. Policy makers and the elite have a responsibility to make sure that endangered cultures do not disappear. All of us in privileged positions have a responsibility to protect these cultures. Failing to do so will be not only be a disservice to humanity but will make us willing participants in ethnocide.

## References

Buruma, Ian & Avishal Margalit. (2004). Occidentalism: The West in the Eyes of the Enemy. Penguin Press.

Harmon, Amy. (2004). *An answer, but not a cure, for a social disorder.* New York Times, Vol. CLIII: No.52, 834.

Harris, Lee. (2004). Civilization and Its Enemies: The next stage of history. New York: The Free Press.

Huntington P. Samuel. (1993). *The clash of civilizations.* Foreign Affairs Vol.72, No. 3, pp. 22–28.

Kagame, Alexis. Indyoheshabirayi. www.kimenyi.com/indyohesha-birayi.php

Kimenyi, Alexandre. Cow metaphor in Kinyarwanda. www.kimenyi.com/cow-metaphors.php

Kimenyi, Alexandre. The Role of Symbols in Nation Building: The Case of Rwanda. www.kimenyi.com/the-role-of-symbols-in-nation-building-the-case-of-rwanda.php

Kimenyi, Alexandre. Clichés: a Window to the Mind. www.kimenyi.com/cliches.php

Kimenyi, Alexandre. Umuco karande. UKURI and www.kimenyi.com/umuco-karande.php/

Kimenyi, Alexandre. Body Metaphors in Kinyarwanda. www.kimenyi.com/the-body-as-a-human-experience-metaphor-in-kinyarwanda.php

Lakoff, Georges & Mark Johnson. (1980). Metaphors we live by. University of Chicago Press.

Lakoff, Georges & Mark Johnson. (1999). A philosophy in the flesh. New York: Basic Books.

Said, Edward. (1978). Orientalism. New York: Pantheon Books; London: Routledge and Kegan Paul.

Thompson, Ginger. (2003). *Bushmen squeeze money from a humble cactus.* New York Times April 1.

Werthein, Margaret. (2004). *Bursts of Cornets and Evolution Bring Harmony to Night and Day.* New York Times. March 9, 2004.

Dane Morrison
*American Indian Studies: An Interdisciplinary Approach to Contemporary Issues* New York: Peter Lang Publishing 1997.

# Kill the Indian, Save the Child: Cultural Genocide and the Boarding School

*Debra K. S. Barker*

> *You, who are wise must know that different Nations have different Conceptions of things and you will therefore not take it amiss, if our Ideas of this kind of Education happen not to be the same as yours.*
>
> —*Canassatego,*
> *Leader of the Six Nations,*
> *Lancaster, Pennsylvania, 1744*

If you are familiar with the centrality of the oral tradition within American Indian cultures, you will understand how carefully we listen to the stories of our parents and relatives. As they tell us stories about their lives, they bequeath to us a living text of memory to help us structure our understanding of who we are and how we fit into the larger, more encompassing story of our tribe and culture. You will understand, also, that an integral part of the oral tradition is the voices of those offering testimony from their wisdom and experience.

The voices and testimony that follow speak to the family stories a good number of us have heard from our parents, grandparents, and elders; especially, they recall the story of their unwilling participation in the federal government's effort to re-educate on a massive scale thousands of American Indian children. Of course, education is valuable and empowering. Of course, education—in its most positive aspect—can afford all of us the skills and knowledge to help us realize whatever type of success we can imagine, whether we are talking about a conventional Western education or an education grounded in traditional, tribal ways. The key is that the education be undertaken with respect for the dignity of the students and be designed to empower them, not to diminish them. The process of education that I will be discussing here is one that has emotionally and spiritually devastated generations of American Indian people, setting in motion a concatenation of repercussions, including cultural genocide and generations of family pain.

In recent years documentaries and studies on Indian history only briefly touch on the boarding school system, contextualizing it with a host of other oppressive measures taken by the federal government to destroy the cultures of the people who stood in the way of progress. With one exception, however, studies have relied less on the testimony of Indian witnesses than on the published research of white historians. Indian voices, for the most part, have gone unheard. Given the fact that in the last century Indian education became a national political issue, involving Congress, the War Department, and the Department of the Interior, I wanted to counterpoint Native voices with those of the politicians and policymakers whose philosophical positions and decisions so profoundly affected the lives of our ancestors.

Like so many other experiments and policies implemented by the federal government during the past few hundred years in its attempt to deal with "the Indian problem," the boarding school system ultimately did more harm than good. Understanding the point, Fuchs and Havighurst assert that this federal policy, "rooted in forced assimilation, paradoxically grounded in white humanitarianism . . . left a legacy of unpleasant memories that affect attitudes and policies today" (225). This legacy bequeathed more than simply "unpleasant memories" for generations to come, however. Although it appeared to be the solution the federal government had sought to the Indian problem, it became an instrument that emotionally scarred generations of innocent children, leaving them and their children, as well, victims of institutionalized cultural genocide.

If one were to ask those people who endured, fled, or simply survived boarding school about their memories of their teachers and their education, one might hear some surprising answers. John Lame Deer, a Lakota medicine man, relates in his 1972 autobiography that the Catholic mission boarding school he attended on the Rosebud reservation in South Dakota was run like a prison. My own Aunt Margaret, who attended the same school, loved the bread the students made in the bakery and enjoyed the Saturday night movies, especially *King Kong*. Feeling persecuted by the nuns, however, dreading their unceasing unkindness, she made a successful escape to Aunt Mary Cordier's house in St. Francis, never returning to earn her diploma. My mother, an alumna of 1952, also felt quite bitter about her experiences. She recalled constant hunger, incidents of physical abuse, and traumatic public humiliations for even minor infractions of rules. A particularly vivid memory she shared with me was that of one of the youngest girls at school being punished for wetting her bed. Determined to teach her a lesson, one of the nuns wrapped the child up in her wet sheets and threw her down the outdoor fire escape tunnel. Years later, my mother would still recall the child's terrified screams.

In her 1990 autobiography, *Lakota Woman*, Mary Crow Dog compares children who survived Indian boarding schools to "victims of Nazi concentration camps trying to tell average, middle-class Americans what their experience had been like" (28). As a child, I listened to my mother's stories of her own bleak, joyless childhood. Feeling helpless to comfort her, I could not even comprehend what it must have been like to be without one's family and utterly powerless in the hands of a group of people committed to not only controlling one completely, but also to erasing one's personal and tribal identity. Mary Crow Dog is indeed correct in her analogy.

## Extermination by Civilization: Some American History

Indian education in America had been undertaken initially during the colonial period. One of the more successful efforts was that of the Society for Propagation of the Gospel in New England, a London organization which funded the establishment of an Indian college at Harvard during the 1650s. This group also underwrote the expense of books and of Bibles translated into Algonquian, as well as ministers and teachers to convert and educate the "heathen." Yet, as historian Christine Bolt points out, the Native-peoples "were able to educate the whites in the ways of the wilderness without making comparable demands on them and preferred the newcomers' material goods to their culture" (210). Later, in 1701, another English missionary organization, the Society for the Propagation of the Gospel in Foreign Parts, established 170 missions in the colonies (210), inciting a tide of missionization and education that gained momentum as the numbers of Euramericans grew and encroached relentlessly upon Indian land. Even as early as 1744, however, tribal leaders recognized that the curricula and objectives of a Euramerican education were irrelevant to the Indian graduates returning home. Furthermore, colonial educational practices compromised graduates' chances of even surviving in their native environment. Respectfully declining the Euramericans' request to inculcate any more of their young people, the sachems of the Iroquois Confederacy explained:

> Several of our young people were formerly brought up at the colleges of the Northern Provinces; they were instructed in all your science; but when they came back to us, they were bad runners; ignorant of every means of living in the woods; unable to bear either cold or hunger; knew neither how to build a cabin, take a deer, or kill an enemy; spoke our language imperfectly; were therefore neither fit for hunters, warriors, or counselors; they were totally good for nothing. We are, however, not the less obliged by your kind offer, though we decline accepting it; and to show our grateful sense of it, if the gentlemen of Virginia will send us a dozen of their sons, we will take great care of their education, instruct them in all we know, and make men of them. (Qtd. in Franklin 98)

Bolt supports the chiefs' objections and suggests yet another reason why a Euramerican education afforded Indians little benefit in the white world: "Patronized and coerced, required to undertake irksome and sometimes unintelligible tasks and finally offered no secure place in the white world if they wanted, the lot of the small number of educated Indians was an unenviable one" (211).

The federal government and the American public as a whole registered ambivalence when it came to solutions to the Indian problem. In 1792, Benjamin Lincoln, politician and former Revolutionary War general, expressed his hope that Indians would be treated fairly and humanely. Nevertheless, he called for a plan to defoliate the land, thus starving out the "beasts of the forest upon which the uncivilized principally depend for support" (qtd. in Pearce 68). The Trail of Tears, which followed as a result of President Andrew Jackson's deliberate enforcement of the unconstitutional Indian Removal Act of 1830, evoked sympathy among many of those who learned of the death march that claimed thousands of Indian lives as they walked the thousand miles between their homes in the Southeast and Oklahoma. Ironically, the tribes immediately involved, the Five Civilized Tribes, were friendly and "civilized" by Euramerican standards. The Cherokee, for instance, had established their own schools for their children and were printing books and a newspaper in their own language. According to Fuchs and Havighurst, the Choctaw, another of the "Civilized" tribes, had established "a comprehensive school system of their own with twelve schoolhouses and non-Indian teachers, supported by tribal, missionary, and federal funds" (223).

Yet another factor that inflamed public sentiment regarding "the Indian problem" was the phenomenal popularity of the captivity narrative. This was a genre of popular literature which disseminated to the general public the melodramatic image of the Indian as "the consummate villain, the beast who hatcheted fathers, smashed the skulls of infants, and carried off mothers to make them into squaws" (Pearce 58). In accepting this representation, people easily viewed Native people as sub-human and, therefore, undeserving of the same sympathy they might extend to people of their own race. Politicians and philanthropic organizations devoted to the cause of saving this inevitably "vanishing" people would finally conclude that Indians must either conform entirely to the values, religious beliefs, and vocations of white Americans or they would become extinct. As David Adams points out, "The option to maintain a separate cultural identity simply did not exist" (36). Henry Price, the Commissioner of Indian Affairs in 1881, established the position of the federal government in no uncertain terms:

> There is no one who has been a close observer of Indian history and the effect of contact of Indians with civilization, who is not well satisfied that one of two things must eventually take place, to wit, either civilization or extermination of the Indian. Savage and civilized life cannot live and prosper on the same ground. (Qtd. in David Adams 1–2)

In the wake of post-Civil War westward expansion, the growth of the railroad, and Manifest Destiny—the credo buoying up pioneers and entrepreneurs westward in quest of gold and land—the Indian problem became a national issue. Clearly, philanthropists working in behalf of Indian interests would not tolerate all-out extermination; as historian Robert M. Utley points out, "public sentiment overwhelmingly favored destruction by civilization rather than by killing" (35).

A federally controlled policy of civilization through education and aggressive missionization appeared to be the most promising avenue of endeavor. After all, according to one Indian agent's report to Congress, the Brule Sioux, my ancestors, had shown potential to be civilized. Pointing out that, although in the past they had been "splendid animals, having but few human hopes, and much more of the animal than intellectual in their composition," they had begun to live in log cabins (qtd. in David Adams 40). What modern people might not realize, however, was that the Brule Sioux—like other tribes—were given no other choice. The federal government had ordered them to surrender themselves so they could be assigned to reservations.

Indian agents noted in their reports to Congress, however, the apparent futility of civilizing Native children who continued to live within families that persisted in practicing their traditional religion and language. Thomas Morgan, Commissioner of Indian Affairs from 1889 to 1893, warned that if Native children were allowed to grow up within their parents' homes, they would become corrupted by "fathers who are degraded and mothers who are debased." Rather than embrace white Christian values, Indian children would inevitably come to "love the unlovely and to rejoice in the unclean." In Morgan's view, the only way children could "escape the awful doom" of savagery was "for the strong arm of the Nation to reach out, take them in their infancy and place them in its fostering schools . . ." (qtd. in Prucha, *Americanizing the American Indian* 243).

The education of thousands of Indian children became not only a monumental undertaking, but an expensive one, as well. A solution to the problem was offered by Captain Richard Pratt, a former overseer of the Ft. Marion Indian prisoner-of-war camp in Florida and self-styled expert on rehabilitating Indians. His solution was to convert abandoned military forts into boarding schools and then implement an educational program based on a military model. Like others who felt they had special insight into Indian cultures, he thought that Indian people valued neither punctuality nor respect for government authority, clearly hallmarks of "civilized" behavior. The structure and discipline of military training seemed to be the answer to the problem, provided that schools could work with pupils young enough to be successfully indoctrinated.

His first project, the Carlisle Indian School, was established in 1878 in Carlisle, Pennsylvania, and would provide the model upon which federal and mission boarding schools, as well as reservation day schools, based their programs. By 1902, there were ninety reservation boarding schools in existence (David Adams 65), all essentially operating with the ideology espoused by Richard Pratt in an 1881 letter to Senator Henry Dawes. Acknowledging the price the Indian child would have to pay in order to gain the privilege of assimilating into mainstream American life, the Indian would be forced to

> lose his identity as such, to give up his tribal relations and to be made to feel that he is an American citizen. If I am correct in this supposition, then the sooner all tribal relations are broken up; the sooner the Indian loses all his Indian ways, even his language, the better it will be for him and for the government. . . . (Pratt 266)

In an address to a Baptist convention in 1883, Pratt elaborated upon the philosophy of education that guided his work with Indian children: "In Indian civilization I am a Baptist, because I believe in immersing the Indians in our civilization and when we get them under holding them there until they are thoroughly soaked" (Pratt 335).

Even as the ideological groundwork was laid for the detribalization of indigenous nations, no one thought to consult Indian people about the prospect of their cultures being eradicated. In fact, policymakers could not understand why Indians were not eager to embrace "civilization." Bolt suggests the paternalistic ethnocentrism that prompted white policymakers to view their culture as clearly superior to any other, observing that whites quite naturally viewed their "home environment" to be more wholesome than those of African Americans and Indians. Because their "home environment" was "held by whites to be the cause of the 'inferiority' of the two races, educators assumed that they would gratefully abandon their values and institutions when prompted to do so by their 'superiors'" (217). Unfortunately, the time soon came when many parents were given no choices regarding their children's education or even their religious training.

Having no ready pupils for his experiment, Pratt embarked on a recruiting mission that took him to my family's reservation in South Dakota, where he persuaded reluctant parents to hand their children over into his care. Pratt, whom historian Robert M. Utley deems wrongheaded but well-meaning, at least gave Indian parents the choice of rejecting his offer. From 1879 to 1918, the Carlisle Industrial School represented a successful model of Indian education that other schools in the United States and Canada would emulate. According to Utley, "During his twenty-four-year tenure the school educated, in all, 4,903 Indian boys and girls from seventy-seven tribes" (xiii).

What made possible the realization of the Carlisle school, as well as that of other federal boarding schools, reservation day schools, and mission schools, was the intrinsic nature of the reservation system itself. Advocates such as Francis Walker, Commissioner of Indian Affairs in 1872, argued that policymakers needed to be hardheaded when it came to "the treatment of savages by a civilized power." As Walker observed, reservations were necessary to bring "the wild beasts [the Indians] to the condition of supplicants for charity" (qtd. in Thomas 60–61). Assigned to reservations, designated wards of the government, and forced into complete economic dependency, Indians were at the mercy of government attempts to control and coerce them into compliancy. Having conquered them militarily, the federal government could then undertake a well-planned campaign to exterminate Indian cultures, resulting in "devastating cultural implications" for the human beings involved (Utley xvii).

In the years to come, Indian agents, serving on reservations as representatives of the federal government, condoned any means necessary to fill boarding schools, lending new significance to the term, "compulsory education." In fact, Congress enacted legislation in 1892 formally empowering government officials to use force when Native parents balked at the prospect of their children being taken from them, herded onto trains, and transported hundreds of miles away to boarding schools. David Adams notes that not until 1904 were officials required to obtain parental consent to remove their children to non-reservation boarding schools (89).

To enforce compliance with the new compulsory attendance law, Indian agents used whatever means necessary. For example, at the Yankton Agency in South Dakota, the home reservation of my great-grandfather, John Cordier, agents withheld rations to reluctant parents (David Adams 202). Consequently, children at the Pine Ridge agency knew that if they played truant, their parents might starve. J. B. Harrison, of the Indian Rights Association, reported: "When a child was absent from school without a good reason, the rations of the whole family were cut off til he returned" (qtd. in David Adams 203).

During the autumn, agents often supervised what were essentially kidnapping raids. Agency police were ordered to hunt down and seize bodily children who were-hiding or had been hidden by their parents. Fletcher J. Cowart, agent of the Mescolero Agency in New Mexico, described in his annual report for 1886 the cries and "lamentations" of Indian mothers and the stark terror of small, uncomprehending children about to be taken away by impatient strangers, perhaps never seeing their parents again (199). After witnessing such a particularly wrenching scene, one agent understated a dimension of Indian culture that he had observed, noting in his annual report to the Commissioner of Indian Affairs, "I have been impressed with the great fondness Indians have for their children. This may be one cause why they do not like to part from them" (qtd. in David Adams 205). A remarkably empathetic agent, W. D. C. Gibson, reported in 1887,

> It is really a pitiful sight to witness their distress and sorrow at times when they come to talk about the children and ask how many 'moons' before they come home, while their appearance indicates that they had passed a restless night, or perhaps not slept any. (163)

In comparison with the tone and tenor of other agents' reports, this agent appears to be one of the few who viewed Indians as human beings, rather than as obstinate and godless savages.

One of the most dramatic accounts of parents' resisting the kidnapping of their children comes from an annual report filed by an agent at the Yakima agency. In his 1885 report, Agent R. H. Milroy explained that he was forced to arrest and lock up Cotiahan, a Yakima tribal leader who refused to reveal where he had hidden his child. Making an example of him to the other band members, Milroy chained the father's leg and "put him to sawing wood, and told him if he refused to work, he would be tied to a tree and whipped" (200).

Had the children and parents been able to foresee the humiliation, anguish, and deprivation that constituted their children's "education" in these boarding schools, they might have resisted the agents' overtures even more aggressively than they did. As he was being led onto the train bound for Carlisle, Luther Standing Bear recalls thinking at the time that he was being taken away to be killed. "I could think of no reason why white people wanted Indian boys and girls except to kill them, and not having the remotest idea of what a school was, I thought we were going East to die," he writes (*Land of the Spotted Eagle* 230–31).

# Barbed Wire and the Bible

In one sense those children would "die," passing from one life to another: stripped naked of the clothes their mothers had made for them, renamed with the names of American Civil War heroes and famous Indian fighters, and re-educated to adopt the "civilized" values of the race that had conquered them. In a quite literal sense, however, hundreds of children died. Neglect, hunger, disease, homesickness—even suicide—left the testimony of acres of little tombstones at boarding schools all over the United States. Luther Standing Bear tells us that "In the graveyard at Carlisle most of the graves are those of little ones" (*Land of the Spotted Eagle* 234). Chief Standing Bear goes on to say that by the third year Carlisle Indian School was in operation, almost one-half of the Plains children had died. Sadly, anxious parents back home might never be notified that their children were ill, much less dead and buried. Too often, rather than deal with the questions and tears of bereft parents, Indian agents would leave telegrams and letters to gather dust on their desks (*My People, the Sioux* 162–63). Ojibwa scholar Basil Johnston recalls a particularly virulent epidemic at his boarding school that claimed "between thirty to fifty boys at a time: chicken pox, measles and mumps . . ." (82). Not surprisingly, John Cook, Indian agent at the Rosebud reservation, warned that given "the large percentage of deaths among the scholars" at Carlisle, parents would not allow their children to be taken away (*Annual Report* 1881, 52).

When military and prison systems induct a new member into their respective institutions, their first step is to dismantle the individual's identity. Boarding school inductions followed similar lines. When Basil Johnston first met his new class-mates at Peter Claver's Residential School, he was struck by the fact that they all had been shaven bald. In a 1900 article she published in *The Atlantic Monthly,* Dakota writer Zitkala-Ša (Gertrude Bonnin) describes being dragged screaming into a chair, where she was tied and her hair cut. (A shocked student once asked me, "Did they do the same thing to white girls who went away to school?") Zitkala-Ša explained to her readers that in Dakota culture, to have one's hair cut meant two things, both momentous. Either one had been publicly exposed as a coward or one was in the throes of grief at the loss of a dear one. Along with the haircut, the children were then subjected to a further humiliation—delousing—a practice that persisted until the 1960s, according to Mary Crow Dog. An alumna of my mother's school, who attended in the late 1960s, Crow Dog reports in the chapter of her autobiography entitled "Civilize Them with a Stick" that the nuns would "dump the children into tubs of alcohol, a sort of rubbing alcohol, 'to get the germs off' " (35).

Stripped of their clothes, which were usually burned, children were issued uniforms that distinguished them as inmates, so to speak. In the last century, girls were given dresses which were close-fitting and to Zitkala-Ša's thinking, immodest. Boys were issued little military uniforms, which they later learned to sew for themselves and their classmates. Betty Eadie writes in her 1992 memoir that after the haircut and delousing, girls were issued "two dresses each, one color for one week, the other for the following week. These uniforms would help identify runaways" (7).

Just as children were stripped of all outward marks of identity, they were threatened, bullied, and beaten to conform to their teachers' expectations of what constituted civilized behavior. When Congress considered enacting legislation banning corporal punishment in boarding schools, Captain Richard Pratt was incensed, insisting that such a ban "would mean the end of Indian schools" (qtd. in Hyde, *A Sioux Chronicle* 57). Children received a spectrum of punishments for speaking their own language, for instance. Marcella La Beau remembers that children caught speaking Lakota would have their mouths washed out with soap before they were punished (qtd. in Josephy 436). A Klamath man recalls that older boys were forced to walk around a tree stump for an hour, carrying a fence rail on their backs (David Adams 125). One of the most dramatic incidents of punishment is recounted by a Blackfoot student, Lone Wolf, who witnessed the event. Angered at hearing a boy speaking his Native language, a white supervisor threw the boy across a room, breaking his collarbone (qtd. in Josephy 435).

Because the constitutional right of freedom of religion was denied to Indians, Indian children were forced to practice the religion of whatever Christian denomination prevailed at their school. Children were also punished for not worshipping with the zeal the teachers demanded of them. Mary Crow Dog's grandmother told her a story that happened when she was very young and caught by the nuns playing jacks instead of praying. As a punishment, she was locked in a tiny cell in an attic, in the dark, and fed only bread and water for a week (Crow Dog 32). Betty Eadie recalls, "My sister Thelma was often beaten by [the nuns] with a little hose and was then forced to thank the Sister who had done it or be beaten again" (9).

Unable to bear the regimentation, spoiled food, bleak living conditions, and utter lack of emotional support, many children ran away. Consequently, one agent at Cheyenne and Arapaho Agency felt compelled to place bars on the dormitory windows and padlock the doors to prevent children from escaping (David Adams 127). Even in this century, according to Betty Eadie, children were locked in their rooms at night (8). Punishment for running away was usually severe. As Mary Crow Dog explains, her grandmother and her fellow inmates were made examples to other children after they were found and returned to school: "The nuns stripped them naked and whipped them. They used a horse buggy whip on my grandmother. Then she was put back into the attic—for two weeks" (32). One particularly incensed school principal hunted down a group of escaped Ute students, drove them back at gunpoint "like wolves," then threatened to hang them (David Adams 219). Luckily, my Aunt Margaret was never caught. Just last summer, while we were at Rosebud, she pointed out to me the route she took to escape what had become an intensely miserable period of her life.

As I look at old photographs of my mother and Aunt Margaret's school grounds, as well as those of other schools, I am struck by two images that recur with frequency: the barbed wire fences and the rows of little children behind those fences, identically dressed, staring warily into the camera. From all the accounts I have read and heard, from the 1880s to the 1960s, the typical boarding school operated on a daily basis like a military prison for children. Basil Johnston and his classmates objected to the absolute lack of privacy, of having every hour of day scheduled: "The boys resented the never ending surveillance that began in the morning and ended only late at night, after they had all fallen asleep; a surveillance that went on day after day, week after week, month after month, year after year" (137). My mother recalls having only two hours of free time a week outdoors—on Sunday afternoon. She said that boys and girls could mingle and talk on the grounds, but everyone had to remain standing for that time; no one was allowed to sit on the ground, unless the person had a telephone book to sit on. (My mother would later laugh about the irrationality of this stipulation: "Where on earth were we going to get telephone books?") Apparently, the nuns were concerned that students might engage in sexual activity on the school grounds in full sight of everyone. "They treated us like we were savages," my mother said.

Children awoke each morning to reveille and fell asleep to taps. Medicine man John Lame Deer remembers falling in for roll call four times each day. He recalls, "We had to stand at attention, or march in step" (25). His grandson Archie Lame Deer, who is my mother's age and perhaps a classmate of hers at St. Francis, tells us that a priest would order the boys to march around the playground holding sticks as if they were rifles. "If we'd had blond hair and blue eyes," he jokes, "you might have taken us for Hitler youth in Nazi Germany" (49).

Even girls were not exempt from the military regimentation. In her book *Oglala Women,* Marla N. Powers presents testimony from a woman who attended Rapid City Indian School, recounting the bugles and bells that dictated when they awakened, ate, worked, had inspections, and slept. The girls marched, too: "We fell into formations. We had officers for each company . . . a captain and a major. . . . We knew every drill there was to be known, right flank, left flank, forward march, and double time" (111). Thomson Highway adds that he knew of girls getting their heads shaved for "minor infractions" of rules (*War against the Indians*).

The education and training most children received was equally regimented, culturally irrelevant, and ultimately a waste of time, according to a number of disillusioned graduates. Understanding nothing about Indian people, teachers assumed that the children were unfeeling and impervious to humiliation. Charles Eastman, who earned his M.D. at Boston College, writes in his autobiography *From the Deep Woods to Civilization* of the humiliation of class recitation at Dr. Alfred Riggs Santee Training School: "For a whole week we youthful warriors were held up and harassed with words of three letters . . . rat, cat, and so forth . . . until not a semblance of our native dignity and self-respect was left" (46). To make the learning process even more fraught with anxiety, students reciting their lessons were asked to do so "taking the position of a soldier at attention" (Pratt 244).

Christine Bolt notes that in both white and Indian cultures children learned by memorization. However, the rote learning by which Indian children were inculcated with the religion and values of the dominant culture must have been not only tortuous, but bewildering as well. Bolt explains,

> *The Indian mission children were asked to memorize hymns and passages from Scripture which they frequently did not understand and which contradicted all their own learned traditions. Incomprehension was compounded by the fact that pupils of every degree of attainment were at first taught together. . . . (213)*

The ninth-grade students at Pierre Indian School in South Dakota must certainly have puzzled over the usefulness and relevance of *Julius Caesar* and *Lady of the Lake* to the lives they would lead as they adapted to their dramatically changing world. Indeed, how could Shakespeare help a Cheyenne person negotiate the cultural transition from tribal values to those of the American West? No doubt Paiute children in Nevada prior to 1931 were equally mystified by the following lines they were forced to memorize and recite:

> *What do we plant*
> *When we plant the tree?*
> *We plant the ship*
> *That sails the sea. . . . (Qtd. in Szasz 33)*

My aunt Margaret never did have an occasion to use the Latin she was taught after she learned to speak English, although she did point out that Mass and prayers were in Latin, hence the necessity of the hours spent memorizing all those Latin verb conjugations. Studying secretarial skills as a part of her curriculum, my mother at least received an education that would theoretically prepare her to survive and earn economic independence in the white world.

Going on to earn an Associate's Degree from Haskell Institute, a former boarding school which is today a university, my mother managed to surpass the expectations non-Indian teachers and administrators usually had of Indian students. From the inception of the boarding school idea, however, federal officials generally held very low expectations of what Indian students might achieve professionally after they completed school. Secretary of the Interior Henry Teller had articulated a philosophy of education that had been adopted not only by Richard Pratt at Carlisle, but also by boarding schools everywhere up until the middle of this century. Within the curriculum of these schools, Teller declared, "more attention should be paid to teaching them to labor than to read" (qtd. in Prucha, *American Indian Policy* 271).

Students were expected to become laborers or domestic servants. In fact, policymakers envisioned Native people leaving their reservations to join the ranks of what was viewed at that time as a permanent underclass in white society. Captain Pratt's vision was that eventually tribal people would be swallowed up into the melting pot of immigrants that had become mainstream Euramerican culture. What he probably did not foresee, however, was that his philosophy would defeat the aspirations of some Indian people to use their education to secure more fulfilling professions than those in manual labor or domestic service.

Chief Standing Bear's situation is a case in point. Like so many others at the mercy of a paternalistic boarding school, he had little say in determining his own future. Standing Bear had wanted to spend his entire day in the classroom getting an education, rather than devote half of it working in the tinshop learning a profession that would be useless back at Rosebud. Eventually, after pointing out that the government was supplying his reservation with an abundance of tinware, he asked Captain Pratt if he could learn carpentry instead. Pratt refused his request. Standing Bear writes, "What worried me was the thought that I might not be able to work at the trade after I returned home. But Captain Pratt could not understand why I wanted to make a change, and so the matter was dropped" (*My People, the Sioux* 176). In this century, white educators' expectations of their Indian students clearly have not changed. In his 1992 autobiography, *The Gift of Power,* medicine man Archie Lame Deer states that his boarding school teachers held the opinion that "we Indians were only good at menial jobs. They did not prepare us to become teachers, lawyers, or doctors" (49).

According to the testimony of Native people and historians, boarding school students were essentially trained, then treated as indentured servants, not as scholars—a fact that students' parents were unaware of. Making the best of a difficult situation, parents such as those of Luther Standing Bear and Stay at Home Spotted Tail hoped that their sons' white education would afford them both professions and the knowledge they would need to protect and defend both personal and tribal interests. Unfortunately, this was not the case for Chief Spotted Tail's son. Visiting his son at Carlisle in 1880, Spotted Tail talked with the Lakota boys from Rosebud, learning that they were all generally "miserable and homesick" (Hyde 322). However, when he discovered that his son was working at harness making, rather than learning to read, write, and speak English, "the thunder began to roll," George Hyde explains, noting that ordinarily Spotted Tail's son would be back home at Rosebud, "training to become a chief," not a farmhand (322).

Although the students were there ostensibly to earn an education, child labor was vitally important to support the expense of maintaining the boarding school. Indeed, one-half of the pupils' day was devoted to the maintenance and upkeep of their prison, including farming, cooking, sewing their own uniforms, and making their own shoes. In his memoir, *Battlefield and Classroom,* Richard Pratt explains that even children too young to be put to work had to ". . . witness the productions of the older ones in harness making, tin ware, boots and shoes, clothing, blacksmith and wagon making . . ." (259). The prized jobs at his school were those in the kitchen, recalls Basil Johnston, because there students could eat the leftover food from their teachers' plates and at least satisfy their incessant hunger (49). Johnston's recollection of hunger echoes the testimony of students over a range of residential institutions. Not until the publication of the Meriam Report in 1928 and the subsequent investigations of the Red Cross was it widely known that children had to survive on "a diet that was the equivalent of slow starvation" (Szasz 19). The Meriam Report criticized the boarding school system on another charge, as well—

the failure to demonstrate the practices they taught. Girls in home economics classes were lectured on the elements of proper nutrition and meal planning; yet, the schools themselves rarely provided milk, fruit, or vegetables in the children's diets (351).

A cruel irony, of course, was that graduates returning to the reservation might not find an opportunity to use the education or vocational training they received in these institutions. Robert Utley points out that "with the spoils system ascendant, the few government jobs available rarely went to Indians, and few Carlisle graduates found any occupation to utilize their newly learned talents" (xvi). As in the case of Standing Bear, who found no use for his training as a tinsmith, other students, such as those trained as hatmakers and tailors, found few opportunities to become independent and self-supporting once they returned home.

On the other hand, Indian graduates were not always successful in finding a place in the white world, either. My grandfather, Levi Prue, who graduated from Haskell Institute with a degree in accounting, could find only occasional, short-term employment at home—or within a Bureau of Indian Affairs office or other Indian agencies. After finding that white employers in Omaha were not anxious to hire an educated Indian, my grandfather, who loved to read and disliked the mind-numbing tedium of sheer manual labor, went to work in a cold storage company, then a sheet metal plant, before finally trading in his dreams for a bottle. On the advice of Uncle Moses Red Owl, who feared that she would not find a BIA (Bureau of Indian Affairs) job on the reservation, my mother decided not to return to Rosebud to look for work. Instead, she moved to a succession of white towns looking for some kind of meaningful employment. Unfortunately, she never had the opportunity to exercise her college degree or her shorthand skills (taking dictation at 120 words a minute). During the 1950s, racism against Indians had not abated much since my grandfather's day, so my mother also resigned herself to factory work.

At least my mother and grandfather did not have to face the type of racial discrimination that prevented them from securing a residence in the white world. In *My People, the Sioux*, Luther Standing Bear writes of his discouragement at facing racial discrimination in Philadelphia, where he wanted to work as a clerk in Wanamaker's Store. He explains, "I was to prove to all people that the Indians could learn and work as well as the white people . . ." (179). Unfortunately, he was denied the opportunity to prove his equality—white landlords refused to rent a room to him. Chief Standing Bear explains, "When I would find something that seemed suitable, and the people discovered my nationality, they would look at me in a surprised sort of way, and say that they had no place for an Indian boy" (189).

Sadly, many graduates returned to the reservation finding they did not belong there, either. A white education was an acquisition of dubious value for young people returning home expecting to reintegrate into their communities, earn a living, and move on with their lives. As Robert Utley points out, "The result was that they either existed in a shadow world neither Indian nor white, with acceptance denied by both worlds, or they cast off the veneer of Carlisle and again became Indians" (xvi). Commenting upon this predicament from a Native perspective, John Lame Deer writes, "When we enter the school, we at least know that we are Indians. We come out half red and half white, not knowing what we are" (27). For Sun Elk, a Taos Pueblo graduate, his homecoming would be a heartbreaking one. Soon after his arrival, tribal elders came to his parents' home, and, completely ignoring him, made the following pronouncement to his father:

> Your son who calls himself Rafael has lived with the white men. He has been
> far away. . . . He has not . . . learned the things that Indian boys should learn.
> He has no hair. . . . He cannot even speak our language. He is not one of us.
> (Qtd. in Josephy 436)

Alienated from home and family, culturally as well as emotionally, some Indian people have struggled with their ambivalence about claiming a relation to the people of whom they had been taught to be ashamed. Inculcated with white values and taught the Euramerican version of American history, Pequot minister William Apess, for instance, before he went on to work as an Indian rights activist, grew up "terrified" of Indians. LaVonne Brown Ruoff explains that "whites had filled him with stereotypical stories about Indian cruelty but never told him how cruelly they treated Indians" (1781). Albert White Hat, now a professor at Sinte Gleśka University and spiritual leader at Rosebud, recalls having grown so alienated from his cultural roots that when he and his friends would watch western movies, "we cheered for the cavalry" (Beasley 41).

The emotional cost of the boarding school experience upon generations of Native families has been incalculable. When I was a child I would watch my mother brood for hours, chain smoking over memories that intruded insistently upon the present. Passed around from relative to relative, from orphanage to boarding school, she—like so many other Indian children—had to bear the consequences of her parents' shattered lives. Her life story and those of other boarding school survivors remind me of Basil Johnston's description of the youngest children at his boarding school, "the babies":

> They were a sad lot, this little crowd of babies; they seldom laughed or smiled
> and often cried and whimpered during the day and at night. . . . [T]hey were
> hunched in their wretchedness and misery in a corner of the recreation hall,
> their outsized boots dangling several inches above the asphalt floor. And
> though Paul Migwanabe and Joe Thompson and other carvers made toys for
> them, the babies didn't play with their cars and boats; they just held on to them,
> hugged them and took them to bed at night, for that was all they had in the
> world when the lights went out, and they dared not let it go. (60)

Given such testimony, we must ask: What was to be the destiny of children like these? What were the experiences of children who grew up never feeling the nurturing of parents, who emerged from an institution without knowing how to function within a family, without possessing a sense of belonging to a particular group, of sharing a particular history, or of feeling pride in their ancestors? Whom were these individuals allowed to feel proud of? The Pilgrims? Christopher Columbus? These are the queries of the academic researcher, of course. Yet, they are also questions posed with bitterness by those who recognize that their own cultural heroes and tribal identities have been erased out of history by the Colonizers. We have been spiritually dispossessed with that erasure, bereft of our language and our pride in being Indian, diminished by the loss of the cultural knowledge that constitutes the psychic infrastructure of a people. My ancestors made this point more emphatically: A people without a history is like wind across the buffalo grass. A history, after all, is a narrative, a story. And the boarding school robbed generations of Indian children of the stories of their families and tribes, stories that would have otherwise empowered them with knowledge, wisdom, survival skills, and a spiritual foundation.

Aside from being an instrument of cultural genocide, another insidious effect of the boarding school system has been its effectiveness in eroding the foundation of tribal culture, the family. Since the inception of the boarding school system in the last century up to the present, Indian families all over the United States have struggled and are still struggling with healing the pain of generations of family dysfunction. The documentaries, *The War Against the Indians* and *The Native Americans*, both present testimony from Native people explaining that the years of institutionalizing did not foster in children the nurturing skills they would need to be parents. One of the producers of another well-known documentary on boarding schools, *In the White Man's Image*, Matthew "Sitting Bear" Jones, explains how the boarding schools have perpetuated generations of dysfunction within families: "They didn't teach us to be parents at the schools and we didn't have parents to teach us to be parents. When we had children we didn't know how to raise them" ("Boarding Schools" B2).

## Healing Our Hoop

My approach to the subject of the boarding school system, as I have noted, grows out of my desire that the voices of adult children survivors be heard, and that the audiences which listen will understand how this important dimension of Indian history fits into the larger context of factors that have played a role in the attempted cultural genocide of the first Americans. For Indian audiences, I hope that this testimony will bring the kind of healing shock I experienced after reading an interview with Carol Anne Heart Looking Horse in Sandy Johnson's *The Book of Elders*. Her story and those of others have helped me to construct the narrative of my family, as I hope they will for other people.

In her interview, Looking Horse discusses the "historical grief" we bear and its relation to not only the attempted eradication of our culture, but also the trauma our parents experienced as they were forced through this process. As tribal nations regain control over the education of their own children, she observes, Indian teachers have been able to teach our young people about the relationship between this history and our parents' personal experience. In doing so, we are able to help young people to make strides in recovering their culture, learning a history of America that does not demonize their ancestors, and regaining pride in tribal heritage.

An important key to this recovery lies in the tribal college. In sites such as Sinte Gleśka University on the Rosebud reservation, for instance, students have the opportunity to learn from Indian professors and to complete a core curriculum of Lakota studies that includes language, history, and traditional knowledge. At the same time, students can remain in proximity to their families and communities, sustaining the family bonds that have been so cherished within traditional families. A major challenge that tribal colleges all over the United States face, however, is financial. As always, the destinies of Native people have been subject to the seemingly capricious decisions of the federal government. For instance, although Congress had at one time authorized financial support of amounts up to $6,000 for each student attending college, the Reagan administration made cuts in allocations. By 1989 a student might receive only $1,900 of the funds Congress had originally allocated (Wright and Tierney 17). Even now, Congress continues to slash appropriations once promised to Indian tribes—funds which would enable Native people to pursue their dreams of economic independence and self-determination. Thankfully, a handful of tribal communities—not all—are experiencing an economic and cultural renaissance, due to gaming revenues that enable tribes to build new schools and hire qualified teachers to help bring the next generation proudly into the coming century. And, they will be proud, for they will have the choices our parents and grandparents were denied: to walk in either world, in the tracks and in the image not of the Colonizers, but of the ancestors.

# Works Cited

Adams, David Wallace. *The Federal Indian Boarding School: A Study of Environment and Response, 1879–1918.* Diss. Indiana University, 1975.

Adams, Evelyn C. *American Indian Education, Government Schools and Economic Progress.* New York: King's Crown Press, 1941.

*Annual Report of the Secretary of the Interior.* Washington: GPO, 1879–1895.

Beasley, Conger, Jr. "The Return of the Lakota: An Indian People Thrive 500 Years After Columbus." *The Environmental Magazine* Sept.–Oct. 1992: 38+.

"Boarding Schools Likened to Concentration Camps." *Indian Country Today (Lakota Times)* 5 Oct. 1994: B2.

Bolt, Christine. *American Indian Policy and American Reform: Case Studies of the Campaign to Assimilate the American Indians.* London: Allen & Unwin, 1987.

Cowart, Fletcher J. "Reports of Agents in New Mexico." Secretary of the Interior. *Annual Report of the Secretary of the Interior.* Washington: GPO, 1886.

Crow Dog, Mary, and Richard Erdoes. *Lakota Woman.* New York: Harper Perennial, 1990.

Eadie, Betty J. *Embraced by the Light.* New York: Bantam Books, 1992.

Eastman, Charles. *From the Deep Woods to Civilization: Chapters in the Autobiography of an Indian.* 1916. Lincoln: U of Nebraska P, 1977.

Franklin, Benjamin. "Remarks Concerning the Savages of North America." *The Writings of Benjamin Franklin.* Ed. Albert Henry Smyth. Vol. 10. New York: Macmillan, 1907. 10 vols.

Fuchs, Estelle, and Robert J. Havighurst. *To Live on This Earth: American Indian Education.* New York: Doubleday, 1972.

Gibson, W. D. C. "Reports of Agents in Nevada." Secretary of the Interior. *Annual Report of the Secretary of the Interior.* Washington: GPO, 1887.

Hyde, George E. *A Sioux Chronicle.* Norman: U of Oklahoma P, 1956.

———. *Spotted Tail's Folk: A History of the Brule Sioux.* Norman: U of Oklahoma P, 1961.

*In the White Man's Image.* Prod. Christine Lesiak and Matthew Jones. Videocassette. PBS Video. 1991.

Indian Removal Act of 1830. 28 May 1830, c. 148, 4 stat. 411.

Johnson, Sandy. *The Book of Elders: The Life Stories of Great American Indians as Told to Sandy Johnson.* San Francisco: Harper Collins, 1994.

Johnston, Basil H. *Indian School Days.* Norman: U of Oklahoma P, 1988.

Josephy, Alvin M. *500 Nations: An Illustrated History of North American Indians.* New York: Alfred A. Knopf, 1994.

*King Kong.* Dir. Ernest B. Schoedsack. Perf. Fay Wray, Bruce Cabot, Robert Armstrong. Universal, 1933.

Lame Deer, Archie, and Richard Erdoes. *The Gift of Power: The Life and Teachings of a Lakota Medicine Man.* Santa Fe: Bear & Company, 1992.

Lame Deer, John (Fire), and Richard Erdoes. *Lame Deer, Seeker of Visions.* New York: Pocket Books, 1972.

Meriam, Lewis, et al. *The Problem of Indian Administration.* 1928. Introd. Frank C. Miller. New York: Johnson Reprint Corporation, 1971.

Milroy, R. H. "Reports of Agents in Washington Territory." Secretary of the Interior. *Annual Report of the Secretary of the Interior.* Washington: GPO, 1885.

*The Native Americans.* Narr. Joy Harjo. 3 episodes. TBS Productions. 1992.

Pearce, Roy Harvey. *The Savages of America: A Study of the Indian and the Idea of Civilization.* Baltimore: Johns Hopkins UP, 1953.

Powers, Marla N. *Oglala Women: Myth, Ritual, and Reality.* Chicago: U of Chicago P, 1986.

Pratt, Richard Henry. *Battlefield and Classroom: Four Decades with the American Indian, 1867–1904.* Ed. Robert M. Utley. Lincoln: U of Nebraska P, 1964.

Prucha, Francis Paul. *American Indian Policy in Crisis: Christian Reformers and the Indian, 1865–1900.* Norman: U of Oklahoma P, 1976.

———, ed. *Americanizing the American Indians: Writings by the "Friends of the Indian," 1800–1900.* Cambridge: Harvard UP, 1973.

Ruoff, A. LaVonne Brown. "William Apess." *The Health Anthology of American Literature.* Ed. Paul Lauter. Vol. 1, 2nd ed. Lexington, MA: D. C. Heath, 1994. 1780–81.

Standing Bear, Luther. *Land of the Spotted Eagle.* Lincoln: U of Nebraska P, 1933.

———. *My People, the Sioux.* Lincoln: U of Nebraska P, 1975.

Szasz, Margaret Connell. *Education and the American Indian: The Road to Self-Determination Since 1928.* 2nd ed. Albuquerque: U of New Mexico P, 1974.

Thomas, Robert K. "On an Indian Reservation: How Colonialism Works." *The Way: An Anthology of American Indian Literature.* Eds. Shirley Hill Witt and Stan Steiner. New York: Alfred A. Knopf, 1972. 60–68.

Utley, Robert M. Introduction. *Battlefield and Classroom: Four Decades with the American Indian, 1867–1904.* Ed. Robert M. Utley. Lincoln: U of Nebraska P, 1964. ix–xix.

*The War against the Indians.* Narr. Harry Rasky. Canada Broadcasting Corporation. 1992.

Witt, Shirley Hill, and Stan Steiner, eds. *The Way: An Anthology of American Indian Literature.* New York: Alfred A. Knopf, 1972.

Wright, Bobby, and William G. Tierney. "American Indians in Higher Education." *Change.* March–April 1991: 11–18.

Zitkala-Ša. (Gertrude Bonnin). "The School Days of an Indian Girl." *Atlantic Monthly* Feb. 1900: 185–94. Rpt. in *American Indian Stories.* Washington: Hayworth Publishing House, 1921. 52–56.

# The Ethics of Living Jim Crow: An Autobiographical Sketch

*Richard Wright*

 **I**

My first lesson in how to live as a Negro came when I was quite small. We were living in Arkansas. Our house stood behind the railroad tracks. Its skimpy yard was paved with black cinders. Nothing green ever grew in that yard. The only touch of green we could see was far away, beyond the tracks, over where the white folks lived. But cinders were good enough for me and I never missed the green growing things. And anyhow cinders were fine weapons. You could always have a nice hot war with huge black cinders. All you had to do was crouch behind the brick pillars of a house with your hands full of gritty ammunition. And the first woolly black head you saw pop out from behind another row of pillars was your target. You tried your very best to knock it off. It was great fun.

I never fully realized the appalling disadvantages of a cinder environment till one day the gang to which I belonged found itself engaged in a war with the white boys who lived beyond the tracks. As usual we laid down our cinder barrage, thinking that this would wipe the white boys out. But they replied with a steady bombardment of broken bottles. We doubled our cinder barrage, but they hid behind trees, hedges, and the sloping embankments of their lawns. Having no such fortifications, we retreated to the brick pillars of our homes. During the retreat a broken milk bottle caught me behind the ear, opening a deep gash which bled profusely. The sight of blood pouring over my face completely demoralized our ranks. My fellow-combatants left me standing paralyzed in the center of the yard, and scurried for their homes. A kind neighbor saw me and rushed me to a doctor, who took three stitches in my neck.

I sat brooding on my front steps, nursing my wound and waiting for my mother to come from work. I felt that a grave injustice had been done me. It was all right to throw cinders. The greatest harm a cinder could do was leave a bruise. But broken bottles were dangerous; they left you cut, bleeding, and helpless.

When night fell, my mother came from the white folks' kitchen. I raced down the street to meet her. I could just feel in my bones that she would understand. I knew she would tell me exactly what to do next time. I grabbed her hand and babbled out the whole story. She examined my wound, then slapped me.

"How come yuh didn't hide?" she asked me. "How come yuh awways fightin'?"

I was outraged, and bawled. Between sobs I told her that I didn't have any trees or hedges to hide behind. There wasn't a thing I could have used as a trench. And you couldn't throw very far when you were hiding behind the brick pillars of a house. She grabbed a barrel stave, dragged me home, stripped me naked, and beat me till I had a fever of one hundred and two. She would smack my rump with the stave, and, while the skin was still smarting, impart to me gems of Jim Crow wisdom. I was never to throw cinders any more. I was never to fight any more wars. I was never, never, under any conditions, to fight *white* folks again. And they were absolutely right in clouting me with the broken milk bottle. Didn't I know she was working hard every day in the hot kitchens of the white folks to make money to take care of me? When was I ever going to learn to be a good boy? She couldn't be bothered with my fights. She finished by telling me that I ought to be thankful to God as long as I lived that they didn't kill me.

All that night I was delirious and could not sleep. Each time I closed my eyes I saw monstrous white faces suspended from the ceiling, leering at me.

From that time on, the charm of my cinder yard was gone. The green trees, the trimmed hedges, the cropped lawns grew very meaningful, became a symbol. Even today when I think of white folks, the hard, sharp outlines of white houses surrounded by trees, lawns, and hedges are present somewhere in the background of my mind. Through the years they grew into an overreaching symbol of fear.

It was a long time before I came in close contact with white folks again. We moved from Arkansas to Mississippi. Here we had the good fortune not to live behind the railroad tracks, or close to white neighborhoods. We lived in the very heart of the local Black Belt. There were black churches and black preachers; there were black schools and black teachers; black groceries and black clerks. In fact, everything was so solidly black that for a long time I did not even think of white folks, save in remote and vague terms. But this could not last forever. As one grows older one eats more. One's clothing costs more. When I finished grammar school I had to go to work. My mother could no longer feed and clothe me on her cooking job.

There is but one place where a black boy who knows no trade can get a job, and that's where the houses and faces are white, where the trees, lawns, and hedges are green. My first job was with an optical company in Jackson, Mississippi. The morning I applied I stood straight and neat before the boss, answering all his questions with sharp yessirs and nosirs. I was very careful to pronounce my *sirs* distinctly, in order that he might know that I was polite, that I knew where I was, and that I knew he was a *white* man. I wanted that job badly.

He looked me over as though he were examining a prize poodle. He questioned me closely about my schooling, being particularly insistent about how much mathematics I had had. He seemed very pleased when I told him I had had two years of algebra.

"Boy, how would you like to try to learn something around here?" he asked me.

"I'd like it fine, sir," I said, happy. I had visions of "working my way up." Even Negroes have those visions.

"All right," he said. "Come on."

I followed him to the small factory.

"Pease," he said to a white man of about thirty-five, "this is Richard. He's going to work for us."

Pease looked at me and nodded.

I was then taken to a white boy of about seventeen.

"Morrie, this is Richard, who's going to work for us."

"Whut yuh sayin' there, boy!" Morrie boomed at me.

"Fine!" I answered.

The boss instructed these two to help me, teach me, give me jobs to do, and let me learn what I could in my spare time.

My wages were five dollars a week.

I worked hard, trying to please. For the first month I got along O. K. Both Pease and Morrie seemed to like me. But one thing was missing. And I kept thinking about it. I was not learning anything and nobody was volunteering to help me. Thinking they had forgotten that I was to learn something about the mechanics of grinding lenses, I asked Morrie one day to tell me about the work. He grew red.

"Whut yuh tryin' t' do, nigger, get smart?" he asked.

"Naw; I ain' tryin' t' git smart," I said.

"Well, don't, if yuh know whut's good for yuh!"

I was puzzled. Maybe he just doesn't want to help me, I thought. I went to Pease.

"Say, are yuh crazy, you black bastard?" Pease asked me, his gray eyes growing hard.

I spoke out, reminding him that the boss had said I was to be given a chance to learn something.

"Nigger, you think you're *white*, don't you?"

"Naw, sir!"

"Well, you're acting mighty like it!"

"But, Mr. Pease, the boss said. . . ."

Pease shook his fist in my face.

"This is a *white* man's work around here, and you better watch yourself!"

From then on they changed toward me. They said good-morning no more. When I was just a bit slow in performing some duty, I was called a lazy black son-of-a-bitch.

Once I thought of reporting all this to the boss. But the mere idea of what would happen to me if Pease and Morrie should learn that I had "snitched" stopped me. And after all the boss was a white man, too. What was the use?

The climax came at noon one summer day. Pease called me to his work-bench. To get to him I had to go between two narrow benches and stand with my back against a wall.

"Yes, sir," I said.

"Richard, I want to ask you something," Pease began pleasantly, not looking up from his work.

"Yes, sir," I said again.

Morrie came over, blocking the narrow passage between the benches. He folded his arms, staring at me solemnly.

I looked from one to the other, sensing that something was coming.

"Yes, sir," I said for the third time.

Pease looked up and spoke very slowly.

"Richard, *Mr.* Morrie here tells me you called me *Pease.*"

I stiffened. A void seemed to open up in me. I knew this was the show-down.

He meant that I had failed to call him Mr. Pease. I looked at Morrie. He was gripping a steel bar in his hands. I opened my mouth to speak, to protest, to assure Pease that I had never called him simply *Pease,* and that I had never had any intentions of doing so, when Morrie grabbed me by the collar, ramming my head against the wall.

"Now, be careful, nigger!" snarled Morrie, baring his teeth. "*I* heard yuh call 'im *Pease!* 'N' if yuh say yuh didn't, yuh're callin' me a *lie,* see?" He waved the steel bar threateningly.

If I had said: No, sir Mr. Pease, I never called you *Pease,* I would have been automatically calling Morrie a liar. And if I had said: Yes, sir, Mr. Pease, I called you *Pease,* I would have been pleading guilty to having uttered the worst insult that a Negro can utter to a southern white man. I stood hesitating, trying to frame a neutral reply.

"Richard, I asked you a question!" said Pease. Anger was creeping into his voice.

"I don't remember calling you *Pease,* Mr. Pease," I said cautiously. "And if I did, I sure didn't mean. . . ."

"You black son-of-a-bitch! You called me *Pease,* then!" he spat, slapping me till I bent sideways over a bench. Morrie was on top of me, demanding:

"Didn't yuh call 'im *Pease?* If yuh say yuh didn't, I'll rip yo' gut string loose with this bar, yuh black granny dodger! Yuh can't call a white man a lie 'n' git erway with it, you black son-of-a-bitch!"

I wilted. I begged them not to bother me. I knew what they wanted. They wanted me to leave.

"I'll leave," I promised. "I'll leave right *now.*"

They gave me a minute to get out of the factory. I was warned not to show up again, or tell the boss.

I went.

When I told the folks at home what had happened, they called me a fool. They told me that I must never again attempt to exceed my boundaries. When you are working for white folks, they said, you got to "stay in your place" if you want to keep working.

## II

My Jim Crow education continued on my next job, which was portering in a clothing store. One morning, while polishing brass out front, the boss and his twenty-year-old son got out of their car and half dragged and half kicked a Negro woman into the store. A policeman standing at the corner looked on, twirling his night-stick. I watched out of the corner of my eye, never slackening the strokes of my chamois upon the brass. After a few minutes, I heard shrill screams coming from the rear of the store. Later the woman stumbled out, bleeding, crying, and holding her stomach. When she reached the end of the block, the policeman grabbed her and accused her of being drunk. Silently, I watched him throw her into a patrol wagon.

When I went to the rear of the store, the boss and his son were washing their hands at the sink. They were chuckling. The floor was bloody and strewn with wisps of hair and clothing. No doubt I must have appeared pretty shocked, for the boss slapped me reassuringly on the back.

"Boy, that's what we do to niggers when they don't want to pay their bills," he said, laughing.

His son looked at me and grinned.

"Here, hava cigarette," he said.

Not knowing what to do, I took it. He lit his and held the match for me. This was a gesture of kindness, indicating that even if they had beaten the poor old woman, they would not beat me if I knew enough to keep my mouth shut.

"Yes, sir," I said, and asked no questions.

After they had gone, I sat on the edge of a packing box and stared at the bloody floor till the cigarette went out.

That day at noon, while eating in a hamburger joint, I told my fellow Negro porters what had happened. No one seemed surprised. One fellow, after swallowing a huge bite, turned to me and asked:

"Huh! Is tha' all they did t' her?"

"Yeah. Wasn't tha' enough?" I asked.

"Shucks! Man, she's a lucky bitch!" he said, burying his lips deep into a juicy hamburger. "Hell, it's a wonder they didn't lay her when they got through."

## III

I was learning fast, but not quite fast enough. One day, while I was delivering packages in the suburbs, my bicycle tire was punctured. I walked along the hot, dusty road, sweating and leading my bicycle by the handle-bars.

A car slowed at my side.

"What's the matter, boy?" a white man called.

I told him my bicycle was broken and I was walking back to town.

"That's too bad," he said, "Hop on the running board."

He stopped the car. I clutched hard at my bicycle with one hand and clung to the side of the car with the other.

"All set?"

"Yes, sir," I answered. The car started.

It was full of young white men. They were drinking. I watched the flask pass from mouth to mouth.

"Wanna drink, boy?" one asked.

I laughed as the wind whipped my face. Instinctively obeying the freshly planted precepts of my mother, I said:

"Oh, no!"

The words were hardly out of my mouth before I felt something hard and cold smash me between the eyes. It was an empty whisky bottle. I saw stars, and fell backwards from the speeding car into the dust of the road, my feet becoming entangled in the steel spokes of my bicycle. The white men piled out and stood over me.

"Nigger, ain' yuh learned no better sense'n tha' yet?" asked the man who hit me. "Ain't yuh learned t' say *sir* t' a white man yet?"

Dazed, I pulled to my feet. My elbows and legs were bleeding. Fists doubled, the white man advanced, kicking my bicycle out of the way.

"Aw, leave the bastard alone. He's got enough," said one.

They stood looking at me. I rubbed my shins, trying to stop the flow of blood. No doubt they felt a sort of contemptuous pity, for one asked:

"Yuh wanna ride t' town now, nigger? Yuh reckon yuh know enough t' ride now?"

"I wanna walk," I said, simply.

Maybe it sounded funny. They laughed.

"Well, walk, yuh black son-of-a-bitch!"

When they left they comforted me with:

"Nigger, yuh sho better be damn glad it wuz us yuh talked t' tha' way. Yuh're a lucky bastard, 'cause if yuh'd said tha' t' somebody else, yuh might've been a dead nigger now."

## ◼◉ IV

Negroes who have lived South know the dread of being caught alone upon the streets in white neighborhoods after the sun has set. In such a simple situation as this the plight of the Negro in America is graphically symbolized. While white strangers may be in these neighborhoods trying to get home, they can pass unmolested. But the color of a Negro's skin makes him easily recognizable, makes him suspect, converts him into a defenseless target.

Late one Saturday night I made some deliveries in a white neighborhood. I was pedaling my bicycle back to the store as fast as I could, when a police car, swerving toward me, jammed me into the curbing.

"Get down and put up your hands!" the policemen ordered.

I did. They climbed out of the car, guns drawn, faces set, and advanced slowly.

"Keep still!" they ordered.

I reached my hands higher. They searched my pockets and packages. They seemed dissatisfied when they could find nothing incriminating. Finally, one of them said:

"Boy, tell your boss not to send you out in white neighborhoods after sundown."

As usual, I said:

"Yes, sir."

## V

My next job was a hall-boy in a hotel. Here my Jim Crow education broadened and deepened. When the bell-boys were busy, I was often called to assist them. As many of the rooms in the hotel were occupied by prostitutes, I was constantly called to carry them liquor and cigarettes. These women were nude most of the time. They did not bother about clothing, even for bell-boys. When you went into their rooms, you were supposed to take their nakedness for granted, as though it startled you no more than a blue vase or a red rug. Your presence awoke in them no sense of shame, for you were not regarded as human. If they were alone, you cold steal sidelong glimpses at them. But if they were receiving men, not a flicker of your eyelids could show. I remember one incident vividly. A new woman, a huge, snowy-skinned blonde, took a room on my floor. I was sent to wait upon her. She was in bed with a thick-set man; both were nude and uncovered. She said she wanted some liquor and slid out of bed and waddled across the floor to get her money from a dresser drawer. I watched her.

"Nigger, what in hell you looking at?" the white man asked me, raising himself upon his elbows.

"Nothing," I answered, looking miles deep into the blank wall of the room.

"Keep your eyes where they belong, if you want to be healthy!" he said.

"Yes, sir."

## VI

One of the bell-boys I knew in this hotel was keeping steady company with one of the Negro maids. Out of a clear sky the police descended upon his home and arrested him, accusing him of bastardy. The poor boy swore he had had no intimate relations with the girl. Nevertheless, they forced him to marry her. When the child arrived, it was found to be much lighter in complexion than either of the two supposedly legal parents. The white men around the hotel made a great joke of it. They spread the rumor that some white cow must have scared the poor girl while she was carrying the baby. If you were in their presence when this explanation was offered, you were supposed to laugh.

## VII

One of the bell-boys was caught in bed with a white prostitute. He was castrated and run out of town. Immediately after this all the bell-boys and hall-boys were called together and warned. We were given to understand that the boy who had been castrated was a "mighty, mighty lucky bastard." We were impressed with the fact that next time the management of the hotel would not be responsible for the lives of "trouble-makin' niggers." We were silent.

## VIII

One night, just as I was about to go home, I met one of the Negro maids. She lived in my direction, and we fell in to walk part of the way home together. As we passed the white night-watchman, he slapped the maid on her buttock. I turned around, amazed. The watchman looked at me with a long, hard, fixed-under stare. Suddenly he pulled his gun and asked:

"Nigger, don't yuh like it?"

I hesitated.

"I asked yuh don't yuh like it?" he asked again, stepping forward.

"Yes, sir," I mumbled.

"Talk like it, then!"

"Oh, yes sir!" I said with as much heartiness as I could muster.

Outside, I walked ahead of the girl, ashamed to face her. She caught up with me and said:

"Don't be a fool! Yuh couldn't help it!"

This watchman boasted of having killed two Negroes in self-defense.

Yet, in spite of all this, the life of the hotel ran with an amazing smoothness. It would have been impossible for a stranger to detect anything. The maids, the hall-boys, and the bell-boys were all smiles. They had to be.

## IX

I had learned my Jim Crow lessons so thoroughly that I kept the hotel job till I left Jackson for Memphis. It so happened that while in Memphis I applied for a job at a branch of the optical company. I was hired. And for some reason, as long as I worked there, they never brought my past against me.

Here my Jim Crow education assumed quite a different form. It was no longer brutally cruel, but subtly cruel. Here I learned to lie, to steal, to dissemble. I learned to play that dual role which every Negro must play if he wants to eat and live.

For example, it was almost impossible to get a book to read. It was assumed that after a Negro had imbibed what scanty schooling the state furnished he had no further need for books. I was always borrowing books from men on the job. One day I mustered enough courage to ask one of the men to let me get books from the library in his name. Surprisingly, he consented. I cannot help but think that he consented because he was a Roman Catholic and felt a vague sympathy for Negroes, being himself an object of hatred. Armed with a library card, I obtained books in the following manner: I would write a note to the librarian, saying: "Please let this nigger boy have the following books." I would then sign it with the white man's name.

When I went to the library, I would stand at the desk, hat in hand, looking as unbookish as possible. When I received the books desired I would take them home. If the books listed in the note happened to be out, I would sneak into the lobby and forge a new one. I never took any chances guessing with the white librarian about what the fictitious white man would want to read. No doubt if any of the white patrons had suspected that some of the volumes they enjoyed had been in the home of a Negro, they would not have tolerated it for an instant.

The factory force of the optical company in Memphis was much larger than that in Jackson, and more urbanized. At least they liked to talk, and would engage the Negro help in conversation whenever possible. By this means I found that many subjects were taboo from the white man's point of view. Among the topics they did not like to discuss with Negroes were the following: American white women; the Ku Klux Klan; France, and how Negro soldiers fared while there; French women; Jack Johnson; the entire northern part of the United States; the Civil War; Abraham Lincoln; U.S. Grant; General Sherman; Catholics; the Pope; Jews; the Republican Party; slavery; social equality; Communism; Socialism; the 13th and 14th Amendments to the Constitution; or any topic calling for positive knowledge or manly self-assertion on the part of the Negro. The most accepted topics were sex and religion.

There were many times when I had to exercise a great deal of ingenuity to keep out of trouble. It is a southern custom that all men must take off their hats when they enter an elevator. And especially did this apply to us blacks with rigid force. One day I stepped into an elevator with my arms full of packages. I was forced to ride with my hat on. Two white men stared at me coldly. Then one of them very kindly lifted my hat and placed it upon my armful of packages. Now the most accepted response for a Negro to make under such circumstances is to look at the white man out of the corner of his eye and grin. To have said: "Thank you!" would have made the white man *think* that you *thought* you were receiving from him a personal service. For such an act I have seen Negroes take a blow in the mouth. Finding the first alternative distasteful, and the second dangerous, I hit upon an acceptable course of action which fell safely between these two poles. I immediately—no sooner than my hat was lifted—pretended that my packages were about to spill, and appeared deeply distressed with keeping them in my arms. In this fashion I evaded having to acknowledge his service, and, in spite of adverse circumstances, salvaged a slender shred of personal pride.

How do Negroes feel about the way they have to live? How do they discuss it when alone amongst themselves? I think this question can be answered in a single sentence. A friend of mine who ran an elevator once told me:

"Lawd, man! Ef it wuzn't fer them polices 'n' them ol' lynch-mobs, there wouldn't be nothin' but uproar down here!"

# Two Brothers: Two Filipino American Perspectives

*James Sobredo*

As a Filipino American in the 1980s and 1990s, I shall always remember Reaganomics and the "Decade of Greed." Under the Reagan administration, I saw financial aid programs and scholarships for racial and ethnic minority groups dwindle and in some cases disappear all together. I did not approve of Reagan's policies, so through it all, I was always attending demonstrations against the Reagan-Bush policies. In the 1990s, my political activism continued: I was protesting with thousands of people in San Francisco against American military actions in the Persian Gulf War.

The màjority of my undergraduate Filipino friends were not like me. They were more conservative, and after college they became successful engineers, accountants, and health professionals. My Filipino friends had a fairly smooth and successful transition to the privileged professional, middle class, and they fit the media's image of Asians as "model minorities"—that is, people who worked hard, sacrificed, and, in spite of a history of racial discrimination, persevered and succeeded. Upon examination, I too seem to fit this model minority category: my family came to America as poor immigrants from the Philippines and eventually worked their way into the middle class. My father worked as a mechanic for the Navy, my mother a middle school teacher. Their son went on to attend one of the top doctoral programs in the country and received a prestigious fellowship.

Filipino Americans like me and the rest of my college-educated Filipino friends receive all the media's attention. We are the stuff that myths, like the model minority construction, are made of.

Before coming to Berkeley I was attending an Ivy league university. My younger brother Johann was pumping gas at a gas station, which caused for me, to put it mildly, a bit of "psychic disequilibrium." Johann would be dodging the local police who had a warrant out for his arrest for having outstanding tickets for

From *Seven Card Stud with Seven Manangs Wild*, edited by Helen C. Toribio, East Bay Filipino American National Historical Society, 2002. Reprinted by permission of the author.

illegal drag-strip racing. He was the undefeated local drag-strip champion in the quarter-mile. Johann hung out with 15 other teenagers, his buddies (his *barkada*), who formed an informal racing group called the "Eliminators." Outsiders, the media, for example, who didn't know any better, would call the Eliminators a "gang." And it's true that individual members of the Eliminators sold drugs, got involved in fights, and some were even involved in "drive-by" shootings. The crucial term here is "individual members" for they never did any of these acts as a group. In a word, they were not really a gang for they did not defend turf; they did not extort money; they had no formal initiation rites; and they had no formal gang leader who issued orders—although my brother was a sort of informal leader of the group. Fortunately, my brother never dealt drugs, never started fights or shot anyone. The Eliminators were simply a bunch of restless young men who hung out together and didn't know what they wanted in life.

The reality of the matter is, although we both came from the same family, my brother's experience in our family differs greatly from mine. I was born in the Philippines, and when my family came to America, we were very poor. So I understood how difficult life was, and consequently worked very hard to make sure that I don't stay poor and non-privileged for the rest of my life.

My younger brother, on the other hand, never experienced hardship while he was growing up, and by the time he was a senior in high school, he had his own new car complements of my parents. Then, the following year Reagan's decade of greed began. My mother went on strike, and, like the striking airport traffic controllers, whom Reagan fired, she too was fired from her job. At the same time, my father had a stroke and had to quit his job. Hence, during the decade of greed in which the rich got richer, my family dropped out of their middle-class status.

Disillusionment quickly got the better of my brother when he realized that there would be no money for him to attend college and his period of restless searching started. I taught Asian American studies at U. C. Berkeley, and I listened to lots of Filipinos talk about their experiences and also those of their friends. Their stories were similar to my Johann's. Like many young Filipinos who have no direction and consequently no hope for the future, Johann turned to hanging out with his *barkada* who were just as lost as he was.* Unfortunately, as a result of this hanging out with friends, a lot of Filipinos get into trouble, for example, with gangs, the police, drugs, and alcohol.

My brother was one of the lucky ones. On his own volition, he left the Eliminators and now works as a supervisor for Northwest Cargo. He still hasn't figured out what exactly he wants to do with his life, but at least he's planning on returning to college and getting a degree.

Thus, while the education route worked for me because my family could afford to send me to college, in the Reaganomics of the 1980s, however, it was not an option that was available to my brother. Striking workers are fired from their jobs, and scholarship funds and programs were eliminated. My brother's experience shows the reality behind the myth of the "model minority."

**Postscript:** Johann is currently a successful manager of an international air-freight company. He and his wife, Wendy, and their daughter, Angelina, live in Saipan.

---

*barkada,* a social group of close friends, gang.

*N.b. there is no comma after "Filipinos," so this is a restrictive clause, which means I am talking about Filipinos "who have no direction". This is not to say that all Filipino youth have no direction, or that they all get into trouble.

# How White People Became White

## James R. Barrett and David Roediger

> By the eastern European immigration the labor force has been cleft horizontally
> into two great divisions. The upper stratum includes what is known in mill par-
> lance as the English-speaking men; the lower contains the "Hunkies" or "Gin-
> nies." Or, if you prefer, the former are the "white men," the latter the "foreigners."
>
> *John Fitch,* The Steel Workers

In 1980, Joseph Loguidice, an elderly Italian-American from Chicago, sat
down to give his life story to an interviewer. His first and most vivid childhood recollection was of a race riot that had occurred on the city's near north side. Wagons
full of policemen with "peculiar hats" streamed into his neighborhood. But the
"one thing that stood out in my mind," Loguidice remembered after six decades,
was "a man running down the middle of the street hollering . . . 'I'm White, I'm
White!' " After first taking him for an African-American, Loguidice soon realized
that the man was a white coal handler covered in dust. He was screaming for his
life, fearing that "people would shoot him down." He had, Loguidice concluded,
"got caught up in . . . this racial thing."[1]

Joseph Loguidice's tale might be taken as a metaphor for the situation of millions
of "new immigrants" from Eastern and Southern Europe who arrived in the United
States between the end of the nineteenth century and the early 1920s. That this
episode made such a profound impression is in itself significant, suggesting both that
this was a strange, new situation and that thinking about race became an important
part of the consciousness of immigrants like Loguidice. How did this racial awareness and increasingly racialized worldview develop among new immigrant workers?
Most did not arrive with conventional U.S. attitudes regarding "racial" difference, let
alone its significance and implications in industrial America. Yet most, it seems, "got
caught up in . . . this racial thing." How did this happen? If race was indeed socially
constructed, then what was the raw material that went into the process?

How did these immigrant workers come to be viewed in racial terms by others—
employers, the state, reformers, and other workers? Like the coal handler in Loguidice's

*How White People Became White* by James Barrett and David Roediger. Reprinted by permission of
the authors.

story, their own ascribed racial identity was not always clear. A whole range of evidence—laws, court cases, formal racial ideology, social conventions, and popular culture in the form of slang, songs, films, cartoons, ethnic jokes, and popular theatre—suggests that the native born and older immigrants often placed the new immigrants not only *above* African- and Asian-Americans, for example, but also *below* "white" people. Indeed, many of the older immigrants, and particularly the Irish, had themselves been perceived as "nonwhite" just a generation earlier. As labor historians, we are interested in the ways in which Polish, Italian, and other European artisans and peasants became American workers, but we are equally concerned with the process by which they became "white." Indeed, in the U.S. the two identities merged, and this explains a great deal of the persistent divisions within the working-class population. How did immigrant workers wind up "inbetween"? . . .

We make no brief for the consistency with which "race" was used, by experts or popularly, to describe the "new immigrant" Southern and East Europeans who dominated the ranks of those coming to the U.S. between 1895 and 1924 and who "remade" the American working class in that period. We regard such inconsistency as important evidence of the "inbetween"[2] racial status of such immigrants. The story of Americanization is vital and compelling, but it took place in a nation also obsessed by race. For new immigrant workers the processes of "becoming white" and "becoming American" were connected at every turn. The "American standard of living," which labor organizers alternately and simultaneously accused new immigrants of undermining and encouraged them to defend via class organization, rested on "white men's wages." Political debate turned on whether new immigrants were fit to join the American nation and "American race." Nor do we argue that new immigrants from Eastern and Southern Europe were in the same situation as non-whites. Stark differences between the racialized status of African-Americans and the racial inbetween-ness of new immigrants meant that the latter *eventually* "became ethnic" and that their trajectory was predictable. But their history was sloppier than their trajectory. From day to day they were, to borrow from E. P. Thompson, "proto-nothing," reacting and acting in a highly racialized nation.[3]

America's racial vocabulary had no agency of its own, but rather reflected material conditions and power relations—the situations that workers faced on a daily basis in their workplaces and communities. Yet the words themselves were important. They were not only the means by which native born and elite people marked new immigrants as inferiors, but also those by which immigrant workers came to locate themselves and those about them in the nation's racial hierarchy. In beginning to analyze the vocabulary of race, it makes little sense for historians to invest the words themselves with an agency that could be exercised only by real historical actors, or meanings that derived only from the particular historical contexts in which the language was developed and employed.

The word *guinea,* for example, had long referred to African slaves, particularly those from the continent's northwest coast, and to their descendants. But from the late 1890s, the term was increasingly applied to southern European migrants, first

and especially to Sicilians and southern Italians, who often came as contract laborers. At various times and places in the United States, *guinea* has been applied to
mark Greeks, Jews, Portuguese, Puerto Ricans, and perhaps any new immigrant.[4]

Likewise, *hunky,* which began life, probably in the early twentieth century, as
a corruption of "Hungarian," eventually became a pan-Slavic slur connected with
perceived immigrant racial characteristics. By World War I the term was frequently
used to describe any immigrant steelworker, as in *mill hunky.* Opponents of the
Great 1919 Steel Strike, including some native born skilled workers, derided the
struggle as a "hunky strike." Yet Josef Barton's work suggests that for Poles,
Croats, Slovenians, and other immigrants who often worked together in difficult,
dangerous situations, the term embraced a remarkable, if fragile, sense of prideful
identity across ethnic lines. In *Out of This Furnace,* his epic novel of 1941 based
on the lives of Slavic steelworkers, Thomas Bell observed that the word *hunky* be-
spoke "unconcealed racial prejudice" and a "denial of social and racial equality."
Yet as these workers built the industrial unions of the late 1930s and took greater
control over their own lives, the meaning of the term began to change. The pride
with which second- and third-generation Slavic-American steelworkers, women as
well as men, wore the label in the early 1970s seemed to have far more to do with
class than with ethnic identity. At about the same time, the word *honky,* possibly a
corruption of *hunky,* came into common use as black nationalism reemerged as a
major ideological force in the African-American community.[5]

Words and phrases employed by social scientists to capture the inbetween identity of the new immigrants are a bit more descriptive, if more cumbersome. As late
as 1937, John Dollard wrote repeatedly of the immigrant working class as "our
temporary Negroes." More precise, if less dramatic, is the designation "not-yet-
white ethnics" offered by immigration historian John Bukowczyk. The term not
only reflects the popular perceptions and everyday experiences of such workers,
but also conveys the dynamic quality of racial formation.[6]

The examples of Greeks and Italians particularly underscore the new immigrants' ambiguous positions with regard to popular perceptions of race. When
Greeks suffered as victims of an Omaha race riot in 1909 and when eleven Italians
died at the hands of lynchers in Louisiana in 1891, their less-than-white racial status mattered alongside their nationalities. Indeed, as Loguidice's coal handler
shows, their ambivalent racial status put their lives in jeopardy. According to Gunther Peck's fine study of copper miners in Bingham, Utah, the Greek and Italian
immigrants were "non-white" before their tension-fraught cooperation with the
Western Federation of Miners during a 1912 strike ensured that "the category of
Caucasian worker changed and expanded." Indeed, the work of Dan Georgakas and
Yvette Huginnie shows that Greeks and other Southern Europeans often
"bivouacked" with other "nonwhite" workers in Western mining towns. Pocatello,
Idaho, Jim-Crowed Greeks in the early twentieth century and in Arizona they were
not welcomed by white workers in "white men's towns" or "white men's jobs." In
Chicago during the Great Depression, a German-American wife expressed regret

over marrying her "half-nigger," Greek-American husband. African-American slang in the 1920s in South Carolina counted those of mixed American Indian, African-American, and white heritage as *Greeks*. Greek-Americans in the Midwest showed great anxieties about race, and were perceived not only as Puerto Rican, mulatto, Mexican, or Arab, but also as non-white *because of* being Greek.[7]

Italians, involved in a spectacular international diaspora in the early twentieth century, were racialized as the "Chinese of Europe" in many lands.[8] But in the U.S. their racialization was pronounced and, as *guinea's* evolution suggests, more likely to connect Italians with Africans. During the debate at the Louisiana state constitutional convention of 1898 over how to disfranchise blacks, and over which whites might lose the vote, some acknowledged that the Italian's skin "happens to be white" even as they argued for his disfranchisement. But others held that "according to the spirit of our meaning when we speak of 'white man's government,' [the Italians] are as black as the blackest negro in existence."[9] More than metaphor intruded on this judgment. At the turn of the century, a West Coast construction boss was asked, "You don't call the Italian a white man?" The negative reply assured the questioner that the Italian was "a dago." Recent studies of Italian- and Greek-Americans make a strong case that racial, not just ethnic, oppression long plagued "non-white" immigrants from Southern Europe.[10]

The racialization of East Europeans was likewise striking. While racist jokes mocked the black servant who thought her child, fathered by a Chinese man, would be a Jew, racist folklore held that Jews, inside-out, were "niggers." In 1926 Serbo-Croatians ranked near the bottom of a list of forty "ethnic" groups whom "white American" respondents were asked to order according to the respondents' willingness to associate with members of each group. They placed just above Negroes, Filipinos, and Japanese. Just above them were Poles, who were near the middle of the list. One sociologist has recently written that "a good many groups on this color continuum [were] not considered white by a large number of Americans."[11] The literal inbetween-ness of new immigrants on such a list suggests what popular speech affirms: The state of whiteness was approached gradually and controversially. The authority of the state itself both smoothed and complicated that approach.

# Notes

[1]The epigraph is from John A. Fitch, *The Steel Workers* (New York, 1910), 147. Joe Sauris, Interview with Joseph Loguidice, July 25, 1980, Italians in Chicago Project, copy of transcript, Box 6, Immigration History Research Center, University of Minnesota, St. Paul, Minn.

[2]We borrow "inbetween" from Robert Orsi, "The Religious Boundaries of an Inbetween People: Street Feste and the Problem of the Dark-Skinned 'Other' in Italian Harlem, 1920–1990," *American Quarterly*, 44 (September 1992): passim, and also from John Higham, *Strangers in the Land: Patterns of American Nativism, 1860–1925* (New York, 1974), 169.

[3]Lawrence Glickman, "Inventing the 'American Standard of Living': Gender, Race and Working-Class Identity, 1880–1925," *Labor History*, 34 (Spring–Summer, 1993): 221–35; David

Montgomery, *Beyond Equality: Labor and the Radical Republicans, 1862–1872* (Urbana, Ill., 1981), 254.

[4]On *guinea*'s history, see David Roediger, "Guineas, Wiggers and the Dramas of Racialized Culture," *American Literary History,* 7 (1995): 654. On post-1890 usages, see William Harlen Gilbert, Jr., "Memorandum Concerning the Characteristics of the Larger Mixed-Blood Islands of the United States," *Social Forces,* 24 (March 1946): 442; *Oxford English Dictionary,* 2d ed. (Oxford, 1989), 6:937–38; Frederic G. Cassidy and Joan Houston Hall, eds., *Dictionary of American Regional English* (Cambridge and London, 1991), 2: 838.

[5]Tamony's notes on *hunky* (or *hunkie*) speculate on links to *honky* (or *honkie*) and refer to the former as an "old labour term." By no means did *Hun* refer unambiguously to Germans before World War I. See, e.g., Henry White, "Immigration Restriction as a Necessity," *American Federationist,* 4 (June 1897): 67; Paul Krause, *The Battle for Homestead, 1880–1892: Politics, Culture and Steel* (Pittsburgh, 1992), 216–17; David Brody, *Steelworkers in America* (New York, 1969), 120–21. See also the *Mill Hunky Herald,* published in Pittsburgh throughout the late 1970s.

[6]Dollard, *Caste and Class in a Southern Town,* 2d ed. (Garden City, N.Y., 1949), 93; Barry Goldberg, "Historical Reflections on Transnationalism, Race, and the American Immigrant Saga" (unpublished paper delivered at the Rethinking Migration, Race, Ethnicity, and Nationalism in Historical Perspective Conferences, New York Academy of the Sciences, May, 1990).

[7]Albert S. Broussard, "George Albert Flippin and Race Relations in a Western Rural Community," *The Midwest Review,* 12 (1990): 15, n. 42; J. Alexander Karlin, "The Italo-American Incident of 1891 and the Road to Reunion," *Journal of Southern History,* 8 (1942); Gunther Peck, "Padrones and Protest: 'Old' Radicals and 'New' Immigrants in Bingham, Utah, 1905–1912," *Western Historical Quarterly,* (May 1993): 177; Dan Georgakas, *Greek America at Work* (New York, 1992), 12 and 16–17; Yvette Huginnie, *Strikitos: Race, Class, and Work in the Arizona Copper Industry, 1870–1920,* Thesis (Ph.D.) Yale University, 1991.

[8]Donna Gabaccia. "The 'Yellow Peril' and the 'Chinese of Europe': Italian and Chinese Labourers in an International Labour Market" (unpublished paper, University of North Carolina at Charlotte, c. 1993).

[9]George E. Cunningham. "The Italian: A Hindrance to White Solidarity in Louisiana, 1890–1898," *Journal of Negro History,* 50 (January 1965): 34, includes the quotes.

[10]Higham, *Strangers in the Land,* 66; Gary R. Mormino and George E. Pozzetta, *The Immigrant World of Ybor City: Italians and Their Latin Neighbors in Tampa, 1885–1985* (Urbana, Ill., 1987), 241; Micaela DiLeonardo, *The Varieties of Ethnic Experience* (Ithaca, N.Y., 1984), 24, n. 16; Georgakas, *Greek America at Work,* 16. See also Karen Brodkin Sacks' superb "How Did Jews Become White Folks?" in Steven Gregory and Roger Sanjek, eds., *Race* (New Brunswick, N.J., 1994).

[11]Quoted in Brody, *Steelworkers,* 120; W. Lloyd Warner and J. O. Low, *The Social System of the Modern Factory. The Strike: A Social Analysis* (New Haven, 1947), 140; Gershon Legman, *The Horn Book* (New York, 1964), 486–87; *Anecdotal Americana: Five Hundred Stories for the Amusement of Five Hundred Nations That Comprise America* (New York, 1933), 98.

# Life on the Color Line: The True Story of a White Boy Who Discovered He Was Black

*Gregory Howard Williams*

That first Friday, Uncle Jim picked me up at lunchtime. We stopped at every small-town diner between Muncie and Albany dumping rotten meat, fruit, potato rinds, and all types of stinking garbage into large oil drums lashed on the back of his truck. I tried to brace the cans as we raced over the country roads. It all went smoothly until Uncle Jim plunged pell-mell down a dip, sending me a foot in the air. I managed to keep the drums in place, but was drenched with slimy garbage.

Uncle Jim had an extra work shirt in the cab, but by late afternoon when we arrived at a small-town café, I was reeking of garbage. While I wrestled a can to the alley, a middle-aged white man appeared at the rear door. From his long, casual chat with Uncle Jim I guessed he was the owner. My body tensed when I heard the man ask: "Who's that white boy?"

Uncle Jim said I was his nephew.

"He's the whitest colored boy I ever seen. Are you sure he wasn't just caught in the wrong net?" The owner chuckled.

I wanted to smash his face with the can when I lugged it back to the diner, and caught him gaping at me. His sharply pressed long white apron reminded me of the Ku Klux Klan leader I saw on Uncle Osco's new television following the 1954 Supreme Court decision outlawing segregated schools. [*Brown v. Board of Education*, 347 U.S. 483 (1954)—Ed.] That beefy-faced, white-robed Klansman stood in front of a burning cross, railing against black and white children learning together. He claimed that the Supreme Court was encouraging "race-mixing" and the only result would be the "bestial mongrel mulatto, the dreg of human society." In the refuge of Uncle Osco's sitting room, I had laughed at the pale, jowly southerner. In a white sheet and pointed hat, he looked more like the "dreg of society" than any-body I knew. Yet his nasal repetition of "mongrel mulatto" finally hit like a thunderbolt. He was talking about me. I was the Klan's worst nightmare. I was what the violence directed against integration was all about. I was what they hated and wanted to destroy. And that was the biggest puzzle in the world to me because I had absolutely nothing.

The café owner had a different idea. He didn't want to destroy me, he wanted to exhibit me. While I lugged garbage from his rear door, he hovered there beckoning me inside. There were people he wanted me to meet, he coaxed. He tried to engage me in conversation. "Gonna be a pig farmer like your uncle?" he asked with a chuckle.

"I'm gonna be a lawyer," I quipped.

His face reddened with laughter. "You gonna have to shovel a lot of shit to make that happen. Come on, these folks really want to see you. We all wanna see Muncie's first colored lawyer. I even got a piece of pie for you."

I knew he was insulting me, but I was tempted by the pie. When I noticed Uncle Jim frowning, I mumbled "No thanks." Soon the café owner was miles behind, and I was overcome by feelings of self-pity, confusion, and anger. As Uncle Jim turned down a gravel lane, I concentrated more on keeping the garbage off me than on fantasizing about dumping it on the man who had ridiculed my dream.

As the truck slowed, a strange form sprouted on the horizon. Uncle Jim pulled to a stop, and I realized it was the unfinished foundation of a house protruding three feet above the ground. The black tar paper sides and top gave it a sinister aura. It was Uncle Jim's home.

"Boy, I'm sorry about that ol' white man," he said as we carried groceries to the house. "He don't know shit. I learned a long time ago that you just have to laugh at white folks or they'll drive you crazy. Forgit 'bout him. We gonna have us a helluva dinner."

# Anti-Essentialism and Intersectionality: Tools to Dismantle the Master's House

*Trina Grillo*

My father was born in Tampa, Florida, of Cuban Black parents. Much of his life was spent firmly claiming his place among American Blacks. My mother was the daughter of Italian immigrants. I was born in 1948 and soon thereafter moved to the San Francisco Bay Area. There were four children in my family. At times it seemed to me that we were half the biracial population of the Bay Area. We were stared at wherever we went, although it took me a while, probably until I was five, to realize that the stares were not always ones of admiration. Of course, we did not define ourselves as biracial then. Instead, we were considered, and considered ourselves, Black, or Negro as we then said. Still, our skin color and our parents' interracial marriage were always causes for comment. My race and my skin color have been issues that have preoccupied me for a good part of my life, and I see little prospect of this changing anytime soon.

When I began teaching at Hastings Law School in 1977, I knew that I wanted to write about multiraciality. I did a little research and proceeded to write— nothing. At that time there was little interest in the popular culture in that subject, and virtually nothing in the legal literature, so it is easy to see why I gave up on my project. Multiraciality did not seem to matter to anyone but me.

But now I cannot turn on *Oprah* without seeing a segment on multiraciality, right in between the shows on incest and the shows on weight loss. . . . We are everywhere, in numbers hard to ignore. But one thing has not changed. No one knows how to talk about us.

I looked at two newspapers yesterday and saw the racial descriptions of the jurors in the O. J. Simpson trial. One paper said there were "eight Blacks, one Anglo, one Hispanic and two persons of mixed race." The other paper said there were eight Blacks, two Hispanics, one Anglo, and one person who identified himself as half white and half American Indian. There were four items about each juror described in the paper: gender, age, occupation, and racial background. From a more complete description of the racial backgrounds of the jurors, I found out that one of the Hispanics was a Hispanic/Black, classified as mixed race by one paper and as Hispanic by another. Interestingly, neither paper classified this juror as Black, although that would be my "first" classification of myself.

So we have no stable conventions for describing multiracial persons, at least none that match what we perceive to be reality. . . .

[W]e must fully understand that race is not a biological concept but a social and historical construct. The reason that I grew up considering myself, as we then said, Negro, is that a racist system described me in that way. Most Blacks in the United States are persons of "mixed blood," if such a thing can be said to exist, and have both white and Black ancestors. If there were such [a] thing as a biological white, I would be at least half that, and so would many other Blacks. However, the fact that race is a historical and social construct certainly does not mean that it does not exist. Experiences, histories, and communities have all developed around this concept; so if we abandon race, we abandon communities that may have been initially formed as a result of racism but have become something else entirely.

All the scientific literature says that biological races do not exist. Instead, races were created as a mechanism for the oppression of certain groups of people. But once created, they remain. We are then left with these questions: How should we regard people of mixed race? How is it possible to take our experiences seriously without having them turned into a means of separating ourselves from other Blacks or into a means of ranking people of color, with those of mixed race given more power than other Blacks? (I should say that my focus is on mixtures that include Black, because that is the experience with which I am familiar; because the history is different, the issues are surely different for persons of mixed race who are, for example, Asian and white).

If we accept the definition of Black that we have been given—a definition that historically defined anyone with "one drop of Black blood" as Black—we ignore the existence of multiracial people. We ignore people whose experiences may be different from those experiences that have been defined as constituting the Black experience—that is, the "essentialized" Black experience. By so essentializing, we assume that the taxonomy of race proposed by nineteenth-century white supremacists—that human beings can be classified into four races and everyone fits neatly into one slot—is a valid one. On the other hand, if we do classify multiracial people as Black, the potential for group solidarity is much greater. "We are all Black," we say. "You cannot divide us."

. . . Is it possible to create a Black-identified biracial identity? Can one be biracial or multiracial and also be Black? Or is the historical freight still too great for that to be possible? One thing I am sure of: The fact that a person is biracial is an important piece of who she is. It is something I would find of interest if I were reading her work or listening to her speak. We need a way to say that, a way that does not compromise the community of Black people.

# "Melting Pot" or "Ring of Fire"?: Assimilation and the Mexican American Experience

*Kevin R. Johnson*

## I. The Myth of Spain and Assimilation Through Denial

Approaching sixty years, my mother, born Angela Gallardo, has lived a difficult life. Although nobody would or could ever fill me in on all the details, according to family lore my grandmother was born in El Paso, Texas, though instincts tell me she was born in Mexico. Her mother, my great-grandmother (Josephine Gonzales), was a Mexican citizen who lived in Mexico most of her life. My mother was born in 1938 in Brawley, California, a small agricultural town in the Imperial Valley, about an hour's drive from San Diego. About all my family told me about my mother's father, my maternal grandfather (Charles Daniel Swalez), is that he was killed in an automobile accident when my mother was a child. A sprinkling of distant family still lives in the Imperial Valley area, though my mother lost touch with them long ago, something not that uncommon for Latinos in rural communities.

My mother grew up in downtown Los Angeles. With olive-colored skin and gray hair that once was black (she always emphasized that it was "dark brown"), she stands just under five feet tall. In her younger adult years, and intermittently now, she talked incessantly. Her preferred nickname, "Angie," reflects the assimilationist tendencies she shared with my grandmother. . . .

Despite their Mexican roots, my mother and grandmother were ardently assimilationist in outlook. Marrying Anglo men was part of the grand assimilationist strategy. Another aspect of the plan was for my mother and grandmother to claim that they were not of *Mexican* but *Spanish* ancestry. Always the storyteller, one of my grandmother's favorite tales concerned her mixed Spanish-French background, with particular emphasis on the Spanish. This theme, in fact, found itself in many of her stories. My mother also claimed a "Spanish" ancestry.

Over the years, I realized this elusive Spanish heritage was very much an exaggeration. My grandmother, with her indigenous phenotype, and my mother, with her olive-colored skin, seemed no different from the other Mexican Americans in the San Gabriel Valley. My great-grandmother, who never mentioned her Spanish background in my presence, was a Mexican citizen who lived in Mexico. All of our relatives in the Imperial Valley, only a few miles from the U.S.–Mexico border, were Mexican American. "Where are all the Spaniards?" I could only wonder.

A "Spanish" heritage is not an uncommon myth and indeed is one embraced by some Latinos today. Many understand at least implicitly that being classified as Mexican is disfavored in the United States, especially in the Southwest before the development of the civil rights consciousness of the 1960s. The phenomenon of Latinos attempting to "pass" as Spanish, and therefore as White, is a variation of the "passing" of other minorities as White. To many Anglos, being "Spanish" is more European, and therefore more acceptable to Whites, than being of Latin American ancestry. My mother and grandmother knew the southern Californian world in which they lived and the racial hierarchy that existed, even if they recognized it in simple terms (i.e., that many people did not like Mexicans and that they had better convince them they were not Mexicans).

This Spanish mythology was fully consonant with my mother's assimilationist leanings. To this day, rather than pronounce her maiden name (Gallardo) in proper Spanish, which requires a special "ll" sound similar to "y," she says it as it would be said in English, as in the word "fallen." Consequently, the word "lard," and all of the images that the word connotes, sticks out right in the middle. My wife, Virginia, and I laugh about it today. But those efforts served a critical function for my mother and many others of her generation. The Anglicizing, thereby "Whitening," of their Spanish last names was an important step for a Mexican American attempting to pass as White.

In no small part because of her assimilationist nature, my mother consciously avoided teaching her children Spanish. She spoke Spanish, though losing some of it over the years. As for many in her generation, Spanish was considered an educational impediment. The theory was that we needed to master English (which would not be possible if we learned Spanish) so that we could succeed in school, a view held to this day by some Latinos. In my mother's generation, it was not unheard of for public school teachers to punish students for speaking Spanish. When I was growing up, my mother and grandmother spoke Spanish only when they wanted to have a private conversation in our presence. My mother would become irritable—rare for her—when my brother and I teased her for speaking "Mexican." "It is *Spanish*," she would emphasize. "There is no *Mexican* language."

While my mother and grandmother lived in a state of denial, the Anglo men in the family often emphasized their Mexican ancestry, though in dramatically different ways. When my grandmother talked about her Spanish background, my step-grandfather would sarcastically respond: "Get off it. You're a Mexican like the rest of them." Weakly saying that he did not know anything and laughing uncomfortably, my grandmother was visibly wounded. Similar exchanges occurred regularly. In a much more constructive way, my father would emphasize the positive side of my mother's Mexican background to me. He told me as a child that the mixture of his "Swedish" (an exaggeration) and my mother's Mexican bloodlines was good, and that I would be strong.

## II. Race, Ethnicity, and Nationhood for Latinos: Some Assimilation Lessons

Some Latinos, like my mother and grandmother, attempt to "pass" as Spanish in the United States. In the Southwest, to be stigmatized by Anglos as "Mexican" places one at a distinct disadvantage in certain circumstances. A Latino who attempts to live as Anglo suffers in other ways, however. My mother's assimilation ordeals reveal the psychological and related costs. My experiences, though far less severe, reveal the pain suffered by mixed race persons thought to be White.

In essence, the capability of "passing" is a double-edged sword. Adrian Piper eloquently captures the pain she suffered as an African American who might have been able but declined to "pass" as White.[1] Some Blacks demanded proof of her Blackness; others subjected her to White slurs. At the same time, some Whites in academia have suggested that she declared a Black identity to reap affirmative action benefits. This Catch-22 greatly affects the shaping of one's identity as well as life experiences. Over my lifetime, I have experienced both sorts of challenges to my identity. Some Latinos express curiosity about my background, where I come from, my commitment to Latino issues, and Spanish-speaking skills, probing whether I am only a "check-the-box" Latino in pursuit of the benefits of affirmative action. Whites with similar concerns scrutinize my identity as a Latino. Life under a microscope at times is disorienting, uncomfortable, and burdensome.

Piper also offers insights into another layer of complexity. She resented some family members with fair complexions who sealed themselves off from the rest of the family as part of their attempt to pass as White. Although able to achieve higher status, they left their Black family behind, with all the emotional turmoil and sadness that resulted. As has been my experience . . . , minorities who "look White" hear some horrible things about what Whites think about their kinship group. Moreover, attempts to "pass," as my mother and grandmother harshly learned, are not always successful. Not all persons recover from the pain of rejection and sting of defeat. Like Piper, I at times resent yet understand efforts to appear White (and gain its privileges) through adoption of a phantom "Spanish" identity.

# "Ain't That Love?": Antiracism and Racial Constructions of Motherhood

*Andrea O'Reilly*

Dominant ideologies and discourses of mothering and motherhood are racialized and racist; that is, they represent only one experience of mothering, that of white middle-class women, and position this experience as the real, natural and universal one. Any discussion of mothers and antiracism must, therefore, begin with an understanding of how discourses of motherhood become racially codified and constructed. This essay explores how the development and dissemination of one normative discourse of motherhood—that of so-called sensitive mothering—causes other experiences of mothering—working class, ethnic—to be marginalized and delegitimized.

Motherhood is a cultural construction that varies with time and place; there is no one essential or universal experience of motherhood. However, the diverse meanings and experiences of mothering become marginalized and erased through the construction of an official definition of motherhood. Through a complex process of intersecting forces—economics, politics, cultural institutions (what Teresa de Lauretis would call social technologies)—the dominant definition of motherhood is codified as the official and only meaning of motherhood.[1] Alternative meanings of mothering are marginalized and rendered illegitimate. The dominant definition is able to suppress its own construction as an ideology and thus naturalizes its specific construction of motherhood as the universal, real, natural maternal experience.

The dominant discourse of motherhood is, however, historically determined and thus variable. In the Victorian era, for example, the ideology of moral motherhood that saw mothers as naturally pure, pious and chaste emerged as the dominant discourse. This ideology, however, was race- and class-specific: Only white and middle-class women could wear the halo of the madonna and transform the world through their moral influence and social housekeeping. Slave mothers, in contrast, were defined as breeders, placed not on a pedestal, as white women were, but on the auction block.

After World War II, the discourse of the happy homemaker made the "stay-at-home mom and apple pie" mode of mothering the normal and natural motherhood experience. Again, only white and middle-class women could, in fact, experience what discursively was inscribed as natural and universal. In the 1970s, the era in which many baby boomers became parents, a new hegemonic discourse of motherhood began to take shape, one that authors Valerie Walkerdine and Helen Lucey appropriately term "sensitive mothering" in their landmark book *Democracy in the Kitchen: Regulating Mothers and Socializing Daughters.*

Walkerdine and Lucey examine how the maternal behavior of the middle-class became culturally constructed and codified as the real, normal and natural way to mother. Natural mothering begins with the ideological presupposition that children have needs that are met by the mother. To mother, therefore, is to be sensitive to the needs of children, that is, to engage in sensitive mothering. The first characteristic of the sensitive mother, Walkerdine and Lucey explain,

> is that her domestic life is centred around her children and not around her housework. The boundaries between this work and children's play have to be blurred . . . While the mother is being sensitive to the child's needs, she is not doing any housework. She has to be available and ready to meet demands, and those household tasks which she undertakes have to become pedagogic tasks . . . The second feature of the sensitive mother is the way she regulates her children. Essentially there should be no overt regulation; regulation should go underground; no power battles, no insensitive sanctions as these would interfere with the child's illusion that she is the source of her wishes, that she has "free will."[2]

This mode of mothering is drawn from the parenting styles of the so-called baby-boom generation. Today good mothering is defined as child-centered and is characterized by flexibility, spontaneity, democracy, affection, nurturance and playfulness. This mode of mothering is contrasted to the earlier stern, rigid, authoritative, "a child should be seen and not heard" variety of parenting. Today's ideal mother is not only expected to be "at home" with her children—as her mother was with her in the fifties—she is also required to spend, in the language of eighties' parenting books, "quality time" with her children. While the fifties mom would put her children in the pram or playpen to tend to her household chores, today's mom is to "be with" her child at all times physically and, most importantly, psychologically. Whether the activity is one of the numerous structured moms-and-tots programs—swimming, kindergym, dance—or an at-home activity—reading, gardening, cooking, playing—the mother's day is to revolve around the child, not her housework as it was in the fifties, and is to be centered upon the child's educational development. The child is to be involved in any domestic labor performed and the chore at hand is be transformed into a learning experience for the child.

Working-class mothers, Walkerdine and Lucey emphasize, do not practice so-called sensitive mothering; work does not become play nor do power and conflict go underground. Working-class mothers, in the authors' study, do play with their children but only after domestic chores have been tended to. In working-class households, the boundaries between mothering and domestic labor are maintained and the very real work of domestic labor is not transformed—or trivialized—into a game for the child's benefit. Nor does the mother abdicate her power and authority to create the illusion of a family democracy. This type of mothering, however, becomes pathologized as deficiency and deviance because the middle-class style of sensitive mothering has been codified, both socially and discursively, as natural. Working-class mothering is, thus, not simply different, it is deemed unnatural, and working-class mothers are deemed unfit mothers in need of regulation. In other words, "there is something wrong with working-class mothering which should be put right by making it more middle-class."[3]

Lucey and Walkerdine do not specifically look at African-American mothering in their book. The research that has been done on black mothering, however, does suggest that Lucey and Walkerdine's observations may be applied to black women's experiences of mothering, at least among working-class families.[4] Patricia Hill Collins, for example, argues, in her many works on black mothering, that there is a distinct African-American experience of mothering. African-American mothering, what she calls mother-work, is about "maintain[ing] family life in the face of forces that undermine family integrity" while "recognizing that individual survival, empowerment, and identity require group survival, empowerment, and identity."[5] Central concerns of "racial ethnic" (Collins's term) mothers include keeping the children born to you, the physical survival of those children, teaching the children resistance and how to survive in a racist world, giving to those children their racial/cultural history and identity, and a social activism and communal mothering on behalf of all the community's children. What the research on black mothering suggests is that sensitive mothering is not valued or practiced by African-American mothers, particularly if the family in question is urban and working-class.

In her brilliant book *Maternal Thinking*, Sara Ruddick argues that the first duty of mothers is to protect and preserve their children: "to keep safe whatever is vulnerable and valuable in a child."[6] "Preserving the lives of children," Ruddick writes, "is the central constitutive, invariant aim of maternal practice."[7] "To be committed to meeting children's demand for preservation," Ruddick continues, "does not require enthusiasm or even love; it simply means to see vulnerability and to respond to it with care rather than abuse, indifference, or flight."[8] Though maternal practice is composed of two other demands—nurturance and training—this first demand, what Ruddick calls preservative love, is what describes much of economically disadvantaged African-American women's mother-work. For many African-American women, securing food, shelter and clothing, building safe neighborhoods, and fighting a racist world is what defines both the meaning and experience of their mother-work and mother-love. However, because sensitive mothering has been naturalized as the universal normal experience of motherhood, preservative love is not regarded as real, legitimate or "good enough" mothering.

In the mothering of my children and in my teaching on motherhood, I seek to challenge the normative discourse of sensitive mothering by inscribing mothering as a culturally determined experience. I bring to this struggle the experience of being raised in a white, middle-class family by a working-class mother. The stories my mother tells me of my early childhood indicate that my mother's mode of mothering was clearly that of working-class 1950s culture. She used to "air" me on the front porch in the pram and, later, in the playpen each morning—summers and winters—as she tended to her housework and the caring of my infant sister. It was the early 1960s, and my mother had an eight-year-old daughter from her first marriage and three children under the age of three from her second marriage.

My mother grew up poor in a working-class family from, what was called in my hometown of Hamilton, Ontario, the "wrong side of the tracks." In the 1950s she found herself divorced with a young baby to raise. At twenty-eight she married my father, a man from an established middle-class family, and moved to middle-class suburbia. My mother has often told me she never really felt she was a part of the suburban culture of young motherhood—the morning coffees in each other's kitchens, afternoons in the park, recipe sharing, and the borrowing of that cup of sugar.

Having had my children in graduate school with no one to share young motherhood with, I envied my mother and could not understand why she kept herself apart from what I imagined to be a feminist utopia of female solidarity. Only recently have I been able to see my mother's experience for what it was: It was the 1950s, and she was an older divorcee with a young daughter, from a poor, working-class family, among young, newly married women from "good" middle-class families. I can only imagine the culture shock she must have experienced and speculate upon how she was received by those "good" middle-class neighbors of hers. The memories of my later childhood reveal that my mother eventually became part of that middle-class culture and practiced, at least occasionally, the so-called sensitive mothering Walkerdine and Lucey discuss.

The struggles of my mother were replayed when I became a mother thirty years later at the relatively young age of twenty-three. While my class affiliation was middle-class, my spouse was working-class; and though we were educated—both of us were pursuing graduate degrees at the time—we were also very poor. At that time, though, my energies were focused on challenging the oppressiveness of motherhood as a patriarchal institution. As a student of women's studies, my perspective was decidedly feminist, and I sought to imagine and achieve an experience of mothering that was empowering or, at the very least, not oppressive to me or my children. What I had not considered in my feminist practice of mothering was how the philosophy of so-called sensitive mothering to which I subscribed was a regulatory discourse as oppressive as the patriarchal one with which I was familiar.

I became conscious of the class and racial dimensions of discourses on mothering only upon reading *Democracy in the Kitchen* and Toni Morrison's novel *Sula* midway through my early mothering years.[9] What these readings forced me to recognize is that although so-called sensitive mothering is neither real nor universal, it results in the regulation of middle-class mothers and the pathologizing of working-class mothering.

I planned to use the novel *Sula* in my teaching as a way to talk about racist constructions of motherhood and to arrive at an antiracist perspective in the way we perceive and practice mothering. I became more and more convinced that any attempt at teaching antiracism to children and students was doomed to failure as long as our perceptions and practices of mothering were racialized and racist. How can a white middle-class woman who sees her sensitive mothering as more real—and hence superior—possibly teach antiracism to her child? In turn, how can a black mother empower her child to resist racism when that child is encouraged to see her own mother's mode of mothering as insufficient? With these questions in mind I set to work.

I presented a lecture on *Sula* at the conclusion of a first-year humanities course entitled "Concepts of the Male and Female in Western Culture" in March 1995, a class made up mostly of mature and returning students. The perspective of the course was thoroughly feminist and issues of race and racism had been discussed in the classroom. My audience was, thus, a highly informed and, for the most part, receptive one.

I spoke with much passion on how the mother's preservative love in the novel had been pathologized by the critics because it did not fit the bill of sensitive mothering. I stressed the need to deconstruct the hegemony of sensitive mothering so that other expressions of mothering are given legitimacy and validity. With this lecture I hoped to generate discussion on the ways in which black and working-class women's mothering is often delegitimized and how white middle-class women are regulated in trying to achieve this sensitive mothering. Instead, what I got was a hazy fog of incomprehension, bewilderment and indifference.

Interestingly, when I moved from the topic of mothering to other themes in *Sula*—women's friendship, growing up female—I could feel—almost see—a shift in the students' response to my lecture: Suddenly there was connection, interest and understanding. I also observed, though could not account for, a noticeable change in the emotional climate of the lecture hall. Inexplicably, during the first part of my lecture on motherhood the atmosphere was serious and noticeably tense, yet in the latter section the mood was lighthearted and relaxed. When we talked about the lecture and text later in tutorial, the students, much to my dismay, replicated the patronizing stance of the critics regarding Eva's mothering—we can't be too hard on her, it wasn't her fault, she would have done it differently had she had the choice and so on. They had missed the whole point of my lecture.

I was troubled, dismayed and perplexed by my students' misunderstanding/incomprehension; eventually though I attributed it to a weak lecture. Not until I started working on this essay did I think about the experience again and see it from a different perspective. At the same time, a Caribbean student in a course I was teaching told the class about her family experience. This student's mother, like many Caribbean women, came to Canada in the early 1970s to secure work and left her children back home with her parents in the hope of creating a better life for them. The mother sent her earnings home, visited her children on holidays, and several years later, when she had good, permanent work, had her children join her in Canada. The eldest sister had great difficulty adjusting to this change and blamed her mother for being absent all those years. Good mothers, the daughter told her mother, don't leave their children for a day, let alone for many years. Good mothers, like those of her Canadian friends, did things with their kids, were not always so tired and away so much working. What the daughter was saying is: Why can't you be more like other mothers? Why can't you be normal?

Hearing this student's story I began to make sense of my former students' reaction to my lecture. Though sensitive mothering is a recent ideological construction of motherhood—having been around only two decades—it has very successfully taken up residence in the dominant culture. (It reminds one of the aliens in *The Invasion of the Body Snatchers* who enter and take over, en masse, the human population.) Good mothers read to their children, enroll them in ballet and piano lessons, enrich them with theatre, art and culture; they are patient, nurturing, spontaneous, sensitive and—most importantly—child-centered, transforming even the most mundane task into an entertaining and educational experience for their children.

Now no mother can actually live the ideological script of sensitive mothering, though all mothers are judged by it and many mothers seek to achieve it. And most children, very much cultural creatures, interpret their own mother's mothering from the discourse of sensitive mothering. On several occasions my children have responded to my behavior or comments with the statement: Mothers don't do, or say, that. We have embraced so completely this discourse of mothering that we see it as the best, ideal, normal and, ultimately, only way to mother. Hence my students' confusion: Why would I problematize something so good, so natural? Why wouldn't I want the characters in this book to partake in such mothering, given how good it is? And why shouldn't we help others to achieve the same experience of sensitive mothering? Why not indeed?

With my own children I struggle to make conscious to them the ways in which mothering is overdetermined and regulated by cultural discourses, such as sensitive mothering. Discussions about racism and antiracism have always been part of our children's upbringing. What is more difficult to work through with our growing children is, I think, how practices of mothering are racialized and class-specific. After all, kids don't see mothering as a practice. I strive to challenge that perception in my mothering. What I seek to emphasize to my children, both in word and deed, is that my experience of mothering and their experience of being mothered are culturally determined. I want them to know that children are mothered differently and that one way is not any more real, natural or legitimate than any other way.

When my kids respond to something I have said or done with the line "Mothers don't do that" or, conversely, "All the other mothers are . . . so why can't you?" I remind them that there is no one way to mother or be mothered. As I seek to free myself from the regulation of sensitive mothering, I share with my children my critique of this discourse by giving concrete examples of how this discourse is oppressive to me—and by implication to them—and how it results in the "putting down" of other mothers.

In my critique of sensitive mothering I am not suggesting that I am against reading to your child or playing, every now and then, "let's wash the floors" to make enjoyable an otherwise tedious chore. However, what I do find deeply disturbing is the codification of this discourse as the official and only way to mother. Walkerdine and Lucey argue that sensitive mothering is ultimately bad for both mother and child: It trivializes women's domestic labor, causes the mother's workday to be never-ending and compels her to be manipulative with her children—to make them believe that her wishes are really their own—so as to avoid authoritarianism and conflict. It causes the child to confuse work with play and to see the self as completely in control of circumstances—somewhat problematic lessons, particularly for black and working-class kids in a racist and capitalist world. While I agree with Lucey and Walkerdine's observations, I am less interested in debating the pros and cons of sensitive mothering than in deconstructing any normative discourse of mothering that pathologizes difference and seeks to regulate it.

What has this to do with mothers acting against racism? My students' incomprehension at my lecture and my student's moving story have brought home to me the intricate relationship between mothering and racism; mothering and antiracism. If that mother could have told her daughter that her survivalist type of mother-love—mothering as separation—*was* an expression of mothering, as good as, if not better than, the dominant mode, perhaps there would have been less blame and more understanding between mother and daughter. With my own lecture I would have been able to talk about an antiracist perspective with respect to mothering far more effectively had the students not been so thoroughly identified with the dominant discourse of mothering.

Adrienne Rich in her ovarian work *Of Woman Born* discusses how motherhood is an institution that is defined and controlled by patriarchy. I would add that ideologies of mothering, and the institutions they create, are also thoroughly racialized and racist. I believe that the teaching and practice of antiracism through mothering can happen if, and only if, the dominant mode of mothering is identified and challenged as racist. It does not help to build an antiracist household on foundations that are racist.

# ◤ Notes

[1] Teresa de Lauretis, "The Technology of Gender," in *Technologies of Gender* (Bloomington: Indiana University Press, 1987), 1–30.

[2] Valerie Walkerdine and Helen Lucey, *Democracy in the Kitchen: Regulating Mothers and Socializing Daughters* (London: Virago Press, 1989) 20, 23–24.

[3] Ibid., taken from the back cover.

[4] See, for example: Valora Washington, "The Black Mother in the United States: History, Theory, Research, and Issues," in *The Different Faces of Motherhood*, ed. Beverly Birns and Dale F. Hay (New York: Plenum Press, 1988), 185–213; Filomina Chioma Steady, ed., *The Black Woman Cross-Culturally* (Rochester, VT: Schenkman Books, 1981); Patricia Bell-Scott et al., *Double Stitch: Black Women Write About Mothers and Daughters* (New York: HarperPerennial, 1991); Carol B. Stack, *All Our Kin: Strategies for Survival in a Black Community* (New York: Harper & Row, 1974); Patricia Hill Collins, *Black Feminist Thought: Knowledge, Consciousness and the Politics of Empowerment* (New York: Unwin Hyman, 1990); bell hooks, "Revolutionary Parenting" in *Feminist Theory: From Margin to Center* (Boston: South End Press, 1984), 133–46, and "Homeplace" in *Yearning: Race, Gender, and Cultural Politics* (Boston: South End Press, 1990), 41–49.

[5] Patricia Hill Collins, "Shifting the Center: Race, Class, and Feminist Theorizing About Motherhood" in *Mothering: Ideology, Experience, and Agency,* ed. Evelyn Nakano Glenn, Grace Chang and Linda Rennie Forcey (New York: Routledge, 1994), 47.

[6] Sara Ruddick, *Maternal Thinking: Toward a Politics of Peace* (Boston: Beacon, 1989), 80.

[7] Ibid., 19.

[8] Ibid.

[9] Toni Morrison, *Sula* (New York: New American Library, 1973). The contemporary critical responses to a dialogue in the novel brought home to me how thoroughly identified our culture is with the discourse of sensitive mothering. In this novel, Eva, the mother, is left by her husband in 1895 with "$1.65, five eggs, three beets" and three children to feed. After her baby son nearly dies from constipation Eva leaves her children in the care of a neighbor, saying she will be back the next day, only to return eighteen months later with money and one of her legs gone. It was rumored that Eva placed her leg under a train in order to collect insurance money to support her children. Years later, her now adult daughter, Hannah, asks her mother if "[She] ever love[d] us?" The mother responds: "You settin' here with your healthy-ass self and ax me did I love you? Them big old eyes in your head would a been two holes full of maggots if I hadn't." The daughter then asks: "Did you ever, you know, play with us?" Eva replies: "Play? Wasn't nobody playin' in 1895. Just 'cause you got it good now you think it was always this good? 1895 was a killer, girl. Things was bad. Niggers was dying like flies . . . Don't that count? Ain't that love? You want me to tinkle you under the jaw and forget 'bout them sores in your mouth?" (67–69). Many readers of the novel question, with Hannah, whether Eva did in fact mother her children. Her mothering has been called unnatural and untraditional. The words unnatural and untraditional, however, accrue meaning only if both the speaker (writer) and listener (reader) know what is meant by their opposites, the normative terms—in this instance, natural and traditional. When a critic, like Dayle Delancy, laments that Eva has "no time to lavish traditional displays of affection upon her children" or that "she has to work for the survival of her offspring at the expense of having fun with them" ["Motherlove Is a Killer" in *Sage* 8 (fall 1990): 15–18] she is working from a very specific discourse of what constitutes good mothering—namely that of sensitive mothering.

# Is Yellow Black or White?

*Gary Y. Okihiro*

Between 1985 and 1990 in New York City, there were three major protests against Korean storeowners in African communities, while in Los Angeles, as one boycott ended in the summer of 1991, another began, and within a six-month period, five Korean grocery stores were fire-bombed. In a Los Angeles courtroom, the television monitors showed fifteen-year-old Latasha Harlins punch Soon Ja Du and turn to leave the store, when Du lifts a gun and fires pointblank at Harlin's head, killing her. On December 15, 1991, Yong Tae Park died of bullet wounds received during a robbery on his liquor store the previous day; Park was the seventh Korean storeowner killed in Los Angeles by African male suspects that year. "Black Power. No Justice, No Peace! Boycott Korean Stores! The Battle for Brooklyn," the poster read. "Crack, the 'housing crisis,' and Korean merchants is a conspiracy to destabilizing our community. . . . The Korean merchants are agents of the U.S. government in their conspiracy to destabilize the economy of our community. They are rewarded by the government and financed by big business."[1] In south central Los Angeles in April and May 1992, following the acquittal of police officers in the beating of African American Rodney G. King, Koreatown was besieged, eighteen-year-old Edward Song Lee died in a hail of bullets, nearly fifty Korean merchants were injured, and damage to about 2,000 Korean stores topped $400 million. Parts of Japantown were also hit, and losses to Japanese businesses exceeded $3 million. Is Yellow black or white?

In laying the intellectual foundation for what we now call the model minority stereotype, social scientists William Caudill and George De Vos stated their hypothesis: "there seems to be a significant compatibility (but by no means identity) between the value systems found in the culture of Japan and the value systems found in American middle class culture." That compatibility, they cautioned, did not mean similarity but rather a sharing of certain values and adaptive mechanisms, such that "when they [Japanese and white middle-class Americans] meet under conditions favorable for acculturation . . . Japanese Americans, acting in terms of their Japanese values and personality, will behave in ways that are favorably evaluated by middle class Americans."[2] Although Caudill and De Vos tried to distinguish between identity and compatibility, similarity and sharing, subsequent variations on the theme depicted Asians as "just like whites." And so, is yellow black or white?

The question is multilayered. Is yellow black or white? is a question of Asian American identity. Is yellow black or white? is a question of Third World identity, or the relationships among people of color. Is yellow black or white? is a question of American identity, or the nature of America's racial formation.[3] Implicit within the question is a construct of American society that defines race relations as bipolar—between black and white—and that locates Asians (and American Indians and Latinos) somewhere along the divide between black and white. Asians, thus, are "near-whites" or "just like blacks."[4] The construct is historicized, within the progressive tradition of American history, to show the evolution of Asians from minority to majority status, or "from hardship and discrimination to become a model of self-respect and achievement in today's America."[5] "Scratch a Japanese-American," social scientist Harry Kitano was quoted as saying, "and you find a Wasp," and Asians have been bestowed the highest accolade of having "outwhited the Whites."[6] The construct, importantly, is not mere ideology but is a social practice that assigns to Asian Americans, and indeed to all minorities, places within the social formation. Further, the designations, the roles, and the relationships function to institute and perpetuate a repression that begets and maintains privilege. Asian Americans have served the master class, whether as "near blacks" in the past or as "near-whites" in the present or as "marginal men" in both the past and the present. Yellow is emphatically neither white nor black; but insofar as Asians and Africans share subordinate position to the master class, yellow is a shade of black, and black, a shade of yellow.

We are a kindred people, African and Asian Americans. We share a history of migration, interaction and cultural sharing and commerce and trade. We share a history of European colonization, decolonization, and independence under neocolonization and dependency. We share a history of oppression in the United States, successively serving as slave and cheap labor, as peoples excluded and absorbed, as victims of mob rule and Jim Crow. We share a history of struggle for freedom and the democratization of America, of demands for equality and human dignity, of insistence on making real the promise that all men and women are created equal. We are a kindred people, forged in the fire of white supremacy and struggle, but how can we recall that kinship when our memories have been massaged by white hands, and how can we remember the past when our storytellers have been whispering, amid the din of Western civilization and Anglo-conformity?

We know each other well, Africans and Asians. Some of the first inhabitants of South and Southeast Asia were a people called "Negrito," who were gatherers and hunters and slash-and-burn cultivators. They may have been absorbed or expelled by the Veddoids, a later group of immigrants to the Indian subcontinent, but remnants survive today as the Semang of the Malay Peninsula, the Mincopies of the Andaman Islands, and the Negritos of the Philippines. One branch of the Dravidians, who arrived in South Asia probably after 1000 B.C.E., were black people, who at first apparently intermarried with the lighter-skinned Indo-Aryan branch of Dravidians, but who were later denigrated in the caste system that evolved on the Gangetic plains.[7]

Trade, if not migration, between Africa and Asia predated the arrival of Portuguese ships in the Indian Ocean by at least a thousand years. African ambergris, tortoiseshell, rhinoceros horns, and especially ivory left African ports for Arabia, India, Indonesia, and China. The *Periplus of the Erythraean Sea,* a handbook compiled by a Greek-Egyptian sailor sometime during the first three centuries C.E., described Indonesian food crops, such as coconuts, and cultural items, such as sewn boats, along the East African coast perhaps as far south as Mozambique, and historians believe that Indonesians may have settled on Madagascar in the early centuries C.E., but after the time of the *Periplus.*[8] The Chinese Ch'engshih Tuan, in his *Yu-yang-tsa-tsu* written in the ninth century C.E., described East Africa, or the "land of Po-pa-li," where the women were "clean and well-behaved" and where the trade products were ivory and ambergris.[9]

From the eighth through twelfth centuries, the Hindu kingdom of Sri Vijaya, centered on Sumatra, was the dominant mercantile power in the Indian Ocean; it controlled the sea routes between India and China and likely traded directly with people along the East African coast. About the same time, the Chola kingdom in southeast India sent traders to East Africa, where their cowrie currency, system of weights, and trade beads became standard and widespread. By the thirteenth century, both Sri Vijaya and the Chola kingdom fell into decline, and the west Indian Ocean became an Islamic sphere. Still, the Ming dynasty, which gained control of China in 1368, sent a fleet to East Africa in 1417 and again in 1421, and Ming porcelain has been found in abundance among the ruins of mosques, tombs, houses, and palaces on the islands and on the mainland along the East African coast. Fei-Hsin, a junior officer on the 1417 expedition, described the townspeople of Mogadishu: "the men wear their hair in rolls which hang down all round and wrap cotton cloths round their waists" and the women "apply a yellow varnish to their shaven crowns and hang several strings of disks from their ears and wear silver rings round their necks."[10]

Besides the trade in goods, Africans and Asians engaged in a slave trade that was "probably a constant factor" in the Indian Ocean from the tenth to the thirteenth centuries.[11] Much of that trade was conducted by Africanized Muslims, who sent African slaves to the shores of the Persian Gulf, to India, and to China. In the year 1119, "most of the wealthy in Canton possessed negro slaves," and East African slave soldiers were used extensively by the Sassanian kings of Persia during the seventh century and by the Bahmanid kings of the Deccan in India during the fourteenth and fifteenth centuries.[12] Africans in Asia sometimes rose from the ranks of slaves to become military and political leaders, such as Malik Sarvar of Delhi, who became the sultan's deputy in 1389, was appointed governor of the eastern province, and eventually ruled as an independent king. Perhaps most influential was

Malik Ambar, who was born in Ethiopia around 1550, sold into slavery in India, and rose to become a commander and ruler in the Decan. Ferista, a contemporary Arab historian, called Ambar "the most enlightened financier of whom we read in Indian history," and he reported that "the justice and wisdom of the government of Mullik Ambar have become proverbial in the Deccan."[13] The East African slave trade remained small in volume until the nineteenth century, when European colonies in the Americas and the Indian Ocean opened a larger market for slaves.[14]

The creation of that global system of labor and the conjunction of Africans, Asians, and Europeans began long before the nineteenth century. African and Asian civilizations contributed much to the dawning of European civilization in the Greek city-states. The armies of the Islamic Almoravids ranged across the Sudan and North Africa to Carthage and the Iberian Peninsula, and the Mongol armies of Chingiz Khan penetrated the European heartland. The invaders brought not only devastation but also religion, culture, and science. That intimacy would later be denied by the Europeans, who, after crusades to expel the "infidels" from Christendom and after the rise of nationalism and mercantile capitalism, conceived an ideology that justified their expansion and appropriation of land, labor, and resources in Africa, Asia, and the Americas. That ideology, in the name of religion and science, posited the purity and superiority of European peoples and cultures, unsullied by the anti-Christian, uncivilized non-Europeans—the Other—and found expression in European colonization of the Third World.

Seeking first the kingdom of gold, Europeans set sail for Asia down the African coast and around the Cape of Good Hope to India and China, and later west across the Atlantic Ocean to India, where instead they stumbled into the landmass they named the Americas. Colonization followed trade just as surely as capital required labor. European plantations in the Americas devoured the native inhabitants and, unstated, demanded African laborers from across the Atlantic in the miserable system of human bondage that supplied an outlet for European manufacturers and produced the agricultural products that enriched the metropole. The reciprocal of European development was Third World underdevelopment, and the web spun by European capitalism crisscrossed and captured the globe, creating a world-system in which capital and labor flowed as naturally as the ocean currents that circled the Atlantic and Pacific.

Some of the earliest Asians in the Americas came by way of the Spanish galleon trade between Manila and Acapulco in the early seventeenth century. Chinese and Filipino crew members and servants on those Spanish ships settled in Mexico, and Filipino "Manilamen" found their way to Louisiana, where, in 1763, they created the oldest continuous Asian American communities in North America.[15] The Filipinos named their fishing and shrimping settlements Manila Village, St. Malo, Leon Rojas, Bayou Cholas, and Bassa Bassa. But the main body of Asian migration to the Americas came after the termination of the African slave trade in the nineteenth century and the consequent need for a new source of labor for the plantations, mines, and public works in Central and South America, Africa, and the islands of the Pacific and Caribbean.

A forerunner of the nineteenth-century coolie trade and the successor of the earlier East African slave trade was the use of Asian and African slaves on board European ships in the Indian Ocean and a European carrying trade that took Asian slaves from Bengal, southern India and Sri Lanka, the Indonesian archipelago, the Philippines, and Japan to Dutch and Portuguese possessions in Asia and Africa. Beginning in the early sixteenth century, largely because of the debilitating effects of disease upon European sailors, Arab, South Asian, Malay, and African slaves frequently made up the majority of the crews on Portuguese vessels plying Indian Ocean waters.[16] Asian slaves were joined by Africans taken from Madagascar and East Africa and were brought to the Dutch settlement at the Cape of Good Hope after 1658. By 1795, there were 16,839 slaves in the colony, and in 1834, the year slavery was abolished at the Cape, there were approximately 34,000 slaves.[17] The slaves produced mixed offspring with the indigenous San and Khoikhoi and with whites, forming the group the Europeans called the Cape Coloured. South Asians arrived on the East Coast of eighteenth-century America as indentured workers and slaves. Brought to Massachusetts and Pennsylvania on board English and American trade vessels possibly during the 1780s and 1790s, South Asians with Anglicized names such as James Dunn, John Ballay, Joseph Green, George Jimor, and Thomas Robinson served indentures, were sold and bought as slaves, likely married African American women, and became members of the local African American communities.[18]

In 1833, slavery was formally abolished in the British Empire, but during the period of transition, slaves over six years of age served apprenticeships from four to six years as unpaid and later as paid labor. Apprenticeships ended in the British colonies in 1838, leading to the claim by sugar planters of a chronic labor shortage and a determination "to make us, as far as possible, independent of our negro population," according to John Gladstone, father of Robert and William Gladstone and one of the largest slaveholders and proprietors of estates in British Guiana.[19] Slavery, as pointed out by historian Hugh Tinker, produced both "a system and attitude of mind" that enabled a new system of slavery—coolieism—that incorporated many of the same oppressive features of the old.[20]

White planters saw the "new slaves" as subhuman and mere units of production. In 1836, anticipating the end of African slave apprenticeships, John Gladstone inquired about purchasing a hundred coolies from Gillanders, Arbuthnot & Company, who had supplied thousands of South Asians to Mauritius. The firm assured Gladstone that the Dhangars, or "hill coolies" of India, were "always spoken of as more akin to the monkey than the man. They have no religion, no education, and in their present state no wants beyond eating, drinking and sleeping: and to procure which they are willing to labour."[21] In May 1838, the first contingent of what would become a veritable stream of indentured labor arrived in British Guiana. The 396 Asian Indians were contracted to work nine to ten hours a day (as compared with seven and a half hours daily under apprenticeships) for sixteen cents (compared with thirty-two cents for free workers). In addition to economic exploitation, the indentured laborers were subject to disease and harsh treatment, particularly during the "seasoning," or breaking-in, period, resulting in numerous runaways and high mortality rates. From May 1845 to December 1849, 11,437 Asian Indians were indentured on sugar estates in British Guiana. Of that total as of December 1849, 11,437 Asian Indians were indentured on sugar estates in British Guiana. Of that total as of December 1849, only 6,417 still remained on the estates, whereas 643 were listed as sick, vagrants, paupers, or children 2,218 had died on the estates in jails and hospitals or were found dead elsewhere, and 2,259 were unaccounted for, of whom more than half were probably dead. Even those who had served their period of contract were left to wander "about the roads and streets, or lie down, sicken and die" or were castigated as "vagrants" who were stereotyped as "eating every species of garbage . . . filthy in (their) habits, lazy and addicted to pilfering."[23] Little wonder that Asian Indian indentures composed and sang this song as they sailed for Trinidad:

> What kind plate,
> What kind cup,
> With a ticket to cut
> in Trinidad,
> O people of India
> We are going to die there.[24]

Chinese and Asian Indian "coolies" were sold and indentured to European and American ship captains in a barter called by the Chinese "the buying and selling of pigs." The Chinese coolies, or "pigs," were restrained in "pigpens", one such barracoon on Amoy in 1852 was described in a British report "the coolies were penned up in numbers from 10 to 12 in a wooden shed, like a slave barracoon, nearly naked, very filthy, and room only sufficient to lie; the space 220 by 24 feet with a bamboo floor near the roof; the number in all about 500."[25] On the shore, the coolies were strapped naked and on their chests were painted the letters C (California), P (Peru), or S (Sandwich Islands), denoting their destinations. Once on board the ship, they were placed below deck in the hold, where they were usually confined for the duration of the transpacific passage. Overcrowding and a short supply of food and water led to revolts, suicides, and murders. Fearing a revolt, the crew of an American ship, the *Waverly,* drove the Chinese coolies below deck and cosed the hatch on October 27, 1855: "on opening them some twelve or fourteen hours afterwards it was found that nearly three hundred of the unfortunate beings had perished by suffocation."[26] Chao-ch'un Li and 165 other coolies petitioned the Cuba Commission about ill-treatment and abuse: "When quitting Macao," they testified, "we proceeded to sea, we were confined in the hold below; some were even shut up in bamboo cages, or chained to iron posts, and a few were indiscriminately selected and flogged as a means of intimidating all others; while we cannot estimate the deaths that, in all, took place, from sickness, blows, hunger, thirst, or from suicide by leaping into the sea."[27] As many as a third of the coolies died during the journey across the Pacific on board ships bound for the Americas. During the years 1860 to 1863, for example, of the 7,884 Chinese coolies shipped to Peru, 2,400 or 30.4 percent, died en route.[28] The African slave and Asian coolie were kinsmen and kinswomen in that world created by European masters.

Between 1848 and 1874, 124,813 Chinese coolies reached Cuba from Macao, Amoy, Canton, Hong Kong, Swatow, Saigon, and Manila. Within Cuba's plantation system, wrote historian Franklin W. Knight, the Chinese became "coinheritors with the Negroes of the lowliness of caste, the abuse, the ruthless exploitation. . . . Chinese labor in cuba in the nineteenth century was slavery in every social aspect except the name."[29] Coolies were sold in the open market, following advertisements that appeared in the local newspapers. Prospective buyers inspected the human merchandise, lined up on a platform, before the bargaining began, and the Asians were "virtually sold to the planters."[30] Conditions on Cuba's plantations were desperate. Chien T'ang, Chao Chang, A-chao Wen, and about three hundred of their compatriots in labor testified that they worked daily from between 2 and 4 a.m. until midnight, including Sundays, and others described the harsh treatment they received at the hands of overseers and masters. Confinement, shackling with chains, flogging, and cutting off fingers, ears, an limbs were methods employed to ensure docility and productivity in the workplace. A-pa Ho reported that for making a cigarette, "I was flogged with a rattan rod so severely that my flesh was lacerated and the bones became visible." A-chen Lu stated: "I have seen men beaten to death, the bodies being afterwards buried, and no report being made to the authorities"; A-sheng Hsieh told of Chen and Liang, who committed suicide after having been severely beaten. "The administrator accused them of cutting grass slowly," testified Hsieh, "and directing four men to hold them in a prostrate position, inflicted with a whip, a flogging which almost killed them. The first afterwards hanged himself, and the second drowned himself."[30]

In the United States, white planters similarly saw Chinese laborers as the "coinheritors with the Negroes of the lowliness of caste, the abuse, the ruthless exploitation." Before the Civil War, southern planters saw African slaves as a counter to immigration to their region by, in the words of Edmund Ruffin, "the hordes of immigrants now flowing from Europe." After the war, the planters saw free blacks as a troublesome presence and sought to deport and colonize them outside the United States and to replace them with Europeans and Asians.[31] In 1869, Godfrey Barnsley, a Georgia planter and New Orleans factory predicted that Mississippi Valley planters would recruit "large numbers of Chinese to take the place of negroes as they are said to be better laborers[,] more intelligent and can be had for $12 to $13 per month and rations." William M. Lawton, chair of the Committee on Chinese Immigrants for the South Carolina Agricultural and Mechanical Society, put it more bluntly: "I look upon the introduction of Chinese on our Rice lands, & especially on the unhealthy cotton lands as new and essential machines in the room of others that have been destroyed [or are] wearing out, year by year."[32] Africans and Asians, according to that point of view, were mere fodder for the fields and factories of the master class.

Africans and Asians, however, were not the same. After the Civil War, southern employers viewed African Americans not only as essential laborers but also as political liabilities insofar as they voted and voted Republican.[33] The problem, thus, was how to maintain white political supremacy while employing cheap and efficient "colored" workers, thereby ensuring white economic supremacy. William M. Burwell, in an essay published in the July 1869 issue of *De Bow's Review*, described the challenge: "We will state the problem for consideration. It is: To retain in the hands of the whites the control and direction of social and political action, without impairing the content of the labor capacity of the colored race." Asian migrant workers, it seemed to some southerners, provided the ideal solution to the problem in that they were productive laborers and noncitizens who could not vote. Further, Asian workers would be used to discipline African workers and depress wages. On June 30, 1869, the *Vicksburg Times*, a proponent of Asian migration, editorialized: "Emancipation has spoiled the negro, and carried him away from fields of agriculture." The *Times* went on to exult at the impending arrival of several hundred Chinese coolies: "Our colored friends who have left the farm for politics and plunder, should go down to the *Great Republic* today and look at the new laborer who is destined to crowd the negro from the American farm." Arkansas Reconstruction governor Powell Clayton observed: "Undoubtedly the underlying motive for this effort to bring in Chinese laborers was to punish the negro for having abandoned the control of his old master, and to regulate the conditions of his employment and the scale of wages to be paid him."[34]

African and Asian workers, nonetheless, were related insofar as they were both essential for the maintenance of white supremacy, they were both members of an oppressed class of "colored" laborers, and they were both tied historically to the global network of labor migration as slaves and coolies. As anthropologist Lucy M. Cohen has shown, the planters in the American South were members of a Caribbean plantation complex, and the plans they formulated for Chinese migration drew from their cultural bonds with West Indian societies.[35] For example, during the 1850s, Daniel Lee of the *Southern Cultivator* and J. D. B. De Bow of *De Bow's Review*, despite their preference for African slaves, informed their readers about the growing use of Asian coolie labor in the plantations of the West Indies, and after the Civil War in October 1865, John Little Smith, an eminent jurist, reported in several southern newspapers that, according to an American ship captain who had taken Chinese coolies to Cuba, the Chinese were the "best and cheapest labor in the world" and would make good plantation workers and unparalleled servants.[36]

Despite their interest in Asian coolies, southern planters were stymied by the 1862 act of Congress that had prohibited American involvement in the coolie trade. To skirt federal restrictions on the importation of Asian workers, the planters and labor contractors crafted a distinction between coolies, who were involuntary and bonded labor, and Asian migrants, who were voluntary and free labor. That distinction, they noted, enabled the comparatively easy entry of Chinese into California, and when a shipload of Chinese from Cuba was impounded in 1867 at the port of New Orleans, planter Bradish Johnson argued: "What if the government should forbid the employment of the thousands of Chinese who have worked on the railroads, on the mines, and agriculture of California? No reason had been found for their exclusion and they were valuable for that country. The cultivators of cane and cotton would not be made an exception."[37] Johnson won his point, and the case was discontinued. Meanwhile, planters held Chinese labor conventions, such as the 1869 Memphis convention that drew delegates from Alabama, Arkansas, Georgia, Kentucky, Louisiana, Mississippi, Missouri, South Carolina, Tennessee, and California, representing agricultural, railroad, and other business interests, and formed immigration committees and companies, and labor agents continued to bring Chinese workers, under contract, to the South, procuring them from Cuba, California, and China. After 1877, when white supremacist Democrats had broken the grip of Reconstruction through fraud and violence, southern planters reverted to a preference for African American workers, and interest in Asians declined and vanished.[38]

Although advocates of Chinese labor in the South learned to distinguish slave from coolie, and coolie from migrant, the migration of Asians to America cannot be divorced from the African slave trade, or from the coolie trade that followed in its wake. Both trades were systems of bonded labor, and both trades formed the contexts and reasons for the entry of Asians into America. Contract labor was the means by which Chinese and Japanese migrated to the Hawaiian kingdom and the American South, whereas the credit-ticket system was the means by which many Chinese gained admittance into California. But a system that advanced credit to laborers and constrained those workers to a term of service until the debt was paid was a scant advance over the earlier forms of coolie and contract labor,[39] and, perhaps more importantly, all of the successive systems of labor—from slave to coolie to contract to credit-ticket—were varieties of migrant labor and functioned to sustain a global order of supremacy and subordination.[40] The lines that directed Africans and Asians to America's shore converge at that point, and the impetus for that intersection came from the economic requirement and advantage of bonded labor buttressed by the relief in the centrality of whiteness and the marginality of its negation—nonwhiteness.

African Americans recognized early on the wide embrace of racism and equated racism directed at Asians with racism directed at Africans. Frederick Douglass pointedly declared that the southern planters' scheme to displace African with Asian labor was stimulated by the same economic and racist motives that supported the edifice of African slavery. The white oligarchy of the South, he stated, "believed in slavery and they believe in it still." During the late 1870s and early 1880s, when a Chinese exclusion bill was being debated in the Congress, Blanche K. Bruce of Mississippi, the lone African American senator, spoke out and voted against the discriminatory legislation, and the *Christian Recorder,* an African American newspaper in Boston, editorialized: "Only a few years ago the cry was, not 'The Chinese must go,' but 'The niggers must go' and it came from the same strata of society. There is not a man to-day who rails out against the yellow man from China but would equally rail out against the black man if opportunity only afforded."[41]

In his *Observations Concerning the Increase of Mankind*, published in 1751, Benjamin Franklin divided humankind along the color line of white and nonwhite. The number of "purely white people," he noted with regret, was greatly exceeded by the number of blacks and "Tawneys," who inhabited Africa, Asia, and the Americas. Whites had cleared America of its forests and thereby made it "reflect a brighter light"; therefore, argued Franklin, "why should we . . . darken its people? Why increase the sons of Africa, by planting them in America, where we have so fair an opportunity, by excluding all Blacks and Tawneys, of increasing the lovely White. . . .?"[42] According to historian Alexander Saxton, the same racism that sought to increase the "lovely White" and that justified the expulsion and extermination of American Indians and the enslavement of Africans was carried, like so much baggage, west across the American continent, where it was applied to Asians, the majority of whom resided along the Pacific coast.[43]

Franklin's binary racial hierarchy found expression in a book written by Hinton R. Helper of North Carolina, who would become a chief Republican antislavery polemicist. Describing his visit to California in his *The Land of Gold*, published in 1855, Helper wrote of the inhabitants of a small coastal town north of San Francisco: "Bodega contains not more than four hundred inhabitants, including 'Digger' Indians, 'niggers,' and dogs, the last by far the most useful and decent of the concern." Of the Chinese, Helper charged that the "semibarbarians" had no more right to be in California than "flocks of blackbirds have in a wheat field," and he offered his view of American race relations: "No inferior race of men can exist in these United States without becoming subordinate to the will of the Anglo-Americans. . . . It is so with the Negroes in the South; it is so with the Irish in the North; it is so with the Indians in New England; and it will be so with the Chinese in California."[44] Within months after the end of the Civil War, the *New York Times* warned of allied dangers: "We have four millions of degraded negroes in the South . . . and if there were to be a flood-tide of Chinese population—a population befouled with all the social vices, with no knowledge or appreciation of free institutions or constitutional liberty, with heathenish souls and heathenish propensities . . . we should be prepared to bid farewell to republicanism."[45] In popular culture, the stereotype character of the "heathen chinee" made its debut in American theater by way of the blackface minstrel shows, and Chinese were paired with black sambos in Wild West melodramas.[46]

The institutionalization of Africans and Asians as the Other, as nonwhites, was embraced in American law and proposed legislation. California's state assembly passed two companion bills excluding from the state both Chinese and African Americans, modeled on the black codes of midwestern states.[47] In 1854, Justice Charles J. Murray delivered the California Supreme Court's ruling on *The People v. George W. Hall*, in which Hall, a white man, was convicted of murder based upon the testimony of Chinese witnesses. Murray outlined the precedents that established that "no black or mulatto person, or Indian, shall be allowed to give evidence in favor of, or against a white man," and he considered the generic meaning of the terms "black" and "white." The words, Murray contended, were oppositional, and "black" meant "nonwhite," and "white" excluded all persons of color. In addition, the intent of the law was to shield white men "from the testimony of the degraded and demoralized caste" and to protect the very foundations of the state from the "actual and present danger" of "a race of people whom nature has marked as inferior, and who are incapable of progress or intellectual development beyond a certain point . . . differing in language, opinions, color, and physical conformation; between whom and ourselves nature has placed an impassable difference."[48] The Chinese testimony thus was inadmissible, and Hall's conviction was reversed.

Like exclusion, antimiscegenation laws helped to maintain the boundary between white and nonwhite. Virginia banned interracial marriages in 1691.[49] Besides withholding state sanction of interracial cohabitation, antimiscegenation laws sought to prevent race mixing and the creation of "hybrid races" and the "contamination" and lowering of the superior by the inferior race. The issue of Chinese and white parents, predicted John F. Miller at California's 1878 constitutional convention, would be "a hybrid of the most despicable, a mongrel of the most detestable that has ever afflicted the earth." California enacted its antimiscegenation law two years later, prohibiting marriages between whites and nonwhites, "negro, mulatto, or Mongolian."[50] Based on the same reasons for antimiscegenation laws, African, Asian, and American Indian children were excluded in 1860 from California's public schools designated for whites, and the state's superintendent of public instruction had the power to deny state funds to schools that violated the law. Nonwhite children attended separate schools established at public expense.[51]

Asian laborers might have been ideal replacements for African slaves because they were productive and incapable of becoming citizens, but they were also useful in that they were neither white nor black. Although some believed that the addition of yet another group of people to society would only add to the complexity and hence difficulty of race relations, others saw the entrance of Asians as a way to insulate whites from blacks. Asians were simultaneously members of the nonwhite Other, despite their sometime official classification as white, and an intermediate group between white and black. The foundations of that social hierarchy can be found in the economic relations of the plantation system. Franklin Knight informs us that in nineteenth-century Cuba, Asians were classified as whites, yet "their conditions of labor tended to be identical to those of slaves," and on plantations with a mixed labor force, Asians "bridged the gap between black and white," assisting slaves in the fields and factories but, unlike slaves, performing simple semiskilled tasks and handling machines.[52]

In Louisiana before the 1870 census, Chinese were counted as whites in the absence of a separate category for people who were neither white nor black.[53] Despite that classification, whites perceived Asians as belonging to the economic, if not social, caste assigned to Africans. In 1927, taking up a Chinese American challenge by Gong Lum to Mississippi's Jim Crow schools, the U.S. Supreme Court, citing its 1896 landmark decision *Plessy v. Ferguson,* which set forth the "separate but equal" doctrine, affirmed the state supreme court's ruling that Chinese were non-white and hence "colored" and thus could be barred from schools reserved for whites. A Chinese man who married an African American woman during the 1930s recalled: "Before 1942, the Chinese had no status in Mississippi whatever. They were considered on the same status as the Negro. If a Chinese man *did* have a woman, it *had* to be a Negro." Mississippi planter William Alexander Percy described Delta society in his autobiography, *Lanterns on the Levee,* published in 1941: "Small Chinese storekeepers are almost as ubiquitous as in the South Seas. Barred from social intercourse with the whites, they smuggle through wives from China or, more frequently, breed lawfully or otherwise with the Negro."[54]

The Chinese, however, occupied an ambiguous position racially, as reflected in Louisiana's census. In 1860, Chinese were classified as whites; in 1870, they were listed as Chinese; in 1880, children of Chinese men and non-Chinese women were classed as Chinese; but in 1900, all of those children were reclassified as blacks or whites and only those born in China or with two Chinese parents were listed as Chinese.[55] In Mississippi, according to sociologist James W. Loewen, the Chinese were initially assigned "a near-Negro position" with no more legal rights or political power, but neither whites nor blacks "quite thought of them *as* Negroes," and they later served in some respects "as middlemen between white and black."[56] In fact, that function both mediated and advanced the prevailing social relations.

In 1925, two months after the founding of A. Philip Randolph's Brotherhood of Sleeping Car Porters, the Pullman Company hired Filipinos to serve on its private cars as attendants, cooks, and busboys. African Americans, who had for more than fifty years worked in those capacities, were henceforth relegated to the position of porter and denied mobility to easier, more-lucrative positions. At first, the Brotherhood called Filipinos "scab labor" and sought their elimination from Pullman lines; however, during its most desperate years, the 1930s, the Brotherhood, unlike the racist American Federation of Labor that had excluded both Africans and Asians, recognized the hand of capital in dividing workers and saw the common plight of black and yellow: "We wish it understood," explained a policy statement, "that the Brotherhood has nothing against Filipinos. They have been used against the unionization of Pullman porters just as Negroes have been used against the unionization of white workers . . . We will take in Filipinos as members . . . We want our Filipino brothers to understand that it is necessary for them to join the Brotherhood in order to help secure conditions and wages which they too will benefit from."[57]

Amid such examples of solidarity, African Americans were severely tested by the capitalist system, which deliberately pitted African against Asian workers, whereby Asians were used to discipline African workers and to depress their wages. The root cause of African and Asian American oppression was further clouded by mutual ethnocentrism and prejudice that frequently devolved from the ideas and practices of the master class. It is not surprising, therefore, that some African Americans, like Howard University professor Kelly Miller, saw a danger in linking the claims of African and Asian Americans. "The Negro is an American citizen whose American residence and citizenry reach further back than the great majority of the white race," wrote Miller. "He has from the beginning contributed a full share of the glory and grandeur of America and his claims to patrimony are his just and rightful due. The Japanese, on the other hand, is the eleventh hour comer, and is claiming the privilege of those who have borne the heat and burden of the day."[58]

What is surprising, instead, was the extent and degree of solidarity felt by African Americans toward Asian Americans. The *Chicago Defender* explained that Chinese and Japanese learned from racist America, having been "taught to scorn the Race or lose the little footing they may now boast," and Mary Church Terrell believed that Japanese shunned African Americans in an attempt to avoid the stigma of inferiority that whites had placed upon blacks.[59] And despite dismay over Asian American ethnocentrism, African Americans steadfastly realized that the enemy was white supremacy and that anti-Asianism was anti-Africanism in another guise. Thus, in 1906 and 1907, when the San Francisco school board ruled that Japanese children had to attend "Oriental schools" and when President Theodore Roosevelt intervened to avoid an international incident, the *Colored American Magazine* declared: "We are with the President in the California muddle, for as California would treat the Japanese she would also treat the Negroes. It is not that we desire to attend schools with the whites at all, per se, but the principle involved in the attempt to classify us as inferiors—not because we are necessarily inferior, but on the grounds of color—forms the crux of our protest."[60]

The Philippine-American war, like many of America's imperialist wars, provided an extraordinary test for American minorities. The late nineteenth century, America's period of manifest destiny and expansionism overseas, was a time of severe repression at home for African Americans. Shouldering the white man's burden was an opportunity for making domestic claims and gains, but at the expense of peoples of color with whom African Americans identified: the Cubans, Puerto Ricans, and Filipinos. Bishop Henry M. Turner of the African Methodist Episcopal church characterized the U.S. presence in the Philippiaes as "an unholy war of conquest" against "a feeble band of sable patriots," and Frederick L. McGhee, a founder of the Niagara Movement, observed that America was out "to rule earth's inferior races, and if they object make war upon them," and thus concluded that African Americans could not support the war against the Filipinos.[62] From the Philippines, an African American soldier wrote home to Milwaukee, where his letter was published in the Wisconsin Weekly Advocate on May 17, 1900:

> *I have mingled freely with the natives and have had talks with American colored men here in business and who have lived here for years, in order to learn of them the cause of their (Filipino) dissatisfaction and the reason for this insurrection, and I must confess they have a just grievance. . . . (Americans) began to apply home treatment for colored peoples: cursed them as damned niggers, steal (from) and ravish them, rob them on the street of their small change, take from the fruit vendors whatever suited their fancy, and kick the*

*poor unfortunate if he complained, desecrate their church property, and after fighting began, looted everything in sight, burning, robbing the graves.*

*I have seen with my own eyes carcasses lying bare in the boiling sun, the re-sults of raids on receptacles for the dead in search of diamonds. The white' troops, thinking we would be proud to emulate their conduct . . . One fellow . . . told me how some fellows he knew had cut off a native woman's arm in order to get a fine inlaid bracelet. . . . They talked with impunity of "niggers" to our soldiers, never once thinking that they were talking to home "niggers" and should they be brought to remember that at home this is the same vile epithet they hurl at us, they beg pardon and make some elfiminate (sic) excuse about what the Filipino is called.*

*I want to say right here that if it were not for the sake of the 10,000,000 black peo-ple in the United Sates, God alone knows on which side of the subject I would be.*

General Robert P. Hughes, a commander in the Philippines, entertained some doubt over "which side of the subject " African American troops fell when he re-ported: "The darkey troops . . . mixed with the natives at once. Whenever they came together they became great friends." And according to a contemporary report, white troops deserted because they found the Army irksome, whereas black troops deserted "for the purpose of joining the insurgents," whose cause they saw as the struggle of all colored people against white domination. Perhaps the most famous African American deserter was David Eagan of the Twenty-fourth Infantry, who joined the Filipino freedom fighters and fought the Yankee imperialists for two years.[63] After the war—the war in which General "Howlin' Jake" Smith ordered his men to "kill and burn, kill and burn, the more you kill and the more you burn the more you please me" and the war that cost over 600,000 Filipino lives for the sake of "civilizing" those who remained—about 500 African Americans, many of whom had married Filipino women, chose to stay in the Philippines.[64]

Asians, like African Americans, resisted their exploitation and subjugation, and in the shared struggle for equality secured the blessings of democracy for all peoples. On this point we must be clear. Inclusion, human dignity, and civil rights are not "black issues" nor are they gains for one group made at the expense of another. Like-wise, the democratization of America fought for by African and Asian Americans was advantageous for both groups. The "separate but equal" doctrine of *Plessy v. Fergu-son,* for instance, was a basis for the 1927 case Gong *Lum v. Rice,* and both were cited as precedents in the *1954 Brown v. Board of Education* decision.[65] In addition to those parallel and conjoining struggles for freedom, African and Asian American lives con-verge like rivers through time. In full knowledge of intergroup conflicts and hatreds among America's minorities and their sources and functions, I will recall here only acts of antiracialism and solidarity between Asian and African Americans.[66]

During the late 1840s and early 1850s, African Americans gathered with Chi-nese and whites at San Francisco's Washerwoman's Bay to wash clothes, and rela-tions between Chinese and Africans were apparently friendly. William Newby, a prominent African American leader in the city, reported to Frederick Douglass "that the Chinese were the most mistreated group in the state and that blacks were the only people who did not abuse them." Both shared with Indians, Newby pointed out, the "same civil rights disabilities," insofar as they were denied the franchise and debarred from the courts." In 1869, the first Japanese settlers arrived in California and established the Wakamatsu Tea and Silk Farm Colony near Sacramento. The colony failed, but among that group of adventurers was Masumizu Kuninosuke, who married an African American woman, had three daughters and a son, and operated a fish store in Sacramento for many years. Sacramento Chinese shared their church with African Americans for some time during the nineteenth century, and in San Francisco, Jean Ng, an African American married to a Chinese American, was buried in a Chinese cemetery. In 1913, Charley Sing, a Mobile, Alabama, Chinese laundryman, tried to get permission to marry Lillie Lambert, an African American. A Filipino band made sweet music under the baton of its African American conductor, Walter Loving, at the San Francisco Panama-Pacific International Exposition in 1915, and touring African American musicians sometimes stayed at Chinese-owned lodging houses in San Francisco. In 1927, Lemon Lee Sing, a sixty-eight-year-old Chinese laundryman in New York City, sought permission to adopt Firman Smith, an abandoned African American child he had found sleeping in a hallway. Sing fed and clothed Firman, enrolled him in school, and ultimately won from the courts custody of the child. Sam Lee, a Chinese restaurant owner in Washington, D.C., refused to fire one of his African American employees, despite threats on his life, while in Chicago, in 1929, a Chinese restaurant was dynamited for serving African Americans.

Many of us, Asian and Pacific Americans, several generations native-born, came of age during America's imperialist war in Vietnam and the African American freedom struggle of the 1960s. Many of us found our identity by reading Franz Fanon and Malcolm X, Cheikh Anta Diop and W.E.B. Du Bois, Leopold Senghor and Langston Hughes. Many more of us, however, have migrated to the United States since 1965; we came of age in Reagan's America, the era of yuppies and yappies, and wasn't that the time when history came to an end?—announced, significantly, by an Asian American. During fall semester 1990, I asked my Asian American students with whom they felt a closer kinship: African or European Americans? They almost universally expressed affinity with whites, and I recalled how in 1944, amid strident, anti-Japanese wartime propaganda and concentration camps for Japanese Americans, the *Negro Digest* conducted a poll among its readers. To the question, "Should negroes discriminate against Japanese?" 66 percent in the North and West and 53 percent in the South answered "No." During spring semester 1991, I asked my Asian American students the same question, and all of them claimed kinship with African Americans, and I recalled how in 1960, Yuri Kochiyama, born in San Pedro, California, and interned during the war at the Jerome concentration camp in Arkansas, and her husband, a veteran of World War II, enrolled in the Harlem Freedom School established by Malcolm X to learn African American history and to engage in the struggle for civil rights."

We are a kindred people, African and Asian Americans. We share a history of migration, cultural interaction, and trade. We share a history of colonization, oppression and exploitation, and parallel and mutual struggles for freedom. We are a kindred people, forged in the fire of white supremacy and tempered in the water of resistance. Yet that kinship has been obscured from our range of vision, and that common cause, turned into a competition for access and resources. We have not yet realized the full meaning of Du Bois's poetic insight: "The stars of dark Andromeda belong up there in the great heaven that hangs above this tortured world. Despite the crude and cruel motives behind her shame and exposure, her degradation and enchaining, the fire and freedom of black Africa, with the uncurbed might of her consort Asia, are indispensable to the fertilizing of the universal soil of mankind, which Europe alone never would nor could give this aching world."

Is yellow black or white? In 1914, Takao Ozawa, a Japanese national, filed for naturalization on the basis of his over twenty-eight-year residence in the United States and the degree of his "Americanization." Further, Ozawa contended, Asians were not specifically excluded under the naturalization laws, and thus he should be considered a "free white person." The U.S. Supreme Court rendered its decision on November 13, 1922, rejecting Ozawa's application and claim. Only whites and Africans were accorded the privilege of naturalization, wrote Associate Justice George Sutherland, and although the founding fathers might not have contemplated Asians within the meaning of either black or white, it was evident that they were not included within the category of "free white persons." Ruled Sutherland: "the appellant is clearly of a race which is not Caucasian, and therefore belongs entirely outside the zone on the negative side."[76] The marginalization of Asians—"entirely outside the zone"—was accompanied by their negation as "nonwhites"—"on the negative side"—in this institutionalization of the racial state. Yellow is not white.

But yellow is not black either, and the question posed is, in a real sense, a false and mystifying proposition. The question is only valid within the meanings given to and played out in the American racial formation, relations that have been posited as a black and white dyad. There are other options. Whites considered Asians "as blacks" or, at the very last, as replacements for blacks in the post-Civil War South, but whites imported Chinese precisely because they were not blacks and were thus perpetual aliens, who could never vote. Similarly, whites upheld Asians as "near-whites" or "whiter than whites" in the model minority stereotype, and yet Asians experienced and continue to face white racism "like blacks" in educational and occupational barriers and ceilings and in anti-Asian abuse and physical violence. Further, in both instances, Asians were used to "discipline" African Americans (and other minorities according to the model minority stereotype). That marginalization of Asians, in fact, within a black and white racial formation, "disciplines" both Africans and Asians and constitutes the essential site of Asian American oppression. By seeing only black and white, the presence and absence of all color, whites render Asians, American Indians, and Latinos invisible, ignoring the gradations and complexities of the full spectrum between the racial poles. At the same time,

Asians share with Africans the status and repression of nonwhites—as the Other—and therein lies the debilitating aspect of Asian-African antipathy and the liberating nature of African-Asian unity.

On November 27, 1991, about 1,200 people gathered outside Los Angeles City Hall to participate in a prayer vigil sponsored by the African-Korean American Christian Alliance, a group formed the previous month. A newspaper reporter described the "almost surreal" scene:

> *Elderly Korean American women twirling and dancing with homeless men in front of the podium. Koreans and street people in a human chain, holding hands but not looking at each other. Shoes and clothing ruined by cow manure, which had been freshly spread over the rally grounds in an unfortunate oversight. Alliance co-chair Rev. Hee Min Park startled rally-goers when he began quoting from Marther Luther King's famous "I have a dream" speech. Black homeless people listened in stunned silence at first, as the pastor's voice with a heavy immigrant accent filled the slain black minister's familiar words. Then a few began chanting "Amen" in response to Park's litany.*[77]

Park's articulation of King's dream reminds me of Maxine Hong Kingston's version of the story of Ts'ai Yen, a Han poetess kidnapped by "barbarians," in her book *The Woman Warrior.* Although she had lived among them for twelve years, Ts'ai Yen still considered the people primitive, until one evening, while inside her tent, she heard "music tremble and rise like desert wind." Night after night the barbarians blew on their flutes, and try as she Africans were apparently friendly. William Newby, a prominent African American leader in the city, reported to Frederick Douglass "that the Chinese were the most mistreated group in the state and that blacks were the only people who did not abuse them." Both shared with Indians, Newby pointed out, the "same civil rights disabilities," insofar as they were denied the franchise and debarred from the courts.[66] In 1869, the first Japanese settlers arrived in California and established the Wakamatsu Tea and Silk Farm Colony near Sacramento. The colony failed, but among that group of adventurers was Masumizu Kuninosuke, who married an African American woman, had three daughters and a son, and operated a fish store in Sacramento for many years.[67] Sacramento Chinese shared their church with African Americans for some time during the nineteenth century, and in San Francisco, Jean Ng, an African American married to a Chinese American, was buried in a Chinese cemetery. In 1913, Charley Sing, a Mobile, Alabama, Chinese laundryman, tried to get permission to marry Lilie Lambert, an African American.[68] A Filipino band made sweet music under the baton of its African American conductor, Walter Loving, at the San Francisco Panama-Pacific International Exposition in 1915, and touring African American musicians sometimes stayed at Chinese-owned lodging houses in San Francisco.[69] In 1927, Lemon Lee Sing, a sixty-eight-year-old Chinese laundryman in New York City, sought permission to adopt Firman Smith, an abandoned African American child he had found sleeping in a hallway. Sing fed and clothed Firman, enrolled him in school, and ultimately won from the courts custody of the child.[70] Sam Lee, a Chinese restaurant owner in Washington, D.C., refused to fire one of his African American employees, despite threats on his life, while in Chicago, in 1929, a Chinese restaurant was dynamited for serving African Americans.[71]

Many of us, Asian and Pacific Americans, several generations native-born, came of age during America's imperialist war in Vietnam and the African American freedom struggle of the 1960s. Many of us found our identity by reading Franz Fanon and Malcom X, Cheikh Anta Diop and W. E. B. Du Bois, Leopold Senghor and Langston Hughes. Many more of us, however, have migrated to the United States since 1965; we came of age in Reagan's America, the era of yuppies and yappies, and wasn't that the time when history came to an end?—announced, significantly, by an Asian American.[72] During fall semester 1990, I asked my Asian American students with whom they felt a closer kinship: African or European Americans? They almost universally expressed affinity with whites, and I recall how in 1944, amid strident, anti-Japanese wartime propaganda and concentration camps for Japanese Americans, the *Negro Digest* conducted a poll among its readers. To the question, "Should negroes discriminate against Japanese?" 66 percent in the North and West and 53 percent in the South answered "No."[73] During spring semester 1991, I asked my Asian American students the same question, and all of them claimed kinship with African Americans, and I recalled how in 1960, Yuri Kochiyama, born in San Pedro, California, and interned during the war at the Jerome concentration camp in Arkansas, and her husband, a veteran of World War II, enrolled in the Harlem Freedom School established by Malcom X to learn African American history and to engage in the struggle for civil rights.[74]

# Notes

[1]Poster of the December 12th Movement, Brooklyn Chapter, 1990.

[2]William Caudill and George De Vos, "Achievement, Culture and Personality: The Case of the Japanese Americans," *American Anthropologist* 58 (1956): 1107.

[3]For a definition of racial formation, see Michael Omi and Howard Winant, *Racial Formation in the United States: From the 1960s to the 1980s* (New York: Routledge & Kegan Paul, 1986), pp. 57–86.

[4]See, e.g., James W. Loewen, *The Mississippi Chinese: Between Black and White* (Cambridge: Harvard University Press, 1971).

[5]*U.S. News & World Report,* December 26, 1966. See also Dan Caldwell, "The Negroization of the Chinese Stereotype in California," *Southern California Quarterly 53* (June 1971): 123–31, on the convergence of the Chinese and African American physiognomy; and Dennis M. Ogawa, *From Japs to Japanese: The Evolution of Japanese-American Stereotypes* (Berkeley: McCutchan Publishing, 1971), on the progression of Japanese American stereotypes.

[6]"Success Story: Outwhiting the Whites," *Newsweek,* June 21, 1971.

[7]Hugh Tinker, *South Asia: A Short History* (Honolulu: University of Hawaii Press, 1990), pp. 1–5.

[8]J. E. G. Sutton, *The East African Coast: An Historical and Archaeological Review* (Dar es Salaam: East African Publishing House, 1966), p. 8.

[9]G. S. P. Freeman-Grenville, ed., *The East African Coast: Select Documents from the First to the Earlier Nineteenth Century* (London: Oxford University Press, 1962), p. 8.

[10]Gervase Mathew, "The East African Coast until the Coming of the Portuguese," in *History of East Africa,* ed. Roland Oliver and Gervase Mathew (London: Oxford University Press, 1963), 1:116, 120–21.

[11]Ibid., p. 106.

[12]Ibid, pp. 101, 108, 121.

[13]Joseph E. Harris, *The African Presence in Asia: Consequences of the East African Slave Trade* (Evanston: Northwestern University Press, 1971), pp. 78–79, 91–98.

[14]Ibid., pp. 7–10; and Edward A. Alpers, *The East African Slave Trade* (Dar es Salaam: East African Publishing House, 1967), pp. 4–5.

[15]Marina E. Espina, *Filipinos in Louisiana* (New Orleans: A. F. Laborde & Sons, 1988), p. 1.

[16]Arnold Rubin, *Black Nanban: Africans in Japan during the Sixteenth Century* (Bloomington: African Studies Program, Indiana University, 1974), pp. 1–2, 9.

[17]R. L. Watson, *The Slave Question: Liberty and Property in South Africa* (Hanover: Weslyan University Press, 1990), pp. 9–10; and Robert Ross, *Cape of Torments: Slavery and Resistance in South Africa* (London: Routledge & Kegan Paul, 1983), pp. 11, 13.

[18]Joan M. Jensen, *Passage from India: Asian Indian Immigrants in North America* (New Haven: Yale University Press, 1988), pp. 12–13.

[19]Alan H. Adamson, *Sugar without Slaves: The Political Economy of British Guiana, 1838–1904* (New Haven: Yale University Press, 1972), pp. 31, 41.

[20]Hugh Tinker, *A New System of Slavery: The Export of Indian Labour Overseas, 1830–1920* (London: Oxford University Press, 1974), p. 19. For overviews of Asian Indian and Chinese migration and indentureship in the Caribbean, see K. O. Laurence, *Immigration into the West Indies in the 19th Century* (Mona, West Indies: Caribbean Universities Press, 1971); and William A. Green, *British Slave Emancipation: The Sugar Colonies and the Great Experiment, 1830–1865* (London: Oxford University Press, 1976), pp. 276–86, 289–93.

[21]Tinker, *New System of Slavery,* p. 63.

[22]Adamson, *Sugar without Slaves,* p. 48. Asian Indian and Chinese indentured laborers inherited, in the minds of the white planters, the alleged vices of African slaves in Trinidad. See David Vincent Trotman, *Crime in Trinidad: Conflict and Control in a Plantation Society, 1838–1900* (Knoxville: University of Tennessee Press, 1986), pp. 69, 87–88.

[23]Noor Kumar Mahabir, *The Still Cry: Personal Accounts of East Indians in Trinidad and Tobago during Indentureship (1845–1917)* (Tacarigua, Trinidad: Calaloux Publications, 1985), p. 41. For life on the sugar estates, see Adamson, *Sugar without Slaves,* pp. 104–59; and Judith Ann Weller, *The East Indian Indenture in Trinidad* (Rio Piedras, P.R.: Institute of Caribbean Studies, University of Puerto Rico, 1968).

[24]Cited in Ching-Hwang Yen, *Coolies and Mandarins: China's Protection of Overseas Chinese during the Late Ch'ing Period (1851–1911)* (Singapore: Singapore University Press, 1985), p. 59.

[25]Shih-shan H. Tsai, "American Involvement in the Coolie Trade," *American Studies* 6, nos. 3 and 4 (December 1976): 54. For a more detailed account of U.S. involvement in the coolie trade and coolie resistance, see Robert J. Schwendinger, *Ocean of Bitter Dreams: Maritime Relations between China and the United States, 1850–1915* (Tucson: Westernlore Press, 1988), pp. 18–62.

[26]Yen, *Coolies and Mandarins,* pp. 61–62.

[27]Persia C. Campbell, *Chinese Coolie Emigration to Countries within the British Empire* (London: P. S. King & Son, 1923), p. 95; and Watt Stewart, *Chinese Bondage in Peru* (Durham: Duke University Press, 1951), pp. 62, 66, 97. See also Yen, *Coolies and Mandarins,* p. 62.

[28]Franklin W. Knight, *Slave Society in Cuba during the Nineteenth Century* (Madison: University of Wisconsin Press, 1970), p. 119. African slavery in Cuba, of course, was governed by slave codes

that differed significantly from the institutions that regulated the coolie system. On the complementarity and distinctions between African slavery and Chinese indentured labor, see Rebecca J. Scott, *Slave Emancipation in Cuba: The Transition to Free Labor, 1860–1899* (Princeton: Princeton University Press, 1985), pp. 29–35, 109–10.

[29]Yen, *Coolies and Mandarins,* p. 63; and Knight, *Slave Society,* p. 116.

[30]Yen, *Coolies and Mandarins* pp. 64, 66–68. For a comparison, see Jan Breman, *Taming the Coolie Beast: Plantation Society and the Colonial Order in Southeast Asia* (Delhi: Oxford University Press, 1989); and Wing Yung, *My Life in China and America* (New York: Henry Holt, 1909), p. 195, on Chinese coolies in Peru.

[31]James L. Roark, *Masters without Slaves: Southern Planters in the Civil War and Reconstruction* (New York: W. W. Norton, 1977), p. 165. See also Rowland T. Berthoff, "Southern Attitudes toward Immigration, 1865–1914," *Journal of Southern History* 17, no. 3 (August 1951): 328–60; and George E. Pozzetta, "Foreigners in Florida: A Study of Immigration Promotion, 1865–1910," *Florida Historical Quarterly* 53, no.2 (October 1974): 164–80.

[32]Roark, *Masters without Slaves* p. 167.

[33]Loewen, *Mississippi Chinese,* pp. 21–24.

[34]Ibid., p. 23.

[35]Lucy M. Cohen, *Chinese in the Post-Civil War South: A People without a History* (Baton Rouge: Louisiana State University Press, 1984); idem, "Entry of Chinese to the Lower South from 1865 to 1879: Policy Dilemmas," *Southern Studies* 17, no. 1 (Spring, 1978): 5–37; and idem, "Early Arrivals," *Southern Exposure,* July/August 1984, pp. 24–30.

[36]Cohen, "Entry of Chinese," pp. 8–12.

[37]Ibid., p. 20.

[38]Loewen, *Mississippi Chinese,* p. 26.

[39]Cohen, *Chinese in the Post–Civil War South,* p. 44; and Gunther Barth, *Bitter Strength: A History of the Chinese in the United States, 1850–1870* (Cambridge: Harvard University Press, 1964), p. 67. See also Shih-shan Henry Tsai, *The Chinese Experience in America* (Bloomington: Indiana University Press, 1986), pp. 3–7; idem, "American Involvement"; Roger Daniels, *Asian America: Chinese and Japanese in the United States since 1850* (Seattle: University of Washington Press, 1988), pp. 13–15; and Sucheng Chan, *This Bitter-Sweet Soil: The Chinese in California Agriculture, 1860–1910* (Berkeley and Los Angeles: University of California Press, 1986), pp. 21, 26.

[40]June Mei, "Socioeconomic Origins of Emigration: Guangdong to California, 1850 to 1882," in *Labor Immigration under Capitalism: Asian Workers in the United States before World War II,* ed. Lucie Cheng and Edna Bonacich (Berkeley and Los Angeles: University of California Press, 1984), p. 220; and Sucheng Chan, *Asian Americans: An Interpretive History* (Boston: Twayne Publishers, 1991), p. 4.

[41]David J. Hellwig, "Black Reactions to Chinese Immigration and the Anti-Chinese Movement: 1850–1910," *Amerasia Journal* 6, no. 2 (1979): 27, 30, 31. See also Philip S. Foner, "Reverend George Washington Woodbey: Early Twentieth Century California Black Socialist," *Journal of Negro History* 6, no. 2 (April 1976): 149–50. In their 1943 struggle for repeal of the exclusion laws, Chinese Americans recognized a common cause with African Americans in their quest for equality. Renqiu Yu, "Little Heard Voices: The Chinese Hand Laundry Alliance and the *China Daily News'* Appeal for Repeal of the Chinese Exclusion Act in 1943," in *Chinese America: History and Perspectives, 1990,* ed. Marlon K. Hom et al. (San Francisco: Chinese Historical Society of America, 1990), pp. 28–29, 31–32.

[42]Quoted in Takaki, *Iron Cages,* p. 14.

[43]Alexander Saxton, *The Indispensable Enemy: Labor and the Anti-Chinese Movement in California* (Berkeley and Los Angeles: University of California Press, 1971), pp. 19–45; and idem, *The Rise and Fall of the White Republic: Class Politics and Mass Culture in Nineteenth Century America* (London: Verso, 1990). See also Luther W. Spoehr, "Sambo and the Heathen Chinese: Californians' Racial Stereotypes in the Late 1870s," *Pacific Historical Review* 42, no. 2 (May 1973): 185–204; and Miller, *Unwelcome Immigrant.*

[45]Saxton, *Indispensable Enemy,* p. 18; and Caldwell, "Negroization of the Chinese Stereotype," p. 127.

[46]Cited in Ronad Takaki, *Strangers from a Different Shore: A History of Asian Americans* (Boston: Little, Brown & Co., 1989), pp. 100–101.

[47]Saxton, *Indispensable Enemy,* p. 20.

[48]Ibid., p. 19–20. For comparision of Chinese and African American intelligence, see U.S. Congress, Senate, *Report of the Joint Special Committee to Investigate Chinese Immigration,* 44th Cong., 2d sess., 1877, pp. 942, 1133–34.

[48]Quoted in Wu, "*Chink!*" pp. 36–43.

[49]George M. Fredrickson, *The Arrogance of Race: Historical Perspectives on Slavery, Racism, and Social Inequality* (Middletown: Wesleyan University Press, 1988), p. 196. Cf. Takaki, *Strangers from a Different Shore,* p. 101, who, like Winthrop Jordan, claims that a 1664 Maryland law that discouraged the marriage of "Negro slaves" with "freeborne English women" by imposing a penalty requiring such women and their children to be consigned into slavery should be viewed as ban on interracial marriage. Fredrickson, however, argues that before the 1690s, bans of interracial unions were largely class as opposed to race-based.

[50]Takaki, *Strangers from a Different Shore,* pp. 101–2.

[51]Elmer Clarence Sandmeyer, *The Anti-Chinese Movement in California* (Urbana: University of Illinois Press, 1973), p. 50; Victor Low, *The Unimpressible Race: A Century of Educational Struggle by the Chinese in San Francisco* (San Francisco: East/West Publishing Co., 1982), pp., 6–37; and Charles M. Wollenberg, *All Deliberate Speed: Segregation and Exclusion in California Schools, 1855–1975* (Berkeley and Los Angeles: University of California Press, 1976), pp. 30, 31, 39–43.

[52]Knight, *Slave Society,* p. 71.

[53]Cohen, *Chinese in the Post-Civil War South,* p. 167.

[54]Loewen, *Mississippi Chinese,* pp. 59, 61, 66–68.

[55]Cohen, *Chinese in the Post-Civil War South,* pp. 167–68. Sociologists Omi and Winant point out that racial classification is "an intensely political process" and is not a mere academic exercise but denies or provides access to resources and opportunities (Omi and Winant, *Racial Formation,* pp. 3–4).

[56]Loewen, *Mississippi Chinese,* p. 60. Similarly, the biracial offspring of Africans, Europeans, and American Indians occupied an ambiguous social and legal position in the South. See Adele Logan Alexander, *Ambiguous Lives: Free Women of Color in Rural Georgia, 1789–1879* (Fayetteville: University of Arkansas Press, 1991).

[57]Barbara M. Posadas, "The Hierarchy of Color and Psychological Adjustment in an Industrial Environment: Filipinos, the Pullman Company, and the Brotherhood of Sleeping Car Porters," *Labor History* 23, no. 3 (1982): 363.

[58]Kelly Miller, *The Everlasting Stain* (Washington, D.C.; Associated Publishers, 1924), p. 163.

[59]David J. Hellwig, "Afro-American Reactions to the Japanese and the Anti-Japanese Movement, 1906–1924," *Phylon* 38, no. 1 (March 1977: 103.

[60]*The Colored American Magazine* 12, no. 3 (March 1907): 169.

[61]Willard B. Gatewood, Jr,. *"Smoked Yankees" and the Struggle for Empire: Letters from Negro Soldiers, 1898–1902* (Urbana: University of Illinois Press, 1971), p. 13; and William Loren Katz, *The Black West* (Seattle: Open Hand Publishing, 1987), pp. 323–24. On African American soldiers and the Vietnam War, see Byron G. Fiman, Jonathan F. Borus, and M. Duncan Stanton, "Black-White and American-Vietnamese Relations among Soldiers in Vietnam," *Journal of Social Issues* 31, no.4 (1975): 39–48.

[62]Gatewood, *"Smoked Yankees,"* pp. 14, 15.

[63]Luzviminda Francisco, "The First Vietnam: The Philippine-American War, 1899–1902," *in Letters in Exile: An Introductory Reader on the History of Philipinos in America,* ed. Jesse Quinsaat (Los Angeles: UCLA Asian American Studies Center, 1976), pp. 15, 19; and Gatewood, *"Smoked Yankees,"* p. 15.

[64]Richard Kluger, *Simple Justice: The History of* Brown v. Broad of Education *and Black America's Struggle for Equality* (New York: Vintage Books, 1975), pp. 120–22, 191, 423, 448, 554, 565–66, 670, 703–4.

[65]On African and Asian American conflicts, see Arnold Shankman's three publications: " 'Asiatic Ogre' or 'Desirable Citizen'? The Image of Japanese Americans in the Afro-American Press, 1867–1933," *Pacific Historical Review* 46, no. 4 (November 1977): 567–87; "Black on Yellow: Afro-Americans View Chinese-Americans," *Phylon* 39, no. 1 (Spring 1978): 1–17; and *Ambivalent Friends: Afro-Americans View the Immigrant* (Westport: Greenwood Press, 1982).

[66]Rudolph M. Lapp, *Blacks in Gold Rush California* (New Haven: Yale University Press, 1977), pp. 104–5.

[67]Bill Hosokawa, *Nisei: The Quiet Americans* (New York: William Morrow, 1969), pp. 31–33.

[68]Lapp, *Blacks in Gold Rush California,* pp. 104–5, 109–10; Douglas Daniels, *Pioneer Urbanites: A Social and Cultural History of Black San Francisco* (Philadelphia: Temple University Press, 1980), p. 97; and Shankman, *Ambivalent Friends,* pp. 31–32. On marriages between Africans and Asians in the South, see Loewen, *Mississippi Chinese,* pp. 135–53; Cohen, *Chinese in the Post-Civil War South,* pp. 149–72; and Doris Black, "The Black Chinese," *Sepia,* December 1975, pp. 19–24.

[69]Kenneth G. Goode, *California's Black Pioneers: A Brief Historical Survey* (Santa Barbara: McNally & Loftin, 1974), p. 110; and Shankman, *Ambivalent Friends,* p. 30.

[70]Shankman, "Black on Yellow," pp. 15–16.

[71]Ibid., p. 16.

[72]Francis Fukuyama, "The End of History?" *National Interest* 16 (Summer 1989): 3–18. The symbol of a man of color, particularly a man of Japanese ancestry, schooled in the West proclaiming "the triumph of the West" added substance to the finality of that "triumph," especially to those dubbed by Allan Bloom "we faithful defenders of the Western Alliance" (Allan Bloom, "Responses to Fukuyama," *National Interest* 16 [Summer 1989]: 19).

[73]*Negro Digest,* September 1944, p. 66.

[74]Yuri Kochiyama, "Because Movement Work is Contagious," *Gidra,* 1990, pp. 6, 10.

[75]W. E. B. Du Bois, *The World and Africa, An Inquiry into the Part Which Africa Has Played in World History* (New York: International Publishers, 1965), p. 260.

[76]Frank F. Chuman, *The Bamboo People: The Law and Japanese-Americans* (Del Mar, Calif.: Publisher's Inc., 1976), pp. 70–71. See also Yuji Ichioka, *The Issei: The World of the First Generation Japanese Immigrants, 1885–1924* (New York: Free Press, 1988), pp. 210–26.

[77]*Korea Times,* December 9, 1991. In Los Angeles, after meeting between the Korean American Grocers Association and several African American gang leaders on May 25, 1992, the merchants announced plans to hire gang members, and a participant in the negotiations reported a "total bond between the two groups," which included the widely feared gangs the Bloods and the Crips (*Asian Week,* May 29, 1992; and *Korea Times,* June 8, 1992).

[78]Maxine Hong Kingston, *The Woman Warrier: Memories of a Girlhood among Ghosts* (New York: Alfred A. Knopf, 1976), pp. 241–43.

# Response and Responsibility

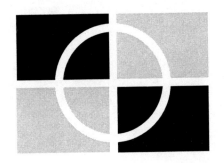

# Introduction

*Eric Vega*

Ethnic Studies concerns itself with both abstract ideas and social justice. It presents historical and sociological information regarding race, ethnicity, gender and class. At the same time Ethnic Studies also discusses strategies for confronting unequal social relations in our community and nation. These discussions and dialogs offer us a chance to think critically about how others have confronted questions of power and privilege. This is both tricky and complex because the subject matter of inequality is not purely abstract or academic.

The specific struggles of women and people of color for liberation and respect are in themselves political controversies. Simply raising the issue of race or ethnicity is for many people an unsettling political terrain. But this is exactly the world of ideas and social struggle that informs this book. Both parts are integral to Ethnic Studies research and both parts continue to reanimate our lectures and study. In other words, this book is not just a data dump of terms and abstract ideas to memorize for the teacher. That is because the subject consistently breaks the bounds of objective analysis. This is sometimes uncomfortably true.

A few years ago our Department of Ethnic Studies received racially motivated death threats. The caller felt deeply threatened by the intersection of people of color analyzing questions of race and ethnicity. This immersion in political controversy is not likely to be found in the Geology or Math Department. That is not to suggest Ethnic Studies has the "truth" or even complete answers to the difficult questions that surround us. It is more true to say our readings and our study are precisely about going deeper and learning how we can use language and ideas to inform our strategies for making the world a better place. As an example, this book asks the reader to move away from shallow or simplistic responses to racism. In our classes it is not enough to observe that the Ku Klux Klan makes you feel bad or sad. It is more important to ask questions regarding the historical and ideological context for white supremacist organizations. How do you respond to hate organizations when they work to insert themselves into popular consciousness? When you move beyond their cartoon like imagery, to what extent are their ideas accepted? These are difficult questions rooted in both theory and practice.

On the theoretical side, there are many explanations for the reoccurring controversies and issues connected to racial and ethnic relations. One way of approaching this topic is to examine identity. Who are we? Do we socially construct ourselves? What is the history of identity and what is its connection to the order of the nation? Historically, in the social sciences, intellectuals have formulated classic questions to help us examine popular ideas regarding identity. People like Freud, Marx and Nietzche have argued that we must examine the subconscious, money relations or the will to power if we want to honestly examine how people see themselves and relate to others. Ethnic Studies continues this tradition of observation and questioning. It asks the following kinds of questions. How have racial and ethnic groups been silenced or marginalized? What is the relationship of identity to power? In what ways do we have a fixed identity? What are the consequences of a constructed identity? As we work our way through these complex questions we rely on basic terms and theories. Stereotypes, ethnocentrism, assimilation and theories of prejudice and discrimination are the building blocks for examining questions related to racial and ethnic identity. But again it is critical to acknowledge that these words and ideas arise out of the struggles of historically subjugated peoples. That is not to suggest that social struggles are limited to problems associated with oppression and victimization. It is instead to say that our ideas about ourselves and about the world around us are fundamentally connected to the actual struggles of people. This means that an accurate description of the ethnic experience in this country must include an examination of social movements, political demands, styles of organizing, legal information and strategies that people of color have used historically to achieve their objectives.

This section of the book offers examples of how scholars, activists and communities have responded to the challenge of identity and power relations. Ward Churchill analyzes problems associated with stereotypes by examining the ongoing controversy regarding Native American mascots in *Crimes Against Humanity*. In California and throughout the nation state agencies and community organizations help people understand the laws and their rights under the law. In this section we provide information on how you can challenge discrimination by using the complaint process of the Department of Fair Employment and Housing. In the post 9/11 world many immigrants, Arab and Muslim people are learning about their rights. Both the American Civil Liberties Union and the National Lawyers Guild have been at the forefront of providing information, as in the case of *Know Your Rights*. Also included is an example of a local community effort in Sacramento, California. Activists successfully persuaded the City Council to take a stand against discriminatory and unconstitutional provisions of the U.S Patriot Act. In *Gender Inequality Within the Movement* Barbara Ransby examines the contributions of civil right advocate Ella Baker. Her emphasis on poor people of color leading their own organizations and formulating their own strategies continues to be an important contribution to the civil rights movement in this country. Finally, this section gives an example of faculty and students participating in Ethnic Studies classes at Hiram Johnson High School. The work of James Sobredo, Linda Revilla and Gregory Yee Mark in *An Ethnic Studies Model of Community Collaboration* highlights the responsibility of an Ethnic Studies Department committed to bridging the gap between theory and practice to address local needs.

# Facing the Demon Head On: Race and the Prison Industrial Complex

*Manning Marable*

> *We know through painful experience that freedom is never voluntarily given by the oppressor; it must be demanded by the oppressed.*
>
> —*Martin Luther King, Jr.*
> "Letter from Birmingham Jail," April 16, 1963

 **I**

When I was a child, the only two prisons I had ever heard about were Alcatraz and Sing Sing. Alcatraz was the formidable, stone citadel, perched on a small island in the middle of the San Francisco Bay. I saw *The Birdman of Alcatraz* starring Burt Lancaster, and the film left a deep impression about prison life. I suppose my knowledge of Sing Sing was acquired in a similar fashion. My images of crime and punishment were derived from Edgar G. Robinson, or perhaps some obscure character actors who were usually cast as hoodlums. Somehow, though, I knew that the phrase "to send him up the river" meant a one-way trip along the Hudson River to the infamous Sing Sing Prison.

Nothing I have seen or experienced prepared me for the reality of Sing Sing. The prison itself seems literally carved out of the side of a massive cliff that hovers just above the Hudson River. Parking is usually difficult to find near the prison, so you have to walk a good distance before you come to the outer gate, the first of a series of razor sharp barriers. The main entrance looks remarkably small, compared to the vast size of the prison. Entering the front door, you find yourself in a relatively small room, with several guards and a walk-through metal detector. Your clothing and other personal items are carefully checked. Permission to go inside the prison is severely restricted, and you must be approved through a review process well before your visit.

From *The Meaning of Race in America* by Manning Marable. Reprinted by permission of the author.

On the other side of the entrance area, shielded by rows of steel bars, is a hallway that is lined with wooden benches on either side. It is here that inmates wait before being summoned to their hearings to determine whether they have merited early release. During my first time visiting Sing Sing, there were about a half dozen young males, all African Americans and mostly in their twenties, who were sitting nervously on the benches. Most would be forced to wait for hours in order to have fifteen minutes before the parole board. In fifteen short minutes, they would learn whether they would be released, or ordered to serve another term of years behind bars. You could see clearly the hopeful anxiety in each man's face, trying to anticipate the queries of their inquisitors. The right answer at the right moment could bring their suffering to an end.

The prisoners also know that the parole board's decisions are directly influenced by authorities in political power. Under former Governor Mario Cuomo, for instance, approximately 54 percent of violent offenders received parole on their first appearance before a parole board. Since 1995 under Governor George Pataki, only one-third of violent offenders were granted parole after their first review. As Robert Gangi, the director of the Correctional Association of New York, observed, "Given the practice of the parole board, there are more and more long-termers that no matter how well they behave, no matter how many programs they complete, the parole board is not going to let them out."

As you walk through the prison, you go down a series of hallways, separated by small containments that have two sets of steel bars on either side, and secured by a prison guard. Only one set of doors opens at a time. The guard must lock and secure the first door before you're permitted to walk through the second door. Because the prison was constructed on a side of a cliff, there are also a series of steps that must be climbed to go from one area to another.

At the end of one hallway is the infamous, seventy-year-old structure, Cell Block B. The guards informed me, with considerable pride, that Cell Block B was one of the largest enclosed incarceration areas of its kind in the world. One must first walk through a series of double barred steel doors separated by a small interlocking security chamber. Once passing through the second door, one enters a vast open space, surrounded by massive concrete walls and ceiling. In the center of this chamber, filling up nearly the entire space, is a solid iron cage, five stories high. Every story or tier contains 68 separate prison cells, front and back, for a total of 136 cells on each level. Each tier is separated by small-railed catwalks and narrow stairwells.

Each cell is a tiny confined space, with barely enough room for a prisoner's toilet, sink, and bed. Prisoners are not allowed to place any clothing or items covering the front of their cells, except when using their toilets. In effect, personal privacy is nonexistent. The massive metal structure is like a huge iron and steel echo chamber, where every sound from tier to tier resonates and can be easily heard. The whole oppressive environment—the pungent smells of sweat and human waste, the absence of fresh air, the lack of privacy, the close quarters of men who have been condemned to live much of their natural lives in tiny steel cages—

is so horrific that I find it even now impossible to express in words its awesome reality. Perhaps the only word for it is evil.

Ted Conover, the author of *Newjack: Guarding Sing Sing*, who worked for nine months as a correctional officer at the prison, had a similar experience when he spent his first day on the job in Cell Block B. Conover was immediately overwhelmed by the constant level of noise, the demands of his supervisors, and the general chaos. "Being a new face," Conover noted, "was like being a substitute teacher. They test you. They defy you. And your job is to get them to comply." Conover questioned the ability of anyone to withstand the psychological stresses and physical levels of brutality that permeated the entire character of life in Sing Sing. "Every day is terrifying," Conover observed. "From the first minute, you're presented with challenges no one prepared you for. It's like working in an explosives factory. You think you're going to get killed. But you have to put it out of your mind."

Violence against prisoners is a daily occurrence. Conover described the process of carrying out a "shakedown" of solitary confinement cells. The guards go from cell to cell, demanding that each individual prisoner strip, turn around, raise his arms, and permit himself to be body searched. For prisoners who refused to be humiliated by this demeaning procedure, a group of guards pushed their way into their cells and forcibly carried out body searches. It was months after Conover was working in Sing Sing, however, that he realized that prisoners who resisted being physically searched were trying to hold on to some element of self-respect, to refuse to participate in their own violation. "If enough people did that together," Conover recognized, "the correctional system would come tumbling down."

In this man-made hell-on-earth, something within the human spirit nevertheless flourishes. About two decades ago, the prisoners of Cell Block B somehow managed to overwhelm their guards, protesting their inhumane conditions. For several days seventeen correctional officers were held as hostages. But in the end, the prisoners recognized that escape was impossible, and that this act of resistance was more symbolic than anything else. To demand to be treated as a human being in an inhumane environment is to be a revolutionary.

Seven years ago I received an invitation to visit Sing Sing from the Reverend George William ("Bill") Webber, who in 1982 had started the master's degree program at New York Theological Seminary (NYTS). When Bill began visiting Sing Sing on a regular basis, he observed that there were a small but highly motivated number of prisoners who had finished their bachelor's degrees and wanted to take more advanced courses. NYTS began to offer a graduate program designed for long-term prisoners at the facility. As the NYTS program developed, inmates at various correctional facilities throughout New York State were selected for admission and then transferred to Sing Sing. About fourteen to sixteen men were selected every year, with a waiting list of one or more years.

I was escorted to the rear quarters of the prison, which consist of religious quarters and chapels of different denominations. At the bottom of a stairwell was the entrance to a classroom. The students were already waiting there and were eager to introduce themselves. There was Louis, a twenty-nine-year-old man of Puerto Rican descent, who had already spent twelve years of his brief life inside penal institutions; Kevin, a middle-aged African-American man, articulate and serious, who had been in Sing Sing for nineteen years, and who was now actively involved in AIDS awareness and antiviolence programs within the inmate population; "Doc," a thirteen-year prisoner who planned to be a counselor; Paul, a seventeen-year inmate interested in working with teenagers and young adults after his release; and Felipe, a prisoner for nineteen years, who was preparing himself for the ministry.

The NYTS program is basically designed to prepare these men for community service. There is a rigorous academic program, where lectures and classroom discussions are held three hours a day, five days a week. Forty-two credit hours must be taken to complete the degree. Inmates are also required to perform an additional fifteen credit hours of field service within the prison, which can range from working in the AIDS ward to tutoring other prisoners. Since the program was established, more than 200 men have graduated with master's degrees. Only 5 percent of those inmates who have completed the program and were released were subsequently returned to prison.

The NYTS program is exceptional, in part, because so few educational programs of its type exist in U.S. prisons. In 1995, only one-third of all U.S. prisons provided college course work, and fewer than one in four prisoners were enrolled in some kind of educational or tutorial program behind bars. There are only about 11,000 paid teachers who are currently employed by penal institutions, or about one teacher per ninety-three prisoners.

One can only imagine the personal courage and determination of these men, most of whom entered prison without a high-school diploma or GED. From the first day of their sentences inside Sing Sing, they experienced what the NYTS 1994 program graduates accurately described as "social death": "We are told what we can eat, when we can eat it, and how we must eat it. We are told what type of clothing we can wear, when to wear it, and where we can wear it; when we can sleep and when we cannot sleep; where we can walk and where we cannot walk; when we can show affection to our families and when we cannot show affection; where we can sit and where we cannot sit; where we can stand and where we cannot stand." Despite the hostility of many prison guards, most of whom come from the same oppressed classes of those whom they are employed to guard, the men involved in the program withstand the daily abuse and harassment. In their own words, "We see ourselves as agents of change."

## II

For a variety of reasons, rates of violent crime, including murder, rape, and robbery, increased dramatically in the 1960s and 1970s. Much of this increase occurred in urban areas. By the late 1970s, nearly one-half of all Americans were afraid to walk within a mile of their homes at night, and 90 percent responded in surveys that the U.S. criminal-justice system was not dealing harshly enough with criminals. Politicians like Richard M. Nixon, George Wallace, and Ronald Reagan began to campaign successfully on the theme of law and order. The death penalty, which was briefly outlawed by the Supreme Court, was reinstated. Local, state, and federal expenditures for law enforcement rose sharply. Behind much of anticrime rhetoric was a not-too-subtle racial dimension, the projection of crude stereotypes about the link between criminality and black people. Rarely did these politicians observe that minority and poor people, not the white middle class, were statistically much more likely to experience violent crimes of all kinds. The argument was made that law-enforcement officers should be given much greater latitude in suppressing crime, that sentences should be lengthened and made mandatory, and that prisons should be designed not for the purpose of rehabilitation, but punishment.

Consequently, there was a rapid expansion in the personnel of the criminal-justice system, as well as the construction of new prisons. What occurred in New York State, for example, was typical of what happened nationally. From 1817 to 1981, New York had opened thirty-three state prisons. From 1982 to 1999, another thirty-eight state prisons were constructed. The state's prison population at the time of the Attica prison revolt in September 1971 was about 12,500. By 1999, there were more than 71,000 prisoners in New York State correctional facilities.

In 1974, the number of Americans incarcerated in all state prisons stood at 187,500. By 1991, the number had reached 711,700. Nearly two-thirds of all state prisoners in 1991 had less than a high-school education. One-third of all prisoners were unemployed at the time of their arrests. Incarceration rates by the end of the 1980s had soared to unprecedented rates, especially for black Americans. As of December 1989, the total U.S. prison population, including federal institutions, exceeded 1 million for the first time in history, an incarceration rate of the general population of 1 out of every 250 citizens. For African Americans, the rate was over 700 per 100,000, or about seven times higher than for whites. About one-half of all prisoners were black. Twenty-three percent of all black males in their twenties were either in prison, on parole, on probation, or awaiting trial. The rate of incarceration of black Americans in 1989 had even surpassed that experienced by blacks who still lived under the apartheid regime of South Africa.

By the early 1990s, rates for all types of violent crime began to plummet. But the laws sending offenders to prison were made even more severe. Children were increasingly viewed in courts as adults and subjected to harsher penalties. Laws like California's "three strikes and you're out" eliminated the possibility of parole for repeat offenders. The vast majority of these new prisoners were nonviolent offenders, and many of these were convicted of drug offenses that carried long prison terms. In New York, African Americans and Latinos make up 25 percent of the total population, but by 1999 they represented 83 percent of all state prisoners and 94 percent of all individuals convicted on drug offenses. The pattern of racial bias in these statistics is confirmed by the research of the U.S. Commission on Civil Rights, which found that while African Americans today constitute only

14 percent of all drug users nationally, they account for 35 percent of all drug arrests, 55 percent of all drug convictions, and 75 percent of all prison admissions for drug offenses. Currently, the racial proportions of those under some type of correctional supervision, including parole and probation, are one in fifteen for young white males, one in ten for young Latino males, and one in three for young African-American males. Statistically today, more than eight out of every ten African-American males will be arrested at some point in their lifetime.

Structural racism is so difficult to dismantle in our nation today, in part, because political leaders in both major parties have deliberately redirected billions of our tax dollars away from investments in public education into the construction of what many scholars now describe as a prison industrial complex. This is the terrible connection between education and incarceration.

A 1998 study produced by the Correctional Association of New York and the Washington, D.C.–based Justice Policy Institute illustrated that in New York State hundreds of millions of dollars have been reallocated from the budgets of public universities to prison construction. The report stated: "Since fiscal year 1988, New York's public universities have seen their operating budgets plummet by 29 percent while funding for prisons has increased by 76 percent. In actual dollars, there has nearly been an equal trade-off, with the Department of Correctional Services receiving a $761 million increase during that time while state funding for New York's city and state university systems has declined by $615 million." By 1998, New York State was spending nearly twice what it had allocated to run its prison system a decade ago. To pay for that massive expansion, tuitions and fees for students at the State University of New York (SUNY) and the City University of New York (CUNY) had to be dramatically hiked.

For black and Latino young adults, these shifts have made it much more difficult to attend college than in the past, but much easier to go to prison. The New York State study found: "There are more blacks (34,809) and Hispanics (22,421) locked up in prison than there are attending the State University of New York, where there are 27,925 black and Hispanic students. Since 1989, there have been more blacks entering the prison system for drug offenses each year than there were graduating from SUNY with undergraduate, masters, and doctoral degrees—combined."

The devastating pattern of schools versus prisons in New York exists throughout our country. In California, thousands of black and Latino young adults were denied access to state universities because of the passage of Proposition 209, which destroyed affirmative action. Thousands more have been driven out by the steadily growing cost of tuition and cutbacks in student loans. Meanwhile, hundreds of millions of dollars have been siphoned away from the state's education budget and spent on building prisons.

In 1977, California had 19,600 inmates in its state prison system. By 2000, the number of that state's prisoners exceeded 163,000. In the past two decades of the twentieth century, California has constructed one new state university, but twenty-one new prisons. California's prison system "holds more inmates in its jails and prisons than do France, Great Britain, Germany, Japan, Singapore, and the Netherlands combined." And future trends are worse. The California Department of Corrections estimated in 2000 that it would need to spend $6.1 billion over the coming decade just to maintain the present prison population. There are more employees at work in the American prison industry than in any Fortune 500 corporation, with the one exception of General Motors.

Instead of funding more teachers, we are hiring extra prison guards. Instead of building new classrooms, we are constructing new jails. Instead of books, we now have bars everywhere.

## III

The latest innovation in American corrections is termed "special housing units" (SHUs), but which prisoners also generally refer to as The Box. SHUs are uniquely designed solitary confinement cells in which prisoners are locked down for twenty-three hours a day for months or even years at a time. SHU cell blocks are electronically monitored, prefabricated structures of concrete and steel, about 14 feet long and 8 1/2 feet wide, amounting to 120 square feet of space. The two inmates who are confined in each cell, however, actually have only about 60 square feet of usable space, or 30 square feet per person. All meals are served to prisoners through a thin slot cut into the steel door. The toilet unit, sink, and shower are all located in the cell. Prisoners are permitted one hour "exercise time" each day in a small concrete balcony, surrounded by heavy security wire, directly connected with their SHU cells. Educational and rehabilitation programs for SHU prisoners are prohibited.

As of 1998, New York State had confined 5,700 state prisoners in SHUs, about 8 percent of its total inmate population. Currently under construction in Upstate New York is a new 750-cell maximum-security SHU facility that will cost state taxpayers $180 million. Although Amnesty International and human-rights groups in the United States have widely condemned SHUs, claiming that such forms of imprisonment constitute the definition of torture under international law, other states have followed New York's example. As of 1998, California had constructed 2,942 SHU beds, followed by Mississippi (1,756), Arizona (1,728), Virginia (1,267), Texas (1,229), Louisiana (1,048), and Florida (1,000). Solitary confinement, which historically had been defined even by corrections officials as an extreme disciplinary measure, is becoming increasingly the norm.

The introduction of SHUs reflects a general mood in the country that the growing penal population is essentially beyond redemption. If convicted felons cease to be viewed as human beings, why should they be treated with any humanity? This punitive spirit was behind the Republican-controlled Congress and President Clinton's decision in 1995 to eliminate inmate eligibility for federal Pell Grant awards for higher education. As of 1994, 23,000 prisoners throughout the United States had received Pell Grants, averaging about $1,500 per award. The total amount of educational support granted prisoners, $35 million, represented only 0.6 percent of all Pell Grant funding nationally. Many studies have found that prisoners who participate in higher education programs, and especially those who complete college degrees, have significantly lower rates of recidivism. For all prison inmates, for example, recidivism averages between 50 percent and 70 percent. Federal parolees have a recidivism rate of 40 percent. Prisoners with a college education have recidivism rates of only 5 to 10 percent. Given the high success ratio of prisoners who complete advanced degree work and the relatively low cost of public investment, such educational programs should make sense. But following the federal government's lead, many states have also ended their tuition benefits programs for state prisoners.

The economic consequences of the vast expansion of our prison industrial complex are profound. According to criminal-justice scholar David Barlow at the University of Wisconsin at Milwaukee, between 1980 and 2000 the combined expenditures of federal, state, and local governments on police have increased about 400 percent. Corrections expenditures for building new prisons, upgrading existing facilities, hiring more guards, and related costs increased approximately 1,000 percent. Although it currently costs about $70,000 to construct a typical prison cell, and about $25,000 annually to supervise and maintain each prisoner, the United States is still building hundreds of new prison beds every week.

The driving ideological and cultural force that rationalizes and justifies mass incarceration is the white American public's stereotypical perceptions about race and crime. As Andrew Hacker perceptively noted in 1995, "Quite clearly, 'black crime' does not make people think about tax evasion or embezzling from brokerage firms. Rather, the offenses generally associated with blacks are those . . . involving violence." A number of researchers have found that racial stereotypes of African Americans—as "violent," "aggressive," "hostile," and "short-tempered"— greatly influence whites' judgments about crime. Generally, most whites are inclined to give black and Latino defendants more severe judgments of guilt and lengthier prison sentences than whites who commit identical crimes. Racial bias has been well established, especially in capital cases, where killers of white victims are much more likely to receive the death penalty than those who murder African Americans.

The greatest victims of these racialized processes of unequal justice, of course, are African-American and Latino young people. In April 2000, utilizing national and state data compiled by the FBI, the Justice Department and six leading foundations issued a comprehensive study that documented vast racial disparities at every level of the juvenile justice process. African Americans under age eighteen constitute 15 percent of their national age group, yet they currently represent 26 percent of all those who are arrested. After entering the criminal-justice system, white and black juveniles with the same records are treated in radically different ways. According to the Justice Department's study, among white youth offenders, 66 percent are referred to juvenile courts, while only 31 percent of the African-American youth are taken there. Blacks make up 44 percent of those detained in juvenile jails, 46 percent of all those tried in adult criminal courts, as well as 58 percent of all juveniles who are warehoused in adult prison. In practical terms, this means that young African Americans who are arrested and charged with a crime are more than six times more likely to be assigned to prison than white youth offenders.

For those young people who have never been to prison before, African Americans are nine times more likely than whites to be sentenced to juvenile prisons. For youths charged with drug offenses, blacks are forty-eight times more likely than whites to be sentenced to juvenile prison. White youths charged with violent offenses are incarcerated on average for 193 days after trial; by contrast, African-American youths are held 254 days, and Latino youths are incarcerated 305 days.

Even outside of the prison walls, the black community's parameters are largely defined by the agents of state and private power. There are now approximately 600,000 police officers and 1.5 million private security guards in the United States. Increasingly, however, black and poor communities are being "policed" by special paramilitary units, often called SWAT (Special Weapons and Tactics) teams. Researcher Christian Parenti cited studies indicating that "the nation has more than 30,000 such heavily armed, military trained police units." SWAT-team mobilizations, or "call outs," increased 400 percent between 1980 and 1995, with a 34 percent increase in the incidents of deadly force recorded by SWAT teams from 1995 to 1998.

What are the practical political consequences for regulating black and brown bodies through the coercive institutional space of our correctional facilities? Perhaps the greatest impact is on the process of black voting. According to the statistical data of the Sentencing Project, a non-profit research center in Washington, D.C., forty-eight states and the District of Columbia bar prisoners who have been convicted of a felony from voting. Thirty-two states bar ex-felons who are currently on parole from voting. Twenty-eight states even prohibit adults from voting if they are felony probationers. There are eight states that deny voting rights to former prisoners who had been serving time for felonies, even after they have completed their sentences: Alabama, Florida, Iowa, Kentucky, Mississippi, Nevada, Virginia, and Wyoming. In Arizona, ex-felons are disfranchised for life if they are convicted of a second felony. Delaware disfranchises some ex-felons for five years after they finish their sentences, and Maryland bars them from voting for an additional three years.

The net result to democracy is devastating. The Sentencing Project released these statistics in 2002:

● An estimated 3.9 million Americans, or one in fifty adults, have currently or permanently lost their voting rights as a result of a felony conviction.

● 1.4 million African-American men, or 13 percent of black men, are disfranchised, a rate seven times the national average.

● More than 2 million white Americans (Hispanic and non-Hispanic) are disfranchised.

- Over half a million women have lost their right to vote.

- In seven states that deny the vote to ex-offenders, one in four black men is *permanently* disfranchised.

- Given current rates of incarceration, three in ten of the next generation of black men can expect to be disfranchised at some point in their lifetime. In states that disfranchise ex-offenders, as many as 40 percent of black men may permanently lose their right to vote.

- 1.4 million disfranchised persons are ex-offenders who have completed their sentences. The state of Florida had at least 200,000 ex-felons who were unable to vote in the 2000 presidential elections.

The Sentencing Project adds that "the scale of felony voting disenfranchisement is far greater than in any other nation and has serious implications for democratic processes and racial inclusion." In effect, the Voting Rights Act of 1965, which guaranteed millions of African Americans the right to the electoral franchise, is being gradually repealed by state restrictions on voting for ex-felons. A people who are imprisoned in disproportionately higher numbers, and then systematically denied the right to vote, can in no way claim to live under a democracy.

The consequence of such widespread disfranchisement is what can be called "civil death." The individual who has been convicted of a felony, serves time, and successfully completes parole nevertheless continues to be penalized at every turn. He/she is penalized in the labor force, being denied certain jobs because of a criminal record. He/she has little direct access or influence on the decision-making processes of the political system. He/she may be employed and pay taxes, assuming all of the normal responsibilities of other citizens, yet may be temporarily or permanently barred from the one activity that defines citizenship itself—voting. Individuals who are penalized in this way have little incentive to participate in the normal public activities defining civic life because they exercise no voice in public decision making. Ex-prisoners on parole are also frequently discouraged from participation in public demonstrations or political meetings because of parole restrictions. For many ex-prisoners, there is a retreat from individual political activity; a sense of alienation and frustration easily leads to apathy. Those who experience civic death largely cease to view themselves as "civic actors," as people who possess the independent capacity to make important changes within society and within governmental policies.

Criminal-justice scholars have described prison as a metaphor for the most oppressive and socially destructive conditions of structural racism in America. As Alvin J. Bronstein observed in the *Prisoners' Rights Sourcebook* (1981), edited by Ira Robbins:

> In a very real sense, the prison is the outside world, squeezed into a very small space. The total and largely self-contained society that is prison contains all of the evils of that outside world, only much more concentrated. . . . Hence, militancy is especially great in prison, not because of a few agitators, but because

*the repression—whether justified or not—is harsh and undiluted. Because prison is one of the most severe sanctions in our society, the subjects of that sanction include the most alienated and the most aggressive members of society. And since the sense of injustice is most developed where the penalties are the greatest, the resentment and bitterness . . . [are] deep and pervasive.*

Many women and men who do manage to survive incarceration often acquire critical insights about the nature of the legal process and the criminal-justice system that could provide important and powerful lessons for young people in racialized minority communities. Like Frederick Douglass and Fannie Lou Hamer before them, they frequently do not have formal educational credentials or middle-class privileges. Yet from theorizing about their practical day-to-day experiences within the prison system, they come to a richer understanding of how that system actually works and how to develop innovative and creative ways to subvert it. As Bronstein noted, "It is no coincidence that many of the classics of black literature, such as those by Malcolm X, Eldridge Cleaver, Bobby Seale, and George Jackson, are prison memoirs, in whole or in part." Paradoxically, such strong personalities, who were able to survive the system, found ways to learn its lessons and to become empowered in the process. An essential step in transforming this system is in "reproducing" leaders like Malcolm X. The site of the most extreme oppression could have the greatest potential for creating the most effective leadership.

## IV

It is absolutely clear that a new leviathan of racial inequality has been constructed across our country. It lacks the brutal simplicity of the old Jim Crow system, with its omnipresent "white" and "colored" signs. Yet it is in many respects potentially far more brutalizing, because it presents itself to the world as a correctional system that is theoretically fair and essentially color-blind. The Black Freedom Movement of the 1960s was successful largely because it convinced a majority of white middle-class Americans that racial segregation was economically inefficient and that politically it could neither be sustained nor justified. The movement utilized the power of creative disruption, making it impossible for the old system of white prejudice, power, and privilege to function in the same old ways it had for nearly a century. How can Americans who still believe in racial equality and social justice stand silently while millions of our fellow citizens are being destroyed all around us?

It is abundantly clear that the political demand for mass incarceration and the draconian termination of voting rights to ex-felons will only contribute toward a more dangerous society. No walls can be constructed high enough, and no electronic surveillance cameras and alarms sophisticated enough, to protect white middle- and upper-class American families from the consequences of these policies. Keep in mind that approximately 600,000 people are released from prison every year; that about one-sixth of all reentering ex-prisoners, 100,000 people, are being released without any form of community correctional supervision; that about 75 percent of reentering prisoners have substance abuse histories; and that an estimated 16 percent suffer from mental illness. Nearly two-thirds of this reentering prison population will be arrested again within three years. The madness of our penal policies and of the criminal-justice system places the entire society at risk. Dismantling the prison industrial complex represents the great moral assignment and political challenge of our time.

During my last visit to Sing Sing, I noticed something new. The prison's correctional officials had erected a large, bright yellow sign over the door at the prison's public entrance. The colorful sign reads: "Through these doors pass some of the finest corrections professionals in the world."

I stood frozen for a second, immediately recalling the chillingly brutal sign posted above the entrance gate at Auschwitz and other concentration camps: *Arbeit Macht Frei* ("Work Makes Us Free"). I later asked Bill Webber and a few prisoners what they thought about the new sign. Bill thought a moment, then said simply, "demonic." One of the M.A. students, a thirty-five-year-old Latino named Tony, agreed with Bill's blunt assessment. But Tony added, "Let us face the demon head on." With more than 2 million Americans who are now incarcerated, it is time to face the demon head on.

# Crimes Against Humanity

## Ward Churchill

*If nifty little "pep" gestures like the "Indian Chant" and the "Tomahawk Chop" are just good clean fun, then let's spread the fun around, shall we?*

During the past couple of seasons, there has been an increasing wave of controversy regarding the names of professional sports teams like the Atlanta "Braves," Cleveland "Indians," Washington "Redskins," and Kansas City "Chiefs." The issue extends to the names of college teams like Florida State University "Seminoles," University of Illinois "Fighting Illini," and so on, right on down to high school outfits like the Lamar (Colorado) "Savages." Also involved have been team adoption of "mascots," replete with feathers, buckskins, beads, spears, and "warpaint" (some fans have opted to adorn themselves in the same fashion), and nifty little "pep" gestures like the "Indian Chant" and "Tomahawk Chop."

A substantial number of American Indians have protested that use of native names, images and symbols as sports team mascots and the like is, by definition, a virulently racist practice. Given the historical relationship between Indians and non-Indians during what has been called the "Conquest of America," American Indian Movement leader (and American Indian Anti-Defamation Council founder) Russell Means has compared the practice to contemporary Germans naming their soccer teams the "Jews," "Hebrews," and "Yids," while adorning their uniforms with grotesque caricatures of Jewish faces taken from the Nazis' anti-Semitic propaganda of the 1930s. Numerous demonstrations have occurred in conjunction with games—most notably during the November 15, 1992 match-up between the Chiefs and Redskins in Kansas City—by angry Indians and their supporters.

In response, a number of players—especially African Americans and other minority athletes—have been trotted out by professional team owners like Ted Turner, as well as university and public school officials, to announce that they mean not to insult but to honor native people. They have been joined by the television networks and most major newspapers, all of which have editorialized that Indian discomfort with the situation is "no big deal," insisting that the whole thing is just "good, clean fun." The country needs more such fun, they've argued, and "a few disgruntled Native Americans" have no right to undermine the nation's enjoyment of its leisure time by complaining. This is especially the case, some have argued, "in hard times like these." It has even been contended that Indian outrage at being systematically degraded—rather than the degradation itself—creates "a serious barrier to the sort of intergroup communication so necessary in a multicultural society such as ours."

Okay, let's communicate. We are frankly dubious that those advancing such positions really believe their own rhetoric, but, just for the sake of argument, let's accept the premise that they are sincere. If what they say is true, then isn't it time we spread such "inoffensiveness" and "good cheer" around among *all* groups so that *everybody* can participate *equally* in fostering the round of national laughs they call for? Sure it is—the country can't have too much fun or "intergroup involvement"—so the more, the merrier. Simple consistency demands that anyone who thinks the Tomahawk Chop is a swell pastime must be just as hearty in their endorsement of the following ideas—by the logic used to defend the defamation of American Indians—should help us all really start yukking it up.

First, as a counterpart to the Redskins, we need an NFL team called "Niggers" to honor Afro-Americans. Half-time festivities for fans might include a simulated stewing of the opposing coach in a large pot while players and cheerleaders dance around it, garbed in leopard skins and wearing fake bones in their noses. This concept obviously goes along with the kind of gaiety attending the Chop, but also with the actions of the Kansas City Chiefs, whose team members—prominently including black team members—lately appeared on a poster looking "fierce" and "savage" by way of wearing Indian regalia. Just a bit of harmless "morale boosting," says the Chiefs' front office. You bet.

So that the newly-formed Niggers sports club won't end up too out of sync while expressing the "spirit" and "identity" of Afro-Americans in the above fashion, a baseball franchise—let's call this one the "Sambos"—should be formed. How about a basketball team called the "Spearchuckers?" A hockey team called the "Jungle Bunnies?" Maybe the "essence" of these teams could be depicted by images of tiny black faces adorned with huge pairs of lips. The players could appear on TV every week or so gnawing on chicken legs and spitting watermelon seeds at one another. Catchy, eh? Well, there's "nothing to be upset about," according to those who love wearing "war bonnets" to the Super Bowl or having "Chief Illini-wik" dance around the sports arenas of Urbana, Illinois.

And why stop there? There are plenty of other groups to include. "Hispanics?" They can be "represented" by the Galveston "Greasers" and San Diego "Spics," at least until the Wisconsin "Wetbacks" and Baltimore "Beaners" get off the ground. Asian Americans? How about the "Slopes," "Dinks," "Gooks," and "Zipperheads?" Owners of the latter teams might get their logo ideas from editorial page cartoons printed in the nation's newspapers during World War II: slant-eyes, buck teeth, big glasses, but nothing racially insulting or derogatory, according to the editors and artists involved at the time. Indeed, this Second World War-vintage stuff can be seen as just another barrel of laughs, at least by what current editors say are their "local standards" concerning American Indians.

Let's see. Who's been left out? Teams like the Kansas City "Kikes," Hanover "Honkies," San Leandro "Shylocks," Daytona "Dagos," and Pittsburgh "Polacks" will fill a certain social void among white folk. Have a religious belief? Let's all go for the gusto and gear up the Milwaukee "Mackerel Snappers" and Hollywood "Holy Rollers." The Fighting Irish of Notre Dame can be rechristened the "Drunken Irish" or "Papist Pigs." Issues of gender and sexual preferences can be addressed through creation of teams like the St. Louis "Sluts," Boston "Bimbos," Detroit "Dykes," and the Fresno "Fags." How about the Gainesville "Gimps" and Richmond "Retards," so the physically and mentally impaired won't be excluded from our fun and games?

Now, don't go getting "overly sensitive" out there. None of this is demeaning or insulting, at least not when it's being done to Indians. Just ask the folks who are doing it, or their apologists like Andy Rooney in the national media. They'll tell you—as in fact they *have* been telling you—that there's been no harm done, regardless of what their victims think, feel, or say. The situation is exactly the same as when those with precisely the same mentality used to insist that Step 'n' Fetchit was okay, or Rochester on the Jack Benny Show, or Amos and Andy, Charlie Chan, the Frito Bandito, or any of the other cutsey symbols making up the lexicon of American racism. Have we communicated yet?

Let's get just a little bit real here. The notion of "fun" embodied in rituals like the Tomahawk Chop must be understood for what it is. There's not a single non-Indian example used above which can be considered socially acceptable in even the most marginal sense. The reasons are obvious enough. So why is it different where American Indians are concerned? One can only conclude that, in contrast to the other groups at issue, Indians are (falsely) perceived as being too few, and therefore too weak, to defend themselves effectively against racist and otherwise offensive behavior.

Fortunately, there are some glimmers of hope. A few teams and their fans have gotten the message and have responded appropriately. Stanford University, which opted to drop the name "Indians" from Stanford, has experienced no resulting drop-off in attendance. Meanwhile, the local newspaper in Portland, Oregon recently decided its long-standing editorial policy prohibiting use of racial epithets should include derogatory team names. The Redskins, for instance, are now referred to as "the Washington team," and will continue to be described in this way until the franchise adopts an inoffensive moniker (newspaper sales in Portland have suffered no decline as a result).

Such examples are to be applauded and encouraged. They stand as figurative beacons in the night, proving beyond all doubt that it is quite possible to indulge in the pleasure of athletics without accepting blatant racism into the bargain.

## Nuremberg Precedents

On October 16, 1946, a man named Julius Streicher mounted the steps of a gallows. Moments later he was dead, the sentence of an international tribunal composed of representatives of the United States, France, Great Britain, and the Soviet Union having been imposed. Streicher's body was then cremated, and—so horrendous were his crimes thought to have been—his ashes dumped into an unspecified German river so that "no one should ever know a particular place to go for reasons of mourning his memory."

Julius Streicher had been convicted at Nuremberg, Germany of what were termed "Crimes Against Humanity." The lead prosecutor in his case—Justice Robert Jackson of the United States Supreme Court—had not argued that the defendant had killed anyone, nor that he had personally committed any especially violent act. Nor was it contended that Streicher had held any particularly important position in the German government during the period in which the so-called Third Reich had exterminated some 6,000,000 Jews, as well as several million Gypsies, Poles, Slavs, homosexuals, and other untermenschen (subhumans).

The sole offense for which the accused was ordered put to death was in having served as publisher/editor of a Bavarian tabloid entitled *Der Sturmer* during the early-to-mid 1930s, years before the Nazi genocide actually began. In this capacity, he had penned a long series of virulently anti-Semitic editorials and "news" stories, usually accompanied by cartoons and other images graphically depicting Jews in extraordinarily derogatory fashion. This, the prosecution asserted, had done much to "dehumanize" the targets of his distortion in the mind of the German public. In turn, such dehumanization had made it possible—or at least easier—for average Germans to later indulge in the outright liquidation of Jewish "vermin." The tribunal agreed, holding that Streicher was therefore complicit in genocide and deserving of death by hanging.

During his remarks to the Nuremberg tribunal, Justice Jackson observed that, in implementing its sentences, the participating powers were morally and legally binding themselves to adhere forever after to the same standards of conduct that were being applied to Streicher and the other Nazi leaders. In the alternative, he said, the victorious allies would have committed "pure murder" at Nuremberg—no different in substance from that carried out by those they presumed to judge—rather than establishing the "permanent benchmark for justice" which was intended.

Yet in the United States of Robert Jackson, the indigenous American Indian population had already been reduced, in a process which is ongoing to this day, from perhaps 12.5 million in the year 1500 to fewer than 250,000 by the beginning of the 20th century. This was accomplished, according to official sources, "largely through the cruelty of [EuroAmerican] settlers," and an informal but clear governmental policy which had made it an articulated goal to "exterminate these red vermin," or at least whole segments of them.

Bounties had been placed on the scalps of Indians—any Indians—in places as diverse as Georgia, Kentucky, Texas, the Dakotas, Oregon, and California, and had been maintained until resident Indian populations were decimated or disappeared altogether. Entire peoples such as the Cherokee had been reduced to half their size through a policy of forced removal from their homelands east of the Mississippi River to what were then considered less preferable areas in the West.

Others, such as the Navajo, suffered the same fate while under military guard for years on end. The United States Army had also perpetrated a long series of wholesale massacres of Indians at places like Horseshoe Bend, Bear River, Sand Creek, the Washita River, the Marias River, Camp Robinson, and Wounded Knee.

Through it all, hundreds of popular novels—each competing with the next to make Indians appear more grotesque, menacing, and inhuman—were sold in the tens of millions of copies in the U.S. Plainly, the Euro-American public was being conditioned to see Indians in such a way as to allow their eradication to continue. And continue it did until the Manifest Destiny of the U.S.—a direct precursor to what Hitler would subsequently call Lebensraumpolitik (the politics of living space)—was consummated.

By 1900, the national project of "clearing" Native Americans from their land and replacing them with "superior" Anglo-American settlers was complete: the indigenous population had been reduced by as much as 98 percent while approximately 97.5 percent of their original territory had "passed" to the invaders. The survivors had been concentrated, out of sight and mind of the public, on scattered "reservations," all of them under the self-assigned "plenary" (full) power of the federal government. There was, of course, no Nuremberg-style tribunal passing judgment on those who had fostered such circumstances in North America. No U.S. official or private citizen was ever imprisoned—never mind hanged—for implementing or propagandizing what had been done. Nor had the process of genocide afflicting Indians been completed. Instead, it merely changed form.

Between the 1880s and the 1980s, nearly half of all Native American children were coercively transferred from their own families, communities, and cultures to those of the conquering society. This was done through compulsory attendance at remote boarding schools, often hundreds of miles from their homes, where native children were kept for years on end while being systematically "decultured" (indoctrinated to think and act in the manner of Euro Americans rather than Indians). It was also accomplished through a pervasive foster home and adoption program—including "blind" adoptions, where children would be permanently denied information as to who they were/are and where they'd come from—placing native youths in non-Indian homes.

The express purpose of all this was to facilitate a U.S. governmental policy to bring about the "assimilation" (dissolution) of indigenous societies. In other words,

Indian cultures as such were to be caused to disappear. Such policy objectives are directly contrary to the United Nations 1948 Convention on Punishment and Prevention of the Crime of Genocide, an element of international law arising from the Nuremberg proceedings. The forced "transfer of the children" of a targeted "racial, ethnical, or religious group" is explicitly prohibited as a genocidal activity under the Convention's second article.

Article II of the Genocide Convention also expressly prohibits involuntary sterilization as a means of "preventing births among" a targeted population. Yet, in 1975, it was conceded by the U.S. government that its Indian Health Service (IHS) then a subpart of the Bureau of Indian Affairs (BIA), was even then conducting a secret program of involuntary sterilization that had affected approximately 40 percent of all Indian women. The program was allegedly discontinued and the IHS was transferred to the Public Health Service, but no one was punished. In 1990, it came out that the IHS was inoculating Inuit children in Alaska with Hepatitis-B vaccine. The vaccine had already been banned by the World Health Organization as having a demonstrated correlation with the HIV-Syndrome which is itself correlated to AIDS. As this is written, a "field test" of Hepatitis-A vaccine, also HIV-correlated, is being conducted on Indian reservations in the northern plains region.

The Genocide Convention makes it a "crime against humanity" to create conditions leading to the destruction of an identifiable human group, as such. Yet the BIA has utilized the government's plenary prerogatives to negotiate mineral leases "on behalf of" Indian peoples paying a fraction of standard royalty rates. The result has been "super profits" for a number of preferred U.S. corporations. Meanwhile, Indians, whose reservations ironically turned out to be in some of the most mineral-rich areas of North America, which makes us, the nominally wealthiest segment of the continent's population, live in dire poverty.

By the government's own data in the mid-1980s, Indians received the lowest annual and lifetime per capita incomes of any aggregate population group in the United States. Concomitantly, we suffer the highest rate of infant mortality, death by exposure and malnutrition, disease, and the like. Under such circumstances, alcoholism and other escapist forms of substance abuse are endemic in the Indian community, a situation which leads both to a general physical debilitation of the population and a catastrophic accident rate. Teen suicide among Indians is several times the national average.

The average life expectancy of a reservation-based Native American man is barely 45 years; women can expect to live less than three years longer.

Such itemizations could be continued at great length, including matters like the radioactive contamination of large portions of contemporary Indian Country, the forced relocation of traditional Navajos, and so on. But the point should be made: Genocide, as defined in international law, is a continuing fact of day-to-day life (and death) for North America's native peoples. Yet there has been—and is—only the barest flicker of public concern about, or even consciousness of, this reality. Absent any serious expression of public outrage, no one is punished and the process continues.

A salient reason for public acquiescence before the ongoing holocaust in Native North America has been a continuation of the popular legacy, often through more effective media. Since 1925, Hollywood has released more than 2,000 films, many of them rerun frequently on television, portraying Indians as strange, perverted, ridiculous, and often dangerous things of the past. Moreover, we are habitually presented to mass audiences one-dimensionally, devoid of recognizable human motivations and emotions; Indians thus serve as props, little more. We have thus been thoroughly and systematically dehumanized.

Nor is this the extent of it. Everywhere, we are used as logos, as mascots, as jokes: "Big-Chief" writing tablets, "Red Man" chewing tobacco, "Winnebago" campers, "Navajo" and "Cherokee" and "Pontiac" and "Cadillac" pickups and automobiles. There are the Cleveland "Indians," the Kansas City "Chiefs," the Atlanta "Braves" and the Washington "Redskins" professional sports teams—not to mention those in thousands of colleges, high schools, and elementary schools across the country—each with their own degrading caricatures and parodies of Indians and/or things Indian. Pop fiction continues in the same vein, including an unending stream of New Age manuals purporting to expose the inner works of indigenous spirituality in everything from pseudo-philosophical to do-it-yourself styles. Blond yuppies from Beverly Hills amble about the country claiming to be reincarnated 17th century Cheyenne Ushamans ready to perform previously secret ceremonies.

In effect, a concerted, sustained, and in some ways accelerating effort has gone into making Indians unreal. It is thus of obvious importance that the American public begin to think about the implications of such things the next time they witness a gaggle of face-painted and war-bonneted buffoons doing the "Tomahawk Chop" at a baseball or football game. It is necessary that they think about the implications of the grade-school teacher adorning their child in turkey feathers to commemorate Thanksgiving. Think about the significance of John Wayne or Charleton Heston killing a dozen "savages" with a single bullet the next time a western comes on TV. Think about why Land-o-Lakes finds it appropriate to market its butter with the stereotyped image of an "Indian princess" on the wrapper. Think about what it means when non-Indian academics profess—as they often do—to "know more about Indians than Indians do themselves." Think about the significance of charlatans like Carlos Castaneda and Jamake Highwater and Mary Summer Rain and Lynn Andrews churning out "Indian" bestsellers, one after the other, while Indians typically can't get into print.

Think about the real situation of American Indians. Think about Julius Streicher. Remember Justice Jackson's admonition. Understand that the treatment of Indians in American popular culture is not "cute" or "amusing" or just "good, clean fun."

Know that it causes real pain and real suffering to real people. Know that it threatens our very survival. And know that this is just as much a crime against humanity as anything the Nazis ever did. It is likely that the indigenous people of the United States will never demand that those guilty of such criminal activity be punished for their deeds. But the least we have the right to expect—indeed, to demand—is that such practices finally be brought to a halt.

# Legacies of War: The United States' Obligation Toward Amerasians

*Robin S. Levi*

## The U.S. Government's Attitude Toward Relationships with Asian Women

### A. Vietnam

In contrast to the popular perception held in Vietnam and the United States (and reinforced by *Miss Saigon*), most Amerasian children came from long-term relationships between servicemen and Vietnamese women who were not bargirls. These women usually worked around military bases as launderers, hotel clerks, or menial laborers in other occupations.

Soldiers in Vietnam frequently felt the need to find solace in women and liquor. The U.S. military encouraged this behavior with a tacit "bread and circuses" attitude. The government encouraged "R & R" as a way to escape from the rigors of jungle warfare. But while the military flew married men to meet their wives in Hawaii, it sent single men to other exotic cities. Unmarried servicemen were sent to Asian locales, which led them to believe the U.S. government expected them to conduct their "R & R" with Asian women.

The U.S. military also facilitated the use of local prostitutes. For example, after monthly trips to town resulted in chaos, Marine commanders at Danan decided to restrict their men's sexual activity to areas surrounding the base. Military brothels could be found within the perimeter of at least three U.S. base camps. The military brothels were set up by military commanders and were under the direct operational control of a brigade commander with the rank of colonel. Further, the military periodically checked the health of the prostitutes to curtail the spread of sexually transmitted diseases. The military also regulated prices. If women requested more than a certain price, the military would declare their brothel off-limits.

From 29 *Stanford Journal of International Law* 459 (1993) by Robin S. Levi. Copyright © 1993 by Board of Trustees of the Leland Stanford Junior University. Reprinted by permission.

The U.S. Army officially disapproved of U.S. servicemen living with Vietnamese women, and at times the military police sanctioned soldiers. But unofficially, the U.S. Army allowed many of these living situations (which the soldiers called "liv[ing] on the economy with a national") to continue in order to preserve the soldiers' morale.

Once a serviceman completed his tour of duty, the military's disapproval of his relationship with a Vietnamese woman resurfaced. It was incredibly difficult for servicemen to maneuver through the U.S. bureaucracy to bring their children, girl-friends, or wives back to the United States. Some servicemen tried for many years to get their children out of Vietnam, while others gave up before they left. Some were so busy preparing to end their "year abroad" that they forgot to try to return with those who had been their families there. Some men did not care, and some did not know that they had children. Regardless of what stood in the serviceman's way (government, bureaucracy, confusion, or indifference), the result remained the same: tens of thousands of children left in Vietnam after 1975, rejected by Vietnamese society and dreaming of their unknown father and his land.

## B. South Korea and the Philippines

The relationships in South Korea and the Philippines are fairly similar to those that existed in Vietnam. In South Korea the troops are now on one-year tours similar to those soldiers had in Vietnam and the Philippines. Most of the men come through for short stays while their ships are repaired. About eighteen thousand registered women work in the bar or club areas near U.S. bases in South Korea. Registered women have identification cards and are the only ones allowed to work in the clubs. In order to get an ID card, a woman must have a chest X ray and blood test every six months and an AIDS test every three months. In addition, the women are tested every week for sexually transmitted diseases [STDs]. The Korean police conduct spot checks to ensure that all women have proper ID cards; women without cards can receive jail sentences of up to twelve months. Furthermore, the clubs themselves are checked for cleanliness and STD rates among the women.

The bases in the Philippines had a similar system of registering sex workers. Fifteen thousand to seventeen thousand sex workers were employed around Subic Bay, approximately nine thousand of whom were registered. As in South Korea, unregistered sex workers could be jailed. The U.S. military provided medicine and technical assistance to the clinics. Here, as in South Korea, the military deemed a club "off-limits" for U.S. servicemen if too many women tested positive for sexually transmitted diseases. Most of the U.S. servicemen did not take responsibility for the children born from their relationships, whether short- or long-term, with sex workers. Furthermore, the U.S. government failed to instruct its servicemen regarding possible parental responsibility. Instead, the government focused on teaching servicemen to avoid venereal disease.

# ⦿ The Lives of Amerasians

## A. Amerasians in Vietnam

Vietnam does not accept Amerasians either legally or socially and subjects them to mistreatment that leads to severe emotional trauma. Because nationality, race, and personal identity derive from the father in Vietnamese society, the Vietnamese government considers Amerasians U.S. nationals. In Vietnam the father registers the birth in the family registry, claims paternity, registers the child for school, and procures employment for the child. Without a father to perform these essential functions (at times a stepfather has assisted the Amerasian), a child in Vietnam will have difficulty becoming a functioning part of Vietnamese society. Amerasians are told they are not Vietnamese, although the person who is supposed to give them their identity is not present. The fact that Vietnamese social and legal institutions make it difficult for Amerasians to establish an identity intensifies the identity crisis that mixed race children inherently face.

Vietnam has a Confucian, patriarchal family system, where a person's identity is derived more from the family group, including both the living members and ancestors, than from the individual self. Therefore, an Amerasian child lacks not only a father but also a father's family and ancestors. A child in Vietnam without a supporting familial group is seen as something less than a full person, which increases the Amerasians' lack of identity.

Another factor that contributes to discrimination against Amerasians in Vietnam is homogeneity. Mixed racial ancestry is easily noticed, and Vietnamese society considers people with mixed ancestry as contributing to "racial impurity in the nation." An official from Ho Chi Minh City's Department of Social Welfare stated, "Our society does not need these bad elements."[1]

The final factor contributing to the ostracism of Vietnamese Amerasians is that they are living reminders of the foreign occupation of Vietnam. For some of them, even their names, given by their families, *My Lai* (American half-breed) or *My Phuong* (Vietnamese American), are insults. Vietnamese society faults Amerasians' mothers for consorting with the enemy and considers the mothers prostitutes. Amerasians are considered the children of the enemy: "It was not unusual for an Amerasian child to be singled out by a teacher or a police officer as the offspring of the enemy who had bombed the village."[2] Because communist education emphasizes the evils of the United States, it is very difficult for Amerasians to attend school. Students are taunted in school and by the public and are sometimes told to go back to their "country." Many Amerasians quickly drop out of school; thus a large number of them are illiterate. Amerasian children's identity crises are often intensified by the fact that many mothers destroyed all mementos of their relationships with their children's fathers so that the government would not send them to reeducation camps as punishment for fraternizing with the enemy.

Regardless of the destruction of documentary evidence linking Amerasians to their American fathers, their non-Asian features frequently betray the children's mixed heritage. Some mothers try to disguise the children's American features by putting shoe polish in their hair and powder on their skin. The Amerasians who have experienced the greatest discrimination and whose identities have been the most difficult to hide are the children of African American servicemen. One example is the story of a young black Amerasian: "Vinh Doan came to expect rejection. His father was a black serviceman whom he never met. His Vietnamese mother spent years telling him he was ugly because he looked like his father, then gave him to a neighbor when he was seven years old."[3] Black Amerasians are lowest in the hierarchy of Vietnamese society due to the traditional prejudice against dark skin found in all Asian societies, as well as racial prejudice brought by the European and American presence.

Although the Vietnamese government officially denies discriminating against Amerasians, it prevents many mothers from participating in certain government programs. Mothers of Amerasians are often rejected by their families due to the humiliation the mother has caused the family. A significant percentage of mothers, refusing to live under these conditions, give up their children for adoption, sell their children for their potential value as a ticket to the United States, or simply abandon them. Many Amerasians have ended up in orphanages. Since Vietnamese orphanages are often run badly and have severe overcrowding problems, most Amerasian children have ended up on the streets, and many have turned to prostitution.

## B. Amerasians in South Korea

South Korea is also a homogenous and Confucian nation with a strict class hierarchy. A more dramatic disparity between the upper and lower classes exists there than in Vietnam, and it is very difficult to be successful unless one attends one of the top universities, which are expensive and exclusive. As in Vietnam, the father is the cornerstone of family life and the conduit to public life. Without a father, it is impossible to carry out the traditional responsibilities of ancestor worship. While the religious importance of ancestor worship has decreased with modernization, some symbolic value remains, and the Amerasian who is not able to conduct ancestor worship naturally will be viewed as "different." In recent years, nationalism and cultural pride, along with economic clout, have increased in South Korea. Koreans equate citizenship with their homogenous racial ancestry. Thus, Amerasians remain only marginal members of Korea's society, because without fathers they are prevented from fully participating in Korean culture and religion.

Official discrimination against Amerasians is formally outlawed in South Korea, but covert discrimination continues. The most egregious example is that Amerasians are not allowed to serve in the Korean military. In a nation that considers itself consistently on the brink of war, exclusion from military service serves as a serious obstacle to being accepted by the society and obtaining a good job. Further, most Amerasians cannot afford to go to the better universities. The cumulative effect of not having fathers, military service capability, education credentials, and economic power relegates Amerasians to the lower classes of Korean society.

The degree to which Korean Amerasians encounter discrimination depends on the race of the father. If the father was black, racial discrimination is more blatant. If the father was white, the Amerasian child has a better chance of adoption by society. Nonetheless, all Amerasians are taunted for their American-looking features and are immediately branded as children of imperialists and prostitutes.

Although it should be acknowledged that the U.S. and South Korean governments have taken some financial responsibility for the few registered Amerasians in South Korea, Korean Amerasians have lives similar to Vietnamese Amerasians, filled with poverty, discrimination, and solitude. It is unlikely that financial support from the United States or South Korea will continue once the U.S. military leaves.

## C. Amerasians in the Philippines

Filipino Amerasians were excluded from previous Amerasian immigration laws because of the perception that Filipino Amerasians did not experience discrimination at significant levels. This perception could have been generated by the belief that the Philippines support a very diverse population and therefore mixed race children would be easily accepted. Indeed, Amerasians are capable of being accepted and succeeding in the Filipino society; for example, the mayor of Olongapo, Richard Gordon, is a white Amerasian. Some white Amerasians have become big performing stars in the Philippines, prized for their light skin.

Nevertheless, Filipinos consider themselves a homogenous population, despite their history of intermarriages over the centuries. They also have a strong belief in kinship relations. Because most Filipino Amerasians are interracial children from single-parent households, they are left at a disadvantage with regard to both of these traditions.

The most significant obstacle to Filipino Amerasians is that they are often judged by the circumstances of their birth. Amerasians from certain parts of the Philippines are immediately assumed to be the children of prostitutes and U.S. servicemen, and they are treated as such. Therefore, even though in the past Amerasians have been functioning members of society, Amerasians with U.S. servicemen for fathers are not so lucky. Further, because most are born into a life of poverty next to the bases, many end up working in the bar system that facilitated their birth. Others are sold by their mothers or abandoned. Amerasians in the Philippines experience discrimination and hardship remarkably similar to that experienced by the Amerasians discussed above. Most struggle to survive in the bar scene near the base.

Since the U.S. military withdrew, these children have become subject to increased anti-American sentiment. The closing of the bases also removed the main source of health services and income for the Amerasians and their mothers. Like

Vietnamese Amerasians, Filipino Amerasians are now the remaining traces of U.S. intervention in the Philippines. Any residual resentment against the U.S. presence in the Philippines can easily be vented against Filipino Amerasians. They are without resources and discriminated against in a country that is itself poor.

# VI. The U.S. Government's Treatment of Amerasians

## A. Amerasians under U.S. Immigration Law

A child born in the United States can elect U.S. citizenship regardless of the nationality of her parents. Attaining citizenship is more difficult when the child is born outside the United States. A child born outside the United States to married parents can be a U.S. citizen if one parent is a U.S. citizen who has fulfilled certain age and residency requirements. However, children born out of wedlock, like most Amerasian children, face significantly more stringent citizenship requirements. This factor has made it unlikely that more than a small percentage of Amerasians could receive U.S. citizenship through their parents.

Amerasian children are in the lowest preference category for emigration to the United States because they are usually unable to prove officially that they are related to any U.S. citizen. Rarely can they find U.S. citizens to sponsor them.

## B. Statutes Assisting Amerasians

1. Orderly Departure Program

The first U.S. effort to help Amerasians began inadvertently, after the government became concerned with the plight of the boat people fleeing Vietnam. The media attention given to the Vietnamese refugees in rickety boats on unsafe seas, and their subsequent unpleasant treatment by unwelcoming Southeast Asian countries, led the U.S. government in 1979 to develop the Orderly Departure Program (ODP) under the auspices of the United Nations.[4] The United Nations designed the ODP to give people a safe method of exit from Vietnam. Vietnam agreed to grant exit visas, and the UN High Commissioner for Refugees (UNHCR) agreed to be the processor.

Under the ODP, Vietnamese Amerasians are in a better position to immigrate to the United States than they were under the conventional immigration regulations. Amerasians must fill out applications to participate in the ODP, but the U.S. government no longer requires supporting documents from them. Further, President [Ronald] Reagan accorded priority status to Amerasians by including them in one of three categories of refugees given priority for orderly departure.

Nevertheless, the ODP as it relates to Amerasians has several problems. First, since the United States government and Vietnam do not have diplomatic relations, the United States has been hampered by not having a processing office in Ho Chi

Minh City. Moreover, Amerasians often do not have the knowledge necessary to successfully apply. Many of them, living in the streets, may not even have heard about the ODP. Second, because the ODP classifies recipients as refugees, the Vietnamese government does not think Amerasians should be included; it considers them U.S. citizens. Thus their exclusion from official services, according to the Vietnamese government, does not constitute discrimination.

## 2. The Refugee Act of 1980

The 1980 Refugee Act, implementing the 1951 [United Nations] Convention Relating to the Status of Refugees and its updated Protocol,[5] did little to help Amerasians. The Refugee Act characterized a refugee as a person fleeing a country "because of persecution or a well-founded fear of persecution on account of race, religion, nationality, [or] membership in a particular social group." . . . However, the U.S. government did not direct this legislation specifically at Amerasians, and it has several proof requirements and forms. The act is likely to benefit mainly the more educated Asians who are able to fulfill the specific requirements and successfully complete the forms and interviews. . . . In the case of South Korea and the Philippines, the U.S. government tends to be unwilling to grant Amerasians refugee status, as they are from countries with governments friendly to the United States. Therefore, the Refugee Act is rarely used by Amerasians.

## 3. 1982 Amerasian Amendments

The United States' next effort to assist Amerasians was the enactment of the 1982 Amerasian Amendments.[6] These amendments were the result of a concerted effort by some legislators—who saw the Amerasians as the United States' responsibility—to help those children. The amendments cover Amerasian children from Korea, Vietnam, Laos, Cambodia, and Thailand. They put qualified children into the highest preference category for immigration. In order to qualify, children must petition the Attorney General and give [his or] her reason to believe that they were fathered by a U.S. citizen and were born between 1950 and October 22, 1982. The physical appearance of the Amerasian is to be considered, along with documentary proof. By expanding coverage to Amerasians in some nations, the amendments have helped the non-Vietnamese Amerasians who did not benefit under the ODP. Also, the amendments expand eligibility to those born as late as 1982, taking account of the fact that not all Amerasians are born during military conflicts.

Several problems remain. First, the amendments still force Amerasians to emigrate alone, often leaving loved ones behind. In addition, although Amerasians from several countries can take advantage of the amendments, the strict provisions of the amendments and the lack of diplomatic relations between the United States and Vietnam combine to make it particularly difficult for Vietnamese Amerasians to qualify. Moreover, the amendments do not cover the many Amerasians in the Philippines, and the 1982 cutoff date eliminates Amerasians who were subsequently born in Asia. Finally, the financial sponsor requirements are difficult to fulfill and defy the obligation of the United States to take responsibility for Amerasians.

4. 1984 Amerasian Initiative

President Reagan attempted to ameliorate some of the damaging effects of the 1982 amendments on Vietnamese Amerasians through the 1984 Amerasian Initiative. In contrast to earlier policy, the Initiative allows Vietnamese Amerasians using the ODP to emigrate with qualifying family members. This provision has encouraged more Amerasians to emigrate, because they need not leave their families behind. It has also increased their chances of building successful lives in the United States, because they will have familial support with them.

Unfortunately, the U.S. government offended Vietnam by claiming that the Vietnamese government was using the ODP to facilitate emigration of ethnic Chinese rather than Vietnamese Amerasians, and that as a result the quotas set by the Initiative for Vietnamese Amerasians remained unfilled. Vietnam claimed that the United States was trying to make the Vietnamese government the "bad guy." As a result, Vietnam suspended the ODP program to the United States in 1986 but resurrected it eighteen months later after a sharp increase in the number of people trying to escape Vietnam by boat. Thus the Initiative suffered from both poor United States–Vietnam relations and its limited scope.

# The Homecoming Act

The most recent and comprehensive legislation concerning Amerasians is the Indochinese Refugee Resettlement and Protection Act of 1987 (Homecoming Act).[7] The purpose of the Homecoming Act was to fulfill the United States' legal and moral obligations to Vietnamese Amerasians. . . .

The Homecoming Act, enacted in March 1988, stated that all Amerasian children born in Vietnam between January 1, 1962, and January 1, 1976, could emigrate to the United States, accompanied by either immediate family, guardians, or a spouse. The act set a deadline of two years for all Amerasians to arrive in the United States and exempted them from immigration quotas. Congress included the two-year deadline to speed the processing of Amerasian immigrants, because processing under the ODP had been so slow. The State Department claimed that the deadline was too stringent to allow for adequate processing of all Amerasians. Nonetheless, comparing the speed of processing under the Homecoming Act with the speed under previous acts shows that the deadline did accelerate processing.

In 1990, Congress indefinitely extended the deadline for allowing Amerasians into the United States and removed the provision that had forced them to choose between spouse and family for immediate immigration. The act's original budget and timetable were based on an estimate of twelve thousand to fourteen thousand Amerasians remaining in Vietnam, but this estimate was later revised to forty thousand. Finally, the act did not characterize Amerasians as refugees, which appeased the Vietnamese government.

After Congress passed the Homecoming Act, [its two Congressional co-sponsors—Ed.] traveled to Vietnam to reach an agreement with Vietnamese Foreign Minister Nguyen Co Thach. The agreement stated that the Vietnamese government would allow the Amerasians to emigrate to the United States. This new spirit of cooperation stems from Vietnam's desire for the U.S. government to end its trade embargo, as Vietnam is willing to make the necessary efforts to improve its relationship with the United States. Vietnam has also tried to assist the U.S. government in processing Amerasians by transporting them from outlying areas to Ho Chi Minh City and by increasing the number of carriers that are permitted to fly emigrants out of Vietnam.

## B. Problems Faced by Amerasians in the United States: Squawking like a Chicken

In Asia, most Amerasians lived in the street, frequently surviving through criminal means and having little education and limited familial support. As a result of their background and lack of identity, Amerasian immigrants are at higher risk for problems such as drug use, crime, and suicide than previous Indochinese immigrants.

Although many other refugee groups have similar problems, these problems are more acute among Amerasians. One important reason is that upon arrival in the United States, Amerasians are, on average, eighteen years old, much older and less adaptable than French Eurasians who emigrate to France. Amerasians in the United States have a saying: "I was born like a duck but lived with the chickens. Now I live with the ducks but I squawk like a chicken."

Many Amerasians thought that once they arrived in the United States they would find their fathers and their identities. They also thought that they would be welcomed by their fathers, like lost children finally finding their way home. In short, Amerasians hoped to find the answers to all their problems in the United States.

The Amerasian dream least likely to be fulfilled is that of finding one's American father in the United States. Very few Amerasians have clear identifying information about their fathers; most just have names and hometowns. The U.S. government has led Amerasians to believe that it will help them contact their fathers and give the fathers the option of caring for their children. But due to a combination of domestic privacy laws and government inactivity, that help has not materialized.

As a result of the Freedom of Information Act and a British case concerning children fathered by U.S. soldiers in Great Britain, the U.S. government must allow limited access to records about U.S. servicemen. Other organizations, such as the Red Cross, the Amerasian Registry, and the Buck Foundation, use that information to assist Amerasians searching for their fathers. However, this information is frequently too limited to be useful. Even if Amerasians do find their fathers, often the fathers do not want them or the reunions otherwise fail to work out. Amerasians find such rejections devastating because they expected their fathers to help them find their identities and fill the role Vietnamese fathers play. Although there have been some success stories, many workers at volunteer agencies do not think they make up for the countless other rejections. In fact, some mothers have tried to prevent their children from even beginning the search for their fathers.

The presence of racism in the United States also surprises Amerasians, especially black Amerasians. Further, the Vietnamese community that rejected them in Vietnam continues to reject them in the United States, although the rejection is less severe. As one unemployed Amerasian said, "[I]f the discrimination in Vietnam was 100, the discrimination here is about 50." Many examples exist of Amerasians trying to talk with Vietnamese people in Vietnamese and being snubbed. These rejections increase the Amerasians' sense of alienation; even though they are in the United States, the old problem of discrimination continues to plague them.

Another problem that many Vietnamese Amerasians face is not having attended school in Vietnam. Many stopped attending school as a result of taunts from their schoolmates and teachers. Most are illiterate in Vietnamese and unaccustomed to school, which makes it difficult for them to learn in the United States. Further, as a result of their Vietnamese illiteracy, it is very difficult for them to learn to read and write English.

The street is an environment with which most Amerasians are familiar. [M]any survived by living on the street; they robbed, prostituted themselves, and participated in other illegal activities. In Asia, they supported themselves on the street without any help from the government. When Amerasians in the United States begin having problems in school, finding jobs, or living on welfare, some of them revert to the familiar methods of street survival. This leaves Amerasians at a high risk for becoming criminals and suffering the consequences of criminal activity.

All of the problems discussed above are easily noticed and measured. Less quantifiable, but just as serious, is the general feeling of depression and alienation that affects many Amerasians, leaving them at high risk for suicide. Unfortunately, not nearly enough counselors are available to talk with them about their emotional problems.

## Conclusion and Recommendations

The problems facing Amerasians are daunting but not insurmountable. The settlement of Vietnamese Amerasians in the United States has been fairly effective and can provide guidance for programs to assist other groups of Amerasians. The federal government and volunteer organizations have worked as partners and have shown that the government, when willing, can rectify its wrongs. Based on its international obligations, however, the United States still has a long way to go in helping Amerasians.

# Notes

[1]Marilyn T. Trautfield, Note, *America's Responsibility to Amerasian Children: Too Little Too Late*, 10 Brooklyn Journal of International Law 55, 61 (1984).

[2]*See* Anne Keegan, *Children of Vietnam Find Few Fathers at U.S. Doors*, Chicago Tribune, May 13, 1987, at C1.

[3]Lisa Belkin, *Children of Two Lands in Search of Home*, New York Times, May 19, 1988, at A20. . . .

[4]*See* Marykim DeMonaco, Note, *Disorderly Departure: An Analysis of the United States Policy toward Amerasian Immigration*, 15 Brooklyn Journal of International Law 641, 653–57 (1989).

[5][United Nations] Convention Relating to Status of Refugees, July 28, 1951, 189 U.N.T.S. 137; [United Nations] Protocol Relating to the Status of Refugees, *entered into force*, January 31, 1967, 19 U.S.T. 6223.

[6]8 U.S.C. § 1154 (1988).

[7]Indochinese Refugee Resettlement and Protection Act, Pub. L. No. 100-202, 101 Stat. 1329–40 (1987).

# Department of Fair Employment and Housing: Housing Discrimination

*California Department of Fair Employment and Housing*

**Question:** How does a person file a complaint of housing discrimination?

**Answer:** To file a complaint of housing discrimination, call the appropriate telephone number found by viewing the *DFEH Contact Information*. If the matter falls within the Department's jurisdiction, you, or the person you represent, is sent a *questionnaire* to complete and return to the Department.

Once the completed questionnaire has been received, the Department will contact you and arrange a telephone interview. If the Department has jurisdiction, a formal complaint will be prepared and mailed to you for signature.

**Question:** Is there a time limit for filing a housing complaint with the Department?

**Answer:** Yes. A complaint must be filed within **one year** of the date of the alleged discrimination.

**Question:** If a person has already filed a complaint with the Federal Department of Housing and Urban Development (HUD), can he/she also file with the Department?

**Answer:** If a complaint has been filed with HUD, it will automatically be filed with the Department as well. In most instances, HUD will send the complaint to the Department for investigation. Similarly, if a complaint is filed with the Department and is jurisdictional with HUD, it will also be filed with that agency. Filing the complaint with both agencies benefits the parties by providing a second level of review.

**Question:** How does the Department conduct an investigation?

**Answer:** The Department is a neutral fact-finding agency. Department staff conduct impartial investigations in which records are reviewed and

California Department of Fair Employment and Housing

relevant witnesses are interviewed. An investigation may be conducted on site and/or through telephone interviews. The Department has the authority to take depositions, issue subpoenas and interrogatories and seek Temporary Restraining Orders during the course of its investigation. All evidence gathered is analyzed to determine if a violation of the Fair Employment and Housing Act has occurred. In making its determination the Department considers evidence from both sides as well as from any neutral parties the Department may have contacted.

**Question:** What remedies are available to persons who file complaints of housing discrimination?

**Answer:** The remedies available for housing discrimination include:

- Sale or rental of the housing accommodation
- Elimination of the discriminatory practice
- Policy changes
- Out-of-pocket expenses
- Actual damages, including damages for emotional distress
- Civil penalty (up to $10,000)
- Reasonable accommodation

If the case is pursued in court, civil remedies are identical with one exception:
- Instead of a civil penalty, unlimited punitive damages may be awarded

Remedies may also include the payment of attorney's fees and other court costs.

**Question:** Does a person have to file a complaint with the Department before filing a complaint in court?

**Answer:** No. A person may file directly in court without first filing a complaint with the Department. The time limit for filing in court is **two years** from the date of the alleged discrimination. If a complaint has been filed with the Department, the two-year time period does not include the time that the Department spent processing the case. If the Department has completed its investigation and issued an accusation, either party (the person who filed the complaint or the person against whom the complaint was filed) may elect to have the case transferred to court. The Department's attorneys will prosecute the case in court on behalf of the Department.

**Question:** Can a landlord refuse to rent to families with children?

**Answer:** Generally, a landlord cannot refuse to rent to an applicant because there are children in the family. Moreover, the requirements for rental and the terms and conditions must be the same for families with children as for any other applicant or tenant. The one exception to this rule involves housing that has been specifically designed for senior citizens (persons 55 and older or 62 and older). To qualify as "senior housing", a housing accommodation must meet specific legally-defined requirements which may include a minimum number of units, age-based residency limits and design features.

**Question:** If a tenant with a disability needs to modify his/her unit, is the landlord required to pay for the modification?

**Answer:** Normally not. In most instances, the tenant is responsible for all costs connected to the modification. Moreover, under certain circumstances the tenant may be required to restore the premises to the condition that existed before the modification (other than for reasonable wear and tear). There are, however, certain types of HUD subsidized housing programs that require a landlord to pay for disability-related reasonable modifications.

**Question:** Does the Department help persons find housing or resolve problems connected with their current housing?

**Answer:** No. Finding housing and resolving landlord/tenant problems are not handled by the Department. The Department only handles problems related to discrimination and housing.

# Know Your Rights: What to Do if Questioned by Police, FBI, Customs Agents or Immigration Officers

*American Civil Liberties Union*

The Immigration and Naturalization Service (INS) is now part of the Department of Homeland Security (DHS) and has been renamed and reorganized into:

1. The Bureau of Citizenship and Immigration Services (BCIS)
2. The Bureau of Customs and Border Protection (CBP)
3. The Bureau of Immigration and Customs Enforcement (ICE)

All three bureaus are part of the DHS and will be referred to as "DHS" for the purposes of this brochure.

## I. What if the Police, FBI or DHS Agents Contact Me?

**Q: Do I have to answer the questions asked by the agents?**

**A:** You have the constitutional right to remain silent. It is not a crime to refuse to answer questions. It is a good idea to talk to a lawyer before agreeing to answer questions. You do not have to talk to anyone, even if you have been arrested or are in jail. Only a judge can order you to answer questions.

**Q: Can I talk to a lawyer?**

**A:** You have the right to talk to a lawyer before you answer questions, whether or not the police tell you of that right. The lawyer's job is to protect your rights. Once you say that you want to talk to a lawyer, officers should stop asking you questions. If you do not have a lawyer, you may still tell the officer you want to speak to one before answering questions. If you do have a lawyer, keep his or her business card with you. Show it to the officer, and ask to call your lawyer. Remember to get the name, agency and telephone number of any investigator who visits you, and give that information to your lawyer.

**Q: Can agents search my home or office?**

**A:** Police or other law enforcement agents cannot search your home unless you give them permission, or unless they have a search warrant. A search warrant is a court order that allows the police to conduct a specified search. Interfering with the search probably will not stop it and you might get arrested. But you should say clearly that you have not given your consent and that the search is against your wishes. Your roommate or guest can legally consent to a search of your house if the police believe that person has the authority to give consent. Police and law enforcement need a warrant to search an office, but your employer can consent to a search of your workspace without your permission.

**Q: What if agents have a search warrant?**

**A:** If you are present when agents come for the search, you can ask to see the warrant. The warrant must specify in detail the places to be searched and the people or things to be taken away. Call your lawyer as soon as possible. Ask if you are allowed to watch the search; if you are allowed to, you should. Take notes, including names, badge numbers, what agency each officer is from, where they searched and what they took. If others are present, have them act as witnesses to watch carefully what is happening.

**Q: Do I have to answer questions if the police have a search warrant?**

**A:** No. A search warrant does not mean you have to answer questions.

**Q: What if agents do not have a search warrant?**

**A:** You do not have to let the police search your home, and you do not have to answer their questions. The police cannot get a warrant based on your refusal.

**Q: What if agents do not have a search warrant, but insist on searching my home even after I object?**

**A:** Do not get in the way of the search. If someone is there with you, ask him or her to witness that you are not giving permission for the search. Call your lawyer as soon as possible. Get the names and badge numbers of the searching officers.

**Q: What if I speak to government agents anyway?**

**A:** Anything you say to law enforcement can be used against you and others. Keep in mind that lying to a government official is a crime. Remaining silent until you consult with a lawyer is not. Even if you have already answered some questions, you can refuse to answer other questions until you have a lawyer.

**Q: What if the police stop me on the street?**

**A:** Ask if you are free to go. If the answer is yes, consider just walking away. If the police say you are not under arrest, but are not free to go, then you are being detained. The police can pat down the outside of your clothing if they have reason to suspect you might be armed and dangerous. If they search any more than this, say clearly, "I do not consent to a search." They may keep searching anyway. You do not need to answer any questions if you are detained or arrested with one important exception. The police may ask for your name once you have been detained, and you can be arrested in some states for refusing to provide it.

**Q: What if police stop me in my car?**

**A:** Keep your hands where the police can see them. You do not have to consent to a search. But if the police have probable cause to believe that you have been involved in a crime or that you have evidence of a crime in your car, your car can be searched without your consent. Clearly state that you do not consent. Officers may separate passengers and drivers from each other to question them and compare their answers, but no one has to answer any questions.

**Q: What if the police or FBI threatens me with a grand jury subpoena if I don't answer their questions?**

**A:** A grand jury subpoena is a written order for you to go to court and testify about information you may have. If the police or FBI threatens to get a subpoena, you should call a lawyer right away. Anything you say can usually be used against you.

**Q: Do I have to answer questions if I have been arrested?**

**A:** No. If you are arrested, you do not have to answer any questions. Ask for a lawyer right away. Repeat this request to every officer who tries to talk to or question you. You should always talk to a lawyer before you decide to answer any questions.

**Q: What if I am treated badly by the police or the FBI?**

**A:** Write down the officer's badge number, name or other identifying information. You have a right to ask the officer for this information. Try to find witnesses and their names and phone numbers. If you are injured, seek medical attention and take pictures of the injuries as soon as you can. Call a lawyer or contact your local ACLU office.

# II. What if I am not a Citizen and the DHS Contacts Me?

*Assert your rights.* If you do not demand your rights or if you sign papers waiving your rights, the DHS may deport you before you see a lawyer or an immigration judge. **Never sign anything without reading, understanding and knowing the consequences of signing it.**

*Talk to a lawyer.* If possible, carry with you the name and telephone number of a lawyer who will take your calls. The immigration laws are hard to understand and there have been many recent changes.

Based on today's laws, regulations and DHS guidelines, non-citizens usually have the rights below, no matter what their immigration status.

The following information may change, so it is important to contact a lawyer.

The following rights apply to non-citizens who are inside the U.S. Non-citizens at the border who are trying to enter the U.S. have additional restrictions and do not have all the same rights.

**Q: Do I have the right to talk to a lawyer before answering any DHS questions or signing any DHS papers?**

**A:** Yes. You have the right to call a lawyer or your family if you are detained, and you have the right to be visited by a lawyer in detention. You have the right to have your attorney with you at any hearing before an immigration judge. You do not have the right to a government-appointed attorney for immigration proceedings, but if you have been arrested, immigration officials must show you a list of free or low cost legal service providers.

**Q: Should I carry my green card or other immigration papers with me?**

**A:** If you have documents authorizing you to stay in the U.S., you must carry them with you. Presenting false or expired papers to DHS may lead to deportation or criminal prosecution. An unexpired green card, 1–94, Employment Authorization Card, Border Crossing Card or other papers that prove you are in legal status will satisfy this requirement. If you do not carry these papers with you, you could be charged with a misdemeanor crime. Always keep a copy of your immigration papers with a trusted family member or friend who can fax it to you, if need be. Check with your immigration lawyer about your specific case. You may be required to show your identification to police officers, border patrol agents and aircraft pilots as well.

**Q: Am I required to talk to government officers about my immigration history?**

**A:** Once you have shown evidence of your status, you do not have to talk to officers further–it is up to you. You may be better off remaining silent and talking to a lawyer first, depending on your situation. Immigration law is very complicated. You may have a problem without realizing it. A lawyer can protect your rights, advise you and help you avoid giving answers that might hurt you. If DHS asks anything about your political and religious beliefs, groups you belong to or contribute to, things you have said, where you have traveled or other questions that do not seem right, you do not have to answer them. An officer may not request evidence of your immigration status in your home or another private place unless he or she has a warrant.

**Q: If I am arrested for immigration violations, do I have the right to a hearing before an immigration judge to defend myself against deportation charges?**

**A:** Yes. In most cases only an immigration judge can order you deported. But if you waive your rights or take "voluntary departure," agreeing to leave the country, you could be deported without a hearing. If you have criminal convictions, were arrested at the border, came to the U.S. through the visa waiver program or have been ordered deported in the past, you could be deported without a hearing. Contact a lawyer immediately to see if there is any relief for you.

**Q: Can I call my consulate if I am arrested?**

**A:** Yes. Non-citizens arrested in the U.S. have the right to call their consulate or to have the police tell the consulate of your arrest. The police must let your consulate visit or speak with you if consular officials decide to do so. Your consulate might help you find a lawyer or offer other help.

**Q: What happens if I give up my right to a hearing or leave the U.S. before the hearing is over?**

**A:** You could lose your eligibility for certain immigration benefits, and you could be barred from returning to the U.S. for a number of years. You should always talk to an immigration lawyer before you decide to give up your right to a hearing.

**Q: What should I do if I want to contact DHS?**

**A:** Always talk to a lawyer before contacting the DHS, even on the phone. Many DHS officers view "enforcement" as their primary job and will not explain all of your options to you.

# III. What are My Rights at Airports?

**IMPORTANT NOTE: It is illegal for law enforcement to perform any stops, searches, detentions or removals based solely on your race, national origin, religion, sex or ethnicity.**

**Q: If I am entering the U.S. with valid travel papers can a U.S. customs agent stop and search me?**

**A:** Yes. Customs agents have the right to stop, detain and search every person and item.

**Q: Can my bags or I be searched after going through metal detectors with no problem or after security sees that my bags to not contain a weapon?**

**A:** Yes. Even if the initial screen of your bags reveals nothing suspicious, the screeners have the authority to conduct a further search of you or your bags.

**Q: If I am on an airplane, can an airline employee interrogate me or ask me to get off the plane?**

**A:** The pilot of an airplane has the right to refuse to fly a passenger if he or she believes the passenger is a threat to the safety of the flight. The pilot's decision must be reasonable and based on observations of you, not stereotypes.

**IF YOU HAVE BEEN PROFILED** at the airport, please fill out the Passenger Profiling Complaint Form that can be found in the Racial Equality section of our Web site at **www.aclu.org/airlineprofiling**

AMENDED

# RESOLUTION NO. 2003-795

### ADOPTED BY THE SACRAMENTO CITY COUNCIL

ON DATE OF _____ **NOV 1 3 2003** _____

### RESOLUTION BY THE SACRAMENTO CITY COUNCIL
### AFFIRMING CIVIL LIBERTIES AND OPPOSING THE INFRINGEMENT
### OF SUCH LIBERTIES BY THE FEDERAL GOVERNMENT

WHEREAS, the City of Sacramento is the capital of California, the most diverse state in the United States; and

WHEREAS, the City of Sacramento is proud of its national reputation as the most integrated city in the United States and a model of tolerance for the state and for the nation; and

WHEREAS, the diverse population of the City of Sacramento includes immigrants, students, farm workers, union members and other men and women of various ancestry, color, ethnicity, national origin, ages, sex, sexual orientation, marital status, physical and mental disability, and religion whose contributions to the community are vital to its economy, culture and civic character; and

WHEREAS, on previous occasions, the people of Sacramento, including its elected officials, law enforcement, and community leaders have gathered together in unity to affirm solidarity with victims of hate crimes and to denounce hate violence; and

WHEREAS, the preservation of civil liberties is crucial to the political and social health of the community, state, and nation; and

WHEREAS, federal laws and policies were hastily adopted in the aftermath of the September 11, 2001 terrorist attacks which threaten fundamental rights and liberties; and

WHEREAS, that federal legislation known as the USA PATRIOT ACT was passed by Congress without sufficient study or debate and gives the federal government unprecedented powers that threaten the civil rights of Sacramento residents and especially those community members of Arab descent or Muslim faith as well as immigrants and those who question government policies; and

WHEREAS, the Sacramento City Council believes that there is no inherent conflict between national security and the preservation of liberty; and

WHEREAS, notwithstanding the Sacramento City Council's concerns about the USA Patriot Act as expressed in this Resolution, the Sacramento City Council acknowledges and commends the Office of the U.S. Attorney General for the Eastern District of California for its

---

**FOR CITY COUNCIL USE ONLY**

Credit Line:    Sacramento City Council

RESOLUTION NO.: __2003-795__

DATE ADOPTED: __NOV 1 3 2003__

diligent and sincere efforts to uphold the U.S. Constitution and the laws of this nation in a respectful, lawful and nondiscriminatory manner.

WHEREAS, more than 200 other patriotic communities throughout California and the United States have enacted resolutions reaffirming support for the civil rights and civil liberties in the face of government policies threaten these core values;

BE IT THEREFORE RESOLVED BY THE SACRAMENTO CITY COUNCIL THAT,

THE CITY OF SACRAMENTO REAFFIRMS its strong support for the fundamental constitutional rights and its opposition to federal measures that infringe on these rights; and

THE CITY OF SACRAMENTO REAFFIRMS its strong support for the rights of immigrants and opposes measures that single out individuals for legal scrutiny based on their country of origin, religion, or immigration status, and

THE CITY OF SACRAMENTO calls on agencies and employees of the City not to engage in any activities that would violate any city ordinance or the laws and constitution of the State of California or of the United States; and

THE CITY OF SACRAMENTO calls upon the Sacramento public schools to provide notice to individuals whose education records have been obtained by law enforcement agents pursuant to section 507 of the USA PATRIOT ACT; and

THE CITY OF SACRAMENTO calls upon public libraries to post in a prominent place within the library a notice warning patrons that under Section 215 of the USA PATRIOT ACT records or books and other materials borrowed from the library may be obtained by federal agents; and

THE CITY OF SACRAMENTO reaffirms its commitment to unbiased policing and endorses the principle that no law enforcement or other city agency may profile or discriminate against any person solely on the basis of ancestry, color, ethnicity, national origin, ages, sex, sexual orientation, marital status, physical or mental disability, or religion.

BE IT FURTHER RESOLVED that copies of this resolution be transmitted to United States Senators Dianne Feinstein and Barbara Boxer and Congressman Robert Matsui along with a letter urging them to monitor federal anti-terrorism tactics and work to repeal those provisions of the USA PATRIOT ACT and other laws and policies that infringe upon the rights and liberties of the residents of the City of Sacramento.

HEATHER FARGO
_____
MAYOR

ATTEST:

VIRGINIA HENRY
_____
CITY CLERK

_____

FOR CITY COUNCIL USE ONLY

RESOLUTION NO.: __2003-795__

DATE ADOPTED: ___NOV 1 3 2003___

# Ella Baker & the Black Freedom Movement

*Barbara Ransby*

## Gender Inequity within the Movement

Ella Baker launched SCLC's Crusade for Citizenship with a greater margin of success than one might have expected given the time and resource constraints, demonstrating that she had the skills and commitment the nascent organization required. Yet Baker felt that she was never seriously considered for the job of permanent executive director. At one meeting, a minister from Nashville proposed that Baker be considered as a candidate for the job, but his suggestion fell on deaf ears. "The officialdom didn't take it seriously," Baker recalled.[41] The attitudes that King and other ministerial leaders of the SCLC held toward Baker were not unique to her situation; rather, they were a manifestation of the larger problem of sexism within the church, the organization, and the culture. By this time, Baker was well aware that the SCLC ministers were not ready to welcome her into the organization on an equal footing. That would be to go too far afield from the gender relations they were used to in the church. Baker observed that "the role of women in the southern church . . . was that of doing the things that the minister said he wanted to have done. It was not one in which they were credited with having creativity and initiative and capacity to carry out things."[42] While Baker may have slightly overstated her case—women did have some power and agency—the basic point still had a great deal of merit.

Clearly, women were instrumental forces in the church, but male leaders seldom fully acknowledged women's power and often attempted to limit the authority women exercised.[43] Many of Baker's male colleagues, like their counterparts in white society, viewed women as subordinates and helpmates. Even though African American women have historically worked both inside and outside the home and engaged in public, political activity, the culture that prevailed in the 1950s, especially among the black middle class, as among their white counterparts, emphasized the primacy of women's domestic roles.[44] According to Baker, the majority of the ministers in SCLC wanted to relate to women in this very limited capacity. They were most comfortable talking to women about "how well they cooked, and how beautiful they looked," she complained.[45] Baker's deliberate avoidance of conventional femininity made a number of her male clerical colleagues rather uneasy. "I wasn't a fashion plate," she remarked, "[and] I made no bones about not being a fashion plate."[46] More importantly, "I did not hesitate in voicing my opinion and . . . it was not a comforting sort of presence that I presented."[47] The conditions under which she worked, especially the sexist and often dismissive treatment she endured from her male co-workers, annoyed and offended Baker. Some days she could barely justify persevering in such an adverse situation.[48] "I live to serve" was the tongue-in-cheek way that Baker once described herself to a cousin.[49] This sarcastic statement had a sad ring of truth.

The work that Ella Baker and other women did for SCLC was consistently undervalued. As the organization grew and additional female staffers were hired, Baker protested that these women were taken for granted and treated unfairly as well.[50] A rhetoric of racial equality marked the public pronouncements of SCLC leaders, while old hierarchies based on gender inequities endured within their ranks. Baker refused to accept the situation in silence. She criticized ministerial leaders who came to meetings late and left early, disregarding the inconveniences they caused for the female clerical staff. They expected the women workers to cater to them, Baker complained.[51] Although she never publicly named names, Baker also alluded to unprincipled sexual behavior on the part of some male ministers involved in the movement. She confided to one researcher that certain SCLC ministers would come into the office in the afternoon "after spending the morning at some sister's house doing what they shouldn't have been doing . . . you see, I know too many stories."[52] The ministers' arrogant assumption that they stood above the moral rules they preached to others cost them Baker's respect as ministers and as men.

Despite her frustrations and resentments, Ella Baker assisted SCLC leaders in recruiting, screening, and selecting candidates for the executive director post, which they had tacitly deemed her unqualified to fill. She approached several prospective candidates with whom she had worked in the past. John Tilley, who was hired as executive director was among them. Tilley was a Shaw alumnus and the pastor of a church in Baltimore.[53] Baker thought he was a good candidate because he "had a clear voice and good thinking" and some political experience in Baltimore.[54] Baker and Stanley Levison met with Tilley at an ice cream parlor in Harlem to discuss the organization and the job.[55] When King met Tilley, he was impressed and agreed to bring him on as the new executive director in May 1958.

The first SCLC meeting after Tilley joined the staff took place in Clarksdale, Mississippi, that same month. The gathering was well attended by some 200 delegates, indicating that in many places the organization's work was gaining support.[56] Convening the group in Mississippi was a bold gesture. Mississippi was so well known for antiblack violence that for many southerners it served as a symbol of the crudest and most brutal brand of white racism. Mississippi continued to hold that distinction as the civil rights movement progressed. It was in Mississippi that young Emmett Till had been murdered only three years earlier. It was in Mississippi that three young civil rights workers—Andrew Goodman, Michael Schwerner, and James Chaney—would be ambushed and murdered in 1964. But on the weekend of May 29, 1958, the town of Clarksdale was the site of something hopeful: serious discussions, debates, and strategy sessions about the future direction of the Black Freedom Movement.

Baker went to Clarksdale a few days early to help set up for the meeting.[57] She was optimistic that things were finally coming together for the new coalition. A permanent director was in place; local NAACP leaders such as Evers had agreed to attend the meeting, despite tensions between SCLC and the national NAACP office; and there were sparks of activity in several cities.[58] The participation of Evers and Aaron Henry, a fellow NAACP activist, reflected the willingness of NAACP leaders at the state and local level to work with whatever forces were in motion on the ground, often in direct opposition to national directives.[59] The men and women under attack in the South did not always subscribe to the grandiose objectives and long-term strategies of the national offices and high-level leaders of the organizations with which they worked. Medgar Evers and Aaron Henry never fully agreed with the decision by the NAACP leaders in New York not to form alliances with other civil rights groups, and both men worked closely with SCLC and other groups on particular campaigns.[60] Baker was pleased with the outcome of the 1958 Clarksdale meeting.[61] She hoped Tilley would be a hands-on leader who would expand the base of supporters beyond the church and embrace some of the more militant community-based leaders, both secular and church-related. Toward that end, she invited him to stay on in Mississippi for a few days after the Clarksdale meeting and familiarize himself with the work Amzie and Ruth Moore were doing in Cleveland, Mississippi, which he did. But even putting Tilley in contact with some of the most embattled freedom fighters in the South could not reinvigorate the coalition.[62]

The internal problems of SCLC continued after the meeting in Clarksdale. Tilley did not prove to be the stabilizing force that Baker and King had hoped for. Rev. Tilley continued to head his congregation in Baltimore after assuming his new responsibilities in Atlanta, and he was unable to combine or balance these two demanding positions. His commuting back and forth took its toll on Tilley and on the SCLC's work. In less than a year, King was forced to fire him. Again, by default, Baker was asked to take over as acting or interim director; both titles were used.

Internal problems were compounded by external crises. In September 1958, while Martin Luther King Jr. was on a speaking tour to promote his new book, *Stride toward Freedom,* he was stabbed by a mentally ill woman. Ella was in town at the time, trying to recover from her own health problems. Suffering from acute back pain, she was stretched out on her living room floor when she heard the shocking news of King's stabbing on the radio.[63] Baker immediately rushed to the hospital to see what she could do to help. King survived the attack, but his recuperation took months. Once again, Baker had to pick up the slack. She filled in for King as a speaker on several occasions, answered his correspondence, explained his inca-pacitation, and served as publicist and accountant for the sale of his book, a job she did not relish.

After a year of hard labor in the SCLC's trenches, Baker was disappointed that so little had been achieved in terms of regionwide coordinated work. She blamed the clerical leaders. They had not given her the resources necessary to run an office or a campaign efficiently. She had to beg for a working mimeograph machine, an air conditioner in the summer, and secretarial help. She then had to deal with the added frustration of King's veto power within the organization. Nothing could be done, she complained, without his approval.[64] And, to add insult to injury, she was saddled with the responsibility of all promotions of and sales for King's book. Still, Baker did not see too many other political options for herself in 1958–59, espe-cially if she wanted to be based in a black southern community, which she did. So, she persevered.

Baker's 1958 report to the Administrative Committee of SCLC reflected the goals that she would fight to implement throughout her tenure. Baker urged her SCLC colleagues to develop programs for mass action and to target women for ac-tivist campaigns. She specifically called for the formation of youth and action teams to help ignite the work. This report was her effort to rally the troops, but the results were modest. Everyone nodded and continued on as they had before. With-out support from the principal decision makers in the organization, there was little Baker could do.[65]

On some level, she and the ministers—at least the core of them—were not too far apart in the kind of action they envisioned, but together they could not seem to make it happen. Historian Glenn T. Eskew suggests that Baker was at least in part to blame. He even sees the growing "cult of personality" surrounding King as partly due to the absence of a sustained mass-based campaign, a campaign Baker was re-sponsible for getting off the ground. For Baker, the inverse was true. King's larger-than-life persona inhibited the emergence of local struggles and local leaders.

In December 1958, at the third annual Montgomery Improvement Association Institute on Nonviolence, the program theme was "A Testimonial to Dr. King's Leadership." Taylor Branch maintains that "[t]o Ella Baker, frustrated by SCLC's bare solvency and its paralyzed registration campaign, this sort of activity was not mere froth but a harmful end in itself." She asked King directly why he allowed such hero worship, and he responded simply that it was what people wanted.[66] This answer did not satisfy Baker in the least.

Baker felt that SCLC's increasing reliance on King's celebrity and charisma had all sorts of hidden dangers. Less polished leaders were likely to receive less recog-nition and might become disaffected from the struggle. For example, E. D. Nixon, the labor and civil rights activist who played a pivotal role in the Montgomery bus boycott, resented the way that an outsider eclipsed local leaders. In a 1958 letter to a friend, Nixon complained bitterly about King's fame and his own diminished stature in the movement. It is disheartening, he explained, "when people give all recognition to one because of his academic training and forge[t] other[s] who do not have that kind of training but are making a worthwhile contribution."[67] Furthermore, no one person could possibly meet the needs of a growing and increasingly complex movement. Even leaders who were motivated by high ideals rather than personal ambition and adopted a humble rather than top-down style had to make way for many others to assume leadership roles. According to Baker, organizations had to alter their very concept of leadership: "Instead of the leader as a person who was supposed to be a magic man, you could develop individuals who were bound together by a concept that benefited the larger number of individuals and provided an opportunity for them to grow into being responsible for carrying out a program."[68]

Ella Baker believed that all their lives poor black people had been spoonfed the notion that the key to their emancipation was something external to themselves: ostensibly benevolent masters, enlightened legislators, or skillful and highly educated lawyers. Such dependency reinforced poor people's sense of helplessness, Baker felt. Her message was quite the opposite. "Strong people don't need strong leaders," she argued.[69] In Baker's view, oppressed people did not need a messiah to deliver them from oppression; all they needed was themselves, one another, and the will to persevere. The clerical leaders of SCLC, King included, held a very different notion of leadership. As Baker put it, they saw themselves as the new "saviors."[70] As early as 1947, she had insisted that "the Negro must quit looking for a savior and work to save himself."[71] She was even more convinced of this by 1958.

Crisis after crisis and sacrifice after sacrifice, Baker's dissatisfaction with her circumstances grew. She became especially annoyed that many SCLC ministers viewed her as a glorified secretary who was there to simply "carry out King's orders."[72] Although the SCLC needed Baker's skills, it was not willing to recognize or affirm her leadership. As Eugene Walker put it in an interview with Baker, SCLC ministers seemed to "respect your abilities on the one hand, and fear your independence on the other."[73] To be fair, not all of the SCLC board members felt this way, which in part was what kept Baker going. By 1959, she had built strong ties with SCLC activists in Shreveport and Birmingham, and she had alliances with NAACP people in Mississippi. Yet, despite her independent base, Baker felt so suffocated by the magnitude of King's personality and presence that she could not make herself comfortable within the organization.

## Baker and King

The relationship between Ella Baker and Martin Luther King Jr. is doubly significant. First, the incompatibility between the civil rights movement's most charismatic national spokesperson and one of its most effective grassroots organizers had significant consequences for the development of the movement itself. Baker's decision to leave the SCLC staff in 1960, her choice to support mass-based, grassroots organizations, and her determination to defend the autonomous, democratic decisions made by militant activists changed the course of the Black Freedom Movement, not least by ensuring that the nascent Student Nonviolent Coordinating Committee was not taken over by established civil rights organizations, including SCLC and the NAACP. Second, the conflict between these two civil rights leaders reveals more fundamental conflicts within black politics and African American culture over the meanings of American democracy and the pathways toward social change. If Baker's criticisms of King were overly harsh and unforgiving, that may be because they were intensified by her disappointed hopes in King himself and by her accumulated outrage against the male leaders who had treated her in demeaning ways over many decades.

In some of her harshest, perhaps even gratuitous, criticisms of King, Baker described him as a pampered member of Atlanta's black elite who had the mantle of leadership handed to him rather than having had to earn it, a member of a coddled "silver spoon brigade."[74] He wore silk suits and spoke with a silver tongue. His followers were in awe of him, struggling in vain to imitate him or just seeking to be near him. Young ministers would try to dress like him, even sound like him, Baker observed, and their unsuccessful attempts only reinforced the perception that he deserved the deference and adulation he received. King was, in her words, "the man of the hour . . . [and others] got the reflective glory."[75] In Baker's eyes, King did not identify closely enough with the people he sought to lead. He did not situate himself among them but remained above them. What Baker does not give King credit for is the fact that while he may have allowed others to applaud his leadership skills and oratory talents, he did not hesitate to take risks, putting himself and his family in danger repeatedly for the sake of the cause. So, while attention centered on him, so did the rage of those who, like his assassin, blamed him for the movement's success.

Still, Baker felt the focus on King drained the masses of confidence in themselves. People often marveled at the things King could do that they could not; his eloquent speeches overwhelmed as well as inspired. This disturbed Baker. While she appreciated King's many contributions to the struggle and valued the considerable talents he brought to bear, she was angered and frustrated by the hero worship that surrounded him. Baker challenged King on this matter repeatedly, arguing that the tolerated, even if he did not encourage, such adulation.[76]

In gauging the fairness of Ella Baker's criticisms of King, one should keep in mind that she was known for her patience, tolerance, and willingness to work with individuals of diverse ideologies. She had collaborated with other men who were well known for their inflated egos, from George Schuyler to Walter White. And, as King's biographers have noted, he was in many ways quite humble, given the attention and flattery he received from others. He lived modestly and was initially quite ambivalent about all the attention and accolades that were directed his way.

Why did King provoke Baker so much? Some of her friends and colleagues have asserted that Baker's conflicts within SCLC resulted as much from different personal styles as from political disagreements. Septima Clark, who admired Baker greatly, felt that sometimes she responded too angrily to insults and slights from the male clerics in SCLC, when these situations could have been handled more effectively in a less confrontational manner. There was undoubtedly a subjective component to Baker's criticisms of King and the other SCLC ministers whom she felt did not respect her as an equal. Anne Braden, who was much closer to Baker than to King personally and politically, admitted that "Ella had a blind spot when it came to King. It was just something about him. She and I differed on this."[77]

It would be misguided to view Baker's analysis of King's political flaws too narrowly, however. She did not see King as unique; rather, she saw what she defined as his weaknesses as reflective of prevalent tendencies in American society. At the same time, she insisted that her criticism never translated into personal animus, as some have alleged. Baker remarked that "some of the King family have said that I hated him, but I didn't."[78] King and Baker were bound together, from the very inception of SCLC, by manifold political ties and real interdependence. Their working relationship was close enough—even with King in Montgomery most of the time and Baker in Atlanta—that their fundamental differences became a recurring source of friction.

Still, King and Baker were more alike than Baker was ever prepared to admit. Both were southerners by birth, and both had grown up in the social and spiritual circles of the southern black Baptist church. Both were college-educated intellectuals, articulate spokespersons for the cause of black freedom and social justice, and eloquent public speakers. And both came from class positions of relative advantage. But Baker and King had made very divergent choices about how to utilize their skills and privileges. They translated religious faith into their political identities in profoundly different ways. Above all, they defined the confluence of their roles as individuals and their roles as participants in a mass movement for social change quite distinctly. Baker was a militant egalitarian, and King was a sophisticated southern Baptist preacher.

In Baker's view, the celebrity status that the movement afforded King was not an aberration but rather a product of a dominant culture that promoted individualism and egocentrism. People "just have to have these high-powered individuals to worship," Baker pointed out.[79] "It's the culture we're in," she insisted. "When the newspaper people come around, what do they look for? They don't look for the solid organizational drive . . . they look for a miracle performer."[80] Baker believed that when ordinary people elevate their leaders above the crowd, they devalue the power within themselves. Her message was that we are all, as individuals, products of the larger society, even as some of us struggle to change it. And all leaders, however well intentioned, are susceptible to the corruption of personal ambition. According to Baker, "We on the outside, we want to be important . . . so we ape the insiders."[81] She argued that activists often unwittingly replicate the values and attributes of those they oppose, which becomes a detriment to the movement. While many black leaders criticized racial hierarchies in the dominant society, they recreated hierarchies based on class, gender, and personality within the movement itself.

Baker insisted that leaders live by the principles they espouse. In this sense, she argued, not only is the personal political, but the political is inescapably personal. Transformation has to occur at the societal and institutional level, but also at the local and personal level.

Ironically, Ella Baker could not see in King what other colleagues and his many biographers saw: a young man, talented, brilliant, eager to serve a greater good but reticent about being lionized, and being pushed and pulled in many directions all at once. In Baker's view, he was indeed a talented young man who had been given a precious opportunity to help organize large numbers of people into a fighting force for change, and instead, she lamented, he settled for mesmerizing them.

## Missionaries and Messiahs

King and Baker had been introduced to politics through the same institution: the southern black Baptist church. Since slavery, the black church had been an influential pillar in the African American community and an important arena for black politics. The church provided blacks with the technical skills to enter the political arena: literacy, fund-raising, public speaking, management, and organization. In addition, the church provided its members with a powerful moral language within which to frame political issues, if they so chose. In a high school essay, Baker wrote eloquently, and uncritically, about the important leadership role played by the black church.[82] Her ideas and analysis of the role of the black church, and of the clergy in particular, had changed considerably over the years, but her understanding of the centrality of the institution in African American life and culture remained intact.

Baker's political awakening began within the black Baptist women's missionary movement in the early 1900s. Her mother was a devoted activist who dragged Ella and her two siblings to missionary meetings throughout their home state of North Carolina. These churchwomen celebrated strength, piety, and quiet, selfless service. Egos and individual accomplishments were downplayed. Humility was a virtue. In contrast, King was groomed from an early age to follow in his father's footsteps into the ministry. Playing a visible leadership role in the church, and thereby occupying a prominent place in the black community, was an honorable career goal for a young man from such a deeply religious family.

King's and Baker's respective orientations within the church could not have been more different. Ministers were trained to be shepherds of their flocks. The metaphor itself suggests the differences between the notions of leadership that ministers practiced and those that missionary women adhered to. Ministers directed their flocks; missionaries gathered people together. In Baker's view, most ministers expected to say their piece and have their congregations obediently carry out their decisions. Baker saw no model for collective or democratic decision making within the mainstream ministerial tradition. The preacher's presumed authority did not trouble men like King, however. As he himself put it, "Leadership never ascends from the pew to the pulpit, but . . . descends from the pulpit to the pew."[83] But Baker saw this flow of authority as a weakness, not a virtue. The socialization of women missionaries meant that they practiced a more democratic and decentralized style of religious service than male ministers did.

Another philosophical position that distinguished Baker from King was the issue of nonviolence. Baker accepted nonviolence as a tactic, but she never internalized the concept as a way of life or made it a defining feature of her worldview. Contrasting herself to her friend Bayard Rustin, Ella Baker remarked: "He had a history of dedication to the concept of nonviolence. I have no such history; I have no such commitment. Not historically or even now can I claim that because that's not my way of functioning."[84] Rustin's pacifism was rooted in his Quakerism, while Baker's Christian faith carried no imperative to turn the other cheek or love your enemies. For her, nonviolence and self-defense were tactical choices, not matters of principle. "Mine was not a choice of non-violence per se," Baker reiterated.[85]

Indeed, Baker questioned the capacity of nonviolence to serve as a philosophical basis on which to build a movement, even while she was working for the SCLC. She later questioned "how far non-violent mass action can go" as a mobilization strategy.[86] Her critique of the limitations of nonviolence was informed by her connections with the militant struggles of the 1930s and the self-defense ethos of those she worked with in the 1940s, and it foreshadowed her support of revolutionary militancy in the late 1960s. Baker consistently gave voice to a radical vision for social transformation and encouraged others to join her in the struggle necessary to realize that vision. The realist in her understood that such a struggle might, at times, become heated and even physical. Engaging in determined conflict entailed utilizing a variety of tactics. Baker felt that oppressed people needed to tap whatever resources they had at their disposal to forge a viable strategy for resistance, especially in the dangerous and violent climate of the Jim Crow South. She was not alone in this view. Some of SCLC's most notable grassroots leaders, including C. O. Simpkins and Daisy Bates, admitted to having firearms for self-defense purposes.[87]

Baker differed with King and other SCLC leaders on questions besides nonviolence and the meaning of leadership in militant mass movements. Bernice Johnson Reagon has suggested that Baker's worldview and political practice can best be defined as a type of radical humanism.[88] It was radical, in that she advocated fundamental social transformation, and it was humanistic, because she envisioned that transformation coming about through a democratic, cooperative, and localized movement that valued the participation of each of its individual members. Baker's unfaltering confidence in the common people was the bedrock of her political vision. It was with them that she felt the locus of power should reside. This confidence was rooted in her understanding of the complex dialectical relationship between deference and defiance in southern black culture. Despite the facade of subservience and acquiescence to white rule and Jim Crow indignities on the part of southern African Americans, many black people embodied a fighting spirit that needed only a viable outlet to demonstrate and to express itself in subtle ways every day. It was important for political organizers to understand and decode the culture of everyday life, and to tap the reservoir of resistance that resided there, in order to pull people into collective action.[89] In Baker's assessment, assuming that people were quiescent was a misreading of southern black culture.

In this respect, Baker's views parallel those of the anthropologist James Scott, who writes eloquently about the "hidden transcript" of opposition within oppressed populations and about the danger of not reading that transcript carefully. Scott warns:

> *So long as we confine our conception of the political to activity that is openly declared, we are driven to conclude that subordinate groups essentially lack a political life or that what political life they do have is restricted to those exceptional moments of popular explosion. To do so is to miss the immense political terrain that lies between quiescence and revolt and that, for better or worse, is the political environment of subject classes. It is to focus on the visible coastline of politics and miss the continent that lies beyond.*[90]

Scott's theoretical work on the nature of popular culture and resistance resembles many aspects of the politics that Ella Baker lived but rarely wrote about. From her point of view, it was a semi-spontaneous action from below—Rosa Parks's reasoned decision to violate a segregation ordinance—that had sparked the Montgomery boycott. It was another semi-spontaneous action—a handful of college students sitting in at a lunch counter in Greensboro, North Carolina, in 1960—that would ignite the next phase of movement activity. These actions were thought through and conscious, but they were both examples of leadership coming from below (the metaphorical pews) rather than from the political pulpits above. These actions also tapped into a subterranean oppositional culture and gave it a political outlet.

Baker's political views were profoundly shaped by her analysis of the complex class dynamics within the black community. As she put it, "There's always a problem in the minority group that's escalating up the ladder in this culture . . . it's a problem of their not understanding the possibility of being divorced from those who are not in their social classification."[91] For this reason, she argued, "I believe firmly in the right of the people who were under the heel to be the ones to decide what action they were going to take to get [out] from under their oppression."[92] She held fast to her conviction that the most oppressed sectors of society had to be in the forefront of the struggle to change society.

Ella Baker's job tenure with SCLC was more frustrating than fruitful. She was unsettled the entire time, politically, physically, and, to a certain extent, emotionally. She had no solid allies in the SCLC office that she could rely on daily as she had done during her years with the NAACP. Her close and increasingly critical view of King put some distance between Baker and her old In Friendship allies, Levison and Rustin, who adored King. Moreover, she had never really settled into her semi-furnished apartment in Atlanta and found herself on the road more than she was there. Emotionally, there were some disconnects as well. Jackie was in college.

Baker's marriage had ended in divorce in the summer of 1958 while she was in Atlanta.[93] And her health had begun to effect her work. Her eyes were bothering her, as were her back and encroaching arthritis. Still, there were pockets of activity among some SCLC affiliates that persuaded Baker to stay with the organization a little bit longer.

# Notes

[41] Baker, interviewed by Walker 17–18.

[42] Ibid., 18.

[43] Higginbotham, *Righteous Discontent*, 3, writes: "Male-biased traditions and rules of decorum sought to mute women's voices and accentuate their subordinate status vis-à-vis men. Thus, tainted by the values of the larger society, the black church sought to provide men with full manhood rights, while offering women a separate and unequal status."

[44] See Shaw, *What a Woman Ought to Be and To Do,* and Kevin Gaines, *Uplifting the Race,* for more discussion of the politics of respectability as they relate to gender and black protest and activism in the early twentieth century. See also May, *Homeward Bound,* for a discussion of gender and the Cold War.

[45] Baker, interview by Walker, 20.

[46] Ibid., 19.

[47] Ibid., 15–16.

[48] Ella Baker, letter to "Dear Mattie," June 3, 1958, EBP.

[49] Ella Baker, letter to Vincent (Baker), Mar. 22, 1960, EBP. He appears to have been a cousin of Baker's with whom she had not been in close touch.

[50] Ella Baker, memo to SCLC Administrative Committee on office procedures and personnel, June 2, 1960, EBP, SCLC files.

[51] Baker, interview by Morris, 31B. A call for democratizing the movement's clerical work was analogous to women's demand that men share in household chores. Baker was critical of the gendered division of labor between primarily female clerical staff and primarily male "professional" staff. This issue recurred in SNCC in 1964 when female staffers—half serious and half teasing—"called a strike in the Atlanta [SNCC] office to protest always being asked to take minutes." Richardson, interview by author.

[52] Baker, interview by Morris, 31B. King's alleged extramartial affairs are discussed by Garrow in his biography of King. *Bearing the Cross,* and by Abernathy in his autobiography, *And the Walls Came Tumbling Down.*

[53] Baker, interview by Walker, 11–12.

[54] Ibid., 11, 14.

[55] Ibid, 12.

[56] Branch, *Parting the Waters,* 233.

[57] Alethea Wyatt, letter to Ella Baker, May 27, 1958, SCLC Papers, King Center, box 32, folder 7.

[58] SCLC Papers, box 32, folder 7.

[59] See Green, *Before His Time.*

[60] See Dittmer, *Local People,* 76–78, for details on Evers and NAACP-SCLC rivalry in Mississippi.

[61] Baker, interview by Walker, 13.

[62] John Tilley to Amzie Moore, Oct. 30, 1958, Amzie Moore Papers, box 1, folder: 1958 Correspondence, State Historical Society of Wisconsin, Madison.

[63]Baker, interview by Morris, 81A.

[64]Ibid., 83A.

[65]SCLC Administrative Report, July 3, 1958, EBP, SCLC files.

[66]Eskew, *But for Birmingham*, 28: Branch, *Parting the Waters*, 247.

[67]Quoted in Tyson, *Radio Free Dixie*, 117.

[68]Baker, interview by Morris, 42A.

[69]Cantarow and O'Malley, "Ella Baker," 53.

[70]See Morris, *Origins of the Civil Rights Movement*, 115.

[71]"U.S. Warned to Make Democracy Work at Home," *Atlanta Daily World*, Jan. 2, 1947, I.

[72]Baker, interview by Walker, 5.

[73]Ibid., 19.

[74]Baker, interview by Morris, 65A.

[75]Ibid., 80A.

[76]Branch, *Parting the Waters*, 247.

[77]Clark, interview by Hall, 87; Braden, interview by author, June 1991.

[78]Baker, interview by Britton, 36.

[79]Baker, interview by Morris, 39A.

[80]Ibid., 55A.

[81]Ibid., 48A.

[82]Ella Baker, "The Negro Church, the Nucleus of the Negroes Cultural Development," unpublished high school paper (circa 1923), EBP.

[83]Fairclough, *Martin Luther King, Jr.*, 19.

[84]Baker, interview by Baker, 32.

[85]Ibid., 24.

[86]Baker, interview by Walker, 32.

[87]Tyson, *Radio Free Dixie*, 153; Simpkins, interview by author.

[88]Bernice Johnson Reagon, interview by author.

[89]Ella Baker, letter to Ruth Tinsley, Richmond, Va., ca. Dec. 1942 or 1943, EBP, NAACP files.

[90]Scott, *Domination and the Arts of Resistance*, 199.

[91]Cantarow and O'Malley, "Ella Baker," 70.

[92]Ibid., 84.

[93]Divorce decree, City Clerk's Office for the Borough of Manhattan, N.Y., file number 30849-1958.

# Asian Americans and Debates about Affirmative Action

## L. Ling-Chi Wang

In the past two years, both proponents and opponents have written extensively on the topic of affirmative action. But a national dialogue has yet to take place because both sides are locked in intractable positions, unwilling and unable to listen to and understand each other. Since the beginning of 1995, the national debate has become increasingly acrimonious and polarized. The July 20, 1995 decision of the Regents of the University of California to abolish its long standing affirmative action policy on admissions, faculty and staff hiring, and contracts, as well as the anti-affirmative action California initiative, known as the California Civil Rights Initiative (CCRI), to be placed on the November 1996 ballot, have contributed to the polarization of the national debate. The recent Republican victory in the 1994 elections and several U.S. Supreme Court decisions have greatly strengthened the forces opposed to affirmative action. Despite clear demographic and political shifts in the past three decades, there is a conspicuous absence of any critical, yet constructive, appraisal of the policy.

As one who has supported and worked on issues related to affirmative action during the past 28 years in the Asian American community, I would like to share my understanding and appraisal of the policy and the position I think Asian Americans should take in the national debate. While Asian Americans have slowly become more visible in the political debate, both proponents and opponents of affirmative action have largely misrepresented and marginalized the perspectives and positions of Asian Americans. I shall begin by briefly placing affirmative action in historical and political perspectives, at the risk of being redundant, since misinformation and confusion over both the intents and objectives of affirmative action policy still exist. I shall then outline where Asian Americans are situated in the unfolding national debate. Finally, I shall conclude with a critique of affirmative action as it has been practiced in the past thirty years and what Asian Americans can do to help reconfigure affirmative action within the context of a re-envisioned multiracial America. Asian Americans are central to this debate and play a vital role in shaping its outcome.

## Affirmative Action in Perspective

The issue of fairness and justice in the distribution of scarce resources in our race- and class-conscious society lies at the heart of the current debate over affirmative action. Scarcity invariably creates competition and conflict. In this competition, political and economic elites have the power to define universalistic and meritocratic criteria for distributing scarce resources. For example, access to a University of California (UC) education is considered a scarce resource—in 1993, only 20,413 out of 272,800 high school graduates, which is less than ten percent, were admitted into the nine-campus system. The criteria established by the Regents of the University—grade point average (GPA) and standardized test scores—are assumed to be both fair and reliable and, therefore, universal.

The Johnson administration introduced affirmative action policies, pursuant to Executive Order 11246 in 1965, to help dismantle entrenched segregation and discrimination based on race and gender and to promote racial equality and integration. Opponents of affirmative action argue that it is unfair because it subverts meritocracy, condones mediocrity, promotes group rights, racial quotas, reverse discrimination, and above all, invites big government intrusion. Following the logic of the US Supreme Court decision in *Bakke v. the University of California* (1978), they argue that affirmative action in college admissions is morally wrong and un-American, despite its good intentions, because it grants *group rights* based on race and gender at the expense of *individual rights and merits*.

The July 20, 1995, decision by the UC Regents illustrates the argument against affirmative action policies in college admissions. Writing in defense of his anti-affirmative action resolution, UC Regent Ward Connerly declared,

> We have not "killed" or "scrapped" affirmative action. We have not adopted an academic meritocracy. Instead, the regents have eliminated what amounts to a racial Monopoly board in which students are allowed to proceed with their college educations on the basis of their color or the origin of their ancestors. . . . The University of California still has the "welcome mat" out for students of all races. We cherish our diversity and want more of it; we just want to achieve it *naturally* rather *than* artificially.

Likewise, explaining his anti-affirmative action position, UC Regent Stephen Nakashima wrote,

> The Regents' decision to terminate the discriminatory preference accorded to "minority" persons in hiring and contracting resulted from an increasing awareness that discrimination should not beget discrimination. The history books are full of tragedies born of what someone sincerely thought was justified to correct some prior wrong or to enhance the position of some groups. . . .

*In the popular vernacular, "the playing field has been leveled" after years of requiring only Asians and white males to bear the burden of a tilted field.*

The arguments of Connerly and Nakashima are based on the following major assumptions: (1) the US is and should be a *naturally* color-blind society; (2) granting group rights or privileges based on race or gender in the distribution of scarce resource(s) is *artificial* and discriminatory to Asian Americans and whites and, therefore, illegal and wrong; (3) affirmative action policies condone mediocrity and sacrifice merit and excellence; and (4) the sole criteria for the distribution of scarce resources are those based on individual merits and rights.

All four assumptions are flawed. The US has never existed *naturally* as a color-blind society. From the framing of its Constitution to its past and present policies for women and communities of color, the US has created *artificial* social barriers and relied on institutionalized segregation based on race and gender. For example, Harvard University denied admissions to qualified women and minorities for the first 328 years of its 358 year history, artificially protecting and perpetuating the group rights and privileges of white male gentiles. Its policy of excluding women and minorities can be characterized as affirmative action for white males or a policy that condoned mediocrity. Harvard invoked the concept of individual merit only when its protected privileged status for the white male group was challenged in the 1960s. Thus, throughout US history, artificial group rights or privileges have been used to favor white males at the expense of minorities and women.

Under intense pressure from the civil rights movement, universities reluctantly adopted affirmative action policies for minorities and women in the late 1960s as a token concession. Thus, affirmative action was introduced as a device to lend Harvard and other universities an appearance of fairness and integration. Harvard redefined "merit" by adding an "ethnic docket" to its list of other dockets, including wealthy alumni, athletes, and graduates of preparatory schools, in the admission process. This policy was never intended to promote substantive equality or integration; rather, it was designed to allow a small number of token minorities and women into white male dominated universities and work places.

Consequently, under the guise of affirmative action, elite universities like Harvard and the University of California admit more children of well-connected alumni than underrepresented minorities under "affirmative action." It seems that benefactors of "affirmative action" include *all* students admitted by non-competitive criteria, such as legacy, leadership qualities, athletic ability, disability, and historical racial or gender discrimination.

After 30 years of affirmative action, the racial divide in the US remains as wide and deep as that identified by President Johnson's Commission on Civil Disorder in the wake of urban riots in 1967. The Commission concluded in 1968,

*What white Americans have never fully understood—but what the Negro can never forget—is that white society is deeply implicated in the ghetto. White institutions created it, white institutions maintain it, and white society condones it.*

That was in 1968. Today, "white Americans" still do not understand the racial divide. Despite federal measures to abolish racial discrimination, such as the 1954 *Brown v. Board of Education* decision and the Civil Rights Act of 1964, the US has not succeeded in eliminating racial fissures. Yet many continue to believe that the US is a color-blind society. The opponents of affirmative action rest their case on this presumption of color-blindness and demand that public policies be carried out without distinction of race, gender, color, or national origin.

## Asian Americans in the Affirmative Action Discourse

I will now discuss how opposing sides view and treat Asian Americans and then offer a more inclusive and multiracial vision of the US. Asian Americans have become a major focus of the national debate as both sides of the affirmative action issue use Asian Americans to advance their respective arguments. These arguments point to the complexity of race relations in the US and the need to rethink race and race relations. Among the examples of unfairness cited most frequently by opponents of affirmative action is the policy's adverse impact on Asian Americans. For example, in the 1980s, the opponents of affirmative action seized Asian American complaints of discriminatory admission policies in several top research universities as a means to dismantle affirmative action. More recently, the opponents of affirmative action have cited the lawsuit against San Francisco Unified School District action, the *Brian Ho* case, as an example of injustice engendered by affirmative action. Opponents exploit the "model minority" myth, in which Asian Americans are portrayed as highly motivated and hardworking people, by depicting them as victims of an unfair policy that favors group rights over individual merits.

Anti-affirmative action arguments rely on three major flawed assumptions. First, they assume that Asian Americans are a homogeneous group, ignoring the diverse composition of the group—which ranges from recent refugees from Southeast Asia to descendants of California's Chinese pioneers. Secondly, they assume that a legacy of historical and institutional racism against Asian Americans does not exist. They assume that Asian Americans are intergrated into the mainstream and do not face discrimination nor experience anti-Asian sentiment. Lastly, they assume that Asian Americans no longer need affirmative action programs to overcome past injustice and racial discrimination. Thus, they assume that Asian Americans, in departure from the past, no longer constitute a racial minority and are fully integrated into the white majority.

Defenders of affirmative action also view Asian Americans as a model minority; two perspectives have emerged from them. Some claim that Asian Americans no longer need or deserve to be included in affirmative action programs. With good intention, supporters use the "success of Asian Americans" as an argument for reserving affirmative action for other minorities. They argue that, while Asian Americans once experienced discrimination, they now compete on a level-playing field because of affirmative action and, therefore, no longer need affirmative action programs. In other words, affirmative action has become a sound, temporary public policy which can outlive its usefulness once those who have experienced discrimination in the past have achieved success.

Other proponents of affirmative action presume that all Asian Americans oppose affirmative action since they are already a "model minority." They see the Asian American presence in the debate as a monkey wrench in their "black-versus-white" paradigm of racial discourse. In their view, there is no room for an Asian American presence in both their theories and public policy formulations. In short, they want to exclude Asian Americans from racial discourse, even in times of backlash against affirmative action. They marginalize, if not exclude, those Asian Americans who strongly support affirmative action in public forums and protest rallies. In my opinion, their exclusionary posture aids and abets opponents of affirmative action.

Thus, while opponents of affirmative action divide the Asian American communities by national origin and class and pit Asian Americans against other minorities, a tactic which is both divisive and racist, supporters of affirmative action also deliberately exclude and marginalize Asian Americans in a fashion just as divisive and racist. Both sides incorrectly view Asian Americans as a model minority and erroneously assume their homogeneity and uniform success. While about half of the Asian American population is successful according to educational, occupational, and income measures, the other half—many of whom are non-English-speaking recent immigrants and refugees—is not and needs public assistance and affirmative action. Nonetheless, both halves need affirmative action—they are equally susceptible to racism and discrimination which pose a constant threat to their lives, human dignity, and basic rights.

Asian Americans should not allow themselves to be used or marginalized in intellectual discourses, policy formulations, and political debates over affirmative action. They need to speak out against these misrepresentations promoted by both sides of the debate and articulate their positions forcefully. Their presence is essential for understanding the complexity of current race relations in the US and to re-thinking race and race relations in the 21st century.

## Re-Envisioning Multiracial America

The nation is at a critical juncture in its history. After five hundred years of racial oppression and exclusion, fundamental questions remain. What kind of society should historically oppressed communities seek for themselves and their children? What should be the vision for the US as a whole in the 21st century?

The social progress made through integration and affirmative action, including the creation of a sizable black middle class, has fallen far short of the substantive changes necessary to create a truly equal society which is free of racism and sexism. As much as one-half to two-thirds of African Americans still live in near or dire poverty. For millions of Americans of all races, the dream of racial equality and economic justice remains unfulfilled.

The integrationist paradigm and strategy used in the past three decades failed for five important reasons. First, affirmative action, in the final analysis, is a token concession which was granted under tremendous political pressure during the height of the civil rights movement. It promotes integration for some and alienation for most, including poor whites. It is a temporary and discretionary policy of political expediency which can be taken back at any time. Second by adopting the terms and conditions of integration, affirmative action is judged as fair and universal when it ensures advantages to white males. Furthermore, beneficiaries of affirmative action are deemed less qualified and undeserving, even if they are fully qualified. For these reasons, affirmative action, in its current form, is denounced as a program that unfairly privileges minorities and women at the expense of white males. Third, by adopting the terms and conditions of integration, affirmative action also requires women and minority groups to fight for their own shares of the token concession. Built into these terms is a self-defeating, divide-and-conquer strategy based largely on identity politics in which minorities and women are pitted against each other in a contest to determine which group faces greater discrimination and victimization. While identity politics and victimology are necessary and empowering, they pose limits and present pitfalls. Fourth, the dominant race relations paradigm assumes a black versus white dichotomy which marginalizes other racial minorities. Under this bipolar paradigm, civil rights is a black issue, relegating the civil rights issues of Asian Americans, Chicanos/Latinos, Native Americans, and women to the fringe. This paradigm prevents a multiracial vision of America from emerging, promotes inter- and intra-minority conflict, and, above all, undermines solidarity among racial minorities, women, and poor whites in their efforts to combat racism, sexism, and economic injustice. Last but not least, the race-based policy obscures the significance of class within each racial group, especially within the Asian American communities. As a result, class interests are frequently confused with or manipulated as race-based interests and vice versa. For these five reasons, it is important to re-think race relations and civil rights. It is time to reformulate affirmative action and to re-envision America as a multiracial democracy.

The political backlash which began during the Nixon era has now become a tsunami sweeping across the nation. The backlash has been greatly reinforced by a growing sense of vulnerability among the predominantly white population as the US loses its dominant position in the global economy and its population becomes increasingly multiracial through immigration from Asia and Latin America. This backlash is particularly evident in California, as exemplified by legislative strategies such as Proposition 187, the English-only proposition, and gerrymandering reapportionment.

There is, however, a legacy of the 1960s that has long been forgotten which deserves our attention and support. I am referring to the Third World legacy which united racial minority and white students in the fight against racial oppression and created the ethnic studies departments now found in various universities across the nation. For the first and only time in US history, racial minority groups joined hands with whites in a common cause to transform institutions of higher education. They steadfastly refused to be divided and conquered. The concept of Third World may be passé but the vision of multiracial democracy and the idea of solidarity among oppressed groups are more urgent than ever if the US is to transform itself.

Racial minorities and women in California have an opportunity and an obligation to build a new society for the US. This is especially true in multiracial cities like Los Angeles and San Francisco, where racial minorities and women are clearly in the majority. But, it is also in these cities that they are hopelessly divided and against each other, compelled by the current power structure to accept and live with political domination and economic injustice. This situation must be reversed. It must, however, also go beyond simply chipping away power and privilege from the white males and striving for group gains, and in turn, using the same power and privileges to exclude and oppress others. I hope for a new society and new government which will not repeat the same mistakes and atrocities of the past.

Toward this end, America needs a bold new vision for itself. I suggest a critical re-examination of affirmative action, especially its limits, and an attempt to learn from past mistakes. It is certainly important to build a united force of minorities, women, and white males to defeat the racially motivated backlash against affirmative action and other progressive programs. I cannot overemphasize the importance of coalition building. The backlash, however, cannot be defeated simply to return to business as usual. The nation should return to the promise of equality and justice embodied in the Declaration of Independence and mandated in our Constitution. America must re-envision itself and become a political and economic democracy that is truly multiracial, what historian Harold Cruse called "democratic ethnic pluralism." This means that the US identity is not simply conceptualized as black and white, but as multicolor, including Asian Americans, Chicanos/Latinos, Native Americans, women, and gay of all colors and classes.

The anti-affirmative action forces issue a rare challenge for Asian Americans. They occupy a unique position in meeting this challenge and can help break the deadlock between the opposing sides of the affirmative action debate. Asian Americans could not have asked for a better opportunity and vehicle to take up this challenge. To take full advantage of this opportunity, they must have the courage to critically examine their past actions as well as their successes and failures. They must avoid repeating past mistakes and be prepared to modify past policies, including affirmative action policy. To achieve a multiracial political and economic democracy, a multiracial vision and coalition is needed. Asian Americans must join with others who share this vision to defeat the forces of reaction and to re-envision, transform, and rebuild America.

# ◼◉ Further Reading

Aguilar-San Juan, Karin, ed. *The State of Asian America: Activism and Resistance in the 1990s* (1994).

Asian Women United of California, ed. *Making Waves: An Anthology of Writings by and About Asian American Women* (1989).

Eng, David, and Alice Hom, eds. *Q & A: Queer in Asian America* (1998).

Gee, Emma, et al., eds. *Counterpoint: Perspectives on Asian America* (1976).

Ho, Fred. *Legacy to Liberation: Politics and Culture of Revolutionary Asian/Pacific America* (2000).

Hune, Shirley. "Opening the American Mind and Body: The Role of Asian American Studies," *Change* 21, no. 6 (November/December 1989): 56–63.

Kibria, Nazli. "The Racial Gap: South Asian American Racial Identity and the Asian American Movement," in *A Part Yet Apart: South Asians in Asian America*, ed. Lavina Dhingra Shankar and Rajini Srikanth (1998), 69–78.

Kondo, Dorinne. "Art, Activism, Asia, and Asian Americans," in *About Face: Performing Race in Fashion and Theater (1997)*, 227–260.

Leadership Education for Asian Pacifics: Asian Pacific American Public Policy, *The State of Asian Pacific America: Policy Issues to the Year 2020* (1993).

Lee, Wen Ho, with Helen Zia, *My Country Versus Me* (2000).

Leong, Russell, ed. *Asian American Sexualities: Dimensions of the Gay and Lesbian Experience* (1996).

Lim-Hing, Shirley, ed. *The Very Inside: An Anthology of Writing by Asian and Pacific Island Lesbian and Bisexual Women* (1994).

Ling, Susie. "The Mountain Movers: Asian American Women's Movement in Los Angeles," *Amerasia Journal* 15, no. 1 (1989): 51–67.

Morales, Royal F., *Makibaka, the Pilipino American Struggle* (1974).

Nakanishi, Don. "Linkages and Boundaries: Twenty-Five Years of Asian American Studies," *Amerasia Journal* 21, no. 3 (1995/96): xvii–xxv.

National Asian Pacific American Legal Consortium, *Selected Incidents of Anti-Asian Violence in 1993* (1993).

Ong, Paul, ed. *The State of Asian Pacific America: Economic Diversity, Issues and Policies* (1994).

Root, Maria P. P., ed. *The Multiracial Experience: Racial Borders as the New Frontier* (1996).

———. *Racially Mixed People in America* (1992).

Shah, Sonia, ed *Dragon Ladies: Asian American Feminists Breath Fire* (1997).

Stober, Dan, and Ian Hoffman. *A Convenient Spy: Wen Ho Lee and the Politics of Nuclear Espionage* (2001).

Tachiki, Amy, et al., eds. *Roots: An Asian American Reader* (1971).

Takagi, Dana Y. *Retreat from Race: Asian-American Admissions Policies and Racial Politics* (1992).

Trask, Haunani-Kay. *From a Native Daughter: Colonialism and Sovereignty in Hawaii* (1993).

Umemoto, Karen. "On Strike': San Francisco State College Strike 1968–69: The Role of Asian American Students," *Amerasia Journal* 15, no. 1 (1989), 3–41.

Wei, William. *The Asian American Movement* (1993).

Yamamoto, Eric. *Interracial Justice: Conflict and Reconciliation in Post-Civil Rights America* (1999).

Zia, Helen. *American Dreams: The Emergence of an American People* (2001).

# The Rebirth of Rainbow Politics in California

*Robert Stanley Oden*

On October 7, 2003 two distinct and historic political events occurred. One was the recall of California governor Gray Davis and the election of Arnold Schwarzenegger, which garnered the majority of the media attention. The other was the overwhelming victory of the No on 54 campaign, resulting in the defeat of the measure that would have banned the collection of racial and ethnic data in areas of health, education, law enforcement, and civil rights enforcement.

The recall election was a mobilization of the California populace from the center to the right, and the No on 54 campaign was a mobilization of the California populace from the center to the left. The recall election was fueled by the conservative forces in and out of the state, while the No on 54 campaign was led by progressive forces assisted by mainstream political consultants. Both campaigns had to define a message and frame it for media electoral consumption. For Schwarzenegger and the recall forces that message involved political change from a corrupt Gray Davis administration. For the No on 54 forces, the message focused on the defeat of the information ban on health-related data and other pertinent data in education, law enforcement and civil rights compliance. Both messages resonated with the voting populace.

However, while the recall of Gray Davis became a political tidal wave for Arnold Schwarzenegger, funded by top corporate dollars and embedded with former California governor Pete Wilson operatives, the No on 54 campaign came from out of nowhere. That campaign overwhelmingly defeated the Yes on 54 Racial Privacy Initiative that became the Classification by Race, Ethnicity, and National Origin Initiative. The final vote was impressive: 64% voted No and only 36% voting Yes. The success of the No on 54 campaign was due to its grassroots, multicultural character. Also significant was the Internet-driven campaign coordinated by Coalition for an Informed California, and Californians for Justice. And a major boost to the campaign was the infusion of $3 million plus for media publicity, funds that came from the Indian tribes who were funding Lieutenant Governor Cruz Bustamante's campaign to become governor if the effort to recall Gray Davis were to succeed. After a heated dispute over the allocation of the money, Bustamante's

"The Rebirth of Rainbow Politics in California" by Robert Oden. Reprinted by permission of the author.

campaign was ordered by the state court to not use funds donated by the Indian tribes because of the fact that he had tried to keep the funds in a prior campaign fund. This money was then used to promote the No on 54 campaign in commercials featuring Bustamante. While these commercials did much to publicize the No on 54 message, it was the grassroots, multiethnic effort that was the significant factor which led to the defeat of Proposition 54. This grassroots effort was broadly based and highly inclusive, involving organized labor, non-profit organizations, racial advocacy groups from the NAACP, to MALDEF, to the many Asian American organizations throughout the state.

Several major political forces were significant in defeating Proposition 54: (1) Coalition for an Informed California based in Los Angeles, and Californians for Justice out of Oakland provided literature and information through the Internet which kept progressive forces connected, (2) Organized labor particularly in Sacramento, after realizing the connection between defeating the recall and defeating Proposition 54 decided to release its resources to the No on 54 campaign, (3) Grassroots efforts by organizations that spanned the array of racial ethnicities in California and (4) Strong support in the form of media advertisements from the Indian communities through the use of gaming revenue for campaign purposes.

The forces within the No on 54 campaign articulated a discourse that was both oppositional and mainstream. These two discourses kept the Proposition 54 proponents off-guard in futile attempts to respond to these discourses, which ultimately framed the defeat of Proposition 54. The oppositional discourse was directed at Ward Connerly, one of the authors of Proposition 54. Connerly has been a lightning rod to progressive forces since his successful campaign to end affirmative action through U.C. Regent actions and passage of Proposition 209 the ballot measure ending so-called racial preferences in hiring, education, etc. It was evident to many in the progressive community that passage of the then Racial Privacy Initiative would have put the civil rights and social justice agenda up in flames. The discourse evident with the No on 54 campaign was essentially the importance of not turning back the clock on civil rights, but instead fighting for an end to the assault on group rights. The oppositional discourse was important in mobilizing and informing the base of minority and liberal and progressive supporters, for it explained the ways in which Proposition 54 was another step by the conservative right to further its agenda. In this case, the agenda would involve eliminating the basis for enforcing the equality of life chances for millions of Californians who are of color, as well as millions more who were women or individuals with specialized medical and education needs.

The focus of the No on 54 campaign on the medical implications of the passage of the "information ban" was the centerpiece of the mainstream discourse that utilized to inform Californians of the deleterious aspects of Proposition 54 as they related in health matters. The initiative stated that it would exempt "medical research" from the information ban, but at the same time left it clear that statistics kept by health authorities at the county level and state level would not be exempt. This would efficiently exclude such information as that indicating the high rate of

African Americans contracting asthma because they live close to an oil refinery, or data related to breast cancer rates for women of any race but particularly those races and ethnicities that are underrepresented in health care systems. This mainstream discourse was articulated by many in the health professions, including the California Medical Association, the California Nurses Association, Kaiser Permanente, and other health care providers, as well as county and state health care officials who came out in opposition to 54. The No on 54 campaign was winning the hearts and minds of middle-class suburban Californians because the information ban was seen as going too far particularly in the area of health. This was evident in a "lobbying day" activity at the State Capitol when the author was involved in a conversation between a group of No on 54 advocates and the Chief of Staff of Republican and Minority Leader Dave Cox. The Chief of Staff stated that Assemblyman Cox was also concerned with the ban on information as it related to health because the Asssemblyman had personal issues related to the need for health information. The subsequent silence from this powerful Republican as well as from others in his party helped spell the doom of this measure.

Both of these discourses evolved as the campaign became fully engaged in those hectic three months from the time it was clear that the recall election was going to get certified and a date was established as October 7, 2003. It was, however, the force of the oppositional discourse that was most significant in the victory to defeat Proposition 54, a discourse that was well organized by multiracial and trans-ethnic cooperation. In Sacramento, as well as elsewhere, progressive forces used an oppositional discourse to energize individuals and groups in their respective communities. Each racial and ethnic group shared a similar fate if Proposition 54 passed. The information ban focused on no single color or ethnicity. In Sacramento and other communities, coalitions were forming in order to defeat 54. The oppositional discourse was that of defeating the right-wing forces that brought the state into an anti-affirmative action environment. The oppositional discourse focused on Connerly's assertion of the need for a color-blind society, and contrasted Connerly's assertion to the risk of setting civil rights in California back to the pre 1954 days before *Brown v. Board of Education.*

At the statewide level, fundraising was occurring that would help build a media-focused campaign. Working alongside the Coalition for an Informed California was a group out of Oakland called Californians for Justice. They had been involved in local organizing efforts and connected directly to other social justice organizations and individuals. The statewide steering committee was directed by seasoned social movement individuals and legal minds, which included, Attorney Eva Paterson of the Equal Justice Society, who along with others directed fundraising efforts that exceeded $4 million. Attorney Paterson also debated Connerly and proved to be an influential spokesperson for the No on 54 forces.

In Sacramento as in other California communities, the local group (United Sacramento Citizens Against the Information Ban) worked closely with the Sacramento Central Labor Council. The labor council donated office space, which included phone bank lines. Our committee, as well as others organized fund-raisers and distributed information about the proposition. More than 50 volunteers came out of communities as well as from labor organizing, staffed phone banks at our locations, and there were also other phone bank operations occurring at various sites throughout the city. There was no rivalry between organizations, only multi-racial cooperation focused on the goal of defeating Proposition 54. This occurred throughout the state, because progressive organizations in communities of color knew that this issue would affect each organization regardless of race or ethnicity. Evidence of this cooperation were demonstrated in the reports given in weekly conference call sessions sponsored by the steering committee made up of statewide activists, led by Josh Pulliam an attorney and statewide coordinator of the No on 54 campaign. It was clear that this type of multi-racial and multi-cultural cooperation happened across the state, for these calls included numerous reports of campaign efforts, ranging from voter registration to fund-raising to precinct walking to phone banking, as well as various other efforts.

Ward Connerly and his right-wing forces provided an opportunity for a rainbow coalition of interests to come together, and to succeed in defeating Proposition 54. It was the grassroots forces that turned the election around, with the assistance from the statewide steering committee. In July 2003 the polls stated that 50% of the registered population was voting Yes on Proposition 54 (*Sacramento Bee*, August 19, 2003). It also indicated that four out of five persons did not know about Proposition 54. By early September those figures changed dramatically, with No on 54 in a statistical deadheat with Yes on 54 at 40% each. During that time period there was very little statewide advertising on No on 54 campaign. Grassroots publicity and organizing against 54 was primarily conducted by local organizations such as the one in Sacramento and other groups such as the NAACP, ACLU, the National Lawyers Guild and many other local groups, which put their reputations, resources and money against this measure.

The results of the victory on Proposition 54 were stunning. The exit poll data from the *Los Angeles Times* (*Los Angeles Times*, October 9, 2003) provides the magnitude of the victory:

No on 54—Democrats—80%
Independents—64%
Republicans—44%
Whites—62%
Blacks—88%
Latinos—75%
Asians—75%
Union household—68%
Nonunion household—62%
White men—58%
White women—65%
First time voters—66%

An overwhelming number of California counties (54 out of 58) voted No on 54. The only counties that voted Yes on 54 were in the Sierra foothills and Lassen county. The above categories only represent a few of the categories in which a majority vote went for voting No on 54.

This was a widespread victory across the board, and represents a new beginning for racial and ethnic politics in California. While the mainstream discourse of the dangers of banning information related to health was an important factor in defeating Proposition 54, it is clear that the oppositional discourse utilized by progressive grassroots organizations and forces brought about a multi-racial, multicultural victory. This victory provides an opportunity to maintain the contacts developed during the campaign. Organizations that became energized in the fight against 54 are staying energized through the early stages of the Schwarzenegger administration. As this governor attempts to eliminate health, education, and social programs that are vital to the state's ability to enhance opportunities to communities of color and the poor in California as opposed to sharing the budget deficit with the state's wealthiest citizens, these groups are taking concerted and continued actions.

The battle for a California that will reflect the vast multicultural landscape continues to be waged. But with a victory over the Connerly-led right-wing forces by the progressive, labor and communities of color bods well for future battles in California.

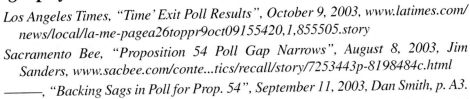

# Bibliography

*Los Angeles Times,* "Time' Exit Poll Results", October 9, 2003, www.latimes.com/news/local/la-me-pagea26toppr9oct09155420,1,855505.story

*Sacramento Bee,* "Proposition 54 Poll Gap Narrows", August 8, 2003, Jim Sanders, www.sacbee.com/conte...tics/recall/story/7253443p-8198484c.html

———, "Backing Sags in Poll for Prop. 54", September 11, 2003, Dan Smith, p. A3.

———, "48% in Poll Back Racial Data Measure", April 23, 2003, Dan Smith, p. A4

# Ethnic Studies Community Collaboration & Activism: Bridging Theory and Practice[1]

*James Sobredo, Linda Revilla, & Gregory Yee Mark*

## ⟡ Abstract

Ethnic Studies programs can trace their formal genesis to the Third World strikes at San Francisco City College and UC-Berkeley. In 1968 students from the Third World Liberation Front at San Francisco City College walked out on a general strike. One of their demands was for the College to develop an "ethnic studies" college that teaches ethnic studies classes. A few months later, students at UC-Berkeley also went on strike for similar reasons. Ethnic Studies was founded on the principle that the history of racial and ethnic groups should be reflected in education, particularly at high schools, colleges and universities. More than 30 years later, major universities across the country offer an ethnic studies degree program. This article describes the Ethnic Studies Department at California State University, Sacramento, a program that emphasizes community activism and collaboration.

## ⟡ I. Introduction

California has one of the most diverse ethnic and linguistic communities in the United States. Examining demographic data gathered in the 2000 Census, researchers at UCLA's Lewis Clark Center for Regional Policy Studies concluded that "California is the most diverse of the 50 states."[2] In California, the "minority population" is now "squarely in the majority."[3] According to the *San Francisco*

---

[1] We are thankful for the generous grant support from the Corporation for National and Community Service in providing funding for our program.

[2] Carol Ness, "S. F.'s Diversity Comeuppance," in *San Francisco Chronicle*, 1 April 2000.

[3] Tanya Schevitz, "California Minorities Become Majority Census reflects surge among Latinos, Asians," in *San Francisco Chronicle*, 30 August 2000.

*Chronicle,* "California's Anglo population has officially dipped under 50 percent and is no longer a majority."[4] Hispanics now make up 34.4% of California's population (ibid.). At 10.8% of the state's population, Asians are now the second largest ethnic group in California (ibid.). The significance of this diversity, however, is rarely integrated successfully in a K-12 school curriculum. Furthermore, "Diversity" curricula are generally inadequate because of their brevity and lack of in-depth analysis.

In December 2001, the Department of Ethnic Studies at California State University at Sacramento (**CSUS**), Hiram Johnson High School (**HJ**), and Healthy Start (**HS**), a Sacramento school district program, Program teamed up to develop and incorporate an "ethnic studies service learning project" **[ES/SL project]** which involved creating a comprehensive program of teaching an ethnic studies curriculum and providing tutoring and mentorship for Sacramento high school students. In spring 2003, Will C. Wood Middle School (**WCW**), a feeder school to Hiram Johnson, joined our ES/SL collaborative project.

## II. Background

Built in 1958, Hiram Johnson High School was a high school with a solid academic curriculum serving a predominantly middle-class neighborhood. Named after the former governor of California (1910–1916) who later became a US Senator, Hiram Johnson High School currently serves an ethnically diverse, multilingual, working class community in Sacramento. The neighborhood was heavily affected by a booming aerospace industry and the nearby military air base, which contributed to its middle-class population. In the late-1960s and throughout 1970s, however, the demographic composition of the neighborhood and the high school changed.

One major factor that caused the change was the burgeoning redevelopment programs occurring in the downtown Sacramento area. Sprawling concrete buildings were being constructed to accommodate the growth of state government, which led to further economic expansion, and until the late-1990s, the State of California remained the largest employer in the Sacramento metropolitan area. Aside from government building projects, housing redevelopment was also displacing many African Americans from the downtown area. As they moved away from the downtown area, blacks were moving into the outlying affordable neighborhoods such as Oak Park, Tahoe Park, and Del Paso Heights. These changes in the neighborhood eventually caused a white flight out to newer, more middle-class suburban developments.

The changing demography around the Hiram Johnson community was also affected by the civil rights movement, affirmative action policies, and major changes

---

[4] Carol Ness, "33,871,648 Hispanics Now Make Up Third Of Californians" in *San Francisco Chronicle,* 30 March 2000.

in immigration laws. People of color were able to afford to move into this middle-class neighborhood and wanted to send their kids to a decent high school. The demographic changes in the community were accelerated in the 1980s as more ethnically diverse populations were moving into the surrounding neighborhoods around Hiram Johnson. Today, areas along main arteries such as Stockton Boulevard and Franklin Boulevard hold a large concentration of newly arrived Asian Americans of Vietnamese, Cambodian, Hmong, and Mien origins. The Elder Creek and Oak Park neighborhood continue to receive African Americans and Southeast Asians residents. The community's demographic changes were also represented in the ethnic composition of Hiram Johnson. Established teachers were not prepared to deal with an ethnically diverse student population. To make the process more complicated, in the last 30 years, there were no new high schools built in the City of Sacramento. The State's budget crisis and shifting educational priorities have further exacerbated the school system. Hiram Johnson was used as a dumping ground for incoming new students. Overcrowding became a familiar experience. The overcrowding led to a high student teacher ratio. Furthermore, cultural and linguistic gaps between students and teachers exacerbated the learning process. As a consequence, talented and experienced teachers left the high school and went to more racially monolithic institutions. The new incoming teachers were inexperienced, and also often times ill-prepared. Those teachers who were well-prepared and talented would not stay at Hiram Johnson and transferred out to more stable, middle-class schools, leading to a "revolving door" system of teachers. These combined factors led to an educationally under-performing school and increased tensions among students, which in turn led to many and frequent cases of student violence.

Today, students at Hiram Johnson have low scores on standardized tests, have low graduation rates, few college-bound students, and the school has severe overcrowding—in Fall 2002, for instance, a school designed for 1,700 students had an opening day registration of over 3,300 students. Not surprisingly, students have a high rate of truancy and incidence of youth violence (fights and youth gang activities). One recent television report referred to Hiram Johnson as a "gladiator school" where things are "just plain scary." In fall 2002 it was within this context that Dr. Gregory Yee Mark, Chair of the Department of Ethnic Studies, approached Dr. Andre Douyon, then Principal of Hiram Johnson, with the plan of creating a community partnership and service-learning program between CSUS and HJ.

Mark had initially surveyed principals in Sacramento with the purpose of developing a community collaboration and service learning project. After meeting Dr. Douyon, however, Dr. Mark chose Hiram Johnson High School as our principal partner for a community collaboration and service learning project.

Mark is one of the key participants of the "Third World" student movement at UC-Berkeley, which culminated in the famous 1969 Third World strike for the purpose of establishing an "ethnic studies" curriculum and program at the University.

One of the key goals of the strike was to bridge the divide between university and community by establishing a "community service" component to the academic curriculum, a goal which grew out of the recognition that ethnic communities were in dire need of social services. Mark would spend a life-time of serving ethnic communities—in his case, focusing on the Asian American community—beginning with establishing the East Bay Chinese Youth Council in Oakland, citizenship programs in Honolulu, and eventually being Principal Investigator/ Director of the Asian Pacific Islander Youth Violence Prevention Center at the John Burns School of Medicine, University of Hawaii.

Demographically, Hiram Johnson goes against the common perception of inner-city schools as being comprised mostly of African Americans and Hispanics. At Hiram Johnson, it is Asian/Pacific Islanders and white students who comprise the majority: 27.9% Asian Americans, 2.5% Pacific Islanders, 1.7% Filipinos for a total of 32.1%. European Americans, particularly those of Russian descent, make up the next largest student group at 27.2%. In contrast, Hispanics comprise 22.4% of the school's population and African Americans comprise 16.3%.

In terms of academic performance, in 2001, only 18% of 9th graders were achieving at the "Proficient" or "Advanced" level in English Language Arts, 24% of 10th graders, and 21% of 11th graders. In Reading, only 25% of 9th graders scores above the 50th percentile, 26% of 10th graders, and 29th percent of 11th graders. In Mathematics, 46% of 9th graders scored above the 50th percentile, 42% of 10th graders, and only 42% of 11th graders. In one of our classroom visits to Hiram Johnson, a 9th grade teacher stated that some of the students in class were only at a 5th grade reading level. In 2001, the school suspended 597 students and expelled six students. Not surprisingly, the school has a very low graduate rate of 45%.

Will C. Wood Middle School, a feeder school to Hiram Johnson, also has similar statistics (2001). It has an ethnically diverse student population with Hispanics and Asians comprising the majority: 32.1% Hispanics, 29.1% Asian Americans (predominantly Southeast Asians), 18.1% African Americans, 15.8% Caucasians, 2.6% Native Americans and .9% for both Pacific Islanders and Filipinos. In 2001, it had a population of 1,210, of which 958 students were suspended and one student was expelled. Only 13% of 7th and 8th graders were achieving at the "Proficient" or "Advanced" level in English Language Arts; 28% of 7th graders and 27% of 8th graders were scoring above the 59th percentile in Reading, and 32% of 7th graders and 28% of 8th graders scored above the 50th percentile in Mathematics.

The major goals of this ES/SL collaborative program are (1) to provide a Service-learning component to the Ethnic Studies curriculum at California State University at Sacramento, (2) to provide an integrative and community-based approach to teaching Ethnic Studies, (3) to prevent youth violence and promote tolerance of different ethnic groups, and (4) to bring a community-based research model into practice at an ethnically diverse community.

# III. Service-Learning Research Project

Our research project goal was to assess the needs and assets of an ethnically diverse, working class community and then conduct both a short-term and a long-term longitudinal study of the effectiveness of our service-learning program. Our research tools were surveys (multi-lingual format), focus groups comprised of community members and students (also multi-lingual format), oral history interviews, as well as participant observation.

Our ES/SL collaborative project started in early 2002, when a needs assessment research project [NAR] was conducted from March to April. The research project was in partnership with Healthy Start Program, a Sacramento school district program designed to help schools that are officially classified as having high poverty and crime rates. Healthy Start is based on the recognition that educational achievement, physical and emotional health and family strength all depend upon each other. Its mission is to promote and facilitate the integration of community and school resources to better serve students and their families and to promote academic success. Healthy Start encompasses an array of prevention and intervention services for youth and their family members. During the 2001–2002 school year, the Healthy Start program at Hiram Johnson served 370 students, over 75% of whom were low income. Mary Struths is the Healthy Start coordinator at Hiram Johnson.

The NAR project was intended not only to assess needs of the community but also the *assets* of the neighborhoods around Hiram Johnson High School and Will C. Wood Middle School. On Saturday, 16 March 2003, a four-hour "walk-the-block" community survey was conducted by CSUS students (many of whom are multilingual), Healthy Start staff, VISTA, AmeriCorps, and the National Civilian Community Corps, who worked in teams of two's and three's. Dr. Mark and Mary Struths were on-site supervising the 57 volunteers. The community survey teams took advantage of several community events occurring that day— a community health fair at Lincoln Village, a neighborhood association pancake breakfast at the Colonial Heights Library, and a Southeast Asian community resident forum at the George Sim Community Center. At the end of the day, 359 surveys were completed.

Students in Dr. Gregory Mark's "Research Methodology" course (Ethnic Studies 194) were trained to assist Healthy Start to design, conduct, and analyze a field survey. After the survey, Struths noted the invaluable research assistance and translation skills provided by CSUS students. The survey was distributed in English, Vietnamese, Chinese and Spanish. Because they were able to speak Vietnamese, Hmong, Mien, Laotian, Cambodian, Chinese, and Spanish, CSUS students were better able to approach non-English speakers, provide translation for Hmong, Cambodian and Mien speakers, and explain the importance of the survey. Here are the results of the needs assessment research project.

**TABLE 3-1**   Provides the Ethnic Composition of the Respondents

| Ethnic Composition of Respondents | Percentage |
|---|---|
| Asian | 15% |
| Native Hawaiian or Pacific Islander | 2% |
| African American or Black | 11% |
| Hispanic or Latino | 26% |
| American Indian or Alaska Native | 2% |
| Caucasian/White | 39% |
| Other | 6.8% |

**TABLE 3-2**   Provides the Figures for Languages Spoken at Home

| Language Spoken Most Often at Home | Percentage |
|---|---|
| English | 73% |
| Spanish | 18% |
| Russian | .3% |
| Vietnamese | 4% |
| Mien | 3% |
| Cantonese | 3% |
| Laotian | .3% |
| Other | 3% |

**TABLE 3-3**   Provides the Age and Gender of the Respondents

| Age of Survey Respondents | Percentage |
|---|---|
| Under 20 years of age | 11% |
| 21–30 years old | 16% |
| 31–40 years old | 19% |
| 41–50 years old | 15% |
| 51–60 years old | 10% |
| 61–70 years old | 3% |
| 71 years and older | 5.6% |

| Gender | Percentage |
|---|---|
| Female | 55% |
| Male | 40% |
| Unknown (left blank) | 5% |

**TABLE 3-3** Provides the Survey Results for the "Top 10" Serious Issues Facing Youth in Their Neighborhoods

| Top 10 Most Serious Issues Facing Teens in Your Neighborhood | Percentage |
|---|---|
| Drinking/drugs | 69% |
| Fighting/violence | 47% |
| Lack of safe places to play and hang out | 44% |
| Lack of supervision/parental involvement | 43% |
| Gang involvement | 42% |
| Family problems | 40% |
| Early sexual activity | 40% |
| School failure/dropping out | 37% |
| Lack of employment | 30% |
| Suicide | 25% |

Of the respondents surveyed, 13% mentioned that they or their children attended Hiram Johnson High School, and 11% for Will C. Wood Middle School. The survey respondents were most concerned about drinking and drugs (69%) followed by fighting/violence (47%). These results were similar to the results of the student focus group conducted at Hiram Johnson.

Aside from a field survey, CSUS students also conducted several focus groups from March to May 2002: Four groups at WCW for 24 students and four groups at HJ for 36 students. CSUS students facilitated the focus group discussions, half of which were for students only and the other half for parents only. The research goals of the focus group were to gain student perceptions of the needs, strengths and challenges facing students and their families.

For both WCW and HJ students, the top concerns were gang violence and fighting at school and in the neighborhood. Next were street safety concerns for WCW students, and mental health and health access issues for the HJ high school students. When asked the question, "What is your estimate of the percentage of students at your school that are involved in gangs?" the average response for both schools was 50%. Students in both schools also referred to the very low level of parent participation in school activities and indicated how discouraging this is to them. Many of the students expressed concerns that they were not respected by most school staff, that their individual needs were of little consequence to the majority of their teachers.

Partly as a result of the NAR project, Healthy Start received a $9 million Department of Education federal grant for the Sacramento Unified School District. Mary Struths specifically mentioned and acknowledged the important role that CSUS students played.

> *I could not have pulled off something this broad-based and labor- and time-intensive without the direct involvement of the Ethnic Studies Research class.*

*My program, although a program of Sacramento City Unified School District, is in many respects, very similar to a grassroots nonprofit organization. At the moment, we have very few actual dollars to implement programs and services. My staff is small. . . The partnership with Professor Mark and his class has allowed me to reach far more people with the needs assessment than I had initially envisioned and has provided me with the technical support and expertise that I needed. I've been so impressed with his students that I'd like to recruit a few of them for AmeriCorps positions at my Healthy Start for next year. Of course, it is only through Professor Mark's leadership and support of community engagement that my contact with the Research class was made possible. The nice thing for me is that I foresee an on-going relationship with the Ethnic Studies Department and Healthy Start long after the needs assessment project is completed.*

# IV. An Ethnic Studies Model of Community Collaboration

As a result of the Healthy Start survey, an immediate need at Hiram Johnson was a tutorial program for students in Math and English. Other programs would develop in response to the needs identified by professors, teachers, administrators, and CSUS student teaching interns. Here are our programs along with a brief description. .

STUDENT TUTORING. A key component to our community collaboration and service learning project involves a tutorial program in which CSUS students tutor in Math, Science and English at HJ and WCW. In Spring 2003 semester we started out with 35 CSUS student interns providing tutorial services at HJ, and the following semester WCW was added to our tutorial program.[5]

The major goals of the program are:

1. To tutor the students of Hiram Johnson High School in predominantly English and Math.

2. To promote inter-ethnic agency, community and university collaboration.

3. To raise the consciousness of college students concerning the issues facing the youth in inner-city schools.

4. To promote and facilitate the empowerment of the youth and communities at large.

## Training Workshops

It is difficult for any program to succeed without the proper orientation and training. In this light, we created three "training workshops" to provide an introduction to our ES/SL project, to explain how CSUS got involved with HJ, to pro-

---

[5] "Hiram Johnson High School & Will C. Wood Tutorial Program," a report by Kyle Meador, Project Coordinator. Ethnic Studies Department, California State University, Sacramento: Fall 2003. The following information regarding the tutorial programs at Hiram Johnson and Will C. Wood is taken from Meador's report.

vide training on teaching in high school versus college/university, and to meet the CSUS faculty and HJ faculty. Mark and Fabionar presented and facilitated the major portion of the training workshops, and they were assisted by CSUS and HJ faculty and "veteran" CSUS student teaching interns. Students were also introduced to the CSUS students who were coordinating our ES/SL program in HJ and WCW. In order to participate in the student teaching internship, tutorial, and peer mentorship programs, all CSUS students were required to attend the three workshops.

CSUS student tutors were recruited from Ethnic Studies classes to serve between 20–30 hours peer week as tutors. The first of these training sessions was designed to familiarize the potential tutors with the schools' history and culture. This training session discussed the racial and economic shifts that have occurred at Hiram Johnson and the surrounding communities. The second training session focused on the history of service learning in Ethnic Studies. Students were given a detailed account of the creation of Ethnic Studies and the Third World Liberation Front, and its strong ties to serving the community. The third training session provided students with the tools they would need when they entered the classroom. At this point students were introduced to the principal and teachers and preliminary tutoring assignments were given. Students were also given instructions concerning common lesson planning structures and participated in workshop sessions with teachers to discuss common issues facing instructors in the classroom. At the end of the semester, all tutors were required to attend a "reflection session" to discuss and share any observations and problems that may have arisen in the course of the semester.

Because both HJ and WCW students perform below the "proficient level" of the California Standards Test, Principal Lynne Tafoya of HJ and Principal James Wong of WCW requested that CSUS interns also provide service as tutors in math, science, and English. Our tutorial program at HJ and WCW provided direct tutoring services to approximately 900 students. We are currently in the midst of evaluating the effectiveness of our tutorial program, and hope to have more substantial survey results as well as demonstrate a rise in test scores.

## Small Learning Communities

This academic year, Hiram Johnson switched to a "Small Learning Communities" [SLC] model. The idea is that students will receive more personalized instruction when they belong to a small learning community that, aside from fulfilling the necessary educational requirement for graduation, will also provide instruction in their areas of interest. For instance, HJ has these Small Learning Communities: Arts, Multimedia & Entertainment; Business & Information Technology; Health and Medical Services; Human and Legal Services; Humanities, Education and Leadership; Engineering and Industrial Technologies; Government and Public Administration; and International Cultural Community. Our collaboration with HJ has led to the creation of a "Community Studies" [CS] Small Learning Community, which is based on an ethnic studies community-studies model of conducting research: "The

Community Studies SLC focuses on the cultural, historical, and social experience of ethnic groups both nationally and within the Hiram Johnson surrounding community. This SLC will be a collaboration with CSUS and includes Ethnic Studies classes."

## Community Studies SLC

Aside from teaching the basics of math, science, social science, English, and language, the CS SLC also teachers Ethnic Studies and a Documentary Arts curriculum. Mr. James Fabionar, our community partner from the inception of the ES/SL project, is the lead instructor of the Community Studies SLC. In fall 2002, he taught the first ethnic studies class, which had an enrollment of 100 students. Fabionar was assisted by 15 student teaching interns from CSUS Ethnic Studies Department. ES undergraduates, most of whom were taking Dr. Mark's research methodologies class, helped in designing and implementing an ethnic studies curriculum by planning and creating lesson plans, selecting readings, creating handouts and overheads, and assisting in classroom instruction. CSUS students worked as teaching assistants in the classroom and occasionally lectured on the day's lesson plan. The Ethnic Studies course at Hiram Johnson High School is offered as an elective to 9th grade students. The class is a year-long course, with Part I in the Fall, and Part II completed in the Spring.

## Community Celebration

At the end of the 2002–2003 academic year, CSUS students planned a "Community Celebration," which was intended as a celebration of implementing the first ethnic studies class at HJ as well as thanking students, faculty, and staff for their help and participation in the ES/SL project. CSUS students sent letters home to parents and did follow-up telephone calls to personally invite parents and students to the community celebration. HJ teacher, James Fabionar, had to prepare CSUS students to make sure to say the correct greetings in their phone calls. Most HJ parents are so accustomed to hear only bad news when the high school calls, so CSUS students were coached on how to inform parents that the phone call is for the purpose of delivering "good news" about their son or daughter. At the community celebration, CSUS students served food from the cafeteria and provided dinner to the evening's participants, which included the ES faculty, CSUS administrators and staff, and principals from HJ and WCW. Aside from faculty, staff and CSUS students, more than 200 HJ parents and students attended the event. This is very significant in the light of the fact that HJ has very low parent participation in school activities, to the extent that there is currently no Parent Teacher Association at HJ. Thus, this was the first time that something close to a PTA meeting was held in recent years.

## Documentary Arts

In Fall 2003, a "Documentary Arts" component was added to the CS curriculum. The goal is to make the class enjoyable for students and allow them to utilize their assets in conducting the documentation of communities. The course is being taught by Ms. Teresa Barnett, a Computer teacher and graduate of CSUS, who worked in close collaboration with Dr. James Sobredo, assistant professor in Ethnic Studies, in designing and implementing the curriculum. The Documentary Arts curriculum includes these four main components: (a) Oral Histories, (b) Photo Editing; (c) Community Photo-documentary; (d) Video documentary and production. Under the guidance of Dr. Sobredo, CSUS teaching interns lectured on the background and importance of oral histories, gave workshops and demonstrations on conducting oral histories, explained the importance and proper procedure to obtain signed consent forms, demonstrated how to type transcripts and narrative summaries, and gave workshops on how to scan/digitize photographs, edit and crop photographs, and prepare and mount documents and photographs for public exhibition. At the end of this winter semester, students will give a public exhibit of their oral history projects, which include edited oral history narratives accompanied by family photographs. The entire oral history project will be made available to the general public in CD-ROM form and archived at the CSUS Multimedia Library. Excerpts from the project will also be made available on our Ethnic Studies Department website (www.csus.edu/ethn).

## Peer Helpers

This semester we started our student "peer helper" program. Under the guidance of Ms. Julia Hedstrom, English teacher at HJ, and with the help of Mr. Andres Victorio, a CSUS major and associate pastor at a community church, we have 35 students who are participating in a "Peer Helping" course. Students study and examine basic principles of counseling and peer mentorship, role-play scenarios that cause conflict (especially among students, teachers and parents), and learn effective, nonviolent ways of dealing with the situation. A major goal of this program is to reduce the level of conflict and violence in HJ, which is especially needed given the amount of violence occurring at HJ, as well as students indicating that violence and fights are among their top concerns at school.

## V. Significance and Relevance

The majority of research in ethnic studies remains a top-down model: Scholars research their subject in the comfort of a university, institute, or library. Furthermore, when the research project is completed, it generally has very little application or benefit to the community. In contrast, this ESHS community-based research project has measurable and beneficial applications: Research data that CSUS Ethnic Studies students collected and analyzed was instrumental in the District receiving the $9 million federal grant. Our community-based research project utilized community surveys and focus group discussions. We are currently in the midst of implementing an oral history project and a longitudinal study of the effectiveness of the ESHS program. Smaller versions of our project have been implemented by other professors in other CSU departments. Several universities have individual professors working on internship programs with community organizations (schools, nonprofits, businesses, and government agencies). What is unique and significant about our ES/SL project, however, is that it involves the participation and commitment of the *entire department.* We are recognized system-wide by the California State University Chancellor's Office as an "engaged" department; that is, the entire faculty, not just a few individuals, are involved in a collaborative, service learning project. What is unique about our ESHS program is it is a collaboration between professors, university students, high school teachers, high school counselors, social service providers, and high school students. For Ethnic Studies student teaching interns, their participation in the ESHS project has changed their traditional views of "ethnic community" and Ethnic Studies "activism." As one CSUS teaching intern stated, "Teaching can be a radical and revolutionary act."

Here are some of the comments from teachers regarding CSUS tutors:

This is a very beneficial program. The students really gain from individual attention.
-Kara Synhorst, Language Arts & Reading, Will C. Wood Middle School

My students looked up to the college students. They are good role models to high school kids. Thanks.
-Lorene Matsumoto, Algebra, Hiram Johnson High School

Here are the comments that CSUS students shared regarding their experience as tutors:

These students taught me things about myself. This class has changed my life, and I hope [the students I worked with] can say the same of me.
-Kara Meador

I found that when I allowed myself to open up to these students most did the same in return. I think this affected the way they acted in class after this. Knowing that they could relate to me in a number of ways in which they probably never imagined, made them a little more comfortable with me and settle in class.
-Silva Martinez

For many of the Spanish-speaking students, I have become something more [than a tutor], perhaps a friend or maybe someone they know will listen.
-Eduardo Sevill

To be able to reach out to these students and know that I've gained a new level of respect from them, really meant a lot to me.
-Jason Kondi

Through end-of-semester course evaluations handed out to high school students, we plan to evaluate the effectiveness of our Ethnic Studies student teachers and the Hiram Johnson High School seniors who will assist them as teaching assistants. Using Hiram Johnson records, we also plan to evaluate the effectiveness of the program in terms of the incidence of youth violence and gang activity.

# VI. Theory and Conceptual Framework: Community-Based Research

Historically, ethnic studies programs in the West coast have developed as a result of student and community involvement and participation. This is particularly the case during the 1968 Third World Strike in San Francisco State College, which gave rise to the formal institution of ethnic studies programs (Wei, 1993). Today, as ethnic studies programs have been institutionalized in major research and comprehensive universities, the central role of students and ethnic communities have been diminished. Scholars such as Hirabayashi and Marilyn Alquizola (1994) have pointed out the historical divergence between scholars, students, and community. Moreover, as Hirabayashi points out, some scholars have taken an even stronger view and argued that "in terms of the will to pursue community-oriented, community-based research in the academic setting, Asian American Studies faculty have 'dropped the ball' " (1995).

This ESC service-learning program has tilted the balance back towards student participation, serving the needs of ethnic communities, and conducting community-based research. Hiram Johnson serves a diverse ethnic population of Hispanics, Asians, African American, Native American and Eastern Europeans. Our program involves Ethnic Studies majors taking classes that prepare them for teaching ethnic studies in high school. Under the close supervision of a high school teacher and Ethnic Studies professors, CSUS students began teaching at Hiram Johnson in the fall of 2002. The first Ethnic Studies class was comprised of five 9th grade sections, serving more than 125 students. This semester, we are teaching an Ethnic Studies curriculum to all levels, grades 9th through 12th, and our collaborative program currently serves more than 250 students. CSUS Ethnic Studies students—some of whom are themselves graduates of Hiram Johnson—are teaching Hiram Johnson students history, culture, social science theory, community-based research and photo-documentation, and how to create and exhibit oral history projects. The community documentation projects and oral histories will be made available at our Department web site that will chronicle the growth and development of the project, as well as disseminate all our research findings.

An immediate goal of the service-learning project was to assist the Healthy Start Program conduct a needs and assets assessment of the community, parents, and students. CSUS Ethnic Studies students and Hiram Johnson students participated under the auspices of Healthy Start. Student volunteers conducted more than

368 surveys in the surrounding community; 390 surveys were submitted by Hiram Johnson parents; and so far Ethnic Studies students facilitated eight focus group discussions (four comprised of students only and four parents only). The service-learning participation of Ethnic Studies students and professors filled an immediate research need of Hiram Johnson High School.

# VII. Summary

Our ES/SL project is unique because our *entire department* is "engaged" in the project. In further recognition of our program's success, in 2003 the Corporation for National Service awarded the CSUS Ethnic Studies Department a Serve and Learn Grant of $375,000 to support our community collaboration and service learning project at Hiram Johnson High School and Will C. Wood Middle School.

The ESC program's ultimate goal is to attract Hiram Johnson students to CSUS, and to encourage them to major or minor in Ethnic Studies, earn a teaching degree, and return to their communities as teachers and mentors who promote a community-based model of teaching and learning. This goal will not only produce more college-bound students, promote tolerance and reduce youth violence and address California's pressing need for more teachers, but it will also fulfill the original vision of Ethnic Studies as service to the community.

# Bibliography

Hirabayashi, Lane, "Back to the Future: Re-framing Community-Based Research" (in *Amerasia Journal*, Vol. 21(1–2), 1995).

Hirabayashi, Lane and Marilyn Alquizola, "Asian American Studies: Reevaluating for the 1990s," in *The State of Asian America: Activism and Resistance in the 1990s*, Karin Aguilar-San Juan, ed. (Boston: South End Press, 1994).

Wei, William, *The Asian American Movement* (Philadelphia: Temple University Press, 1993).

# Race, Class
# and Gender

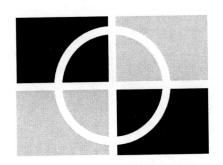

# Introduction

*Boatamo Mosupyoe*

The articles in this section focus on women and their experiences. The accounts about women and their experiences show that women's thinking, knowing and being manifest in multicentric ways. From these multicentric contexts the articles show a) women of different descent's relative position in a hierarchy of status, b) the interactional process that tends to perpetuate inequality, c) the experience resulting from participating in those interactions, d) the importance of relations between women and women, men and women, and men and men, in shaping the character of inequality and dominance, e) the impact of the legacy of the past on the present forms of inequality, f) the function of internalized sexism, classism and racism, and g) how raising level of consciousness to the intersection of race, class, and gender can enhance the understanding and offer hope for reaching solutions. Further, the articles inquire into various social practices, historical processes, and the multiple cultural logics of gender relations.

The intersection of race, class, and gender gives a historical development of thought on the three concepts. The article starts by giving definitions of the terms. The definitions were coined by the dominant group that also benefited from the definitions in real life. Race has been defined as a biological concept when in reality it is a social construct that has functioned to engender systems of inequality that favored groups of Euro descents. Class is described as a system that ranks people according to their relative economic status. Since the top ranking group because of racial classification is the one that controls resources and access, it tends also to be favored by classism. Gender refers to the experiences of women and men, cultural definitions of womanhood and manhood and the interconnections between race, gender, sexual orientation, age, class, and other oppression.

The article cites examples from different communities to illustrate the importance of the intersection of race, class, and gender. The importance of addressing the intersection is emphasized. However, addressing the intersection becomes very difficult since both men of color and women of Euro-descent tend to refuse to acknowledge its existence. Men of color, understandably, also face brutality and discrimination from oppressive Euro-male structures. Consequently, they feel that addressing gender inequality as they practice it is a further unfair attack on them. Similarly, some women of Euro-descent find it difficult to acknowledge that they enjoy privilege because of their skin color, because they too are discriminated against by the male Euro-structures.

Lien Tien continues the dialogue of race, class, and gender with an emphasis on how past history perpetuates negative images in the present. Tien also shows how the laws impacted the public's image of Asian women, thereby affecting their relative position in a hierarchy of status. This article "U.S. Attitudes Towards Women of Asian Ancestry: Legislative and Media Perspectives," further examines how the United States immigration laws have been designed to prevent women of Asian descent and their children from entering the United States, even in cases where they were married to U.S. service men stationed in Asian countries.

The legacy of exclusion dates to pre World War II. Through a series of three Acts: the Chinese Exclusion Act of 1882, the Immigration Act of 1917, and the National Origins Act of 1924, the U.S. effectively barred Asians from becoming U.S. citizens. The subsequent laws, despite their attempts at ending exclusion, created images of women of Asian ancestry as "erotic and sexual beings."

Tien references the play *Miss Saigon* as perpetuating the image of Asian women as temporary romantic and sexual partners for U.S. service men. That the sentiments about women of Asian descent are unacceptable as marriage partners to U.S. service men; and that their children are not U.S. citizens are common, is clearly shown in how the laws have been formulated. Tien argues that the laws also reflect the attitudes and feelings of the U.S. people towards women of Asian descent. Some practices like the "picture bride," which were negating the Euro concept of romance, were not interpreted as different; instead they were used to the advantage of those who were opposed to Japanese immigration. Euro-Americans then interpreted the practice as immoral, a view which underscored the image of Asian women as immoral, debauched, subservient, and depraved.

Tien continues by examining various laws that applied to women of Asian ancestry from different parts of Asia. While laws like The MacCarran-Walter Act passed on June 27, 1952, were designed to eliminate race based exclusion, the Act still contained quotas that favored European immigration and highly disfavored immigration from Asian countries. Even the laws that were formulated to rectify the Vietnamese situation, still had loopholes that ensured the exclusion and sent a message that women of Asian ancestry were not wanted in the United States, Tien contends. The laws functioned to reinforce stereotypic images about women of Asian ancestry. The attitudes contributed towards internalized racists and sexists attitudes in both the dominant and the Asian communities.

Pauline A. Santos's article acknowledges the intersection of race and gender explicitly and of class implicitly. It was only through the realization of their existence and their confluence in her life that was made miserable by her mother, that she was able to constructively address them. While her mother referred to Pauline's dark skin (race) and the fact that she was a girl (gender) as two strikes against her, which they can be, because of sexism and racism, she was consciously determined not to give that message to her daughter, Tanya. Precisely because she was conscious and aware, and did not deny the presence of sexism and racism, she had a better disposition. The disposition allowed her to expose her daughter to better opportunities and to instill in her pride and self confidence. When she faltered and in a moment of anger asked her daughter who did she think she was, she was immediately able to recognize the impact that her statement could potentially have on her daughter. She immediately rectified her mistake. Class comes into play when Pauline who was not rich and not from a rich family, manages to send her daughter to a prep-school.

Devon Mihesuan's article Colonialism and Disempowerment demonstrates how past legacies impact the present. The colonial legacy not only transformed the traditional equitable gender relations among the Native American communities, but also left brutal forms of inequality that are still felt today. Mihensuan like the others elucidates on how class as a variable intersects with gender and race among indigenous societies. This article, like Mankiller's and Corby's, show that women and men experiences are varied and have both similarities and differences because of different backgrounds.

The articles make it clear that women's varied experiences should be seen as mutually interdependent abilities. This mutuality occurs in the process through which individuals and groups act upon forces from within and from without their environment, consciously or unconsciously, to construct themselves and others as cultural and social beings. The latter process is complex and fraught with dynamic tensions.

The articles suggest to us how to mediate the tension. They inform us of the importance of a multicentric approach to gender issues. In a multicentric environment parties will have to exercise the ability to move from the center to the margin in a fashion that will include similarities and differences in a lineal, circular, and spiral fashion. They remind us that the coexistence of multiple centers should also be encouraged. The concept of humanity entails differences and similarities. The reduction of humanity to commonalities has historically ended up in genocides and persecution of those who were different and perceived as inhuman, because they were different.

We have to learn to live with differences. The Euro-centric, sexist, classis, and patriarchal approaches have been unable to do that in many ways. The realities of the differences are obvious. Implicit in these articles is an important message; the construction and reconstruction of relationships, whether they are racial, sexual, or based on class, require a multicentric approach that can engender understanding and resolution of the challenges.

# The Intersection of Race, Class and Gender

*Boatamo Mosupyoe*

## The Purpose

The purpose of this article is to offer an introductory definition and explanation of what the intersection of race, class and gender means. The article will trace the historical development of thought on the three concepts and briefly analyze their impact on men and women relationships and status.

Much has been written about the impact of racism on people of Asian, African, Mexican, Native American descents. The debate about what is important in gender relations has spanned the discourse for ages. Views have varied from looking at race as the most salient, and class and gender as less salient. As time progresses views changed, in other words views moved from isolating the three to putting them on the same par. Progressive feminists and scholars like bell hooks, (1984) Cornell West (1993) and most recently Cole and Guy-Sheftall (2003) have stressed the importance of an analysis that focuses on the confluence of race, class, and gender in understanding the complexities of communities of color in the U.S. and the challenges that they face. In order to fully understand the impact, the three variables have to be considered. Institutionalized racism, economic injustices, and gender all play a role in the relegation of people to secondary status in societies like the United States.

## Explaining the Topic

Historically race has been defined on the basis of how people look. In other words, race has been defined around intrinsic criteria that use phenotypes attributes ascribed by birth to distinguish people from one another. The classifications went a step further to assign and associate certain behavior and skills with certain races. Some scholars of European descent argued that Euro phenotypes reflect highest forms of beauty, in other words people of Euro-descent are the most beautiful of all the people on earth. They are the standards of beauty against which everybody should be measured. Their "fine" hair, sharp noses, "pink skin" which they described and still describe as "white," represented the ultimate forms of beauty. White also came to mean "pure," "innocent," and "less likely to do evil and wrong deeds." Further, it was argued that because of the size of their skulls people of Euro-descent possess superior intellect. The logic centered around the intrinsic nature of the phenotypes, and therefore were presented and explained as biologically determined. Since they are biologically determined, they cannot be changed and have to be accepted as factual and static.

This way of thinking influenced how important political, economic, educational, social, cultural, etc. decisions were made. People of Euro descent were said to be the "norm," the "supreme," the "yard stick," and the "natural." Other people who are not of Euro-descent were not only classified but were also described in comparison with the Euro model in the most unfavorable ways. People were looked upon as inferior precisely because they were not of Euro-descent. Much has been written to dispel the myth of race as a biological construct. Race is a social construct. Although the classification uses obvious physical characteristics to group people, it is very illogical and arbitrary to conclude that the shape of somebody's nose, the color of their skin and the size of their skull give them genetic advantage in terms of intellect, beauty, and behavior over the others.

The definition of race in biological terms was clearly designed to institute and maintain a system of social inequality that ensured and still ensures the preservation of racism. It guaranteed that only people who look a certain way will have access to resources and maintain control. Moreover, this classification influences how people interact with one another. Associating physical characteristics with behavior often leads to discrimination based on race. Joy James in her article "Experience, Reflection, Judgment and Action: Teaching Theory, Talking Community," writes in part:

> "I seem continuously challenged to "prove" that I am qualified. Comparing my work experiences with those of other African American Academics, I notice that in spite of being hired through a highly competitive process, we seemed to be asked more routinely, almost reflectively, if we have Ph.D. We could attribute this and have to our "diminutive" height, youngish appearances, or casual attire. Yet I notice that white women about our height, unsuited, and under sixty seem not to be interrogated as frequently about their qualifications." (D Bell and Klein Radically Speaking, 1996, p 37).

Clearly from this quote Joy James qualifications and credentials are questioned precisely because she is not of Euro descent. In simple terms, the motivation of questioning her qualifications are racist. This explains and indicates the unfair and irrational privilege the color of the skin confers on people of Euro-descent. As much as I want to write about this in the past tense, the fact of the matter is, it still happens today.

Together with race, class can function and has functioned as a form of discrimination. The tendency to socially rank people according to their relative economic system gives rise to classism. The class ranking system, unlike race, is often considered extrinsic to the individual. It is also looked upon as situational and fluid and therefore allows an individual to choose her or his position in the class hierarchy system. This is not necessarily true since class does not happen in a vacuum. It intersects with other variables that influences the status of people in a society. More often than not, in all systems of stratification, the top ranked group controls the economic resources and also enjoys the highest prestige and privilege. Historically, in societies where race has been used to rank people, people who were favored by the race classification as superior, become the people who are also favored by the class system. In societies like the United States and South Africa male of Euro-descent have been the favored group that also defined and determined policies. Policies favored those who looked like them skin wise and gender wise. This favoritism resulted in systems of race and gender inequality that take struggles to penetrate and overcome.

Gender refers to a social construct whereby certain characteristics, behavior, and actions are assigned and associated with people based on their biological sex. "Gender also refers to the experiences of women and men, cultural definitions of womanhood and manhood and the interconnections between race, gender, sexual orientation, age, class, and other oppression." (Cole and Guy-Sheftall, 2003, pxxii). Gender constitutes one of the most salient modes of organizing inequality among the sexes. Vouching for gender as the most quintessential of the three undermines the interconnection of the three, that is, race, class and gender. The three have to be considered in an analysis of discriminatory practices. Experiences of the system and of the intersection of the different systems articulating the actual experiences of inequality, will necessarily be different from man to man, woman to woman, and man to woman. In addition, the experience will be different from one group to another, as well as from groups within a society. Women and men's experiences across class and race have both similarities and differences. It is important not to deny the differences of experiences.

## Feminism as a Concept

This section examines the development of the concept of feminism and global feminism from the 1960's onwards. The examination best exemplifies the complexities of the confluence of race, class, and gender. The efforts of the United Nations Commission on the status of women are well known. Despite sometimes fruitless attempts, the Commission was relentless in its efforts to represent women's issues to the United Nations. It's efforts were eventually successful. The advocates of women's rights eventually managed to convince the United Nations General Assembly to declare 1976–1985 the decade of women. In addition, the advocates and women were able to convince the United Nations to fund an International Women's Conference in 1975 in Mexico City. The theme of the conference was "Equality, Development, and Peace." The theme was intended to be inclusive of world's women's issues; however, what it achieved was a clear picture of dissimilarities of women's experiences world wide.[1]

---

[1]Mosupyoe (1999).

The conference highlighted the differences in thought and experiences between women of Euro-descent, who I will refer to as women of the north and the others, who I will refer to as women of the south.[2] The theme Equality became the focal point of women of Euro descent. Their definition of equality in relation to men formed an important area of focus for them. Other women could not identify with the priorities and the agenda as determined by women of Euro- descent. They looked upon them as, and indeed, they were, part of the oppressive dominant structures that women of the south sought equality from. After all, most of the governing structures where the delegates came from composed of people of Euro-descent. That also meant to most if not all women at the time, women of Euro-descent represented an extension of those oppressive structures. In addition, their priorities were to be liberated from racial oppression and not gender oppression. **At that time,** race and not gender seemed to form the salient variable for women of the south. Of course, later the approach would evolve to recognizing the importance of the intersection of race, class and gender, as this discussion will later illustrate.

Conversations about feminism centered around the definition of the term. To women of the south the term would be irrelevant to their experiences if its translation meant to "be like a man and act like a man." It sounded to women of the south as if women of Euro-descent wanted to be men, in a nutshell. The women of the south did not want to be men; instead they saw an urgent need just to be treated like human beings, to have roofs over their heads, to earn wages that would enable them to feed their children, as priorities. The women of the south's arguments have been articulated outside of the conference by scholars like Lewis (1977). She describes the way in which race is more often a salient feature of oppression in African American women's lives. Lewis **then,** further argued that gender relations in communities of color cannot be interpreted in the Euro-centric terms that reflect the experiences of women of Euro-descent. Historically, African American women have tended to see racial discrimination as a more powerful cause of their subordination. In the 1980's and 1990's scholars like bell hooks also articulate experiences that are similar to those articulated by women of the south at the Mexico conference. In her book *Feminist Theory,* from margin to center (1984), bell hooks writes in part:

> *When I participated in feminist groups, I found that white women adopted a condescending attitude towards me and other non-white participants. The condescension they directed at black women was one of the means they employed to remind us that the women's movement was "theirs"—that we were able to*

---

[2]The north and south characterization follows the debate at the United Nations in the 1970's. The intention was to move away from the political and economic valuation of other countries as inferior. People claimed confusion with New Zealand and Australia. They were both regarded as northern and therefore part of the west. The north in this article refers to "western-Euro" and the south to indigenous and/or different from western-Euro."

*participate because they allowed it, even encouraged it, we were needed to le-gitimate the process. They did not see us as equals. They did not treat us as equals. And though they expected us to provide first hand accounts of black ex-periences, they felt it was their role to decide if these experiences were authen-tic. Frequently, college-educated black women (even those from poor and working class backgrounds) were dismissed as mere imitators. Our presence in movement activities did not count (p 11).*

Sentiments such as these articulated by hooks, were present in the Mexico confer-ence. The agenda and the access were seen as determined by women of Euro-descent. These actions clearly indicated and proved to others that women of Euro descent were oppressive. Others in discussing Chicana women's experiences also confirmed the primacy of race in determining an individual's position in the eco-nomic order in the United States. Similar experiences by women of Asian descent and Native American women also abound.

The other two themes, Peace and Development, seemed to resonate more with women who were not of European descent. The different themes and the different experiences of women in these contexts then brought into question the universal applicability of the term feminism to women's issues. The visibility of the differ-ences intensified during the mid-decade world conference on women held in Copenhagen in 1980. Women were determined to unite and resolve their differ-ences. The determination, notwithstanding, the difference were present and they needed to be confronted. As part of the solution the intersection of race, gender, to-gether with their implication on access and privilege had to be acknowledged. The discourse and the process proved difficult then as it does today in the 21st century. Cole and Guy-Sheftall (2003) notice the difficulty even today. These two remark-able women have been involved both in the civil rights and women's movements, and have been committed to the elimination of racism, sexism, classism and het-erosexism in all of their professional lives. They write in part,

*We have been engaged in difficult dialogues with white feminists about the im-portance of understanding the particular experiences of women of color, and the need to take seriously the intersection of race, class and gender in the lives of all women, not only women of color" (xxviii)*

Arguably, most women of Euro-descent refuse or find it difficult to acknowledge the privilege their skin color confers to them in societies like the United States. Much has been debated about the origin or root of the denial. I will posit the views of two Euro-American women, one that I know personally and have interacted with extensively, and the other who I am acquainted with through her work. The first woman Kyzyl-Fenno-Smith is a respected librarian and scholar; she often articulates how as a woman of Euro-descent she recognizes the tremendous effort spent in maintaining the advantage accorded by the 'pink' Euro skin by Euro-American women.

From Fenno-Smith's point of view the unconscious claim reflects one symp-tom of the concerted effort to maintain the privilege. She succinctly points out that women we are talking about are smart and articulate in ways that demonstrate a deeper level of understanding sexual discrimination, institutionalized and otherwise, what then blinds them to racial discrimination? Fenno-Smith argues that some women of Euro-descent become so skilled in the art of perpetuating their own privilege that they believe it is natural and self perpetuating. What complicates matters is the undeniable fact that women of Euro descent have also been discriminated against by Euro-male dominated structures. However, Fenno-Smith cautions that this should not be confused with or equated to something in the unconscious level. The often uttered phrase "I am doing the best I can," in the discussion of the intersection proves that the domain where the privilege exists is the conscious level. Fenno-Smith also says that it benefits Euro-American women to maintain the privilege, since most of the time Euro-American men, and not women, are blamed for the exclusion and discrimination. It is, she concludes, to the benefit of the women to maintain the status quo.[3]

Peggy Mackintosh in her article "White Privilege, Unpacking the Invisible Knapsack," posits a different view from Fenno-Smith's. Her divergent view is mirrored in her statement:

> *After I realized the extent to which men work from a basis of unacknowledged privilege, I understood that most of their oppressiveness was unconscious. Then I remembered the frequent charges from women of color that white women whom they encounter are oppressive.*

Mackintosh and Fenno-Smith with their divergent views represent those women of Euro-descent who recognize the existence of racism in woman to woman relationship and therefore, offer hope for the achievement of an ideal. Problems of denial or lack of awareness or consciousness resulted in women from the south's reluctance to embrace the term feminism. The problems had linguistic, definition, and substantive implications as well. English constituted the first language of some and not all of the delegates; this impacted the efficacy of translation. The different experiences and agendas impacted the substance of the term.

The controversy surrounding the relevance of the concept feminism to "poor people" precipitated the International Women Tribune Center (IWTC) to hold a forum made up primarily by women from North and South America on "What is Feminism?" These group of women decided that feminism should not be viewed as a list of separate issues, but as a political perspective on women's lives and the problem of domination. Focusing on the problem of domination, then women have to contend with the domination of women of Euro-descent over other women. In the United States, Australia, New Zealand, and South Africa, for example where systems still use skin color to confer privilege, women of Euro-descent had to acknowledge the privilege and its implications. When this is achieved then women

---

[3]ibid.

can work for a definition with the contribution from everybody. This then eliminates confusion and engenders common ownership of the word.

It is worth mentioning here that it is now ten years since South Africa has been freed from a brutal blatant racist system of apartheid that classified and treated people based on the color of their skin. The progress in South Africa remarkable as it is, it takes more than ten years to transform or even eradicate a system that has been in place for 342 years. Further, Euro-Africans will be super humans to just automatically and miraculously rid themselves of the deeply socialization process that taught them that they are superior because of their race. South Africa and the United States are comparable. In spite of the civil rights movement, the U.S. is still battling different manifestations of racism, classism, and sexism.

## Towards the Intersection of Race, Class and Gender

Increasingly, recent scholarship suggests a shift without denying race as one of the important variables in understanding gender and racial relationships. The scholarship has no choice but to shift, since the intersection dates from time immemorial. What has been missing is the acknowledgement of its existence. In the case of the United States like in South Africa, with racist pasts, it became difficult for women and men of color to acknowledge the intersection. Instead, what happened in such situations racial oppression seemed to take primacy over gender oppression. This is true for most communities of color in the United States and elsewhere. Women were faced with a difficult choice, (that should not have been a choice at all), of addressing either gender oppression and risk being labeled collaborators with the Euro enemy or just sticking to addressing racial oppression in the face of patriarchy and sexism from men of color. Anyway, the intersection manifested in various forms. I will first examine the intersection as it found articulation between women and women and then between men and women.

The experiences of Sojourner Truth and Francis Gage best exemplify the intersection that was present in the long history of racial, class, and gender relationships in the United States. Their experiences also prove the complexities of the relationships and the difficulty of assigning hierarchies to oppression. However, I am very much aware that some women of color in the United States will still maintain that in a racially divided society, race and not gender becomes more prominent in creating experiences of discrimination. This paradigm becomes clear in the analysis of Sojourner Truth's experiences in Akron Ohio. At this conference that was attended mostly if not exclusively (except for Sojourner) by Euro-American women and men, men were giving reasons why Euro-American women should not be given the right to vote. One man after the other stood in the podium and justified the exclusion of women from participating in making decisions that affected their daily lives.[4]

---

[4]Mosupyoe, (1999).

Arguments for the exclusion of Euro-American women included the sin of the first mother, Eve was created second and sinned first, that was a powerful reason for the exclusion, one man reasoned. One man referred to the birth of Jesus Christ. Jesus Christ was not a woman; therefore, women should not be given the right to vote. Other arguments pertained to the physical weakness of Euro-American women, since men helped them over puddles of water, opened doors for them, and pulled chairs for them to sit. Arguments about women's inferior intellect were also cited as the reason. After the men made their arguments, Euro-American women were paralyzed into silence, until Sojourner Truth decided to go to the podium to respond. When she stood up, Euro-American women protested, not the men, but the women. They whispered to Francis Gage to stop Ms. Truth from going to the podium because they did not want their course to be mixed up with "the Negro's" course, they declared, very upset.

Francis Gage, an equally remarkable Euro-American woman ignored the Euro-American women's pleas and did not stop Sojourner from going to the podium. Once on the podium Sojourner addressed every argument that men cited. When she said that Jesus Christ was made by a woman and God, and man had nothing to do with it, there was a thundering applause even from those who had earlier on objected. She continued to even more applause when she addressed the sin of the first mother, by saying that, if one woman was able to turn the world upside down like that, then the women of the north and of the south will be able to turn it back right, if men would allow them.

Perhaps the most applause came when she declared that nobody helped her over puddles of water, and nobody opened doors for her; she could work from sun rise to sun set with somebody, a slave owner, beating her up on her back with a lash; not only that, she also saw most of her children sold into slavery and continued to ask, "And, Aint I a woman?" Sojourner rescued Euro-American women from the men that day in Ohio. Initially, her race as an African American woman, invoked rejection from Euro-American women. To them she was a Negro, period, her gender and her support for their course was irrelevant. Sojourner knew that she would not be part of those who would be granted the right to vote. The struggle for the right to vote at that time was for women of Euro-descent. That notwithstanding, she saw the struggle as that of all women. She and Miss Gage saw the intersection that others failed to see. In this context one would be justified to say that race seem more salient here than gender. Be that as it may, they both exist in the equation.

Rollins (1985), in her ethnographic work on black domestics in the United States, shows a different manifestation of the intersection of race, class and gender between women and women. Aspects of inequality as played out in the relationship between an African American woman employee and her Euro-American woman employer manifest in ways that blends the three variables. Phenotype distinctions, that is, race becomes an instrument that the employer uses to dehumanize her African American employee. The Euro-American employee treated the African American as invisible, as though she does not exist. The employers' skin color translated into a symbol of success, which made it easier for her to achieve with her African American employee than with other women of Euro-descent. Further, gender (female to female) blended together with class (/servant/employee to master/employer) and phenotypes (skin color, etc.) in determining the dynamics of the relationship. The African American employee would exhibit extreme forms of deference to the Euro-American employer, on one hand. On the other hand the Euro-American employer will display condescending maternalism towards her African-American employee. In addition, the employer will feel entitled to intrude into her employee's life.

The invasion served to empower the employer and reaffirmed her self worth as she continued to demean her employee who was under pressure to develop affective bonds. One other dynamic that manifested in this relationship was the need for the African American employee to perpetuate the false notion of their employer's superiority and their (African American) inferiority in their employer's mind. They would not reveal their economic successes to their Euro-American women employers, e.g., children in college, owning a car. They understood the need of their employer to feel superior in the face of the Euro-American male patriarchy and sexism. Similarly, Segura (1994) in her discussion of Chicana' women's triple oppression in the contemporary USA also sees race as playing a decisive role in the access of Chicana women to jobs. Segura sees the confluence as important and like the others she acknowledges that racial discrimination sometimes makes race more salient in determining an individual's position in the economic order in the USA.

The intersection of gender relations is very complex. The complexity increases as it relates to men and women of color relationships, especially in a racially divided society like the United States and South Africa. In their book Gender Talk, Cole and Guy-Sheftall (2003) write:

> "We have also been engaged in difficult dialogues with Black men about their sexism, problematic conceptions of Black manhood, and their own gender privilege, even within a culture that continues to be deeply racist and demonizes them" (xxxii).

Confronting sexism and forms of patriarchy in communities of color has historically posed a challenge. The saliency of race functioned to both preclude and undermine the importance of addressing the forms of patriarchy and sexism as practiced by men of color. Both Chicana and African American women talk about how the men in their communities will label them traitors and collaborators with the Euro system that brutalizes them on the daily basis when they attempted to address sexism as they experienced it from the men of color. The same dynamic also manifested in Asian American communities. Chow in her article "The Development of Feminist Consciousness Among Asian American Women" writes:

> As Asian women became active in their communities, they encountered sexism. Even though many Asian American women realized that they usually occupied

*subservient positions in the male-dominated organizations within Asian communities, their ethnic pride and loyalty frequently kept them from public revolt. More recently some Asian American women have recognized that these organizations have not been particularly responsive to their needs and concerns as women. They also protested that their intense involvement did not and will not result in equal participation as long as the traditional dominance by men and the gendered division of labor remain (Ngang-Ling Chow, 1987, p288).*

The arguments varied. In the video *Black is Black Ain't*, (1995) bell hooks clearly articulates the presence of gender inequality in the African American communities and the energy that is directed at making it a taboo subject. She recalls an incident where her father unilaterally ordered her mother to leave the house. The incident confused her and conflicted with her perception of marriage as a partnership. In the same video bell hooks continues to take issue with males of color equating the reclamation of the race to the redemption of an emasculated male identity. Ironically, when male identity is defined as such, it encompasses forms of oppressions that marginalize women of color. In the same video Angela Davis also talks about how women subordination in the African American community needs to be addressed, and how African American males should take equal responsibility.

Often men will cite traditional values to justify sexism, even in the U.S. Chicana women will be told that they are betraying La Rasa. Elizabeth Martinez (1998) notes that in situations where Chicano and Chicana are faced with racism, fighting for women's rights is relegated to secondary status. She states "women will feel an impulse towards unity with rather than enmity towards their brothers" p. 183. Confronting sexism in the communities of color also translated for men into the desire by women of color to be like women of Euro-descent, adopting their values and ideals. This was just another way of silencing the women from addressing the sexism and patriarchy in their communities. Examples of instances where women of color are silenced when they try to address sexism within their own communities are many. Women are often told that they should not air dirty linen in public, because the enemy will use it against the race. Again here this quote from Cole and Guy-Sheftall elucidates the issue; "*whatever differences that we have as Black brothers and sisters should and can be worked out behind closed doors, and not be aired in public, as if we need to be validated by whites or the white media.*" (xxxii). This was said by an African American male journalist, reacting to statements made by an African American woman about O. J. Simpson and Clarence Thomas.

In the Asian American women's protest against sexism within the community will be criticized as "*weakening of the male ego, dilution of efforts and resources in Asian Communities, destruction of working relationships between Asian men and women, setbacks for the Asian American cause, cooptation into the larger society— in short the affiliation with the feminist movement is perceived is perceived as a threat to solidarity within their own community.*" (Ngan-Ling Chow, 1987, p2).

Since there are similarities and also differences in the experience of women of color with South African women, I will in the next section examine the experiences of women in South Africa for comparative purposes.

# The South African Case

For a long time indigenous African women in South Africa faced the same dilemma. It became very difficult for women to address the subordination of women within the movements that were fighting against the racist policies of the South African Apartheid Government. Apartheid was the system that divided people based on the color of the skin and treated them accordingly. The indigenous Africans were placed at the bottom of the ladder in the hierarchical structure of oppression hierarchy and relegated to the margins. It was a brutal racist system that treated Africans as secondary citizens with no rights at all. The apartheid racist system was also very sexist. Women were denied many legal rights. At some point African women were legally denied the right to occupy a house if the husband died and the woman did not have a son. An African woman could not purchase anything on credit unless her husband also co-signs. Outside of the apartheid sexist and racist laws, African women were also faced with forms of patriarchy from within their own culture. Much has been debated about the origin of the sexism and patriarchy. Granted some of it was inherited and imposed by the Euro-Africans during colonialism and apartheid era. Be that as it may, it existed and it impacted women's lives. It needed to be addressed.

The preference was to talk about the contributions of women to the liberation struggle, but not to address the gender inequality among the Africans. Often three different views prevailed. One view preferred that the close door or closet resolution of the problem. In other words, if men and women publicly confronted patriarchy and sexism, the evil apartheid agents will use it against them. The second view opted for the problem to be left to individual couples married or single to resolve. The advocates of the view opposed turning the issues into a systemic problem within the movement. The last view saw women's subordination and exclusion as an important but not as an urgent problem; or as unimportant. To them overthrowing the racist regime superceded any kind of struggle.

The then liberation movements in South Africa made efforts and strides in gender issues. Indeed, the African National Congress Women's Charter and the Women's League bear testimony to this. However, on a daily basis, women did face some of the similar difficulties that women in the United States faced. Shahrazad Ali's ideas in her book *The Black Man's Guide to Understanding Black Women* (1990), about the relationship between African American men and women, echoed what African women had to face when they dared address sexism within their own community. Ali posits that men must rule and women must submit to their natural and traditional roles, as well as to the man's will. These ideas are presented as traditional roles. Any woman who was seen to violate these roles was then described as embracing evil Western ideas. In South Africa women faced the same obstacles as well.

What should be understood is, women experience sexism and patriarchy. The experience and not the western ideas prompts their objection to the dictates that put them in the situation. It is common knowledge that I lost a husband and son on the same day, and at the time when I was expecting one of my daughters. During that period I was required to sit in a very hot room with my head bowed to show my grief. I was pained in the most terrible way; I did not need to have my head bowed all the time. I felt I needed to go outside and get some fresh air. I was pregnant and it was very hot. While my mother was very reluctant to go against the dictates of my late husband's mother, and could not bring herself to rescue me, I was fortunate that my sister was there. Mary Grace, my sister would tell everybody that I needed to take a walk and needed fresh air. That caused a lot of tension that my mother avoided, but to my sister my comfort was most important. She knew I was grieving. She could not even comprehend the extent of my grief, because she said to me after the tragedy, "Ati (my name) I am feeling so much pain, and Simmy (my late husband) and Thami (my late son) are just my brother-in-law and nephew, I cannot even imagine what pain you are feeling right now." My sister knew I was grieving whether my head was bowed 24 hour a day or not. A widow then was not allowed to go outside because that would undermine the extent of her grief, while a widower could go about and even sit under a tree, in a shade. If this was tradition, it was a tradition that was oppressing me and I needed it changed. I was experiencing it as oppressive that is why I wanted it changed, not because some Euro-woman told me it was oppressive. I don't need a Euro-woman to tell me about my experience.

In 1996 I was invited to speak to a multiracial audience at University of Witwatersrand on my research that focused on the mediation of patriarchy and sexism by women in South Africa. During the talk I referred to the differential treatment of widows and widowers, and to this experience. While I love my culture very much, I am aware of oppressive tenants in it. At the end of my talk an African man stood up and berated me on embracing Western values and undermining the fundamentals of the African culture. He told me that he would be damned to listen to somebody who has just come from the US to lecture him on sexism. Needless to say, I did not have to respond to this man, because all the women in the audience of all descents and colors responded to him and lectured him on patriarchy and sexism. The only thing that I said at the end was to ask the women if they have been to the U.S. and the answer was no. That was an attempt to silence me. The man was obviously oblivious to the intersection of racial and sexual oppression.

## Conclusion

Clearly, attempts to silence existed and still exists when the intersection of race, class, and gender are addressed. This should not be the case. Acknowledging the existence of sexism, patriarchy, and gender inequality will lead us to solutions and better relationships. The call to the recognition of the intersection does not constitute an oblivion to women of Euro-descents' subordination. However, it is important for Euro-American women to recognize the existence of privilege for a true sisterhood and brotherhood to be forged. It is in order here that I conclude by referring to MacKinnon (1996) disturbing claims that really prove her lack of awareness to the intersection of race, class and gender.

MacKinnon fails to understand or see the presence of race when she was given the statistics that African American women are raped twice as Euro-American women by Euro-American men. She asked "when African American women are raped twice as white women are they not raped as women." Her question indicates that she marginalizes the racial component in the whole equation. Her lack of awareness becomes even more apparent when she continues to claim that she views the whole experience as a composite rather than a divided unitary whole. Her line of argument still fails to acknowledge the meaning of the intersection of race, class, and gender. To the extent that patriarchal atrocities sometimes affect other women more than the others, points to different contexts created by multiple factors. Those multiple factors, race and class being the two of them need to be addressed together with sexual inequality. The fact that the tendency is to subject women of color with PhD's to more interrogation than women of Euro-descent to proof their qualifications, the fact that Euro-American women ideas will be embraced quicker, the fact that African American or Mexican women are raped twice more than Euro-American women, demand the approach that takes race, class, and gender into account.

Men of color too should take responsibility. Addressing sexism and patriarchy does not mean women hate men. I personally love men to death, and that should not stop me from addressing sexism in as much as it should not stop me from addressing racism, classism, and heterosexism and their intersection.

# References

Cole, J. B. and Guy-Sheftall 2003, *Gender Talk, The Struggle for Women's Equality in African American Communities*, New York: Random House Publishing Group.

hooks, bell 1984, *Feminist Theory from margin to center*, Boston: South End Press.

Joy James 1996, "Experience, Reflection, Judgment and Action Teaching Theory, Talking Community," in D. Bell and Klein *Radically Speaking: Feminism Reclaimed*, p 37 ed. Australia: Spinifex Press.

MacKinnon, P. 1996, "From Practice to Theory, or What is White Anyway" in Bell, D. and Klein, R. *Radically Speaking: Feminism Reclaimed*, pp 45–54 ed. Australia: Spinifex Press.

MacKintosh, P. 1990, White Privilege: Unpacking the Invisible Knapsack" an excerpt from working papers 189. *White Privilege and Male Privilege: A Personal Account of Coming to See Correspondence through Work in Women's Studies.*

Marlon Riggs et al. 1995, *Black is Back Ain't.* California: California Newsreel.

Martínez E. De Colores Means All of Us Latina Views for a Multi-Colored Century. Cambridge: South End Press.

Mosupyoe, B. 1999, *Women's Multicentric Ways of Knowing, Being, and Thinking, 2nd* Edition. New York: McGraw-Hill Companies, Inc.

Ngan-Ling, E 1987, "The Development of Feminist Consciousness Among Asian American Women" in *Gender and Society, Vol. 1. No. 3 September 1987* 284–289, 1987 Sociology for Women Society.

Segura, D. A. 1994 Working at Motherhood: Chicana and Mexican Immigrant Mothers and Employment. London: Routledge.

# U.S. Attitudes toward Women of Asian Ancestry: Legislative and Media Perspectives

*Liang Tien*

The image of women of Asian ancestry as erotic and sexual objects dominated the U.S. entertainment industry for decades. The "exotic Oriental" and her sexual objectification haunted the portrayals of Asian women, from Ah-Choi (the Chinese madam) of the 1880s to the Chinese prostitute in the movie *The World of Suzie Wong* (Mason & Patrick, 1960) and the sultry Indian princess in the movie *Far Pavilions* (Bond, 1984). To what extent does this erotic image of Asian American women portrayed in the media reflect the image and sentiment of the American people?

One method of determining a country's sentiment is to examine its national laws. In a representative government like that of the United States, the process of passing legislation must have popular support, or at least no great opposition. For a bill to become law, there must be a majority of favorable votes in the House of Representatives, the Senate, and acceptance by a president's administration. Legislation both influences and is influenced by the values and attitudes of the American people. To the extent that legislators are elected to represent their constituencies, the laws that they pass can be viewed as an indicator of the sentiment of the majority of the people. To the extent that Americans look to laws for guidance, bills that become law often shape the values and attitudes of the American people. The complex process of lawmaking and the infrequency with which laws are changed result in a relatively stable ideology that can be identified through an examination of U.S. statutes on a particular subject.

To ascertain U.S. sentiment toward women of Asian ancestry, federal legislation on the topic introduced during the past 100-plus years was reviewed. Immigration legislation is one area that has systematically and specifically addressed women of Asian ancestry. Immigration laws govern the admission and exclusion of particular groups of people to the United States. Immigration legislation defines the groups that the United States wishes to include in its citizenry through the granting of and eligibility for immigrant visas. Conversely, immigration legislation also defines those groups that the United States wishes to exclude. Historically, the United States has excluded and kept undesired groups outside of its borders through the denial of legal entry and citizenship and restriction of immigrant status. Consequently, U.S. ideology regarding women of Asian ancestry can be determined through study of its immigration legislation.

This chapter examines federal immigration legislation regarding women of Asian ancestry. Examining U.S. immigration legislation revealed that there have been significant laws addressing Asian women in relationships with U.S. servicemen that defined whether, when, and under what conditions they and their children were allowed to enter the United States.

This review of immigration legislation revealed a continued history of prohibitions against the entry of Asian women, specifically, Asian women who are fiancées or wives of U.S. servicemen stationed overseas and have borne Amerasian (i.e., mixed-race) children. Regardless of the feeling, intent, or wishes of individual servicemen toward the Asian women with whom they became romantically involved, federal legislation established the parameters regarding how they were to behave toward Asian women, and it failed to recognize or legitimatize U.S. servicemen's romantic relationships with women of Asian ancestry. Such exclusionary legislation suggests an American sentiment that Asian women are not acceptable for marriage to U.S. servicemen or that Amerasian children are not American citizens. U.S. laws bar the entry of Asian women and Amerasian children resulting in overseas-duty U.S. servicemen returning to the United States without the product (i.e., fiancée or wife and child or children) of their romantic liaisons with Asian women.

## Before World War II: A Legacy of Exclusion

The United States entered World War II with legislative prohibitions against the entry of people of Asian ancestry. Three immigration laws firmly established the exclusion of people of Asian ancestry: (a) the Chinese Exclusion Act of 1882, (b) the Immigration Act of 1917, and (c) the National Origins Act of 1924.

The Chinese Exclusion Act of 1882 prohibited immigration of any person from China and barred from naturalization those Chinese immigrants who were already in the United States. Given the tendency of Chinese men to immigrate first, this in effect excluded the immigration of Chinese women to the United States. The 1800s were a time of widespread prostitution in the American West due to the paucity of women. Prostitutes of every nationality were abundant in California. However, the Chinese, as a group, were singled out as depraved "Orientals," and Chinese women were characterized as sexually subservient. The newspapers of the day described Chinese women as "reared to a life of shame from infancy and that not one virtuous China woman had been brought to this country. They were also accused of disseminating vile disease capable of destroying the very morals, the manhood and the health of our people" (Yung, 1995, p. 32).

The Immigration Act of 1917 perpetuated this image by naming all people from Asia *inadmissible aliens.* It created the "barred zone of the Asia-Pacific triangle" (U.S. Immigration and Naturalization Service, 1996, p. A-1-5). This legislation barred all Asians from immigration from 1917 until World War II. At that time, this legislation primarily affected the Japanese, given the hostile relations between the United States and Japan. After the earlier U.S. exclusion of Chinese immigrants, there was an influx of Japanese immigrants to the West Coast. Beginning in 1885, Japan permitted laborers to emigrate to the United States. The Japanese from drought ridden Japan could find a place and the United States received much needed workers. Japanese women immigrated some years after the peak years of the immigration of Japanese men. The majority of the Japanese women came as "picture brides," that is, women married in Japan by proxy to Japanese men in the United States through family arrangement. The practice of arranged marriages and marriage ceremonies by proxy with a photograph of the spouse was antithetical to the European practice of romantic marriage. Those who opposed Japanese immigration considered the practice of picture marriage as immoral (Glenn, 1986). Picture brides reinforced the existing image of Asian women as subservient, immoral, and depraved.

The National Origins Act of 1924 established an annual quota for each nation based on the percentage of people from that nation already residing in the United States as of 1920 and specified that aliens ineligible for citizenship could not enter as immigrants. The National Origins Act also specified that natives of Western Hemisphere countries were nonquota persons (U.S. Immigration and Naturalization Service [INS], 1996). This was racially discriminatory in that any people from Europe could immigrate to the United States at will, whereas no one from Asia and the Pacific Islands could immigrate and all other had to wait for visas based on country-specific annual quotas.

These three federal acts effectively prohibited Asians already in the United States from becoming U.S. citizens, barred further immigration of people of Asian ancestry, and prohibited Asian wives from joining their husbands who were already in the United States. Asian American men found themselves permanently separated from their wives and relegated to "bachelor communities." To remedy this situation, legislation was introduced in 1935 to allow for the entry of Asian wives. The intent of the Alien Wife Bill was to "extend that privilege [immigration] to alien wives of other races ineligible for citizenship." This legislation died in committee. It was reintroduced in 1937 and again in 1939, with the same result—reflecting the unwillingness of Americans to accept Asian women.

These three pieces of immigration legislation, together with the defeat of the Alien Wife Bill, ensured that the Asian American community existing in the United States would not expand and that no new Asian American communities could be established. No other group of immigrants was ever targeted as such for exclusion.

The anti-Asian sentiment of the United States reflected in these pieces of legislation, including women of Asian ancestry, was clear. The United States considered any person of Asian ancestry not only unfit for U.S. citizenship, but also unacceptable for entry into the United States.

America entered the World War II era with a firmly established tradition of exclusionary immigration legislation against people of Asian ancestry. Immigration legislation regarding women of Asian ancestry was set within the historical context of the exclusion of all Asians.

# World War II: Splitting Asian Americans

On December 7, 1941, Japan attacked the U.S. naval base at Pearl Harbor, Hawaii, provoking a U.S. declaration of war against Japan the following day. On December 11, 1941, Germany and Italy declared war on the United States. World War II forced the entry of the United States into the global arena, leading to its evolution as a global superpower. Both during and since World War II, substantial numbers of U.S. military personnel were dispatched around the world, including various countries on the Pacific Basin and Asian continent.

During World War II, U.S. servicemen were stationed in Europe, China, and several countries in the Pacific. There were approximately 1 million World War II war brides, that is, women of various nationalities who married U.S. servicemen stationed abroad. Between 1944 and 1950, 150,000 to 200,000 couples married in Europe, and 50,000 to 100,000 couples married in Asia (Shukert, 1988). No legislation was enacted to exclude women of European ancestry from entering the United States to join their husbands. The differential treatment of European and Asian women illustrates the discriminatory image in the United States of women of Asian ancestry.

## China as an Allied Country

The first legislation to address the immigration of Asian women was the repeal of the Chinese Exclusion Act of 1882 in 1943 (Immigration Act of December 17, 1943). During World War II, the enemy on the European front was Germany. On the Asian front, the enemy was Japan, whereas China became an allied nation in 1941. The repeal of the Chinese Exclusion Act, passed in the context of a nation at war, had the effect of splitting Asian groups.

Within the United States, Americans of Japanese ancestry were labeled a potential threat to domestic security and evacuated from the West Coast and imprisoned at alternate locations. This was not done with Americans of German ancestry. Instead of accepting the possibility that security forces were lax on the naval base in Hawaii, the blame for Pearl Harbor was placed on the "otherness" of Asians. Editorial comments like the following expressed the otherness view of Asians held by White Americans:

*We thought he [the Japanese] was bound by certain Western standards of international conduct. . . . They are not of the West, and have nothing to do with what we think is right. So Secretary Hull cried bitterly of "infamy" but the attack was not infamous. It was the Japanese acting according to their code. What earthly reason ever existed for expecting them to act according to our code? None. . . . The Pacific enemy will not change his nature. (Brier, 1994, p. 9)*

Chinese immigrants, on the other hand, were not imprisoned but hailed as the good Asian. They were cast in a positive light by the newspapers of the day. Appearing daily on the front pages of U.S. newspapers were reports like the following: "*American and Chinese airmen of the United States* [italics added] fourteenth Air Force aided in the victory" (*New York Times*, 1943, p. 5). "Brig. Gen. Edgar Flenn, Chief of Staff of the United States Fourteenth United States Air Force, said . . . *American planes* [italics added] were striking from dawn to dusk *to support the Chinese* [italics added]" (*New York Times*, 1943, p. 5). The Chinese were considered brave soldiers worthy of American support.

Throughout the war, U.S. servicemen traveled to and were stationed in China. Concurrently, Chinese units were traveling to the United States for military training. With the friendly interchange, it became unseemly to exclude the immigration of Chinese people. Two years into the alliance with China, the United States passed the Magnuson Act of December 17, 1943 (Immigration Act of December 17, 1943). The Magnuson Act granted eligibility for naturalization to people of Chinese descent; it effectively repealed the Chinese Exclusion Act of 1882. Chinese people were no longer excluded from immigration by their ineligibility for citizenship. Although the act allowed for the immigration of Chinese people, it set an annual quota of only 105 immigrants. Chinese women who were wives or fiancées of U.S. servicemen stationed in China during the war were included as part of this numerical quota; this very low quota made the immigration of Chinese women negligible. In contrast, England, another allied nation, was allowed more than 40% of the annual quota for all countries. This made it possible for the English to migrate without waiting as the quota was so large. This quota system continued the United States's basic policy of excluding Asian women (Kim, 1992).

## Continued Exclusion of Other Asians and Pacific Islanders

During World War II, U.S. servicemen were also stationed in the Philippines and other island countries in the Pacific Ocean. Although the Magnuson Act repealed the exclusion of Chinese immigrants, it let stand the Immigration Act of 1917, that continued to exclude Pacific Islanders and people from other Asian countries from entry into the United States. The romantic relationships that ensued between U.S. servicemen stationed in the Pacific and the women there are depicted in the movie *South Pacific* (Hammerstein & Osborn, 1958). Americans' unwillingness to accept mixed-race relationships legitimized through marriage is well articulated. Despite the large number of U.S. servicemen stationed in the Pacific, no waivers were introduced or passed to allow for the immigration of Pacific Islanders or other Asian women who became involved with U.S. servicemen.

# After World War II: Differential Treatment

On May 8, 1945, Germany unconditionally surrendered to the Allies. On September 2, 1945, Japan also surrendered unconditionally. The victorious Allies included Great Britain and the Commonwealth, France, the United States, the Soviet Union, and China. The U.S. military withdrawal from Europe began in August 1945. Troop withdrawal from Europe and the Far East continued through the end of the year. Immediately following the U.S. troop withdrawal the immigration of the women from various nations who married U.S. servicemen began.

After World War II, U.S. military personnel entered Germany and Japan. The United States participated in the postwar occupation of Germany by stationing U.S. military personnel there. Additionally, the United States, the sole occupying power of Japan, stationed a sizable number of military personnel there.

## The War Brides Act and the G.I. Fiancées Act: Preference for European Women

The next piece of legislation reflecting U.S. attitudes toward Asian women was the War Brides Act of 1945. The war in Europe ended in August of 1945. During the fall and winter of 1945, U.S. troops stationed in Europe began returning home. Every day, long lists of servicemen due to land in various ports around the country were published. Newspapers throughout the country published daily a "Schedule of the Arrival of Troops" derived from information provided by Army ports of embarkation in various cities. The schedules appeared as follows:

> *New York—arrivals, due today, due tomorrow, due Sunday, due Monday, due Tuesday. Newport News, VA, arrived, due today. Boston, arrived, due today. San Francisco, due yesterday, due today. Portland, due yesterday. Tacoma, WA due yesterday. Seattle, WA due yesterday. San Diego, CA due yesterday. Los Angeles, due yesterday. (New York Times, 1945, p. 26)*

At the same time, news of European wives trying to join their American husbands were also being reported in the newspapers. The December 10, 1945, *New York Times* ran the following stories:

> *Since Herbert John Lamoureaux, 22-year-old former American soldier, could not swim to his wife, she is determined to sail to him. So said Mrs. Veronica Lamoureaux, attractive brunette English girl, today. . . . "It would have given him great happiness if we could all have been united this Christmas," the former GI's 23-year-old wife said. She added, however, that she was confident she could book passage to the United States. (p. 26)*

> *Mrs. Yvonne Goppert, 21-year-old Briton, was reunited with her American husband yesterday for the first time in seven months. They were married on May 11 and on May 18 Lieutenant Goppert received orders to go to France on a glider towed by a C-46. Mrs. Goppert hid on the plane in a box eighteen inches high, two feet wide and four and a half feet long. The couple spent two weeks honeymooning. (p. 26)*

These reports systematically excluded women of Asian ancestry.

Beside the columns reporting the daily arrival of troops were announcements about the arrival of their wives. *The New York Times* reported the following on December 27, 1945:

> *War brides of the United States soldiers from the Atlantic area will begin to follow their redeployed husbands in January, according to an official Army announcement today. The brides will embark through Southampton, England, it said. Quotas have not yet been set, but once the movement of brides is started, it will continue until all brides have reached the United States, the War Department orders state. The ship on which brides will sail will be used for this purpose only. (p. 2)*

The next day, December 28, 1945, before the first war veterans were barely home from Europe, the United States passed, without committee hearing or floor debate, the War Brides Act. The purpose of the Act was "to expedite the admission to the United States, of alien spouses and alien minor children of citizen members of the United States armed forces . . . provided they are admissible under the immigration laws." The act waived visa requirements and exclusion based on physical or mental defects for women who had married members of the American armed forces. Within months of U.S. servicemen returning to the United States, their British, European, New Zealander, and Australian wives were able to join them, at the expense of U.S. taxpayers. The War Brides Act was passed while European war brides were on their way to the United States.

One year after passage of the War Brides Act, the G.I. Fiancées Act of 1946 was enacted. Like the War Brides Act, this act was passed without committee hearings or floor debate. The purpose of the Fiancées Act was to "facilitate the admission into the US of the alien fiancées of members of the armed forces of the US . . . provided that the alien is not subject to exclusion from the United States under the immigration laws." With the passage of these two acts, all British, European, New Zealander, and Australian wives and fiancées of U.S. servicemen were allowed to enter the United States.

The image of and attitudes toward women from English-speaking and European countries had to have been positive for these two pieces of legislation to go forth with such speed and so little opposition. The policy of inclusion for women of European ancestry is repeated in both the War Brides Act and the Fiancée Act.

This was in marked contrast to the treatment of wives of Asian ancestry. Missing from the newspaper accounts were the stories of U.S. servicemen's wives from the Pacific Islands and China. Also missing were the wives themselves. Typical is the following story of a Chinese woman who married a U.S. serviceman:

> When she married Sam in China forty years ago, she had to keep the marriage secret at first. If the military found out, they would have shipped Sam out and the couple would have been separated. He could even have been court martialed and dishonorably discharged. The U.S. government discouraged its soldiers from taking war brides in foreign countries and did everything to prevent such marriages. Since Kun-yi lived with Sam, though married in fact, she was called a foreign prostitute. (Sung, 1990, p. 92)

The War Brides Act and the Fiancées Act let stand the exclusion of Asians. This allowed for the Kun-yi situation and thus continued the policy of excluding Asians, including Asian wives and financées.

## Limited Inclusion of Chinese Women: China as an Ally

After World War II, the U.S. withdrew its servicemen from China. Chinese women were still restricted from immigration under the limited 105 persons per year quota. To facilitate the immigration of Asian wives, the Alien Wife Bill was reintroduced, for the third time, in 1939. After the start of World War II, when China became an ally, the same bill was again introduced in 1941, then in 1942. In total, this bill was introduced five times without passage. A restricted version of the bill was finally enacted after the end of World War II. The Immigration Act of August 9, 1946 granted Chinese wives of U.S. citizens nonquota status. The effect of this legislation was the long-awaited entry to the United States of those Chinese women married to U.S. servicemen and civilians stationed in China.

This legislation had limited impact because it affected only the Chinese community. The Immigration Act of 1946 only allowed for American men who served in the armed forces during World War II to return to China, marry a Chinese woman, and bring her back to the United States. The men who took advantage of this were predominantly Chinese Americans. This situation was depicted in the movie *Eat a Bowl of Tea* (Cha & Roscoe, 1989). By providing only for nonquota status for Chinese wives, the bill continued the exclusion of all other wives of Asian ancestry.

## Limited Inclusion of Japanese Women: Occupation of Japan

Between 1944 and 1950, 50,000 to 100,000 couples were married in Asia (Shukert, 1988). Unlike British, European, New Zealander, and Australian women, Asian women married to U.S. servicemen were still barred from entry into the United States. During World War II, U.S. servicemen were stationed in large numbers in the Pacific Islands and later in Japan during the occupation. Both the War Brides Act and the Fiancées Act barred women of Asian ancestry from joining their servicemen husbands and financées in the United States. The War Brides Act provided that alien wives of U.S. citizens who were serving in the U.S. armed forces and were "admissible under the immigration laws, be admitted to the United States." Likewise, the Fiancées Act also included exclusionary language. It provided for the admission of "alien fiancées of members of the armed forces of the US . . . provided that the alien is not subject to exclusion from the United States under the immigration laws."

U.S. forces have been stationed on Japanese soil since 1945. Not surprisingly, a number of men developed romantic relationships with Japanese women. However, Japanese women, regardless of whether or not they were married to U.S. servicemen, could not immigrate to the United States. In an attempt to address the issue of U.S. servicemen in romantic relationships with Japanese women, the initial Alien Wife Bill was reintroduced in 1947 for the sixth time. In 1947, the bill passed as the Soldier Brides Act. It reflected minimal attempts to counteract exclusion based on race. The Act stipulated that an "alien spouse of an American citizen by marriage occurring before 30 days after the enactment of this Act (July 22, 1947), shall not be considered as inadmissible because of race." These time limitations were later extended, then finally removed.

In contrast to the War Brides Act, no exceptions were made to expedite the speedy immigration of these Japanese wives. Instead, placement of tight time restrictions made immigration almost impossible. Although the time restrictions were later extended, the restrictions echoed the earlier exclusion of women of Asian ancestry.

## Differential Treatment and Racial Preference

The differential treatment of women of Asian ancestry compared to women of European ancestry in post–World War II legislation reflected a clear racial preference. The European wives of U.S. servicemen were welcomed and quickly reunited with their husbands in the United States. In contrast, wives of Asian ancestry were initially barred, then later tightly restricted from following their husbands to the United States. The exclusion of women from Asian and Pacific Islander countries resulted in a situation in which servicemen could engage in romantic relationships, even legitimize those relationships with local marriage ceremonies, and still return to the United States without their Asian wives or fiancées. The legislative message about Asian women was that it was acceptable and even expected for servicemen to fraternize with Asian women but not to make them legitimate wives. The legislation protected the overseas servicemen by enabling them to return home unencumbered by their Asian women. This implied that Asian women were acceptable as sexual partners but unacceptable as U.S. citizens or members of U.S. families.

The restrictive legislation regarding women of Asian ancestry perpetuated the myth of the erotic Oriental. The legislation reflected the image of the Asian seductress portrayed in the press and popular media. It relegated Asian women to the images of An-Choi, the Chinese madam of the 1880s; Suzie Wong, the Chinese prostitute in the movie *The World of Suzie Wong* (Mason & Patrick, 1960); and the geisha in the movie *Sayonara* (Mitchner & Osborn, 1957) and the play *The Story of Miss Saigon* (Behr & Steyn, 1989).

## The Cold War Years

### Elimination of Race-Based Exclusions from Naturalization

With the end of the World War II and the spread of Communism from the Soviet Union to China, the United States was into the Cold War years. The nation's security interest was focused on containment of Communism abroad and eradication of Communist influences within the United States. Internationally, the United States was assuming increasing leadership of the Western nations against the perceived expansionist intentions of its former ally, the Soviet Union. As the Cold War heated up, it brought the United States into a military confrontation with Communist forces in Korea and Vietnam.

Within the United States's new role as a world superpower protecting the world from Communism, the 1952 Immigration and Nationality Act, commonly referred to as the McCarran–Walter Act, was passed on June 27, 1952. The McCarran–Walter Act eliminated race as a bar to naturalization. This allowed those people of Asian ancestry who were residing in the United States to become citizens. The act eliminated previous restrictive legislation that barred immigration based on a person's inability to become a U.S. citizen. The Asian wives of U.S. servicemen were no longer subject to exclusion based on race. In response to the elimination of race-based exclusion from naturalization, Japanese women married to U.S. servicemen were able to immigrate. As a result, 85.9% of the immigrants from Japan between 1952 and 1960 were women (Daniels, 1990).

Although it eliminated race-based naturalization discrimination, the McCarran–Walter Act continued the race-based national quota immigration system. The quotas continued the policy of race-based discrimination. For example, "Ireland had a quota of 17,756 and Germany had a quota of 25,814, while quotas for . . . China (105), Japan (185), the Philippines (100), and the Pacific Islands (100) were negligible" (Kim, 1992, p. 1110).

### Elimination of Race-Based Immigration: The Immigration and Nationality Act

Racial equality was in the national spotlight during the 1950s and 1960s. The 1954 U.S. Supreme Court ruling in the case of *Brown v. Board of Education* on the issue of segregation signaled a change in U.S. race relations. Out of this increased focus on civil rights, Congress passed the Immigration and Nationality Act Amendments on October 3, 1965. The 1965 Immigration and Nationality Act eliminated the race-based quotas. For the first time in the history of regulated immigration, each Asian country received the same quota as European countries. Each country received an annual quota of 20,000 immigrant visas, with a ceiling of 170,000 for the Eastern Hemisphere. In addition, immediate relatives of U.S. citizens were not subject to quota restrictions.

With the passage of this Act, there were no longer any legislative restrictions against the immigration of people from Asia, including Asian women. The barriers to Asians established by the Immigration Act of 1917 that created the "barred zone of the Asia-Pacific triangle" were eliminated (Yung, 1995). With the elimination of race-based barriers to naturalization in 1952 and immigration in 1965, Asian wives of U.S. servicemen could not be categorically excluded from immigration into the United States. However, despite the liberal changes in immigration legislation just described, the exclusion of women of Asian ancestry continued in the legislative treatment of wives of U.S. servicemen in the Korean and Vietnam Wars.

## Return to Exclusionary Policies for Amerasians: The Korean and Vietnam Wars

The next immigration legislation to address women of Asian ancestry came in response to the Korean and Vietnam Wars. The Immigration Act of 1982, commonly referred to as the Amerasian Act, excluded women of Asian ancestry in their status as mothers of Amerasians. The idea that Asian women were not acceptable as legitimate spouses for U.S. citizens was thereby continued. *Amerasian* is a term first used by Pearl S. Buck in 1966 to refer to individuals of mixed American and Asian parentage, specifically children fathered by American servicemen stationed in Asia. However, the servicemen, by definition, cannot be U.S. citizens of Asian ancestry because U.S. officials "consider the physical appearance" (Pub. L. No. 97-359, § 1698(3)(B)) to determine parentage. Without mixed-race appearance, American lineage is not established for children of Asian women and Asian American servicemen.

On June 27, 1950, President Truman committed U.S. military forces to aid South Korea against a Communist-backed North Korean invasion. Three years later, on July 27, 1953, an armistice was signed that signaled the end to the shooting part of the war. The conflict ended in a military stalemate, not an end to the war. The United States continues to station military personnel in South Korea to protect it from communist North Korea. Large numbers of U.S. troops have been stationed in South Korea since 1950.

Simultaneously, the United States was involved in armed conflict in the southern tip of the Asian continent. In Vietnam, fighting erupted between France and the Communist-backed Viet Minh in 1947. The United States, in its role as the world defender of democratic freedom against Communism, supported the French. By 1953, the United States was providing 80% of the cost of France's war effort. After the French defeat in 1954, the United States assumed responsibility for the fight in Vietnam. Between 1954 and the U.S. withdrawal in 1975, increasing numbers of military personnel were deployed to Vietnam and the former French Indochina countries in Southeast Asia.

With the large number of U.S. military personnel stationed in Korea and Indochina, romantic relationships between U.S. servicemen and Korean and Vietnamese women inevitably developed. Despite the passage of the Alien Wife Bill, the Soldier Brides Act, the McCarran–Walter Act, and the Immigration and Nationality Act of 1965, the United States still found occasion to continue the exclusion of Asian women.

More than 30 years after the United States dispatched servicemen to Korea, it attempted to address the Amerasian question. This was the first legislative recognition of the United States's responsibility for the Amerasian children of U.S. servicemen. On January 9, 1981, the Amerasian Immigration Act was introduced. The intent of the bill was "to amend the Immigration and Nationality Act to provide preferential treatment in the admission of unmarried or married son or daughter of a citizen of the United States if [the son or daughter] was born in Korea, Vietnam, Laos, or Thailand after 1950, and was fathered by an United States citizen who, at the time of the alien's conception, was serving in the Armed Forces of the United States during active duty for the United States or for the United Nations Organization" (H.R. 808, 97th Congress, 1st Session).

The same year that Congress was considering passage of the Amerasian Immigration Act, Vincent Chin, a Chinese American, was beaten to death in Detroit, Michigan. The U.S. auto industry was beset by the import of more fuel-efficient Japanese cars. Detroit's 16% unemployment rate was blamed on Japan. In June 1982, Chin, a native born American of Chinese ancestry, went to a bar to celebrate his upcoming wedding. In the bar, two White autoworkers shouted, "It's because of you motherfuckers that we're out of work." Outside of the bar, the same two autoworkers bludgeoned Chin to death with a baseball bat.

In the interests of job protection, Simpson-Mazzoli introduced the Immigration Reform and Control Act (IRCA) that was passed in 1982. The target of IRCA was to curb, and eventually eliminate, undocumented aliens working in the United States by establishing employer-based monitoring of INS status (Kim, 1992). Along the same vein of blaming others for U.S. troubles, Congress, in committee hearings, questioned the character of Asian women who were mothers of Amerasians. Committee members were concerned that U.S. servicemen were susceptible to being seduced by Asian women who wished to immigrate if the mothers of Amerasian were allowed immigrant status with their Amerasian children.

Public Law No. 97-359, Section 1698, Preferential Treatment in the Admission of Children of U.S. Citizens, commonly referred to as the Amerasian Immigration Act of 1982, was enacted into law on October 22, 1982. The Amerasian Immigration Act established immigration preference for Amerasians. However, it continued to deny, the special relationship of the mothers of Amerasians with the United States through its servicemen. Two conditions under which Amerasian children could immigrate to the United States resulted in the exclusion of women of Asian ancestry. One condition was that only the minor Amerasian child could immigrate, not the Asian mother or other family members. The second condition was that the mother of the Amerasian had to sign an irrevocable release of family rights for the child to immigrate. The release disallowed the mother any future claims on the child. This not only meant forced separation of the Amerasian child from his or her mother, but also no hope of future reunification. Even after reaching adulthood and gaining citizenship, the Amerasian could not sponsor his or her Asian mother as a nonquota relative. Amerasians who immigrated to the United States came essentially as orphans to be fostered by American families.

The proviso of the irrevocable release made clear the United States intent of total dissociation from those Asian women who had relations with U.S. servicemen. Again, this relegated those relationships between Asian women and U.S. servicemen to the status of temporary sexual liaisons. Asian women were acceptable only as temporary romantic partners for the comfort of U.S. servicemen stationed overseas. This time, the added message was that not only were Asian women unacceptable as legitimate wives, but they also were unacceptable as mothers to rear "American" children.

## Diplomatic Breakdown and Exclusion Following the Vietnam War

The popular image of women involved with U.S. servicemen in Vietnam is depicted in the play *Miss Saigon* (Behr & Steyn, 1989). This image continues the age-old U.S. concept of Asian women as temporary romantic and sexual partners. The Communist Vietnamese victory in 1975 added an additional incentive for Americans to denigrate Asians and Asian women. The loss of the Vietnam War had profound ramifications for the United States. It was a shock to American self-confidence as a military power and world leader. This resulted in the United States severing all diplomatic relations with Vietnam until 1994, thus preventing Vietnamese Amerasians from immigrating under the Amerasian Immigration Act of 1982.

On August 6, 1987, 12 years after the last U.S. servicemen left Southeast Asia, and under pressure from Vietnam, the Amerasian Homecoming Act (H.R. 3171, 100th Congress, 1st Session) was first introduced in Congress. The purpose of the bill was to permit the immigration of Vietnamese Amerasians to the United States. The bill died in the Committee on the Judiciary. It was introduced again on October 28, 1987, but met the same fate. On December 27, 1987, provisions for the immigration of Vietnamese Amerasians were passed as part the Omnibus Budget Reconciliation Act, the Amerasian Immigration Section.

Under extreme pressure from the Vietnamese government, this proviso specifically included the immigration of Vietnamese families. The Amerasian Immigration Section provided for waivers of numerical limitations on immigration for Amerasians and existing exclusionary policies. The waivers meant that adult Amerasians could immigrate and mothers of Amerasians could accompany their children to the United States. However, administrative interpretation of the legislation initially established a condition under which the Vietnamese mother could be excluded. Those family members eligible for immigration with the Amerasian included the Amerasian's spouse, child, *or* natural mother and her spouse or child. If the accompanying family member was a spouse, then the natural mother "shall not be accorded any right, privilege, or status." Amerasians initially had to choose between their mother and their spouse. Again, there existed a loophole to exclude women of Asian ancestry, once again sending the not-so-subtle message that women of Asian ancestry were not wanted in the United States.

# Effects of Lingering Images

As discussed earlier, the persistent image of Asian women as erotic, temporary sexual partners for U.S. servicemen reflects the sentiments of the majority of Americans. In turn, the passage of exclusionary immigration legislation reflects and perpetuates the sexual and erotic image of women of Asian ancestry.

## Stereotypic Images

The image reflected in law is not limited to Asian women living in Asia. This image also affects women of Asian ancestry born in the United States. Asian American women are exposed to the sexualized images of themselves. Two Asian American women described examples of this type of exposure.

> On a tour to Niagara Falls, other passengers kept intimating to Calvert that Yi-fong was just a girl he was taking on an extramarital fling. Although he introduced Yi-fong as his wife, they kept referring to her as his girlfriend and made snide remarks about his leaving his wife at home. People are unable to or refuse to grasp the fact that two people from different backgrounds can be married. (Sung, 1990, pp. 88–89)

> Another attitude that seems especially prevalent is the mail-order-bride mentality. Occasionally when I'm with my boyfriend—who is as Anglo as you can get—total strangers walk up and ask him where I'm from, if I speak English. . . . The same mentality is responsible for a certain class of male that seems to think Asian women are easy to please, utterly subservient and desperately clamoring for Anglo husbands. . . . During lunch in the dorm cafeteria, [a White student] sauntered over and said (this is true), "Hello, Me see you here very long time. Me think you very pretty. I don't like American girls. I only like Asian women." (Kim, 1990, p. M4)

## Erotic Images

The capitulation to this erotic image of Asian American women by the Asian American community influences the stigmatization of Asian American women in interracial relationships. "Chinese feel that women who married Americans are not decent. This is a stereotype. For me, that hurt a lot because I feel that I had to prove my character" (Sung, 1990, p. 92). "Intermarriage between Whites and Asians has been seen in recent times by some Asian Americans as evidence of racial conquest and cultural genocide rather than social acceptance and success for the Asian minority" (Kim, 1982, p. 92).

Repeated exposure to erotic imagery of oneself can have a profound effect on the development of the psychosexual identity. The incorporation of this erotic image by Asian American women has led some to feel ashamed of and reject their Asian ancestry.

> Second-class treatment like this (Asian women are easy to please, utterly subservient and desperately clamoring for Anglo husbands) has made a lot of American-born Asians ashamed of their heritage in a way that other Americans aren't. You'll probably never catch one of us with a button reading, "Kiss me, I'm Korean." In fact, there is a heavy burden on us to deny all ethnicity and to prove we're just like everyone else, i.e., real Americans. The results are sometimes pathetic. I used to present my middle name as "Susan" instead of "Suhn." (Kim, 1990, p. M4)

## Identity Issues

Every Asian American woman, at some level, must contend with the image of the erotic being that is not acceptable as a legitimate partner in a long-term relationship. When Asian American women consider their identities as Americans with the elements of race, ethnicity, and gender, they do not encounter a society that encourages them to be self defined. Anti-Asian immigration legislation denigrates their worth, and erotic and sexual images objectify them. During the many years of their exclusion Asian American women were unable to participate in the legislative and political dialogue about themselves. After so many years of forced silence, Asian American women at last can and should engage in a dialogue with the greater population of U.S. citizens through participation in the legislative process so as to shape their own images.

## Conclusion

Federal legislation of the last 100-plus years articulates enduring images of and sentiments toward women of Asian ancestry. The most common image is that women of Asian ancestry are erotic and sexualized beings. The prevalent sentiment is that women of Asian ancestry are acceptable for temporary romantic liaisons but not as wives or mothers of U.S. citizens. This legislative presentation echoes the erotic, sexualized Asian American woman portrayed in the popular media. In looking to legislation for guidance, many Americans not of Asian ancestry may use these attitudes and images as a priori proof that Asian women are not acceptable for marriage or motherhood. Legislation can then, in turn, be used to legitimize and continue the stereotype of Asian women as erotic sex objects.

The images and sentiments presented through immigration legislation continues to be felt by Asian American women and Asian American communities throughout the United States. More positive images of Asian American women need to be articulated in a number of areas. Scientifically, qualitative research is needed on how Asian American women cope with the erotic images reflected in immigration legislation and the media. Research on the actual self-images of Asian American women is clearly needed. Social scientists need to conduct more research on the confluence of racial, ethnic, and gender identity among Asian American women. Models of identity development are necessary to guide research on gender, race, ethnic minorities, and women in the United States. Finally, more research is needed to examine the effects of these negative images of Asian American women on their relationships.

At the community level, dialogues between Asian American communities and the larger community of U.S. citizens are needed to challenge existing images and sentiments and promote new ones. Institutions of higher education need to support their Asian American female academicians and establish curricula for the teaching of Asian American women. Creative writers and makers of popular media need to develop works that truthfully reflect the lives of Asian American women in all of their complexities. Legislatively, the Asian American community needs to lobby for the elimination of legislation that denigrates Asian American women, such as the Amerasian Immigration Act of 1982. And, as citizens of a representative government, we all need to be vigilant against any legislation that either promotes a derogatory image of Asian Americans or discriminates against anyone on the basis of race, ethnicity, or gender.

# References

Amerasian Homecoming Act, H.R. 3171, 100th Cong., 1st Sess. (1987).

Amerasian Immigration Act of 1982, Pub. L. No. 97-359, 96 Stat. 1716 (1982).

Amerasian Immigration Section of the Omnibus Budget Reconciliation Act of 1987, Pub. L. No. 100-202, § 584 (1987).

Behr, E., & Steyn, M. (1989). [musical] *The Story of Miss Saigon.* London: Jonathan Cape (1991).

Bond, J. (1984). *Far Pavilions.* [television mini-series] P. Duffel (director). Washington, DC: Acorn Media.

Brier, R. (1994). Looking around. *San Francisco Chronicle*, p. 9.

Brown v. Board of Education, 347 U.S. 483 (1954).

Buck, P. S. H. (with Harris, T. F.) (1966). *For spacious skies: Journey in dialogue.* New York: John Day Co.

Cha, L., & Roscoe, J. (1989). *Eat a Bowl of Tea.* [film] W. Wang (director). Burbank, CA: Columbia Pictures.

Chinese Exclusion Act of 1882, 22 Stat. 58.

Daniels, R. (1990). *Coming to America: A history of immigration and ethnicity in American life.* New York: HarperCollins.

G.I. Fiancées Act, 60 Stat. 416 (1946).

Glenn, E. N. (1986). *Issei, Nisei, war bride: Three generations of Japanese American women in domestic service.* Philadelphia: Temple University Press.

Hammerstein, O., & Osborn, P. (1958). *South Pacific.* [film] J. Logan (director). Hollywood, CA: 20th Century Fox.

Immigration Act of August 9, 1946, 60 Stat. 975. (1946).

Immigration Act of 1917, 39 Stat. 874. (1917).

Immigration Act of 1943, 16 Stat. 682. (1943).

Immigration Act of 1982, 96 Stat. 1716. (1982).

Immigration and Nationality Act Amendments of 1965, 79 Stat. 911. (1965).

Immigration and Nationality Act [McCarran–Walter Act], 66 Stat. 163 (1952).

Immigration Reform and Control Act of 1986, 100 Stat. 3359.

Kim, A. (1990). For the last time, darn it, I am not a mail-order bride. *Los Angeles Times,* p. M4.

Kim, E. (1982). *Asian American literature.* Philadelphia: Temple University Press.

Kim, H. -C. (1992). *Asian Americans and the Supreme Count: A documentary history.* Westport, CT: Greenwood Press.

Mason, R., & Patrick, J. (1960). *The World of Suzie Wong.* [film] R. Quine (director). Hollywood, CA: Worldfilm.

Mitchner, J., & Osborn (1957). *Sayonara.* [film] J. Logan (director). Hollywood, CA: MGM Studios.

National Origins Act of 1924, 43 Stat. 153. (1924).

*New York Times.* (1943, November 22, p. 5). *Japanese threat to Changsha seen.*

*New York Times.* (1945, December 10, p. 26). *Chinese press for fleeing Chang Teh.*

*New York Times.* (1945, December 24, p. 4). *Glider Stowaway here with husband.*

*New York Times.* (1945, December 24, p. 6). *Former GI tried to swim to them.*

*New York Times.* (1945, December 27, p. 2). *French brides to begin Sailing for U.S. in month.*

Omnibus Budget Reconciliation Act, 100 Stat. 1329 (1987).

Shukert, E. B. (1988). *The war brides of World War II.* Navato, CA: Predidio Press.

Soldier Brides Act, 61 Stat. 190 (1947).

Sung, B. L. (1990). *Chinese American intermarriage.* New York: Center for Migration Studies.

U.S. Immigration and Naturalization Service. (1996). *Statistical yearbook of the Immigration and Naturalization Service,* 1994. Washington, DC: U.S. Government Printing Office.

War Brides Act of 1945, 59 Stat. 659.

Yung, J. (1995). *Unbound feet: A social history of Chinese women in San Francisco.* Berkeley: University of California Press.

# Policing the Black Woman's Body in an Urban Context

## Hazel V. Carby

*The problem of the unemployed negro woman in New York city is probably more serious than that of any other class of worker. She is unquestionably shut out from many lines of occupation, and through her increasing inefficiency and desire to avoid hard work, the best households and hotels and restaurants are gradually supplanting her with whites. This means in many instances that she must rely upon odd jobs and employment in the questionable house. . . .*

*Negro women who are led into immoral habits, vice and laziness, have in too many instances received their initiative from questionable employment agencies. . . . Some preventive measure must be taken for the colored girl going to work for the first time, and for the green helpless negro woman brought up here from the South—on promises of "easy work, lots of money and good times."*

—Frances A. Kellor, "Southern Colored Girls in the North"

The migration of black people to cities outside of the Secessionist states of the South in the first half of the twentieth century transformed America socially, politically, and culturally. Of course, the migration of black people is not a twentieth-century phenomenon. In the antebellum period the underground railroad was the primary conduit out of the slave-holding states; in the late 1870s there was significant black migration to Kansas and in the 1880s to Oklahoma. Before 1910 there were major changes in the distribution of the black population between rural and urban areas within the South. The proportion of black people in southern cities more than doubled between 1870 and 1910 and, consequently, the proportion of the black population that continued to live in rural areas decreased significantly from 81 to 70 percent.[1] Historians and demographers seem to agree that what is now

---

[1] See Daniel M. Johnson and Rex R. Campbell, *Black Migration in America: A Social Demographic History* (Durham, N.C., 1981).

From *Critical Inquiry*, 18, Summer 1992, "Policing the Black Woman's Body in an Urban Context" by Hazel Carby. Reprinted by permission of The University of Chicago Press.

called the Great Migration needs to be viewed in the context of these earlier migratory patterns and in light of the fact that black people were becoming increasingly urbanized before they left for northern cities.

When considering the complex cultural transformations that not only accompany but are an integral part of these demographic shifts, it is important to challenge simplistic mythologies of how a rural black folk without the necessary industrial skills, untutored in the ways of the city, "green" and ignorant, in Frances Kellor's opinion, were exploitable fodder for the streets of New York, Chicago, Detroit, Cleveland, Philadelphia, and Pittsburgh.[2] Certainly, male and female black migrants suffered economic and political exploitation, but it is important to separate the structural forces of exploitation from the ways in which black migrants came to be regarded as easily victimized subjects who quickly succumbed to the forces of vice and degradation.

I am going to argue that the complex processes of urbanization had gender-specific and class-specific consequences for the production of African-American culture, in general, and for the cultural representation of black women, in particular. The movement of black women between rural and urban areas and between southern and northern cities generated a series of moral panics. One serious consequence was that the behavior of black female migrants was characterized as sexually degenerate and, therefore, socially dangerous. By using the phrase "moral panic" I am attempting to describe and to connect a series of responses, from institutions and from individuals, that identified the behavior of these migrating women as a social and political problem, a problem that had to be rectified in order to restore a moral social order.[3] These responses were an active part of a 1920s

---

[2]Carole Marks argues two important points in her recent book. The first is that the majority of migrants at this stage of migration were from urban areas and left not just to "raise their wages but because they were the displaced mudsills of southern industrial development." Second, the level of a laborer's skill was less important "than institutional barriers in determining migrant assimilation and mobility." While there is a dispute about whether the majority of migrants were from rural or urban areas in the South it is clear that a significant number of migrants were urbanized and had previous experience of wage labor, skilled and unskilled, and that a number were professionals following their clients (Carole Marks, *Farewell—We're Good and Gone: The Great Black Migration* [Bloomington, Ind., 1989], p. 3). See also Johnson and Campbell, *Black Migration in America*, p. 79.

[3]See Stuart Hall et al., *Policing the Crisis: Mugging, the State, and Law and Order* (London, 1978), pp. 16–20. Hall and his coauthors draw on the work of Stanley Cohen, who argues that "societies appear to be subject, every now and then, to periods of moral panic. A condition, episode, person or group of persons emerges to become defined as a threat to societal values and interests; its nature is presented in a stylized and stereotypical fashion by the mass media; the moral barricades are manned by editors, bishops, politicians and other right-thinking people; socially accredited experts pronounce their diagnoses and solutions; ways of coping are evolved or (more often) resorted to; the condition then disappears, submerges or deteriorates and becomes more visible. Sometimes the object of the panic is quite novel and at other times it is something which has been in existence long enough, but suddenly appears in the limelight." [Stanley Cohen, *Folk Devils and Moral Panics: The Creation of the Mods and Rockers* (London, 1972), p. 9]

bourgeois ideology that not only identified this moral crisis but also produced a language that provided a framework of interpretation and referentiality that appeared to be able to explain for all time the behavior of black women in an urban environment. Kellor's indictment of the sexual behavior of black migrant women registers the emergence of what would rapidly become a widely shared discourse of what was wrong with black urban life.

Frances Kellor was the general director of the Inter-Municipal Committee on Household Research in New York City, and her "Southern Colored Girls in the North" appeared in *Charities*, "A Review of Local and General Philanthropy." Her article provides important evidence that as early as 1905 the major discursive elements were already in place that would define black female urban behavior throughout the teens and twenties as pathological.[4] The subjects of Kellor's article are migrating black women who are looking for work, and she implicitly assumes that these women are alone, either single or, at least, without men. Therefore, according to Kellor, they need "protection." On the surface, it looks as if Kellor is inciting moral alarm in defence of the rather abstract quality of female virtue, but it is quickly evident that she does not believe that black women have any moral fiber or will of their own that can be mobilized in the defence of their own interests. On the contrary, she believes that they become prostitutes because they are unable to protect themselves. Kellor's report makes a strong case for the creation of an alternative set of institutions to police the actual bodies of migrating black women. While Kellor is apparently condemning the existence of employment agencies that create a situation of economic dependency and exploitation in order to channel black women into houses of prostitution, she is actually identifying the "increasing inefficiency and desire [of black women] to avoid hard work" as the primary cause of the "problem."

Kellor has three major recommendations to make in addition to the establishment of more respectable and law-abiding agencies. First, she suggests the use of "practical and sympathetic women," like those on Ellis Island "who guide and direct the immigrant women," to "befriend" and act as "missionaries" toward black women when they arrive from the South. Second, she advocates the institution of a controlled system of lodging houses where black women can be sent at night and kept from going off on their own into the streets. Finally, she argues for the creation of training schools to make black women "more efficient."[5] This discourse, however, establishes a direct relationship between the social supervision of black women migrants and the control of their moral and sexual behavior, between the morally unacceptable economics of sex for sale and a morally acceptable policing of black female sexuality. In other words, Kellor characterizes the situation not as the lack of job possibilities for black women with the consequent conclusion that

---

[4]See Frances A. Kellor, "Southern Colored Girls in the North: The Problem of Their Protection," *Priorities*, 18 Mar. 1905, pp. 584–85.

[5]Ibid., p. 585.

the employment market should be rigorously controlled, but, on the contrary, as a problem located in black women themselves, who, given the limited employment available to them and their "desire to avoid hard work," will sell their bodies.[6] Therefore, the logic of her argument dictates that bodies, not economic markets, need stringent surveillance.

The need to police and discipline the behavior of black women in cities, however, was not only a premise of white agencies and institutions but also a perception of black institutions and organizations, and the black middle class. The moral panic about the urban presence of apparently uncontrolled black women was symptomatic of and referenced aspects of the more general crises of social displacement and dislocation that were caused by migration. White and black intellectuals used and elaborated this discourse so that when they referred to the association between black women and vice, or immoral behavior, their references carried connotations of other crises of the black urban environment. Thus the migrating black woman could be variously situated as a threat to the progress of the race; as a threat to the establishment of a respectable urban black middle class; as a threat to congenial black and white middle-class relations; and as a threat to the formation of black masculinity in an urban environment.

Jane Edna Hunter, who was born in 1882 on the Woodburn plantation in South Carolina and trained as a nurse in Charleston and then at the Hampton Institute, arrived in Cleveland in May 1905 with little money. In an attempt to find accommodations she mistakenly arrived at a brothel, and her search for a place to live, she says, gave her an insight into the conditions that a black girl, "friendless and alone," had to face.[7] Hunter reflects that at home on the plantation she was well aware that some girls had been seduced, but she was totally unaware of what she calls a "wholesale organized traffic in black flesh" (*NP*, p. 68). When she goes to a dance she is shocked to see that the saloon on the first floor of Woodluff Hall is "the resort of bad women," and that the Hamilton Avenue area is the home of "vice." Hunter's discovery of what she identifies and criticizes as organized vice is interspersed with a description of her own difficult search for legitimate employment. Although highly trained she cannot find a doctor who wants to employ a black nurse, and she depends on a cousin to find cleaning jobs for her.[8] Eventually, Hunter alternates work as a domestic with temporary nursing assignments until she finds a permanent position in the office of a group of doctors.

In her autobiography, *A Nickel and a Prayer*, Hunter states that her experiences led her to conclude that "a girl alone in a large city must needs know the dangers and pitfalls awaiting her" (*NP*, p. 77). While Hunter never situates herself as a help-

---

[6]Another unspoken assumption here, of course, is that selling sex is not hard but easy work.

[7]Jane Edna Hunter, *A Nickel and a Prayer* (Cleveland, 1940), p. 67; hereafter abbreviated *NP*. I am very grateful to Darlene Clark Hine for telling me about Hunter, her autobiography, and her papers.

[8]Hunter maintains that she was one of only two black professional nurses in Cleveland. See *NP*, p. 87.

less victim she carefully creates a narrative that identifies and appears to account for the helplessness of other black migrating women, and as she does so she incorporates Kellor's analysis, strategies, and conclusions. Hunter turned the death of her mother, from whom she had become estranged, into a catalyst to devote her life to political and social activity on behalf of the black women she designated as helpless. As a young woman Hunter was forbidden to see the man she loved, and she blamed her mother for forcing her into marriage with a man forty years older than herself. However, she walked out of the marriage fifteen months later and went to Charleston to find work, declaring that "a great weight rolled from my mind as I left him, determined to find and keep the freedom which I so ardently desired" (*NP*, p. 50). Hunter's mother died in 1911, after Hunter had lived in Cleveland for four years, and the realization that reconciliation was now impossible occasioned deep despair. In the midst of contemplating suicide Hunter found herself asking the question: "how could I best give to the world what I had failed to give her?" (*NP*, p. 81). Hunter's self-interrogation resulted in her making her mother, rather than herself, a symbol for the helplessness of all migrant women. Hunter characterized her mother as both "immature and impulsive" and imagined that her mother would have been totally helpless if she had been a migrant. What Hunter cannot explicitly acknowledge is that a figure of such helplessness stands in direct contrast to the way she writes with confidence and self-determination about her own need to gain and retain her freedom through urban migration. But the designation of her mother as helpless enables Hunter to occupy the absent maternal space. The daughter becomes mother as Hunter listens to the strains of a spiritual and is moved by the words, "ah feels like a motherless child." At this moment she decided on her "supreme work," dedicating her life to helping "the young Negro girl pushed from the nest by economic pressure, alone and friendless in a northern city; reduced to squalor, starvation; helpless against temptation and degradation" (*NP*, p. 83).

The fruit of Hunter's labors and the institutionalization of her maternal role into that of a matriarch is the formation of the Working Girls' Home Association, which later became the Phillis Wheatley Association, with Hunter as president. The Phillis Wheatley Association was the equivalent of the "controlled system of lodging houses" that Kellor recommended in her report, but under black not white control. In cooperation with the National Association of Colored Women other similar institutions were established in cities across the country with Hunter as chair of the Phillis Wheatley department of the NACW. The board that was established in 1913 to oversee the home included white as well as black patrons, and Hunter argued that the Phillis Wheatley Association was "one of the strongest ties between the Negro and white races in America" (*NP*, p. 165). It was not only at the level of management, however, that Hunter was proud of the association as a model of interracial cooperation. The home was a training ground to prepare young black women for domestic service, and one of Hunter's aims was to improve relations between white mistress and maid by producing a happy and efficient servant. As Hunter states:

> *The most important factor in successful domestic service is a happy and human relation between the lady of the house and the maid—on the part of the maid, respect and affectionate regard for her employer; on the part of the employer, sympathy and imagination. Perhaps it is not going too far to say that the lady of the house should stand in the relation of a foster mother to the young woman who assists her in the household tasks. . . .*
>
> *The girl who is fairly well-trained and well-disposed will become interested in the life of the family that she serves, and will be devoted to its happiness. [NP, pp. 161–62]*

Hunter asserted that the Phillis Wheatley Association was "an instrument for [the] social and moral redemption" of young black women (*NP*, p. 157). A prerequisite for this redemption, Hunter maintained, was surveillance over all aspects of the lives of the girls in the home:

> *In fact it was necessary at all times to guard our girls from evil surroundings. I kept a vigilant ear at the switchboard in my office to catch conversations of a doubtful character, and to intercept assignations. No effort we made to restrict tenancy to girls of good character could exclude the ignorant, the foolish, and the weak, for these had to be protected as well. In the company of a policeman whom I could trust, I would sometimes follow couples to places of assignation, rescue the girl, and assist in the arrest of her would-be seducer. [NP, pp. 128–29]*

There are extraordinary contradictions present in this narrative reconstructing the life of a woman who when young had declared her independence from both the patriarchal power of her husband and the maternal power of her mother by walking away from both of them to "find and keep the freedom [she] so ardently desired," only to find herself in her mature years thwarting the desires of other young women by lurking in hallways to eavesdrop on their telephone calls and marching off into the night accompanied by the police to have their lovers arrested. And, yet, Hunter clearly tries to establish a maternal framework to disguise and legitimate what are actually exploitative relations of power. Exploitation becomes nurturance when Hunter describes the white mistress acting as a "foster mother" to a young black domestic worker and when she herself dominates the lives of her charges in the Phyllis Wheatley Association. Hunter, remembering her own mother as weak and helpless, created the association as a matriarchy that allowed her to institutionalize and occupy a space of overwhelming matriarchal power over younger black women.

Although Hunter is uncritical of and, indeed, manipulates and abuses the possibilities of matriarchal power, she is explicit in her criticism of the ways in which an abusive patriarchal power becomes embedded in the corrupt legal and political machinery of city governance. Hunter is trenchant in her analysis of the mutually beneficial relations between "unscrupulous politicians," the "rapacity of realtors," the creation of the segregated ghetto, and organized vice in Cleveland. But urban blacks are situated as merely the victims of the forces of corruption: the politicians,

Hunter felt, played "upon the ignorance of the Negro voter to entrench themselves in office, and then deliver[ed] the Negro over to every force of greed and vice which stalked around him" (*NP*, p. 121).

Hunter utilizes the forces of matriarchal power to declare war on what she feels to be her most formidable enemy, "commercialized vice." She describes her battle in the most epic of biblical language, a battle in which she joins with a "dreadful monster . . . spawned by greed and ignorance . . . hideous to behold. 'Out of its belly came fire and smoke, and its mouth was as the mouth of a lion . . . and its wages were death' " (*NP*, p. 120). Corrupt city politics enables and maintains the monstrous network that feeds on the young female souls in Hunter's charge, but at its heart is a single patriarchal figure whom she refers to only as "Starlight."[9] If Hunter sees herself as the matriarchal savior of young black women, she describes "Starlight" as the " 'Great Mogul' of organized vice." He is the epitome of the seducer of young black women whom he manipulates, betrays, and then drags as "prisoners" down into the depths of "shame and degradation" (*NP*, p. 122). But, although the war is figuratively between these forces of patriarchal power and maternal influence, Hunter's matriarchal power is aimed directly at other women. Black female sexual behavior, because according to Hunter it is degenerate, threatens the progress of the race: threatens to "tumble gutterward," in her words, the "headway which the Negro had made toward the state of good citizenship" (*NP*, p. 126).

Dance halls and nightclubs are particular targets of Hunter's reformist zeal, and she identifies these cultural spaces, located in the "heart of [the] newly created Negro slum district[s]," as the site of the production of vice as spectacle: "Here, to the tune of St. Louis voodoo blues, half-naked Negro girls dance shameless dances with men in Spanish costumes. . . . The whole atmosphere is one of unrestrained animality, the jungle faintly veneered with civilized trappings" (*NP*, pp. 132–33). Places of amusement and of recreation for black people are condemned as morally dangerous and described as being filled with "lewd men and wretched women" (*NP*, p. 132). Nightclubs where black women perform for a white audience threaten the very foundations of Hunter's definitions of acceptable interracial relations:

> *Interracial co-operation built the Phillis Wheatley Association and is carrying on its work; a co-operation of Negroes and whites for worthy purposes; which can gauge the spiritual contribution the Negro has made to American life, since his arrival in America. But in the meeting of blacks and whites in night clubs*

---

[9]This figure was Albert D. "Starlight" Boyd, whom Katrina Hazzard-Gordon refers to as a "political strongman." He owned and operated Woodluff Hall, the dance hall that Hunter felt was so disreputable, and the Starlight Café. Boyd had numerous estate holdings and links to prostitution and gambling and helped to deliver the black votes of the Eleventh Ward to the Republican boss Maurice Maschke (Katrina Hazzard-Gordon, *Jooking. The Rise of Social Dance Formations in African-American Culture* [Philadelphia, 1990], please see also pp. 128, 130–32, and 136–37).

> *. . . there is to be found only cause for regret and head-hanging by both races.*
> *On the one side an exhibition of unbridled animality, on the other a blasé quest*
> *for novel sensations, a vicarious gratification of the dark and violent desires of*
> *man's nature, a voluntary return to the jungle. [NP, p. 133]*

There are deep fears being expressed in this passage in which the exploitation of black women is only one concern among many. These fears haunt the entire narrative and are also embedded in Kellor's account of young, black migrating women: fears of a rampant and uncontrolled female sexuality; fears of miscegenation; and fears of the assertion of an independent black female desire that has been unleashed through migration. If a black woman can claim her freedom and migrate to an urban environment, what is to keep her from negotiating her own path through its streets? What are the consequences of the female self-determination evident in such a journey for the establishment of a socially acceptable moral order that defines the boundaries of respectable sexual relations? What, indeed, is to be the framework of discipline and strategies of policing that can contain and limit black female sexuality? These are the grounds of contestation in which black women became the primary targets for the moral panic about urban immorality.

St. Clair Drake and Horace Cayton in their history of Chicago, *Black Metropolis*, describe how the existence of residential restrictive convenants made middle-class neighborhoods in Bronzeville "the beach upon which broke the human flotsam which was tossed into the city streets by successive waves of migration from the South."[10] They also describe the deep ambivalence in the attitudes of the black middle class toward the black working class who, as Drake and Cayton insist, perform "the essential digging, sweeping, and serving which make Metropolitan life tolerable" (*BM*, p. 523). This ambivalence, they argue, caused the black upper class to live a contradictory existence. On the one hand they defined their social position by emphasizing their *differentness* from the lower class:

> *But, as Race Leaders, the upper class must [also] identify itself psychologically*
> *with "The Race," and The Race includes a lot of people who would never be*
> *accepted socially. Upper-class Negroes, too, depend upon the Negro masses for*
> *their support if they are business or professional men. The whole orientation of*
> *the Negro upper class thus becomes one of trying to speed up the processes by*
> *which the lower class can be transformed from a poverty-stricken group, iso-*
> *lated from the general stream of American life, into a counterpart of middle-*
> *class America. [BM, p. 563]*

Hunter, clearly, lives this contradiction: her self-definition and her right to control her own behavioral boundaries are beyond question. But, by positioning herself as part of the emergent black bourgeoisie, Hunter secures her personal autonomy in the process of claiming the right to circumscribe the rights of young black working-

---

[10]St. Drake and Horace R. Cayton, *Black Metropolis: A Study of Negro Life in a Northern City* (New York 1946) p. 577) hereafter abbreviated *BM*.

class women and to transform their behavior on the grounds of nurturing the progress of the race as a whole.

What Drake and Cayton fail to recognize, however, is the extent to which the behavioral transformation of this lower class was thought to be about transforming the behavior of black working-class women. Hunter's accounts of the women who represented the success stories of the Phillis Wheatley Association, for example, are narratives of the transformation of the behavior of migrant working-class black women to conform to middle-class norms of acceptable sexual behavior while actually being confirmed in their subordinate, working-class status as female domestics. These success stories represented the triumphant fulfilment of the mission of the Phillis Wheatley Association, a mission that declared itself to be "to discover, protect, cherish, and perpetuate the beauty and power of Negro Womanhood," but which was primarily concerned with shaping and disciplining a quiescent urban, black, female, working-class population.

The texts that draw on aspects of this discourse of black female sexuality as a way to respond to northern urban migration are multiple and varied. In two important novels about Harlem during the twenties, Carl Van Vechten's *Nigger Heaven* (1926) and Claude McKay's *Home to Harlem* (1928), both authors use their female characters as the terrain on which to map a relation between the sexual and class politics of urban black life.[11] While neither author appears to be overtly interested in prescribing a program of social engineering, both novels are fictions of black urban classes in formation. Central to the success of the emergent black middle class in these two novels is the evolution of urban codes of black masculinity. In each text representations of urban black women are used as both the means by which male protagonists will achieve or will fail to achieve social mobility and as signs of various possible threats to the emergence of the wholesome black masculinity necessary for the establishment of an acceptable black male citizenship in the American social order.

The first part of *Nigger Heaven* focuses on Mary Love, a figure of virginal purity. The failure of Byron Kasson, the male protagonist, to recognize the worth of Mary to the social security of his own future leads directly to his social disintegration. Van Vechten, a white patron of black culture and black artists, describes Mary as "cold":

> She had an instinctive horror of promiscuity, of being handled, even touched, by a man who did not mean a good deal to her. This might, she sometimes argued with herself, have something to do with her white inheritance, but Olive [her friend], who was far whiter, was lacking in this inherent sense of prudery. At any rate, whatever the cause, Mary realized that she was different in this respect from most of the other girls she knew. The Negro blood was there,

---

[11]See Carl Van Vechten, *Nigger Heaven* (New York, 1926), hereafter abbreviated *NH;* and Claude McKay *Home to Harlem* (1938 New York, 1987) hereafter abbreviated NH

*warm and passionately earnest: all her preferences and prejudices were on the side of the race into which she had been born. She was as capable, she was convinced, of amorous emotion, as any of her friends, but the fact remained that she was more selective. Oh, the others were respectable enough; they did not involve themselves too deeply. On the other hand, they did not flee from a kiss in the dark. A casual kiss in the dark was a repellent idea to Mary. What she wanted was a kiss in the light. [NH, p. 54]*

Van Vechten appears to dismiss, or put in doubt, the classic nineteenth-century literary explanation of blood "admixture" for these opposing aspects of Mary's fictional personality in favor of using a more contemporary, and urban, explanation that uses Mary's "horror of promiscuity" as a sign of her secure class position.

Mary's middle-class existence is initially defined through her job; she works as a museum curator gathering together collections of African art. But Van Vechten also carefully defines her differentness from migrant and working-class black women in a variety of more complex ways. When Mary attends a rent party, for example, she is figuratively defiled by the gin and juice that is spilled over her and stains her clothes. When she regretfully wonders why she danced at this party until two in the morning Van Vechten has her mentally discipline herself by reflecting on a long, directly quoted passage from Gertrude Stein's "Melanctha." The passage is an extended reflection on the dangers of "colored people" getting excited and "running around and . . . drinking and doing everything bad they can think of" instead of "working hard and caring about their working and living regular with their families and saving up all their money, so they will have some to bring their children up better" (*NH*, p. 57). Mary carefully differentiates herself culturally and ideologically from the black working class. On the one hand, she defines spirituals, which deeply affect her, as a cultural form produced from "real faith," which has the power to "touch most of us . . . and make us want to cry or shout." But on the other hand, she sees the culture of "servant girls and the poor" as being very different. The latter, she is convinced, don't really "feel faith—except as an escape from the drudgery of their lives. They don't really stop playing Numbers or dancing on Sunday or anything else that their religion forbids them to do. They enjoy themselves in church on Sunday as they do in the cabarets on week-days" (*NH*, pp. 60, 59). Mary's disdain of sexual promiscuity is firmly embedded, by Van Vechten, in a middle-class ideology of endlessly deferred gratification.

The counterpoint to Mary is a character called Lasca Sartoris, who uses her sexuality to negotiate her way through her life. Unlike Mary, who has never even been to the South, Lasca, the daughter of a country preacher, "began by teaching school in the backwoods down in Louisiana" and then migrated north when an uncle left her an inheritance. In the city Lasca is to "cut loose" dancing, playing the piano, and singing in Harlem clubs all night (*NH*, pp. 83–84). Lasca's sexuality ensnares a rich and much older husband whose death leaves her a rich heiress. Van Vechten uses Lasca as a figure of overt and degenerate sexuality whose behavior is absolutely outside of all moral boundaries. She attracts, then physically and emotionally destroys and discards a series of male lovers, including Byron Kasson, having embroiled them in an intense bacchanalia of alchoholic, drug, and sexual abuse. For Byron, the would-be intellectual and writer, his choice of the influence of Lasca, rather than Mary, brings a certain end to all his hopes and ambition.

Claude McKay has a rather more subtle but, for women, an equally damning approach to the relation between black sexual politics, masculinity, and the securing of social position. McKay's protagonist, Jake, is ultimately saved by Felice, the woman he loves, in an interesting narrative sleight of hand that transforms Felice from the position of prostitute to a figure of wholesome sexuality. Jake arrives in Harlem and meets Felice in a bar. He spends the night with her, pays her, and leaves the following morning thinking he will never see her again. Wondering if he can afford breakfast Jake discovers that Felice has returned all his money to his pocket, thus proving that her sex is not for sale. This gesture convinces Jake that he must return to Felice, but he is quickly lost in the unfamiliar city streets, and it takes the whole course of the novel for him to find her again. On the journey back toward this "true" woman, however, Jake has to negotiate the vice and temptations of the city, which are embodied in a series of other women that he meets.

McKay has a much deeper, richer, and more complex understanding of the cultural forms of the black urban landscape on which he draws than Van Vechten. But, despite this formal complexity, McKay situates his female figures in a very simplistic manner in various degrees of approximation to an uncontrolled and, therefore, problematic sexual behavior. For Jake's journey is not just a journey to find the right woman; it is, primarily, a journey of black masculinity in formation, a sort of *Pilgrim's Progress* in which a number of threatening embodiments of the female and the feminine have to be negotiated. The most significant of these female figures is Rose, a nightclub singer at a cabaret called the Congo. As its name implies, the Congo is "a real throbbing little Africa in New York. It was an amusement place entirely for the unwashed of the Black Belt. . . . Girls coming from the South to try their future in New York," McKay stresses, "always reached the Congo first" (*HH*, pp. 29–30). These "chippies [that] come up from down home," a male friend of Jake's advises him, represent "the best pickings" in Harlem (*HH*, p. 35). Felice, of course, is never seen there. At the heart of what McKay describes as the "thick, dark-colorful, and fascinating" Congo, he situates the blues and Rose, the blues singer (*HH*, p. 36). As far as Jake is concerned, Rose is "a wonderful tissue of throbbing flesh," though he neither loves nor feels "any deep desire for her" (*HH*, pp. 42, 114). The assumption of the novel is that male love and desire could not be generated for, or be sustained by, a woman like Rose, who is characterized as bisexual because she lacks the acceptable feminine qualities of "tenderness . . . timidity . . . [and] aloofness." Indeed, Rose's sexual ambiguity is positioned as a threat to the very existence of black masculinity, reducing Jake to the role of a "big, good slave" (*HH*, pp. 42, 41). McKay proposes that only a pathological and distorted form of masculine power could exist in such a relationship when Rose makes masochistic demands that Jake brutalize her, confirming his belief "that a woman could always go further than a man in coarseness, depravity, and sheer cupidity" (*HH*, p. 69). Jake's refusal to beat Rose is a triumph of wholesome masculinity over the degenerate female element and allows Jake to proceed on his journey to become a man.

The dance hall and the cabaret, in the texts that I have been discussing, are the most frequently referenced landscapes in which black female promiscuity and sexual degeneracy were described. In William H. Jones's sociological study of black urban recreation and amusement (1927), the dance hall was a complex and a contested social space. Jones could not condemn the dance hall as an "essentially antisocial institution" because it was possible that a dance hall could be a place in which "romantic love of the most idealistic type" could blossom. But dance halls encouraged a quick intimacy that could also lead the young "on the downward path to crime."[12] What Jones condemned without compromise was the dancing that took place in the dance halls. He saw modern dances as nothing more than "sexual pantomimes. They are similar to many of the ancient and primitive methods of publicly arousing human passions in preparation for lascivious orgies." He asserted that the results of his "careful investigation disclosed the fact that . . . a large amount of illicit sex behavior is unquestionably the natural sequence of certain modern forms of dancing" (*RA*, p. 122).

Jones reserved his greatest vehemence for the cabaret, where

> *excess in dancing, jungle laughter, and semi-alcoholic beverages are characteristic features of their life. Here, jazz music is carried to extremes. In general, there is more abandon achieved by the dancers than in the formal dance hall, and more of a tendency toward nakedness on the part of the female entertainers. [RA, p. 131]*

What Jones particularly feared was what he called "social demoralization." He designated these recreational social spaces as places where "the most powerful human impulses and emotions are functioning," impulses and emotions that threatened the deterioration of the fragile social fabric of the black urban community (*RA*, p. 122).

The existence of dance halls and cabarets was particularly dangerous to the moral health of the black middle class, Jones maintained, because of "the rapidity and ease with which the anti-social forms of dancing spread upwards into and engross the so-called higher classes." He viewed the social fabric of the black urban community as fragile because of the lack of "adequate bulwarks against the encroachment of such behavior forms upon the life of the more advanced groups of Negroes" (*RA*, p. 122). "Class stratification" within the black community, Jones continued, only "seems to be strong." If black middle-class public opinion could

---

[12]William H. Jones, *Recreation and Amusement among Negroes in Washington, D.C.: A Sociological Analysis of the Negro in an Urban Environment* (Washington, D.C., 1927), p. 121; hereafter abbreviated *RA*.

generate disapproval of "the vulgar, sexually-suggestive modern dances . . . they would be compelled to confine themselves to the lower anti-social cultural groups in which they originated" (*RA*, p. 123). His appeal to the mobilization of social disapproval appears to be as much about generating a black middle-class ideology of solidarity and coexistence as about challenging threats to the social mores of that group. If middle-class hegemony could be established in the black community it could more effectively discipline the black working class through the implementation of what Jones refers to as "mechanisms of control whereby forces which tend to disintegrate and demoralize the higher forms of culture may be excluded or annihilated" (*RA*, p. 123).

Between Kellor's report for *Charities* and Jones's book the moral panic about the lack of control over the sexual behavior of black women had become absorbed into the fundamental assumptions of the sociological analysis of urban black culture, which thus designated many of its forms of entertainment and leisure "pathological" and in need of greater institutional control.[13] Kathy Peiss, in her recent analysis of white working-women's leisure and recreation in New York, describes how white reformers in the early decades of the twentieth century believed that "the primary purpose of reform for working women was to inculcate standards of respectable behavior." Perceptions of "a rising tide of promiscuity and immorality" and panics over "white slavery and commercialized prostitution," she argues, motivated Progressive reformers whose prime target was increasingly "the growing menace of commercial amusements."[14] But the black urban community was constructed as pathological in very specific ways. Black urban life was viewed as being intimately associated with commercialized vice because black migrants to cities were forced to live in or adjacent to areas previously established as red-light districts in which prostitution and gambling had been contained. The existence of restrictive convenants enforced black residential segregation and limited the expansion of what became identified as black urban ghettos.[15] It was within the confines of East St. Louis, the south side of Chicago, the tenderloin in Kansas City, and Harlem in New York that an entertainment industry that served both a white and a black clientele was located and from which an urban blues culture emerged.

---

[13]Jones acknowledged his greatest debt to Robert E. Park and others of the Department of Sociology at the University of Chicago.

[14]Kathy Peiss, *Cheap Amusements: Working Women and Leisure in Turn-of-the-Century New York* (Philadelphia, 1986), pp. 178–79. The focus of my analysis is rather different than Peiss's. She describes her book as "a study of young working women's culture in turn-of-the-century New York City—the customs, values, public styles, and ritualized interactions—expressed in leisure time" (p. 3). Not only am I concentrating on black women rather than white women, but also I am most interested here in the black woman whom the site of leisure was a place of work rather than recreation.

[15]See William Barlow, *"Looking Up at Down": The Emergence of Blues Culture* (Philadelphia, 1989), pp. 240–43 (on Kansas City), 250–51 (on St. Louis), and 287–92 (on Chicago). See also *Black* 174–213.

On the eve of the depression black women who had migrated to urban areas were still overwhelmingly limited to employment in domestic service and as laundresses. In Chicago, for example, between the First World War and the onset of the depression, over 40 percent of white women workers but only 5 percent of black women workers who entered the labor force obtained "clean" work (see *BM*, pp. 220–29). The category "clean" work referred to jobs like office secretary and department store clerk; "clean" work was the type of employment from which black women were rigorously excluded. From the biographies and autobiographies of the black women who eventually became entertainers it is clear that joining a touring vaudeville troupe or tent show was an important avenue of geographic mobility for young black women who were too poor to pay for train fares and for whom hopping a freight car was dangerous. In addition, being a member of a vaudeville show or performing in a nightclub was not attractive primarily because it offered a mythic life of glamor but because it was a rare opportunity to do "clean" work and to reject the life of a domestic servant.

When she was eight years old Josephine Baker started her first job and discovered that working as a maid for a white mistress was not "the happy and human relation" that Jane Edna Hunter maintained it should be. Baker was assured by her mistress, Mrs. Keiser, that she loved children, and she promised Baker the shoes and a coat that her own family were too poor to provide. However, Baker had to start to work at five in the morning so she could be at school by nine, and when she arrived home in the afternoon she had to work again until ten o'clock at night when she was sent to bed in the cellar to sleep with the dog. One day when Baker made a mistake Mrs. Keiser punished her by plunging the little girl's arms into boiling water. This story and Baker's account of how she watched white people murder and torture her relatives and neighbors during the East St. Louis riot of 1917 are situated in her autobiography as the preface to her decision to leave St. Louis when she was thirteen years old and get on a train with a vaudeville troupe called the Dixie Steppers.[16]

Alberta Hunter left Memphis when she was thirteen because she had heard that young girls in Chicago were being paid ten dollars a week to sing.[17] In 1912 she started working in a club called Dago Frank's, singing to an audience of pimps and prostitutes, and then moved to Hugh Hoskins, a club for "confidence men and their girls who were pickpockets." In many ways Alberta Hunter's story of her early years in Chicago epitomizes the life from which Jane Edna Hunter wanted to save young black women in the name of maternal protection. But Alberta Hunter em-

---

[16]Josephine Baker and Jo Bouillon, *Josephine,* trans. Mariana Fitzpatrick (New York, 1977), pp. 3–4. See also Phyllis Rose, *Jazz Cleopatra: Josephine Baker in Her Time* (New York, 1989), p. 12.

[17]See Frank C. Taylor and Gerald Cook, *Alberta Hunter: A Celebration in Blues* (New York, 1987), pp. 20–23.

phasizes how she found maternal care and nurturance from the prostitutes in her audience and describes how "the prostitutes were so wonderful, they'd always make the 'Johns' give me money you know. . . . They'd go out and buy me little dresses and things to put on me so I'd look nice."[18]

Ethel Waters agreed to join the act of two vaudevillians she met in a Philadelphia saloon because she was offered ten dollars a week playing the Lincoln Theatre when she was "getting three fifty a week as a scullion and chambermaid [at the Harrod Apartments] and a dollar and a quarter more for taking home some of the guests' laundry."[19] Waters grew up in the red-light districts of Philadelphia, and in her autobiography she asserts that she "always had great respect for whores" (*H*, p. 17). Like Alberta Hunter she utilizes the language of maternal nurturance when she describes how her friendship with a young prostitute blossomed:

> *Being hardly more than a child herself, Blanche often played with me, read me stories, and sang little songs with me. Her beauty fascinated me. I loved her. There was a great camaraderie between us, and that young prostitute gave me some of the attention and warm affection I was starving for. Whenever I tipped off the sporting world that the cops were just around the corner I felt I was doing it for Blanche and her friends.* [*H, p. 18*]

Waters reveals a consciousness of being part of a world in which women were under surveillance and has little hesitation in declaring her allegiance. The images and figures of the sources of both exploitation and nurturance in the lives of these young black women are in direct contrast to and, indeed, in direct conflict with the attempts of the black middle class to police and discipline female sexuality.

Black women blues singers, musicians, and performers dominated the black recording industry and vaudeville circuit throughout the twenties, and they are the central figures in the emergence and establishment of an urban blues culture. However, in order to acknowledge their roles as the primary cultural mediators of the conditions of transition and the producers of a culture of migration we have to challenge the contemporary histories of the formation of a black urban culture as a history of the black middle class. The dominance of the conceptual paradigm of the Harlem Renaissance with its emphasis on the practices of literature and fine art relies on a belief that the black middle class did, in fact, accomplish and secure its own cultural and political dominance within black America. However, as Houston A. Baker, Jr., argues, what is called the Renaissance actually marks the historical moment of the failure of the black bourgeoisie to achieve cultural hegemony and to become a dominant social force.[20]

---

[18]Alberta Hunter, quoted in Stuart Goldman (producer), *Alberta Hunter: My Castle's Rockin'* (1988).

[19]Ethel Waters and Charles Samuels, *His Eye Is on the Sparrow* (New York, 1951), p. 72; hereafter abbreviated *H*.

[20]See Houston A. Baker, Jr., *Modernism and the Harlem Renaissance* (Chicago, 1987).

The contradictory nature of the culture that was produced in black urban America between the teens and the depression has not been retained or absorbed within black urban cultural histories. The twenties must be viewed as a period of ideological, political, and cultural contestation between an emergent black bourgeoisie and an emerging urban black working class. The cultural revolution or successful renaissance that did occur stemmed from this terrain of conflict in which the black women who were so central to the formation of an urban blues culture created a web of connections among working-class migrants. The possibilities of both black female liberation and oppression were voiced through a music that spoke to the desires which were released in the dramatic shift in social relations that occurred in a historical moment of crisis and dislocation.[21]

Women's blues was not only a central mechanism of cultural mediation but also the primary means of the expression of the disrupted social relations associated with urban migration. The blues women did not passively reflect the vast social changes of their time; they provided new ways of thinking about these changes, alternative conceptions of the physical and social world for their audience of migrating and urban women and men, and social models for women who aspired to escape from and improve their conditions of existence. I have already described how hopping freight cars, because of the inherent dangers associated with that form

---

[21]Virginia Yans-McLaughlin argues that the new scholarship in immigration and migration studies has moved away from questions about

> individual and group agency toward the social relations of exchange. So, instead of individuals assimilating or achieving, we have group strategies and networks. What we might call a network-exchange theory seems to be emerging as a potential alternative to assimilation and human-capital theory. In network-exchange theory, an ethnic group's human capital is not simply transported from one place to another by individuals who fold their riches into the American system. Although it is true that the groups are sometimes portrayed as holders of assets, these are transformed to new purposes; indeed, immigrant groups seem capable of creating new advantages for themselves. The network structure that originally functioned as the grid connecting Old World kin might, for example, transform itself in ethnic subeconomies to provide jobs, housing, or even business opportunities. [Virginia Yans-McLaughlin, introduction, *Immigration Reconsidered: History, Sociology, and Politics,* ed. Yans-McLaughlin (New York, 1990), p. 12]

Using such a methodology Suzanne Model argues that because of their very limited access to the job market black migrants were unable, or failed to establish such a system of mutual assistance. Although it is clear that networks of exchange did indeed exist within black urban migrant enclaves my argument here is that network-exchange theory is unnecessarily limited if it is applied only to access to the labor market and to alternative economies that existed within migrant communities. I would argue that urban blues culture could profitably be regarded as a network of exchange or web of connection rather than as a conglomeration of individual achievement. See Suzanne W. Model, "Work and Family: Blacks and Immigrants from South and East Europe," in ibid., pp. 130–59. It would seem to me that the role of the *Chicago Defender* would be important in writing a history that documented the system of mutual exchange in black communities that provided information about and access to the job market. See, for example, Emmett J. Scott, "Letters of Negro Migrants of 1916–1918," *Journal of Negro History* 4 (July 1919): 290–340, and "Additional Letters of Negro Migrants of 1916–1918," Journal of Negro History 4 (Oct. 1919):412–65.

of travel, was not a viable option for women and that travelling tent shows and vaudeville on the Theater Owner's Booking Association circuit (TOBA) offered an alternative way to achieve mobility for young women—Mamie Smith, for example, started dancing when she was ten, and Ida Cox left home to join the Black and Tan Minstrel Show when she was fourteen. This increase in their physical mobility parallels their musical challenges to sexual conventions and gendered social roles. However, the field of blues history is dominated by the assumption that "authentic" blues forms are entirely rural in origin and are produced by the figure of the wandering, lone male. Thus the formation of mythologies of blues masculinity, which depend on this popular image, have obscured the ways in which the gendering of women was challenged in the blues. The blues women of the twenties, who recorded primarily in urban centers but who employed and modified the full range of rural and urban blues styles, have come to be regarded as professionalized aberrations who commercialized and adulterated "pure" blues forms. But as Chris Albertson insists, the blues "women were all aggressive women [who] knew what they wanted and went after it."[22] The blues women brought to the black, urban, working class an awareness of its social existence and acted creatively to vocalize the contradictions and tensions of the terrain of sexual politics in the relation of black working-class culture to the culture of the emergent black middle class.[23] In doing so they inspired other women to claim the "freedom [they] so ardently desired."

---

[22]Chris Albertson, quoted in Carole van Falkenburg and Christine Dall (producers), *Wild Women Don't Have the Blues* (1989).

[23]See my forthcoming book, *Women, Migration, and the Formation of a Black Culture.*

# A Mother's Birth

*Pauline A. Santos*

> *The night you were born I ceased being my father's boy and became my son's father.*
>
> — *Henry G. Felsen, To My Son in Uniform*

There is an irony in my commitment to use this quote. Obviously it would be more appropriate to my purposes had it been written by a mother about a daughter. Nonetheless, it is too fitting not to use, for it captures my transition from daughter to mother, a transition that dramatically altered my relationship with racism, with sexism and with my mother. This transition took place over the course of a decade, but it began with the birth of my daughter, when race and gender took on new meanings.

My earliest memory of racism came to me one day when Tonja, my first child, was just weeks old. I was bathing her in the kitchen sink of our apartment. Her small fists and legs were a blur of motion as she cooed and smiled her pleasure. I remember marveling at the perfection of her tiny body, the delicacy of her skin, as soft and as rich as coffee-colored satin. Gently covering her glistening body with the mildest soap on the softest cloth, I was suddenly overcome with sadness. As I squeezed my eyes shut against the unexpected tears, another bathing scene began to emerge.

> *A six-year-old black girl sits on the edge of a cracked, vinyl padded chair in the center of a small kitchen. Her legs dangle as her feet do their best to reach the now nearly cold water in the galvanized tub in which she has just been given her Saturday night bath. She is shivering, and she, too, is squeezing her eyes shut. Perhaps this is because the oil stove cannot adequately heat the three small but drafty rooms. Then, too, it might be because she has just stepped out of the tub, beads of water still visible on her smooth brown skin. The towel she tries to wrap around her naked body is too small and threadbare to offer any absorbency or warmth.*
>
> *Or perhaps the answer to her tears is somewhere else in the picture. There is a small but strong middle-aged white woman muttering under her breath and shaking her head disapprovingly as she scrubs the already-bathed*

*black child–right knee, left knee, right ankle, left ankle–with a scouring pad. Timidly the black child tries to tell the white woman that maybe her knees and ankles are not still dirty—that maybe it's just her color. The white woman scrubs harder. It hurts, and tears begin to fall. This seems to make the white woman angrier, and she scrubs harder still. So the child just shivers and squeezes her eyes shut.*

*What is the relationship between this adult and this child? Who is this woman? A sadistic baby-sitter perhaps? No, the white woman is the black child's mother. Oh. Then she must be the proverbial mean stepmother or an adoptive parent gone bad. Perhaps a burned-out foster parent? No, she is the black child's biological white mother. Oh. Then, the white woman must hate the black man who fathered the child; maybe it was rape? No, the child's father has always been there; he and the woman are married. He's out right now, but it wouldn't make any difference if he were home. Oh, Maybe that's why the child shivers and squeezes her eyes shut against her tears.*

My father was Cape Verdean (or black Portuguese, as natives of then-colony Cape Verde were called), and my mother was white Portuguese. They were married in a small New England town in the 1920s, a place where and a time when interracial unions were an aberration. My father worked until his retirement at a local textile mill; he died in 1983 at the age of eighty-nine. My mother was a housewife and a hypochondriac; she died in 1985 at the age of seventy-four.

I had always heard that when a woman becomes a mother, she develops a new appreciation of her own mother, more respect for a mother's sacrifices, a better understanding of a mother's love. My journey into motherhood took on different dynamics. The more comfortable I became with my role as mother, the more difficult the role of daughter became.

I was not aware of this shift as it occurred, or at least I convinced myself I was not. The quality of the two relationships became more and more polarized over a ten-year period, from 1975, the year Tonja was born, through 1985, the year my mother died. During that time, I managed to suppress any awareness or acknowledgment of what was happening. It was only with my mother's death that I was forced to confront my feelings because I found myself devoid of any emotion except anger. That scared me. What was I so angry about? How could I feel this way about my own mother? What horrible kind of daughter was I? How could I have such anger toward the woman who had "given me everything"?

This was not my first or last experience with death. My father had died two years earlier, and while my sense of loss was profound, our love and respect for each other helped ease my pain. My husband died two weeks before my mother. My grief, while great, was moderated by the anger I felt at the untimeliness of his death following what I still believe to have been an ill-advised liver biopsy. When my oldest friend informed me the following month that she had inoperable ovarian cancer, and when she died seven months later, I mourned the loss of that special relationship. Yet, when my mother died I felt nothing but anger—and guilt about that anger.

My difficulty coping with these feelings resulted in a new relationship. I started to see Sylvia, a therapist. With her sensitive and insightful guidance, I ever so slowly began to understand what had taken place over that past decade—that the more I witnessed how my love for my daughter nurtured her self-esteem and the more I saw her grow and flourish within the safety of that unconditional love, the more I was forced to acknowledge what I had not received from my mother. As bits of awareness rose to the surface, they were entangled in anger, resentment and an overwhelming sense of abandonment and deprivation. The knowing process has often been painful, but with Sylvia's gentle caring and her unwavering positive regard, it has been bearable. More important, it has been freeing.

My mother taught me that my blackness and my femaleness were two strikes against me. She convinced me these two "flaws" were somehow of my own making. She taught me I would get or not get what I deserved based on these two flaws, that I was to be thankful for whatever I did get and that I had to accept the limitations placed on me.

These teachings did not involve structured lessons on her part or conscious learning on mine. Rather, they were taught through the everyday interactions of our lives. Whether she was scrubbing my knees with a scouring pad, or scolding me for my "ashiness" or admonishing me to stay out of the summer sun so as not to get "even darker," the message was the same—my blackness was an embarrassing defect. Whether she was being less than hospitable to my father's relatives or calling him a "black bastard" when she was angry (which was often), the message was the same—the color of one's skin determines the respect to which she or he is entitled.

Sexism was blatant as well. My mother never hesitated to tell anyone, including me, that she wished all her children had been boys because girls were "nothing but trouble." When I turned sixteen, I had to beg to be allowed to complete high school because I was "just a girl." I had less success with my dream of attending college, however. Once again, I was told that not only was this "not necessary for a girl," but it was "foolish" as well.

As a result of this racist and sexist mothering, I fluctuated between no identity and an unacceptable identity. Being nursed on racism and sexism by someone so crucial to one's self-worth left me vulnerable to *anyone's* racism and sexism. In fact, "vulnerable" is too passive a word; it was more an expectation and an acceptance of racism and sexism from whomever and wherever it came. The thought of fighting them, or even questioning them, was as foreign to me as was the thought of fighting or questioning my mother. After all, if you learn at your mother's breast that you are a second-class child, why would you question society's designation of you as a second-class citizen?

And then, on August 13, 1975, everything changed. It was the last time I did anything as my mother had done—I gave birth to a black female child. It was as if until that moment, until I was the birth mother of a black female child, I had been unaware of the impact my race and gender had had on my life. I have often thought that Tonja gave birth to me that day as much as I gave birth to her.

I knew Tonja's life had to be different. She had to be protected from racism and sexism. She had to be free to do as much as she could do, go as far as she could go, without any*one* or any*thing* putting barriers in her way. Initially I would provide that protection, but eventually she would have to protect herself. I had two major tasks. One was to overcome, at least on a functional level, my predisposition to accept racism and sexism, even if it meant acquiring bravado. I had to do this not only to protect Tonja, but to set an example for her as well. My second task was to arm her in such a way that she could protect herself against racism and sexism without limiting herself and without becoming embittered against the sometimes cruel world in which she would have to live. I could not change the external world, but I could help Tonja create an inner space within which self-inflicted-racism and sexism could never take hold, and from which she could recognize, confront and defy external racism and sexism.

I was twenty-nine years old when Tonja was born, old enough to have figured out, to some degree, that it was neither my blackness nor my femaleness that made me such an easy mark for racism and sexism, but rather my low self-esteem and my lack of education. While I assumed it was too late for me (it was not, I would learn!), I vowed to arm Tonja with a positive sense of self and with the best education possible. My instincts told me that with these as a foundation, Tonja could build her life as she chose, not without *experiencing* racism and sexism, but *in spite* of them.

As best I knew how, I nurtured my daughter's self-esteem as she approached school-age. But it took only a moment one day to reinforce my instinct of how fragile a child's ego was. When Tonja was four or five years old, she said something to her older brother that I thought was especially inappropriate. I became very angry. She had stomped off into the living room and was perched, with arms folded across her chest, at the edge of a lounge chair. I marched up to her, bent over, firmly gripped each of her forearms with my strong hands, brought my face to within an inch of hers and asked, with squinting eyes and through clenched jaw, the proverbial "just who do you think you are!?" Unaccustomed to this bullying approach, Tonja instinctively cowered and said, in the smallest voice she could find, what she thought I wanted to hear—"Nobody, Mommy, I'm nobody!" For one horrific moment, I had become my mother, and it was me sitting there cowering. I recovered, and what had started out as a how-not-to-talk-to-your-brother-or-anyone-else lecture was quickly edited into a how-you-are-never-to-believe-you-are-nobody lecture. The memory of that moment has stayed with me, however, as a reminder of the power we, as parents, have over our children's sense of worth. With one thoughtless question, I had risked destroying what had taken years to build.

Through a combination of our good fortune, my tenacity, Tonja's strong academic performance and the school's community scholarship program, I was able to enroll Tonja in Lincoln School, a private, all-female school, which she attended from the sixth through twelfth grades. Tonja's seven years at this exceptional school built on the foundation I had laid for her, teaching her not only to excel academically, but also to believe in herself and to strive to be a leader among women.

For me, those same seven years epitomized my precarious position in life. They highlighted the duality of my world and intensified my struggle to maintain balance as I walked with one foot in each sphere. One sphere was shaped by Tonja's and my day-to-day interactions with her predominantly white, predominantly affluent schoolmates and their families and the school's faculty and administrators, and by my own relationships, as legal secretary to an attorney specializing in estate planning, with a class of people who live very differently from me. The other was colored by my own issues with my race and gender and by the oppression and discrimination inherent in the double-jeopardy of being black and female in our society.

An incident on the day I was asked by the head of my daughter's school to consider serving on its board represents for me the reality of that double life. Although I was honored to have been asked, I knew I had to give it some serious thought, because as a single, working, schooling parent, I was perpetually short on time. I promised to make a decision within the next few days, and I thought about it on and off throughout that day. After work and before going home, I stopped at a local supermarket. As usual, I chose the checkout line that time forgot, and my mind wandered back to the question of whether or not I could effectively serve on this prestigious board. I am not sure how much time had passed when the young man at the register brought me resoundingly back to earth with, "Hey, lady. You got any food stamps?"

So, while it took its toll in heart and soul, I assembled at assemblies, oohed and aahed at yet one more open house, patronized plays, applauded awards, conferred at conferences, grimaced at games, and partook of potlucks. I remember leaving work one day to attend a morning assembly at which Tonja, along with a number of her schoolmates, was to be recognized for some relatively small accomplishment. As she walked across the stage after receiving her ready-for-framing certificate, she lifted her head long enough to scan the audience quickly. I recognized the look; it brought me back to another ceremony many assemblies ago at which another thirteen-year-old girl scanned the audience with that same hopefulness in her eyes.

> *I still can't believe it. Any minute now Miss Carpenter's gonna call my name— my name! 1959 Senior Girl of the Year. I know she'll be here when they do. She just has to be. I mean, this is a real big deal. It isn't just the top award for this playground; it's the top award for every playground in the whole town of Bristol! Yeah, this is big. It's so hard to see into the crowd. The lights are too bright. That's why I can't see her. She's probably out there somewhere. Maybe if I look at each face really slowly I'll see her.*
>
> *Oh, God, I think I'm gonna throw up. What'll I do if that happens? I'll just start running and never come back. Look how far away the table is. When they call my name, I have to walk all the way over there. What if I trip? Oh please, please, please, don't let me trip. I'll just die if I do. I can see my trophy! It's the one in the middle—the one that's taller than all the rest.*
>
> *Wait 'til she sees it. I know she'll be proud.*

*What'll I say? I'll just say "Thank you." That's all I have to say.*

*Where is she? Please let me just see her once before they do it. But what if my voice doesn't work? What if I open my mouth and nothing comes out? Everyone will think I'm stupid.*

*Okay, God. I know I've been bothering you a lot today. But please, this is so important. Please don't let me trip or throw up or lose my voice, okay? I promise I'll be so, so good. I won't tease Rosemary, and I won't steal food in the middle of the night, and I won't say or do anything that'll make Mom have a sugar spell. Just please—this one night!*

*What? Hey, stop pushing, Sarah Paul. Oh, me? She's calling me? Oh my God—listen to them clap. I wonder if I'm blushing? Can they see my heart pounding? I hope not. The table is so far away. I have to watch where I'm going. I can't look around for her, or I'll fall.*

*Finally. It's mine. I'm holding it. Oh, no, she's telling me to stand here. Is it me she's saying all those nice things about? My shoelace is untied. Great. You know what, God? I'll trade—I'll take my chances with falling or throwing up or losing my voice. Just please, please, let her be here hearing this. Please.*

*It's over. All my friends want to see my trophy. That's okay because I'm gonna polish it when I get home anyway. It has my name on it. On a brass plate. Isn't it beautiful? My name will be in the* Phoenix. *I still can't believe it.*

*The lights aren't so bright now. And the crowd is smaller. I can see she's not here. Well, maybe my brother got in trouble again. Or maybe she had to yell at my sister for skipping out last night. Maybe her corns are hurting. I hope she didn't have one of her spells. Maybe she got company and wanted to come really bad but couldn't. I bet she's really sad she's not here. I'd better hurry up home. I bet she can hardly wait to see my trophy. I wonder where she'll put it? She's probably got a spot all picked out.*

Tonja's eyes found mine; the soft, confident smile that appeared on her face said it all.

More than a few times I questioned my good intentions in placing Tonja at the Lincoln School. After all, I was forcing her, too, to straddle two worlds. Was it fair to place her in an atmosphere where she was always "different"? Was I misleading her into thinking that her femaleness would be as much a non-issue in the real world as it was at her school? Was I setting her up for disappointment by immersing her in this college-preparatory environment when I had no idea how I would finance a college education for her?

But my determination to provide her with the best education possible won out, and Tonja graduated from Lincoln in 1993 on a picture-perfect summer's day. Parents, teachers, family and friends looked on proudly as twenty three young ladies in flowing white dresses crossed a green carpet of lawn to take their places beneath the protective branches of a majestic beech tree. The last vestiges of doubt evaporated into the sunlight as I listened to my daughter deliver the graduation address.

Earlier, in Tonja's junior year, I spent some time sitting across from her college advisor as she told me what a strong candidate Tonja was and how she would be able to almost pick her college. When I stammered something about tuitions, she said, "Mrs. Santos, certainly finances are a consideration, but they should not be your first. I'm confident Tonja will be offered a number of attractive packages by the colleges to which I think she should apply—Mount Holyoke, Amherst, Smith, Bryn Mawr, Wellesley . . .

*It is March 1963. A brown-skinned student sits across from Miss Bullock, college advisor. The office is suffocatingly small. The young girl finds it difficult to breathe, partly because of the smell of the polish that makes Miss Bullock's desk glisten, partly because of the overpowering smell of her perfume, which everyone hates, but mostly because the girl is terrified. A short but massively threatening woman, Miss Bullock makes most of the students cower. She glances at this student's file, one hand teasing the handkerchief she keeps tucked between her breasts, the other fondling the chain around her neck that attaches to her glasses. The lump in the young girl's throat swells as Miss Bullock lowers her head, slides her glasses down to the edge of her nose, and peers over them at her:*

*— Well, Pauline, I assume you have a job to go to after you graduate?*
*— You mean for the summer, Miss Bullock? Not yet.*
*— No. No. Not just for the summer. A job. A full-time job. I heard they're looking for help at Smith's. You're seventeen, aren't you?*
*— Not yet, Miss Bullock, but I will be next month. But, uhm, well, I was thinking that maybe I could get a job just for the summer, and then maybe I could go to college in September?*
*— College? For what? And where would you go?*
*— Uhm, maybe Bryant?*
*— Oh. Well. Hmm. I suppose you could get a secretarial job in the city.*
*— Well, umh I was thinking that maybe I could go into the teacher education program? I think I'd like to teach accounting? I love it, and Mr. Candelmo says I'm really good . . .*
*— Teach? You want to teach? Where, Pauline? Where would you teach? You certainly couldn't teach in Bristol. Perhaps in Providence, I suppose . . .*
*— But, why . . .?*
*— And anyway, how could you go to Bryant? Your family doesn't have any money. And speaking of your family, your mother was supposed to be here today!*

. . . Swarthmore, Colby, Bates, Haverford and Middlebury." And we visited each of those colleges that summer. Sometimes my then twelve-year-old daughter came along; more often it was just Tonja and me, or so we thought. It was a summer of rolling green hills, ivy-covered walls, and parking lots that looked like Volvo dealerships. During each visit I donned my bravado long enough to meet the people who were to interview Tonja, and then I would slip into the background (as much as that is possible for a large black woman in such surroundings). Usually I would find my way outdoors where I would wait for Tonja. I let her believe this was for her benefit, that I was giving her the space and the freedom to experience each college for herself. While this was partly true, I needed to be alone as much as Tonja needed to be left alone.

I would leave Tonja to fend for herself in order to deal with another child who managed to sneak along on every trip, no matter how hard I tried to leave her behind. My inner child made each of these trips a bittersweet mix of excitement and resentment, contentment and deprivation, pride and shame, faith and fear. No matter how I tried to reason with this stowaway child, she embarrassed the parent in me with her neediness. And then I remembered another parent who had always been embarrassed by this child. I remembered the origins of this child's neediness. So, instead of trying to send her away, I embraced her. I took what I had learned as a mother and began the ongoing task of undoing what I had learned as a daughter.

# Hard Times

## Wilma Mankiller

*When the first lands were sold by the Cherokees, in 1721, part of the tribe bitterly opposed the sale. They said if the Indians once consented to give up any of their territory, the whites would never be satisfied, but would soon want a little more and a little again, until there would be none left for the Indians. Finding that all they could say was not enough to prevent the treaty, they determined to leave their old homes forever and go far into the West, beyond the great river, where the white men could never follow them. They gave no heed to the entreaties of their friends, but began preparations for the long march, until the others, finding that they could not prevent their going, set to work and did their best to fit them with packhorses loaded with bread, dried venison, and other supplies.*

*When all was ready, they started, under the direction of their chief. A company of chosen men was sent to help them in crossing the great river. Every night until they reached it, runners were sent back to the tribe and out from the tribe to the marching band to carry messages and keep each party posted as to how the other was getting along. At last they came to the Mississippi, and crossed it by the help of those warriors who had been sent with them. These then returned to the tribe, while the others kept on to the west. All communication was now at an end. No more was heard of the wanderers, and in time, the story of the lost Cherokees was forgotten, or remembered only as an old tale.*

*Still the white man pressed on the Cherokees, and one piece of land after another was sold. As years went on, the dispossessed people began to turn their faces toward the west as their final resting place, and small bands of hunters crossed the Mississippi to learn what might be beyond. One of those parties pushed on across the plains, and there at the foot of the great mountains—the Rockies—they found a tribe speaking the old Cherokee language and living as the Cherokees had lived before they had ever known the white man or his ways.*

I experienced my own Trail of Tears when I was a young girl. No one pointed a gun at me or at members of my family. No show of force was used. It was not necessary. Nevertheless, the United States government, through the Bureau of Indian Affairs, was again trying to settle the "Indian problem" by removal. I learned through this ordeal about the fear and anguish that occur when you give up your home, your community, and everything you have ever known to move far away to a strange place. I cried for days, not unlike the children who had stumbled down the Trail of Tears so many years before. I wept tears that came from deep within the Cherokee part of me. They were tears from my history, from my tribe's past. They were Cherokee tears.

People who refuse to put any stock in the adage that history repeats itself undoubtedly do not know any Cherokees. Although most Native Americans have learned hard lessons from the experiences of the bygone years, it seems that as often as not, we are still doomed to revisit some of the bleakest episodes from our tribe's past. Much of the repetition of our history concerns ownership of land and property rights.

*A people without history is like the wind on the buffalo grass.*

*Sioux saying*

From the very start of our relationship with whites, we spent much of the time moving large numbers of our population to appease others. The relocation of the Cherokees certainly did not stop with the punitive terms imposed on us by Andrew Jackson or with the ghastly Trail of Tears. In some ways, that unhappy passage was just the beginning. In more recent times, there are significant examples of how the government meddled with our people and moved them as it had in the past.

Another Cherokee removal occurred three years before I was born. The relocation of 1942 was not nearly as devastating or on the same scale as the tragedy of 1838–1839, but for the native people who were displaced, it was every bit as upsetting and catastrophic. This removal came about in the early days of World War II when the U.S. Army decided to enlarge Camp Gruber, a military installation with an extensive reservation not far from Muskogee, Oklahoma. To accomplish its plan, the government saw to it that eighty tracts of restricted Cherokee property were condemned. The land grab included the homes on allotments of forty-five Cherokee families. Sixteen of those families raised livestock or were self-sufficient farmers. All of them were given only forty-five days to pack up their belongings and abandon their homes.

The Cherokee families affected by the condemnation had no recourse, no means of appeal. So far, the federal government has declined to entertain any legal remedy, despite the clear injustice to those Cherokee families. A tribal attorney is pursuing the matter. Compensation for the appropriated property was grossly inadequate, with the displaced families receiving no financial consideration for improvements that had been made on their property. None of the Cherokees was given any relocation assistance. Altogether, more than thirty-two thousand acres were lost. During the war, many captured enemy troops were transported to Camp Gruber, one of eight POW compounds in Oklahoma. Ironically, the military prisoners, some of whom were German soldiers from the *Afrika Korps,* were treated far better than the native people who had lost their homes and farms. It was evident that Indian affairs still remained among the lowest priorities of the federal government.

Regarding my family, we willingly became part of yet another government scheme for dealing with what was still being referred to in the 1950s as the "Indian problem." It was part of an insidious plan hatched by the Bureau of Indian Affairs. In reality, it was nothing more than another direct assault on Native American rights and tribal identities. This policy was given a name mostly associated with death camps, slaughterhouses, or penitentiaries. It was known as "termination."

The government's primary objectives in launching a policy of termination in the 1950s were to break up the system of Indian reservations across the country and to lure native people from their homeland through a program of "relocation." Although we did not live on a reservation, our family was a primary target for the resettlement plan.

The architect of this brainstorm was Dillon S. Myer. In the early 1950s, he served as commissioner of the Bureau of Indian Affairs. I am quite sure most Native Americans today would get shivers up and down their spines after only a quick glance at Myer's rather dubious record of government service. But Native Americans had little to say about his appointment.

*Many Indians are still primitive.*

*Dillon S. Myer, unpublished autobiography, 1970*

A classic example of a lifelong bureaucrat who had little regard for nonwhites, Myer was named head of the BIA as a reward for having served as director of the Japanese War Relocation Authority during World War II. For three years, Myer and his WRA staff had acted as diligent keepers of more than 120,000 men, women, and children of Japanese descent. At least two-thirds of the "evacuees," as the government called them, were American born. They were innocent United States citizens who had been rounded up and removed from their homes along the West Coast to be confined in tar-paper barracks at WRA camps scattered about the West.

The eleven Japanese-American internment camps hastily constructed on remote federal land, including two on Indian reservations in Arizona, were surrounded by barbed wire. Directors of some of the camps had been recruited from the ranks of Bureau of Indian Affairs reservation superintendents. Behind machine guns in the guard towers were military policemen with orders to shoot any inmates who tried to escape. In fact, the War Relocation Centers, as they were called, were nothing more than concentration camps.

*I sincerely believe, gentleman, that if we don't handle this problem [the presence of Japanese-Americans] in a way to get these people absorbed as best we can while the war is going on, we may have something akin to Indian reservations after the war . . .*

*Dillon S. Myer, Congressional testimony*
*January 20, 1943*

None of those incarcerated had been accused of any crimes, and there was no firm evidence of a single case of Japanese-American espionage throughout the war. But in the months shortly after Japan's attack on Pearl Harbor, the ancestry of all Japanese-Americans was enough to call their allegiance to the United States into question. Japanese-Americans became victims of wartime hysteria, racism, and greed. Many historians now believe that the repeated violations of these people's rights were some of the greatest infringements of the United States Constitution.

The Japanese-American camps were finally disbanded in 1945, after the bombings of Hiroshima and Nagasaki ended the war. Disillusioned and humiliated, many former detainees returned to find their farms and property lost to land speculators. Some people freshly released from the camps went home to find hateful inscriptions such as "No Japs Wanted" painted on their residences.

In 1982, a federal commission concluded that the internment had been wrong and had had no basis in national security. It took until 1988 for Congress to apologize for the relocation camps. It also passed legislation to ensure that individuals who had been interned should be paid damages. By 1992, an additional law was created to increase the amount of monetary compensation for the surviving claimants.

The Cherokees and other native tribes should have recognized that the assorted Trails of Tears of our ancestors served in large part as models for the removal of the Japanese immigrants and Japanese-Americans in the 1940s. In the case of the Japanese, however, the removal was from west to east, and the government used buses and trucks, so there was no need for a forced march. It was a most efficient operation. Dillon Myer would have made Andrew Jackson and Indian fighters Kit Carson and Phil Sheridan very proud.

Myer was even cited for his heinous wartime services. To honor Myer's efficient administration of the War Relocation Authority, President Harry S. Truman presented him with the nation's prestigious Medal of Merit in 1946. For good measure, Truman offered to appoint Myer as governor of Puerto Rico, but he turned it down. Instead, Myer stayed on in Washington. He held governmental posts until May of 1950 when, after declining the offer twice, he finally accepted Truman's proposition to head the Bureau of Indian Affairs. I suppose the reasoning behind the appointment was simple—any person who could handle "the Japanese problem" should certainly be able to take care of the Indians, even if there were, by most counts, almost four times as many of us to oversee.

Given a free hand by Truman and Interior Secretary Oscar L. Chapman on hiring and firing, Myer summarily issued walking papers to many seasoned BIA officials. Many of them had cared about Native Americans and were proven champions of our land rights and tribal self-determination. The reform-minded BIA administrators did not wait for their discharges, but willingly tendered their resignations. As replacements, Myer brought aboard some of his WRA cronies, mostly career government bureaucrats—all of them white—who knew nothing about Indian affairs or law but were proven "yes men."

Shortly after taking office, Myer unveiled several important changes in BIA administrative policy. He pointed out that encouragement of subsistence farming, which had been the policy standard of Franklin Roosevelt's New Deal years, was less viable in the postwar period. That policy had originated when the BIA was headed by John Collier, a committed protector of Indian cultural heritage. According to Myer, the serious unemployment situation on Indian reservations resulted from the return of 113,000 Native Americans who had left their land during the war. To resolve those issues, Myer said, the time had come to stop developing resources on the reservations. Instead, he and his cohorts encouraged tens of thousands of young Indians and their families to relocate in urban and industrial areas.

To Myer, the various Indian reservations and communities were little more than prison camps like those he had maintained for Japanese-American detainees during the war. He treated reservation Indians, whom he labeled as "wily," much as he had treated the inmates of his wartime camps. But even though he felt that some of the native people living on reservations were cunning, Myer was not particularly worried that any Indians were planning acts of sabotage. Instead, he contended that the Native American population had to be released from the confines of tribal communities, where their holdings were assured of government protection from white predators. Myer felt that the government's health service, schools, and other privileges did not permit Indians to behave as individuals. Therefore, he believed we would be much better off if only we could be "mainstreamed" and resettled throughout the general United States population.

A mark of progress, Myer contended, would be for us to move off our tribal and ancestral lands to big cities, where we could work "like white people." To enlighten native people in the ways of the white business world, Myer restricted Indians' access to the already limited credit funds supervised by the BIA, while encouraging them to turn to private banks and lenders for loans. By 1951, Myer had focused on what he labeled "withdrawal programming." When various native people complained about some of his decisions, Myer told his staff to proceed with plans even though they might not have Indian cooperation.

Dwight Eisenhower, the nation's thirty-fourth president, succeeded Truman in 1953. This meant there was also a change of command at the BIA—Myer would be gone. Yet this did not seem to make any difference. Political parties proved to be irrelevant. The new procedures for ending the federal trust responsibility to Native Americans became bipartisan. Termination and relocation policies planned during the Truman years were implemented throughout the Eisenhower administration.

Glenn L. Emmons, a banker and rancher from Gallup, New Mexico, followed Myer at the helm of the BIA. Emmons, as the new commissioner of Indian affairs, acted as his predecessor had. He also shared the belief that the best cures to Indian problems such as unemployment lay in the termination of federal responsibilities for all Indians, and the relocation of substantial numbers of rural Native Americans to large industrial cities. Emmons said this would bring relief for the problem of reservation overpopulation, and it would facilitate rapid assimilation for those of us who did not live on reservations.

On August 1, 1953, the Eighty-third Congress adopted House Concurrent Resolution 108. This legislation, which withdrew the federal commitment for Indian people, stated in part, "It is the policy of Congress, as rapidly as possible to make Indians within the United States subject to the same laws and entitled to the same privileges and responsibilities as are applicable to other citizens of the United States, to end their status as wards of the United States, and to grant them all of the rights and prerogatives pertaining to American citizenship."

> *. . . I have no hesitancy whatever in calling it one of the most valuable and salutary Congressional measures we have had in Indian Affairs in many years.*
>
> *Commissioner Glenn L. Emmons*
> *In praise of House Concurrent Resolution No. 108*

Almost immediately, Utah Senator Arthur V. Watkins, who headed the Senate subcommittee on Indian affairs and was a vigorous proponent of the termination movement, secured the passage of additional legislation to use the policy with specific tribes. Watkins labeled termination as "the Indian freedom program." He and his congressional cronies considered the policy a cure-all for the "Indian problem." Immediately, Congress passed bills seeking termination of various tribes. From 1954 until 1962, Congress imposed the policy on sixty-one tribes and native communities, effectively cutting them off from federal services and protections. It was not until 1970 that Congress censured this detestable policy, too late for most tribes that had been terminated. However, some of the tribes, including the Menominees of Wisconsin, were successful in regaining federal recognition in the 1970s.

The passage and implementation of termination bills during the 1950s shocked many Indian leaders who immediately understood that the United States government again intended to destroy tribal governments. Many of them also realized that the government intended to break up native communities and put tribal land on the market by abolishing its status as nontaxable trust land. Native Americans would soon lose control of their land. Termination also meant the imposition of state civil and criminal authority and the loss of state tax exemptions and special tribal programs. Tribes would find it increasingly difficult to remain sovereign.

The United States policy of Indian relocation did not, in fact, get under way until the mid-1950s. Large numbers of Native Americans began to move en masse from reservations and ancestral lands to targeted metropolitan areas in anticipation of receiving job training, education, and a new place to live. By 1955, about three thousand reservation Indians, mostly from the Southwest, were living in housing developments in Chicago. Many other native people had also made the move to low-rent apartments and public housing in other big cities, including Los Angeles, Detroit, St. Louis, and Seattle.

The following year, my own family experienced the pain of United States government relocation. The year was 1956. It was one month before my eleventh birthday. That was when the time came for our Trail of Tears.

We were not forced to do anything, but that did not matter—not to me. Not when the time came for our family to leave Mankiller Flats. Not when we had to say farewell to the land that had been our family's home for generations, and move far away to a strange place. It was then that I came to know in some small way what it was like for our ancestors when the government troops made them give up their houses and property. It was a time for me to be sad.

Our poverty had prompted the move. In 1955, my father first started talking to Bureau of Indian Affairs officials about the various forms of assistance for Cherokees. Relocation was a possibility. I recall hearing at that time that the relocation program was being offered as a wonderful opportunity for Indian families to get great jobs, obtain good educations for their kids and, once and for all, leave poverty behind. In truth, the program gave the government the perfect chance to take Indian people away from their culture and their land. The government methods had softened since the nineteenth century, but the end result was the same for native people. Instead of guns and bayonets, the BIA used promotional brochures showing staged photographs of smiling Indians in "happy homes" in the big cities.

Some of the BIA people came to our house. They talked to my father, explaining the particulars of the program. They said the government wanted to "get out of the Indian business," and one of the ways to do that was by helping individuals and families relocate in larger cities. Dad listened to their pitch. The BIA people came out to our place a couple of times. I think Dad initially was opposed to our leaving Oklahoma and our land. As a boy, he had been taken from his home against his will to attend Sequoyah Boarding School. He did not want to leave his community and people again. But he talked it over with some Cherokee friends, and eventually he decided it would be a good idea to move. He must have honestly believed that in a distant city he could provide a better life for his children, with all the modern amenities.

I never liked the idea of our moving away. I can still remember hiding in a bedroom in our house of rough-hewn lumber, listening while my father, mother, and oldest brother talked in the adjoining room about the benefits and drawbacks of relocating our family. We younger children tried to listen through the door. We were terrified. They were talking about possible destinations. They spoke of places we had barely heard of—Chicago, New York, Detroit, Oakland, and San Francisco. California seemed to be their favorite. Finally my parents chose San Francisco because Grandma Sitton, my mother's mom, had moved to California in 1943. A widow when she left Oklahoma, she had remarried and settled in Riverbank, a community in the farm belt about ninety miles east of San Francisco.

None of us little kids could visualize California. We had been as far as Muskogee to go to the fair on a school field trip. We had been to Stilwell and Tahlequah, but that was about it. My world lay within a ten-mile radius of our family house at Mankiller Flats. Dad and my oldest brother had traveled to Colorado to cut broomcorn. My mother had been to Arkansas to see her sister, but no farther than that. My mother was scared about leaving, and hated the idea of moving to California. She really opposed it at first, more than anyone else. But finally, knowing she would be living close to her mother, she was convinced to go along with my father, believing that life might be better for us all.

Despite my mother's decision, I still was not ready to leave. Neither was my sister Frances. We asked about the possibility of staying behind with friends, but my folks said we had to go with the others. So then we talked about running away to avoid the move, but we never did that. We kept hoping right up until the day our family left that something would happen—some kind of miracle—and we would stay put and not have to go to San Francisco. We did not have very much materially, but we really did not need much either. We had always managed to get by. From my point of view as a child, I could see no value in leaving our home. If life was not idyllic, at least it was familiar.

Finally, the day arrived in October of 1956 for us to depart for California. That day is branded into my memory. There were nine of us kids then. It was before the last two were born. My oldest sister, Frieda, was attending Sequoyah High School and did not move with us. My folks had sold off everything, including the old car. We all piled in a neighbor's car, and he drove us to Stilwell so we could catch the train headed west to California. As we drove away, I looked at our house, the store, my school. I took last looks. I wanted to remember it all. I tried to memorize the shapes of the trees, the calls of animals and birds from the forest. All of us looked out the windows. We did not want to forget anything.

When we got to Stilwell, Dad took us to a restaurant, and we had bowls of chili. We were not a very happy crew—two adults and eight children leaving everything behind for an unknown place. Just getting aboard the train was terrifying for the smaller children. It was a new experience. We settled in all over the place. Some of the children were more comfortable sleeping on the floor, others stayed on the seats or beneath them. My youngest baby sister was marking the back of a seat with a crayon. We were a wild bunch. We must have looked like a darker version of the Joad family from John Steinbeck's novel, *The Grapes of Wrath*.

My mother was still scared about the move. Dad was also worried, but he was excited about the chance for a better life for all of us. As we got settled on the train, he turned to my mother and said, "I don't think I will ever be back until I come home in a coffin." As it turned out, Dad was right. The next time he came home was more than fourteen years later when he was buried in his native land.

As soon as we were all on the train, my sister Frances started to cry. It seemed as if she cried without stopping all the way from Oklahoma to California, although I am sure she did not. The conductor came along and asked her why she was crying. She could not answer him. I cried, too. All of us did. The train headed north. Then we had to change to another train in Kansas City. The trip took two days and two nights. We finally reached California, passing through Riverbank, where my grandmother lived. We kept on going until we stopped in San Francisco.

My folks had vouchers the BIA officials had given them for groceries and rent. But when we arrived, we found that an apartment was not available, so we were put up for two weeks in an old hotel in a notorious district of San Francisco called the Tenderloin. During the night, the neighborhood sparkled with lots of neon lights, flashily dressed prostitutes, and laughter in the streets. But in the morning, we saw broken glass on the streets, people sleeping in doorways, and hard-faced men wandering around. The hotel was not much better than the streets.

The noises of the city, especially at night, were bewildering. We had left behind the sounds of roosters, dogs, coyotes, bobcats, owls, crickets, and other animals moving through the woods. We knew the sounds of nature. Now we heard traffic and other noises that were foreign. The police and ambulance sirens were the worst. That very first night in the big city, we were all huddled under the covers, and we heard sirens outside in the streets. We had never heard sirens before. I thought it was some sort of wild creature screaming. The sirens reminded me of wolves.

My mother seemed sad and confused. When we went to get breakfast for the first time, we were not acquainted with the kinds of food on the menu. Back in Oklahoma, we usually had biscuits and gravy every morning. My mother scanned the menu, and the only item she could find with gravy was a hot roast beef sandwich. So that is what we all ate for breakfast—beef sandwiches with gravy. My dad left the hotel early every morning to see about obtaining a job and a house—all the things the BIA had promised us. While he was gone, we explored around the hotel. Everything was new to us. For instance, we had never seen neon lights before. No one had bothered to even try to prepare us for city living.

*NO DOGS, NO INDIANS.*

*Popular sign in restaurants, 1950s*

One day, my brother Richard and I were standing by the stairway when we saw some people come down the hall and stop. All of a sudden, a box in the wall opened up. People got inside. Then the box closed and the people disappeared! After a minute or two the box suddenly opened again and a new bunch of people came out. Of course, we had never seen an elevator before. All we knew was that we were not about to get inside that box. We used the stairs.

After a couple of weeks, the BIA was finally able to find us a permanent place to live in San Francisco. We left the hotel and moved into a flat in a working-class neighborhood in the old Potrero Hill District. The apartment was quite small and crowded, but it seemed to be the best location for us. The rope factory where my father was able to get a job was not too far away. He was paid the grand sum of forty-eight dollars a week. There was no way, even then, that a man could support a big family in San Francisco on that salary. That is why my big brother Don also worked in the factory making ropes. He and my father walked to the factory every day and worked long, hard hours. Even with both of them bringing home paychecks, we had a tough time, and our family was growing. My brother James Ray was born while we lived in the Potrero Hill District.

Many Hispanics lived in our neighborhood, and we became good friends with a Mexican family next door named Roybal. They took us under their wing, and made our adjustment a pet project. For example, we had never had a telephone before, so the Roybals showed us how one worked. None of us had ever ridden bicycles, so they taught us how to bike and roller-skate.

Still, I did not like living in the city. I especially hated school. The other kids seemed to be way ahead of us in academic and social abilities. We could hold our own in reading because of what our folks had taught us, but the other students were much more advanced at mathematics and language skills. I spent most of the time trying my best to make myself as inconspicuous as possible.

I was placed in the fifth grade, and I immediately noticed that everyone in my class considered me different. When the teacher came to my name during roll call each morning, every single person laughed. Mankiller had not been a strange name back in Adair County, Oklahoma, but it was a very odd name in San Francisco. The other kids also teased me about the way I talked and dressed. It was not that I was so much poorer than the others, but I was definitely from another culture.

My sister Linda and I sat up late every night reading aloud to each other to get rid of our accents. We tried to talk like the other kids at school. We also thought about our old home in Oklahoma. My big sister Frances and I talked about our life back at Mankiller Flats. We tried to remember where a specific tree was located and how everything looked. That helped a little, but I still had many problems trying to make such a major adjustment. We simply were not prepared for the move. As a result, I was never truly comfortable in the schools of California. I had to find comfort and solace elsewhere.

I was not alone in my feelings. I have met many native people from different tribes who were relocated from remote tribal communities. They discovered, as we did, that the "better life" the BIA had promised all of us was, in reality, life in a tough, urban ghetto. Many people were unable to find jobs, and those who did were often offered only marginal employment. I later learned that many native people endured a great deal of poverty, emotional suffering, substance abuse, and poor health because of leaving their homelands, families, and communities. Children seemed to be especially vulnerable without the traditional support of the extended family at home. Urban Indian families banded together, built Indian centers, held picnics and powwows, and tried to form communities in the midst of large urban populations. Yet there was always and forever a persistent longing to go home. "I was as distant from myself as the moon from the earth," is how James Welch, a native writer, described the sense of alienation he experienced in an urban setting.

The termination and relocation policies of the 1950s clearly failed to solve the "Indian problem." Most of the relocates eventually returned to their communities to live and work, some of them trying even harder to strengthen tribal communities and governments. In the end, we survived.

# Colonialism and Disempowerment

## Devon Mihesuah

> We, collectively, find that we are often in the role of the prey, to a predator so-
> ciety, whether for sexual discrimination, exploitation, sterilization, absence of
> control over our bodies, or being the subjects of repressive laws and legislation
> in which we have no voice. This occurs on an individual level, but equally, and
> more significantly on a societal level. It is also critical to point out at this time,
> that most matrilineal societies, societies in which governance and decision
> making are largely controlled by women, have been obliterated from the face
> of the Earth by colonialism, and subsequently industrialism. The only matri-
> lineal societies which exist in the world today are those of Indigenous nations.
> We are the remaining matrilineal societies, yet we also face obliteration.
>
> —Winona LaDuke, environmental and political activist

Colonialism, a powerful force, continues to affect Indigenous females in countless ways. Women faced the intruders who invaded their lands and watched the
devastation of their ways of life. Their populations decreased from smallpox,
measles, whooping cough, alcoholism, and numerous other diseases, in addition to
warfare and fertility decline. Their lifeways eroded; bison and fur-bearing mammals were over-hunted almost to extinction, and many tribes were removed from
their traditional lands and forced to migrate. Tribes were not allowed to perform religious dances. All Natives became dependent upon material items from the Old
World, and although metal implements and firearms made their lives easier in some
ways, Natives had to compete with other Natives in order to keep in good stead
with the Euro-American suppliers of those items. Indigenous women suffered sexual violence and abuse at the hands of Euro-Americans, and those men created
stereotypes and false images of Natives for their own gain. Although today most
diseases are under control and health care is available, many Native women face
poverty, racism, cultural confusion, and psychological problems, often as a result
of being of mixed heritage.

Traditional gender roles eroded from the impact of patriarchal thought, and
those ideologies still affect Native women's positions within their tribes and the

respect given to them by men. As former Cherokee chief Wilma Mankiller observes, "Our tribe and others which were matriarchal have become assimilated and have adopted the cultural value of the larger society, and, in so doing, we've adopted sexism. We're going forward and backward at the same time. As we see a dilution of the original values, we see more sexism. . . . The thinking that people come to in a patriarchal society is crazy."

Most tribes were egalitarian, that is, Native women did have religious, political, and economic power—not more than the men, but at least equal to men's. Women's and men's roles may have been different, but neither was less important than the other. Females toiled hard at their various "jobs," but they received recognition and compensation, often in the form of controlling the economic output; in addition, they were secure knowing they would always have food, shelter, and support from their extended families and clans.

Prior to contact, men and women performed tasks specific to gender. Perhaps men hunted while women farmed, or men performed heavy labor while women cared for the children. Although the duties were different, none was inferior to the others. All work was necessary, and the tribe needed the hands of both men and women. The influence of Europeans' social beliefs, however, changed the way Natives interpreted the world, themselves, and gender roles.

Many traditional tribal religions include a female divine spirit, a cosmology that positioned Native women in prominent and respected positions. Among Navajos, for example, the term "mother" symbolizes the earth, sheep, and corn—the three major elements of Navajo subsistence—and along with Apaches (the Navajos and Apaches were originally one group), the earth mother is also known as "Changing Woman," a self-renewing entity who symbolizes hope. In spring she is young; she bears her harvest in the summer, grows old in the fall, dies in the winter, and is reborn the next season. White Mountain Apache girls participate in the four-day Sunrise Dance the summer after their first menstrual cycle in order to prepare for their adult life. During the dance, the spiritual presence of Changing Woman endows the girls with strength and health. Navajo girls perform a similar puberty ritual (kinaalda) that was given to the tribe by the Holy People, one of whom is Changing Woman.

Cherokee women believe they came from Corn Mother or Selu. For the Tewa Pueblos, the first mothers were known as Blue Corn Woman and White Corn Maiden. The Shawnees' creator is known to them as "our grandmother." Cheyennes believe their food is supplied by a female who takes the shape of an elder. Iroquois came into the world from mud on the back of Grandmother Turtle. Some Apache tribes are descendants of Child of the Water, who was kept safe by his mother, White Painted Woman. For the Sioux, White Buffalo Calf Woman gave them the gift of the pipe and thus the gift of truth. The Okanagan Nation of British Columbia have a legend that states the earth was once a woman. And so on.

Generally speaking, matrilineal clans within societies determined one's political alignment; furthermore, one received his or her social and political rights from clan membership. Because a person's clan was determined by his or her mother, women possessed much political and social power, in addition to a guaranteed network of female relatives who lent support and companionship.

Some scholars have taken this woman-centered society to mean that homosexuality among women in tribes was commonplace. Paul Gunn Allen posits in *The Sacred Hoop* that "Some distinguishing features of a woman-centered social system include free and easy sexuality and wide latitude in personal style. This latitude means that a diversity of people, including gay males and lesbians, are not denied and are in fact likely to be accorded honor." She goes on to write that women spent "long periods together in their homes and lodges while the men stayed in men's houses or in the woods or were out on hunting or fishing expeditions. . . . In such circumstances, lesbianism and homosexuality were probably commonplace." While Allen's statements may be true for some Native groups, there is too little research on the sexuality of the hundreds of tribal groups to make such sweeping assertions. Personally speaking (and that is what Allen is doing), I have never heard anyone knowledgeable about my tribe's (Oklahoma Choctaw) traditional gender relations speak of such commonplace homosexuality, and neither my husband (Comanche) nor anyone in his family has heard of such things among his tribespeople, either. My Navajo, Apache, and Hopi students (many of whom hail from traditional families), in addition to my Mohawk, Salish-Kootenai, Sioux, Cherokee, and Assinaboine friends and colleagues—both heterosexual and homosexual—also find the notion unsettling. Often, discussions about homosexuality (such as this one) reveal that there is a connection between the authors' personal lives and the topic they write about, rendering the issue interesting but subjective.

Like women in other Iroquois tribes, Mohawk women traditionally had prominent places within their group. Katsi Cook, a Mohawk activist, describes traditional Mohawk women as "having relationships, not roles, within the universe and within society. Within these relationships, there were responsibilities that were met as mothers, grandmothers, aunties, and daughters. From the bodies of women flow the relationship of the generations both to society and to the natural world. In this way is the earth, our mother, the old people said. In this way, we as women, are earth." She is also quick to say that despite this female power pervading the tribe, men and women have equal powers: "The men have their council fire and the women have their council fire. This is a reflection of the balance and harmony between the genders."

In traditional matrilineal societies, the husband left his home to live with his wife close to her extended family. Children belonged to their mother's clan and traced their lineage through their mother's line. Girls received education from their mother and aunts. Boys learned to hunt from their mother's brothers. After divorce, the children could stay with their mother, and women retained family property. Females held responsibility for agricultural activities, while men either hunted or also worked the fields. Elder women among the Iroquois Confederacy (a government created by six northeastern tribes—Onondaga, Oneida, Mohawk, Seneca, Cayuga, and Tuscarora), known as Clan Mothers or Matrons, chose the tribal leaders that in turn represented the tribe on the Grand Council. The Clan Mothers also controlled and divided the agricultural goods, declared and halted war, oversaw burials, and affirmed the agreements between the Iroquois Confederacy and the European powers. Among some tribes, such as the Delaware, Cocopah, Quinault, Yurok, Copper Eskimo, and Southeast Salish, both men and women served as religious leaders.

Some tribes did have females who served in authoritative roles, although they did not wield exclusive authoritative powers like European leaders did. During the colonial period, a Narragansett woman chief named Magnus was executed after their defeat, and a "Massachusetts Queen" headed the Massachusetts Confederacy throughout much of the 1600s. Other tribes such as the Cherokee, Cheyenne, Esophus, Natchez, Nisenan, Osage, Sakonnet, Sinkaietk, Tsimshian, Wampanoag, and Winnebago (Ho Chunk) all reportedly had females as social and/or political leaders at some point.

In some societies, such as many Plains tribes, men were the providers and fighters, and families were centered around men's activity, thereby isolating women from their extended families. Men were the only voices heard in council, and men controlled all aspects of war. Women dealt with domestic duties, but because women were dependent on men for sustenance, Plains men often stood as authority figures. The Plains tribes' cosmology, however, features female figures in their religions (such as the White Buffalo Calf Woman who brings to the Lakotas the Calf Pipe, which, along with the Seven Sacred Rites, comes to their aid in times of hardship), and it is argued that many of these tribes were egalitarian. Ojibwes, Arapahos, Gros Ventres, Winnebagos (Ho Chunks), and Menominees are traditionally male-centered, yet women had considerable freedom socially. Some were medicine women. Female Piegans, Cheyennes, Crows, Kootenais, Modocs, Ojibwes, and Apaches reportedly fought in battle, often beside their husbands or in their place if they died. Other tribes, such as the Nachez and Yuchi, were divided into matrilineal clans, but their organization appears to have been patriarchal.

How much prestige and power women actually held will never be known. Most observations of Indian women in traditional societies were written by Euro-American men, who judged them by the same standards that they judged women of their own societies. Many non-Natives misunderstood tribal kinship systems, gender roles, and tribal spiritual and social values. Their observations also reflected their biases and, perhaps, their desire to manipulate reality to accommodate their expectation that Native women were held in lesser regard in their tribal societies because women were subservient to men in European societies. As Paula Gunn Allen has stated, this lack of proper documentation, including ignoring women's prominent roles altogether, "reinforces patriarchal socialization among all Americans."

For example, almost all the historical and cultural studies of the Choctaws examine only the male tribal members. Choctaw women are rarely mentioned, not even the wives of prominent tribal leaders. When discussed, their roles as

Choctaws are described by non-Native men who evaluate women's roles by their own European, male-oriented standards. Some early commentaries portray Choctaw women as useful tribal members because they prepare food or bear children, but they are also characterized as subservient drudges with no economic, political, or social influence on the tribe.

These viewpoints are incorrect. In the pre-contact period Choctaws were successful agriculturists; the women tilled soil, sowed seed, and harvested crops. Men hunted deer and turkeys and fished the numerous Mississippi and Alabama waterways, while women dressed and prepared the game. In addition, women made clothes, reared children, and held positions of religious importance. Descent was matrilineal, and women retained control over tribal property.

Today, because of movies and television that distort tribal reality, the general public seems to be aware only of prominent Native men. For example, by the mid- to late 1800s (a popular time period for television and movie Westerns), the East was settled and whites continued to move west in search of wealth, land, social prominence, fame, and adventure. Many tribes were surrounded by whites, and they reacted to the encroachments onto their lands in a variety of ways: warfare, negotiation, surrender, migration. The Natives normally portrayed are men who either tried to fight against Americans (e.g., Crazy Horse, Geronimo, Quanah Parker, Manuelito, Captain Jack, Wild Cat, Osceola), tried to lead their people to safe havens (Chief Joseph, Dull Knife), attempted to live peacefully according to treaty terms (Black Kettle), or tried revitalization dances (Big Foot). The Native women the public remains aware of are Sacajawea and Pocahontas.

Other Native women, however, showed intellect and determination in dealing with whites, but little is heard about them except in scholarly literature, which until recently often misinterpreted their actions. Quite often, women such as Paiute Sarah Winnemucca and the LaFlesche sisters of the Omaha tribe had to "dress the part," that is, look like a Native to get attention. These women had to be well versed in the ways of white society before they gained Americans' respect and certainly before whites bothered to listen to them. Sarah Winnemucca (c. 1844–91) dressed as an "Indian Princess" to lecture to white Americans about the injustices against her tribe, including their removal from Nevada to Oregon and Washington. She also founded a school for Indians with her own funds and donations.

The daughter of a Mohawk chief and an English woman, Emily Pauline Johnson (1861–1913), also known as Tekahionwake, was thoroughly bicultural and a prominent figure in Canadian and Native historical literature. She was strongly influenced by Shakespeare, Byron, and theatrical performance, and after attending Central Collegiate School, Johnson began writing poetry. Her first collection, *The White Wampum* (1895), was published by Bodley Head Press in London, and her second set of poems was published in 1903 by a Toronto publishing house. She continued to write stories that featured strong Native women as the protagonists, and she toured throughout Canada as the "Mohawk Princess," enacting her stories through theatrical performances. Some of her later works were *The Legends of Vancouver* (1911), *The Moccasin Maker* (1913), and *The Shagganappi* (1913).

The LaFlesche sisters, Rosalie Farley LaFlesche (1861–1900), Susan Picotte LaFlesche (1865–1915), Marguerite LaFlesche Picotte Diddock (1862–1945), and Suzette Tibbles LaFlesche (1854–1903), were the daughters of Omaha leader Joseph LaFlesche (also known as Insta Maza, or Iron Eye), a mixed-heritage French-Ponca who served as chief of the tribe from 1853 to 1866. Their mother, Mary Gale (Hinnuagsnun, or One Woman), was mixed white and Omaha. Susan, Marguerite, and Suzette were educated in white schools such as the Elizabeth Institute for Young Ladies in New Jersey and the Hampton Normal and Agricultural Institute in Virginia. Susan was the first Native woman to receive her medical degree (the second was Belle Cobb, a Cherokee woman discussed in chapter 7), graduating in 1889 from the Woman's Medical College in Philadelphia. Iron Eye was a proponent of assimilation and pushed to have tribal children educated. Susan continued her father's quest to have Omahas adopt white ways. Although she was not well versed in the culture of the Omahas, she nevertheless dressed in traditional Omaha clothing while traveling the country to speak to non-Natives about tribal issues and treaty rights. Suzette also served her people by lecturing extensively to white audiences about broken treaties, tribal cultural deterioration, and the loss of tribal lands. Interestingly, she also believed in assimilation. Rosalie, on the other hand, pushed for self-government and self-sufficiency. Marguerite believed in education as a means of making the tribe self-sufficient.

The mixed-heritage Christal Quintasket, more commonly known as Mourning Dove (1888–1936), was born in Idaho to a Okanogan father and a Colville mother. Mourning Dove received education in a few government Indian schools. After a 1914 meeting with *American Anthropologist* editor Lucullus V. McWhorter, who became her friend, advisor, and collaborator, she published, most notably, *Co-Ge-We-A, the Half-Blood: A Depiction of the Great Montana Cattle Range* (1927) and *Coyote Stories* (1933). Mourning Dove is known for her desire to preserve her cultural heritages and to retain tribal "secrets" while at the same time creating powerful fiction steeped in reality.

Since contact with Europeans, Native religions have been termed "uncivilized," "barbaric," and "pagan." Foreigners certainly did not understand tribal cultures, much less respect the position women held within their tribal structures. European colonists were influenced by Renaissance ideologies, notably the concept of the "Great Chain of Being," that everything in the universe should be in order (i.e., that God is at the top of the hierarchy, with Hell and chaos at the bottom, or, in politics, the king is at the top and peasants are at the bottom). Natives needed to be placed within the order, and generally they were seen as inferior and therefore positioned at a low rung on the ladder of civilization. As non-Christians (who were lumped into one cultural category instead of being seen as diverse, complex groups), Natives were then dealt with in several ways: they were "civilized" via Christianity, education, farming, allotment, and termination; because many Euro-

Americans believed Natives to be hopelessly "uncivilized," they pushed for policies of destruction and justified brutality by rationalizing it as "God's will" that tribes become extinct so American civilization could spread across the continent; and tribes were moved and/or confined to reservations out of the way of "progress." Among those who preferred to try and "civilize the savages" were Euro-American missionaries, who pressured Natives to convert to Christianity, which, among other things, included them accepting the concept of the male God and thus reinforcing the superiority of males. Females were (and in many Christian traditions still are) expected to submit to the authority and will of men.

Some Natives complied and attempted to acculturate to the ways of white society. Others, however, staunchly resisted and continued with their own beliefs and rituals. Missionaries brought with them the policy of discipline to be used against transgressors, and in the Spanish Southwest, Pueblo medicine men were flogged, burned, or hung for leading religious ceremonies, resulting in the Pueblo Revolt of 1680. Despite non-Natives' lack of appreciation of tribal religious beliefs and their attempts to eradicate them, Natives have continued to practice their beliefs and ceremonies. Although many Natives resisted the lure of converting to Christianity, others were intrigued with the missionaries' promises. Natives had witnessed the destruction of their tribes and loved ones, the loss of their homelands, and the results of alcoholism. Why, they wondered, should they not adopt the ways of the conquerors and, they hoped, avoid these problems? Maybe Christianity was a way to cope with the destruction of their peoples by disease and white intruders. Some Natives were attracted to the ritual of the Catholic church, especially because the beads, incense, and ceremony reminded them of their tribal rituals. Others, like many Pueblos, knew that a strategy for survival was to at least claim they wanted to convert. Regardless of who converted and why, missionaries did manage to instill foreign values into tribes, affecting even those who wanted nothing to do with what Christians had to offer.

Natives on the verge of utter despair because of loss of land, culture, and loved ones turned to the numerous revitalization movements led by prophets such as Wangomen, Handsome Lake, Tenskwatawah, Kenekuk, and Smoholla in hopes that the prophets' promises were true and God would restore the land and peoples as they had existed prior to contact. In 1883 Secretary of the Interior Henry M. Teller introduced the series of laws known as the Indian Religious Crimes Code, which were intended to disallow any Native ceremonies, including dancing, feasts, and giveaways in addition to any "heathenish" practices performed by spiritual leaders, with transgressors punished by imprisonment. Although the laws were not lifted until 1933, Natives continued to hold ceremonial dances, including the "pagan" Sun and Ghost Dances.

Tribes still practice old dances and ceremonies, although they have been forced to alter portions of the rituals. For example, because of the threat of AIDS, at some sun dances, instead of using a communal knife or eagle talon, dancers are required to bring their own scalpels, and dancers are not pierced as deeply as they were traditionally because tearing a large muscle like the pectoral would prevent them from attending work. In the Native American Church, the dwindling supply of peyote causes some ceremonial leaders not to use as much or to be more selective in who gets to use it. There are other examples, of course, but the point is that while the ceremonies may be altered, the symbolism usually remains.

After contact, missionaries seemed to be almost everywhere. Because they had ingratiated themselves into many tribes, tribespeople began to seek the counsel of the missionaries instead of their traditional tribal religious leaders, many of whom were women. By the 1830s, for example, many Cherokees were Christians and began ignoring their *adaehis* (medicine people) when in need of medical attention. Tribal women and men in prominent religious positions quickly became less respected.

Some men among Plains tribes and tribes on the Plateau had more than one wife. With the introduction of European material goods, men could range longer distances to hunt and raid. They killed more animals than before and, because hides had to be tanned and the animals dressed, having more than one spouse alleviated the work burden and helped create more prestige for the male. As they did with other tribes, missionaries objected to the practice of polygamy and pressured Plateau tribes, for example, to change the family social units by encouraging tribespeople to build small homes that could accommodate only the basic nuclear family instead of the traditional longhouse that sheltered extended families.

Because of religious influences and intermarriage with whites, kinship systems among tribes were disrupted. Generally speaking, the status of women diminished as male power increased. For example, by 1808 many white men had intermarried with Cherokee women, and many Cherokees had adopted Christianity. In an effective attempt to undermine the female-dominated clan system, a Council of Headmen declared that the patriarchal family was the norm, not the traditional matriarchal model in which children belonged to their mother's clan and property belonged to the woman. A police force was organized to enforce a new law that stated children were heirs not only to their father's property but to the widow's share as well. Two years later, the council abolished the female-ruled "blood vengeance" and replaced it with the tribal courts. Additionally, a woman who married a white man immediately lost all rights to her land. By the 1830s a dramatic increase in wife abuse was reported. Among Cherokees and Creeks, at least, overuse of alcohol caused men to behave irrationally, which disrupted the male-female balance of respect. Despite laws that declared men the property owners, they still lost their tribal lands to outsiders, and they took their frustrations out on their wives, leading to tribal-wide chaos.

This change from an egalitarian tradition brought numerous problems for Native women. Once men took over as heads of family, women moved to their husband's residence and often lost their relatives' immediate support. A woman's security in all facets of tribal life was diminished. She became less important economically, and when she and her husband divorced the woman lost all her assets.

Men were instated as heads of their families, and children inherited their father's estate.

Among Iroquois tribes, in which women's roles were similar to those of women in the Cherokee tribe, trade with whites increased, which temporarily raised women's status because of their ability to create the desired trade items. Women continued to control the output of corn at least until the early 1800s, when Canadian and American powers attempted to persuade Indian men to farm, thus displacing the women in the fields. Women lost political power after white Europeans convinced Indian men not to listen to females' advice, a move that shifted women into less pivotal positions. By the early nineteenth century the matron-appointed leader system among the Iroquois tribes was gone, replaced with a system of elected representatives—and only men's votes counted.

Unlike women from many of the southern tribes, some Iroquois women did not loose all power within the various tribal spheres; rather, their roles were altered, still allowing them a measure of equality within the tribe. In her 1991 essay "Rise or Fall of Iroquois Women," Nancy Shoemaker concludes that Seneca women traditionally had great influence within the tribe, offering their choices of men for political leadership roles, serving as advisors to the political headmen, and controlling much of the economic production and distribution. Unlike in other tribes that attempted to completely subsume women within the tribes, after contact the Seneca men "defended women's rights as part of the larger effort for community survival."

Like the Cherokees, the Senecas adopted a written constitution. But at least the Senecas allowed the Clan Mothers the right to vote on land issues. Unlike the Cherokees, who disenfranchised women, Seneca women retained their rights in property and divorce settlements. One's tribal membership is still determined through matrilineal heritage (by virtue of one's mother being a tribal member). Shoemaker cautions, however, that just because Seneca women appeared to have numerous powers within the tribe does not mean they were "better off" than white women in regard to women's rights. The high marriage and illegitimacy rates "could support contrary arguments of women's social dependence or independence."

Women of some tribes, like the Muscogees, initially gained status from marrying white men. Women like Mary Musgrove Matthews Bosomworth (also known as Coosaponokeesa) aided their white husbands' efforts to become successful businessmen or traders by serving as interpreters, culture "coaches," and co-partners in business and thus gained financial status and retained security for themselves.

By the 1830s enough time had passed and enough hardships had been endured by white Americans for them to believe that democracy and the American form of government were successful. Because the country was predominately Protestant, many Americans believed that the combination of Protestantism and democracy would serve as the best hope for the world. In addition, the idea of "Manifest Destiny," that Americans were God's chosen people, swept not just through the political system but also through the country. Many Americans believed they could—and should—attempt to absorb the entire land area from coast to coast, although some thought America should expand from pole to pole. This belief in Manifest Destiny was a feeling of superiority, and Indians felt the brunt of Americans' pride and determination.

These ideas about Natives being inferior were especially popular in the early 1800s, when the "scientific" idea of "inherent racial inferiority" gained support. Charles Caldwell, a physician, in *Thoughts on the Original Unity of the Human Race* (1830), presented his theory that there were four distinct human species: Caucasian, African, Indian, and Mongolian. Each possessed differing abilities and intellects, with the Caucasian species being superior to the others. He also attributed any successes among Natives to their intermarriage with Caucasians. Nine years later, Samuel George Morton published *Crania Americana,* a highly influential work that discussed his belief that differences between the races resulted from biology, not environment. Further, Morton asserted that separate creations had taken place for each race in different parts of the world, basing his theory that the Caucasian race was superior on extensive crania studies that included measuring the amount of mustard seeds that could fit into a variety of skulls: the one that held the most had the most room for brains and therefore intelligence. Between 1844 and 1857 Southern surgeon Josiah C. Nott wrote profusely, if not rationally, about the superiority of the Caucasian race. He also was convinced that any achievements made by the Southeastern tribes were solely because of their intermingling with whites.

Not all Natives were aware of these social and "scientific" ideologies, but some, like Cherokees who were educated by teachers from New England schools such as Yale, were. Many Natives, therefore, believed that one way to survive was to imitate their oppressors.

The influence of "scientists" in addition to the ideologies and policies of missionaries created factionalism within tribes, between those who cling to tradition and those who see change as the route to survival, either tribal, familial, or personal. Intratribal factionalism might also be termed "culturalism," a form of oppression that dovetails with racism. Natives in tribal power positions, political, economic, or social, often use expressions of culturalism against those who do not subscribe to their views. "Colorism," the intragroup stratification often associated with blacks, is also an ideology prevalent among tribes. As Potawatomie scholar Terry Wilson discusses in his essay "Blood Quantum: Native American Mixed Bloods," people who identify themselves as Native but do not look phenotypically Native are seen with suspicion, especially by Natives with darker skin.

Among Lakotas, those who do not live on the reservation or do not speak the language do not enjoy the "cultural entirety of being Lakota." A historic example is writer and activist Gertrude Simmons Bonnin (1876–1938), also known as Zitkala-Ša, a Yankton Sioux. Bonnin acquired an education at Earlham College in Indiana and the New England Conservatory of Music in Boston, taught at Carlisle, published stories in prestigious publications such as *Atlantic Monthly* and *Harper's,* and became involved with the American Indian Defense Association, the Indian Rights Association, and the National Congress of American Indians. Despite her strong concerns for her people's welfare and constant travel to educate white America about Natives' problems, she did not live among her tribe, failed to retain strong kinship ties, and therefore lost status among her people.

"Class" is one way to differentiate among Natives, but class does not always refer to money issues. Among Indian people it can also refer to levels of cultural knowledge and blood quantum. Marxist feminists are partially correct in asserting that economics account for Natives women's inferior status. And so are socialist feminists' assertions that a low economic position combined with gender also explains some Native women's status. However, while Native women may be oppressed because of their lesser economic status, capitalism and gender are not the only forces of oppression against them. Native women were gender oppressed (most notably after contact with Euro-Americans) and, like other women of color, they also are subjugated because of their race. Native women, however, because of their varied economic situations, social values, appearances, and gender roles, are oppressed by men and women—both non-Natives and, interestingly enough, other Natives (see chapter 7 for examples among the Cherokees).

Among tribes around the border of the United States and Canada, the demand for beaver pelts especially emphasized the men's roles and lessened women's status. Women also were seen as commodities, valued for their abilities to hunt, trap, skin, and survive in harsh weather and to assist in bringing positive relations between cultures. Jennifer S. H. Brown and Sylvia Van Kirk have shown that northern Native women were adept at trapping, skinning, and curing hides, yet kinship systems unraveled. Like Muscogee women in the Southeast, who played an important role in the deerskin trade and spent long hours at work away from their clan lands, females in the north became dependent on men for material goods essential for survival.

Van Kirk discusses how Cree, Ojibwe, and Chipewyan women contributed to the success of fur trade rivals the Hudson's Bay Company and the North West Company. Natives recognized the marriage of their women to European men as social and economic alliances: traders were given rights to the women, and Natives received rights to the fur trade posts. The trader benefited from the union because his wife was usually adept at canoeing and trapping in addition to knowing how to cook, sew, and make shoes. Despite the women's contributions to their husbands' success, by the early 1800s when the fur-bearing mammals were almost depleted, Native women were not so much in demand as wives. Some white men remained faithful to their Indian wives, and many European men continued to marry Native women into the middle of the century, but many other Native women were abandoned and abused when white women arrived in North America. The mixed-blood female offspring were often sent to boarding schools to learn the ways of white society, resulting in further loss of tribal members and cultural knowledge.

To the south, white men who married into the Cherokee tribe usually demanded that their families adhere to the man's values, which included a market economy dominated by property-owning males. Women of Plains tribes fared the worst. They were basically slaves for a market to which they had no access. Men controlled almost every aspect of tribal life, and women themselves became commodities in the exchanges between their fathers and their new husbands.

The Navajo tribe is traditionally egalitarian, with sheep and wool a focal point of its economy. Both men and women cared for sheep, and along with the matrilocal residence pattern, matrilineal structure of lineage, and prominent female figure in Navajo religious beliefs, women were economically and socially secure. With the imposition of federal mandates to curtail overgrazing of lands by sheep in the 1930s, the amount of wool produced was reduced, thereby reducing women's work as rug weavers. Additionally, demand for rugs lessened because consumers bought cheaper imitations. Women did not ordinarily engage in wage work, while men already worked in construction, mines, and fields and on railroads. Wage work for men increased, wages for women decreased, and men then became the primary earners. Women, especially unmarried and older females, fell victim to financial insecurity, and men often emerged as the authoritative figures in the household because they controlled finances.

Native women have lost more than just social status and political prestige. Florida Seminole and Santo Domingo women who marry white men are disallowed from living on the reservation; however, if a Native man marries a white women, he and his family are permitted to live on the reservation. The Santa Clara Pueblos have a similar law. In 1978 the Supreme Court ruled that it would allow the Santa Clara Tribe to decide on the tribe's rule that states that if a tribal woman marries outside the tribe, the children of that union are not considered full tribal members (they cannot vote or inherit their rights to communal lands); however, if a tribal man marries outside the tribe, the children could be full tribal members. The Indian act in Canada, which stipulated that Native women lose Indian status upon marrying non-Indian men even though the reverse is not true for Native men and Indian status is given to non-Indian women who marry Native men, was not overturned until 1981, in *Sandra Lovelace v. Canada.*

Legal scholar and feminist Catharine A. MacKinnon considers this case and Santa Clara tribal ideology in her essay "Whose Culture? A Case Note on *Martinez v. Santa Clara Pueblo*" and asks the provocative question "Is male supremacy sacred because it has become a tribal tradition?" Roxanne Swentzell, a Santa Clara Pueblo artist, has remarked about her tribe that "Most of the people here at Santa Clara don't have anything to do with the land, with the place, anymore. They go off to work from eight to five just like everybody else and they want their new car and their TV and their VCR. What they really want is to be middle-class white Americans." If she is accurate, then one might consider that the tribe has indeed adopted patriarchal thought.

Men of God, along with the federal government, also established schools throughout Indian country in an attempt to "save souls" and to teach Natives to become civilized. The problems created for Natives by these schools have been well documented. Since the 1600s non-Natives have attempted to educate Indigenes in the ways of Euro-American society. Missionary and secular schools, which aimed to "kill the Indian in order to save the man," were brutal to Native children. In the mid-1880s Native youths were forced to leave their homes and live in boarding schools far from their families. Taught by white teachers and missionaries who assumed they knew what was best for Native children even though they knew nothing about tribal cultures, Native children were forced to wear white clothing, cut their hair, and give up their religious paraphernalia. Students were not allowed to speak their native languages and, as one boarding school alumni comments in the movie *In the White Man's Image,* "My language was beaten out of me." Students were repeatedly told that because they were Natives, they were inferior. The result was depression, confusion, and loss of culture. Some students committed suicide; others died of loneliness. The irony is that after they were educated they were not accepted into white society, and many could not fit into their tribe's society again either.

By 1900 the government maintained at least twenty thousand students in 148 boarding schools and 225 day schools, which were located closer to tribes. The Meriam Report, issued in 1928, revealed that children at the boarding schools faced health problems, poor living conditions, inadequate diets, and extreme punishments, in addition to untrained teachers and impractical curricula that did not pertain to students' needs. Importantly, the Natives whom reformers had hoped to make over in the white man's image clung tenaciously to their identities and cultures. With the passage of the Indian Reorganization Act in 1934, the government focused on tribal self-determination rather than acculturation, and community schools were established in order to help Natives help themselves. This ideology was reversed in the 1950s with the establishment of the government's policy of terminating the tribes' relationships with the federal government. Bureau of Indian Affairs schools under the government's control again adopted the policy of assimilation. Although in the 1960s the tide turned again in favor of Indian self-determination and Natives started to become more active in education affairs, not all schools are adequate today.

Problems at Indian schools are not limited to the past. Numerous schools have inadequate texts and teachers, deteriorating buildings, poorly managed lands, and a legacy of student molestation. In 1984 the Phoenix Indian School in Arizona, for example, was found to use Mace, straightjackets, and shackles as disciplinary tools.

Modern Indigenous mothers still must carefully review their children's textbooks for stereotypical images of Natives, and they also must be diligent about their children's classrooms. Too often kinder-garten teachers will decorate their classrooms with alphabet letters that include images of an animal or object whose name begins with that letter. Even "enlightened" teachers will use the image of an Indian to go with the letter *I* and will use animals dressed in feathers, war paint, and leather to depict other letters. Prior to Thanksgiving, parents must be alert to the probability that teachers will have their students dress as Pilgrims and Indians, a misleading image that gives the impression Indians and colonists always "lived in harmony."

## Abuse and Violence

Various studies have revealed that during the 1970s between 25 and 50 percent of Indigenous women between the ages of fifteen and forty-four were sterilized. These women were not told they were signing consent forms, the surgeon did not wait the requisite seventy-two hours after the woman signed the consent forms before performing the procedure, or the women were not informed what sterilization meant or about the risks of the procedure. Some gave their consent when heavily sedated during another surgical procedure, and some signed forms they did not understand because they did not speak English or because the forms used medical jargon that was difficult for them to read. As a result of being sterilized, many women suffered depression, guilt, and shame and turned to substance abuse. Many divorced or encountered marital problems, and some became overly fearful of losing the children they did have.

Violence against Native women is not committed only by non-Natives. Across the country Native women complain of misogynist behavior by Native men that includes verbal and physical abuse. In her 1992 book, *Death and Violence on the Reservation,* Ronet Bachman wrote that, of 92 women questioned at two women's shelters on two different reservations, 79 percent had been sexually abused by their husbands or boyfriends, 75 percent said that abuser was under the influence of drugs or alcohol at the time the abuse occurred, and 35 percent had received physical injuries from the assault. In another study conducted in 1992, 3,421 abused Navajo women were interviewed, and 52.5 percent cited at least one incidence of domestic abuse by a male. There are only two shelters on the Navajo reservation, the Tohdenasshai Shelter Home in Kayenta and the Native American Family Violence Prevention Project in Shiprock; three "safe houses" exist in three other cities. The reservation has also built two facilities in Chinle to deal with youth problems, but neither is open because of intratribal disputes. According to one study, in New Mexico there is a higher rate of domestic violence–related homicide among Native women than in any other group in the state, and the violence is usually instigated by Native men under the influence of drugs or alcohol.

Perhaps it is frustration and confusion over the loss of traditional gender roles and the adoption of white society's values that has contributed to spousal abuse and tension between the sexes among Natives today. For example, bison was a main source of food for many of the Plains tribes and tribes peripheral to the Plains. With the near extermination of the buffalo during the late 1800s came the disintegration of many tribes' cultures, including the distortion of gender roles. Males, who were the hunters, no longer had bison to hunt and, according to many Natives, their frustration has led to alcoholism, spousal abuse, and "woman hating."

On the Navajo reservation, where violence and gang activity have increased in recent years, it is believed that factors such as the breakup of multigenerational families, the loss of elders and the elders' inability to communicate with youngsters, the "code of silence" among family members that keeps guilty parties from being punished, fewer ties to the land now that many Navajos move to cities to seek employment, and the feeling among young Navajos that their education is of no use on the reservation, contribute to apathy, depression, and boredom.

As Lakota Mary Crow Dog (now Brave Bird) observed about the bad behavior on her reservation: "There is nothing for the young people when they grow up. There is a lot of alcohol. There is a lot of drugs, a lot of young people dying. Like some of those gang members, I talk with them. If you can find unity, you know, even with their own leadership, if you form unity, you can make a strong movement within yourself. Because they are all, you know, fighting over drugs, over women, or whatever. . . . There is nothing in the tribe." Other factors that spur spousal abuse and violence against fellow tribal members include personality disorders and insecurities, unemployment (which is rampant among reservation Natives), lack of formal education and knowledge of tribal culture, drinking, drug abuse, and childhood sexual abuse.

One major cause of the abuse of others (and of the self, for that matter) is what many black scholars refer to as "self-hatred," although other scholars argue that there is no such thing. Nevertheless, as with blacks, numerous Natives point out how many Natives lash out at each other because of insecurity and the desire to have what others possess. Lee Maracle, for example, a member of the Stoh:ilo Nation, writes in *I Am Woman: A Native Perspective on Sociology and Feminism,* "I am so weary of men who, guilt ridden by their own treachery, attack me and accuse me of the very things they are bogged down with." She also writes, in her poem "On Native Resistence":

> In the Third World, Natives resist oppression.
> In America, the Natives resist each other.
> Our loyalty consists of our own self-
> and mutual contempt.

Jimmie Durham, a self-identified Cherokee, writes in "Those Dead Guys for a Hundred Years," "We hate ourselves and each other . . . and now there we all are, out there trying to impress the white folks with one thing or the other. . . . Our regular folks are usually drunk or bad-mouthing their neighbors."

Maracle and Durham state what many Natives think but do not say out loud: Native people do verbally and physically abuse each other—at home, in the academy, and in literature. A common joke among people of color is the "crab joke," in which an enterprising crab manages to make it to the top of the fisherman's bucket. Just as she is about to escape (read: succeed), the other crabs grab her legs and pull her back into the bucket. The metaphor is that when a Native person (or black or Chicana or member of other groups who have adopted this story) succeeds, the other crabs become angry and jealous and try everything they can to keep her from doing so. Natives usually laugh at the joke because they understand the concept. As a Native woman commented to me several years ago, "The most supportive people for me in the university have been Indian women. But at the same time, other Indian women have been the most vicious because of their jealousy and insecurity. Nobody can destroy a person like an Indian woman."

In a competitive society (a reflection of centuries ago when tribes competed for the favors and material goods of the colonial powers), Native men and women often find themselves striving for the same job. In academia, they often are in positions where they evaluate each other's performance, and often they do so with unjustifiable negativity. How, for example, should we deal with the bright, young (and well-published) Native female professor who recently said to me in private that "I can't trust anybody," because she knows from painful experience that trusted male or female Native allies are hard to come by? Other women of color feel the same pain. Gloria Anzaldúa, in *Borderlands/La Frontera: The New Mestiza*, writes about how those who have been "pounced on" may also have pounced on others, and she asserts that all of us need to be accountable for our behaviors, responsibilities, and privileging.

## Stereotypes and Images of Indian Women

Changes in tribal roles, violence, and psychological conflicts are not the only problems Native women faced in the past or in the present. Although all Natives suffer from stereotypes, Native women were and are especially romanticized and abused.

Upon arriving in the New World, the newcomers began speculating on the flora, fauna, and peoples they encountered. They also were entranced with what they perceived as a bountiful land filled with interesting peoples (whom they believed to be inferior). As opposed to portraits of European women, who were shown fully clothed and demure, paintings of the New World included depictions of Native women as symbols of savage sexuality in the wilderness: topless and voluptuous, often carrying a spear, adorned with feathers and tobacco leaves, and surrounded by animals.

Europeans were fascinated with Native women's lack of clothing, and this cultural difference caused misunderstandings about sexuality. Native women were viewed as decadent and sexual—darkskinned whores—while the lighter-skinned, clothed European women were the more "pure," respectable females. Native women were seen as sexual beings free for the taking, and indeed, sexual violence against Native women was common after invasion.

Christianity played a large role in ideas about skin color. Christians' religious beliefs included ideas about dark skin being associated with evil and dark souls, so the Jewish Christ has been depicted in paintings as light-skinned, with blue eyes. In the pre–Civil War South, slavery proponents justified the enslavement of African

Americans by arguing that dark skin was God's punishment for blacks. Indeed, white skin has been desirable among individuals of many cultures around the world during many time periods. In Europe during the Middle Ages and Renaissance, artists depicted their subjects with pale complexions. Women and men powdered their faces and hair and whitened their skin with lemon juice, mercury, and later, arsenic in order to achieve a well-to-do pallid look, and Elizabeth of England painted blue veins on her forehead.

Mormons assert that American Indigenes are descended from Lehi, an individual who allegedly departed Jerusalem in 600 B.C. and came to the Americas and whose children divided into two warring groups here in the New World: the light-skinned Nephites and the evil, dark-skinned Lamanites. The Book of Mormon states that Lamanites are the ancestors of modern Natives and that once those Lamanites convert to Mormonism they will somehow change into "white and de-lightsome" peoples, a claim that has proven a powerful incentive for Natives to join the church. This story also was the rationale for taking Native children from their homes and placing them with Mormon families to be raised as Mormons.

Native women are not the only victims of the "white is right" belief. The award-winning Caribbean poet and novelist Edwidge Danticat states that during her adolescence she was admonished by her uncle to stay out of the sun. "The sun will spoil you," he told her, out of concern not for her health but for her social status. All females are bombarded with images of white beauty everywhere they go—at grocery checkout stands, on television, and in magazines. Many feel that looking white means acceptance by the dominant society, so they submit to dyeing their hair, perming their straight hair into tight ringlets or straightening their "too curly" hair, and wearing the latest clothing styles. In 1990, 20 percent of patients seeking cosmetic surgery were people of color (Jews and blacks altering their noses, Asian women lifting the epicanthic fold, blacks submitting to skin lightening and lip shaving, for example), whereas in 1980 it was less than 2 percent (whether this in-crease is because of increased ability to pay for such surgeries is unknown). Al-though there has been a slight increase in the number of ethnic models on fashion magazine covers, the vast majority of cosmetic, shampoo, and clothing commer-cials in magazines and television and on billboards feature Caucasian women as the ideal. The "ethnic" Barbie dolls may have varying skin tones and wardrobes, but they also have Caucasian features. The recent animated movie *Pocahontas* (1995) set yet another standard difficult for Native women to adhere to: the Native woman as bombshell. Obviously, Native women do not dress like Disney's Pocahontas, nor are the vast majority of Native women built like the animated version (she was, in fact the composite of several models).

A multi-million-dollar enterprise known as "Indian Maiden Art" (marketed on the Web auction site E-Bay, for one place) usually depicts wildly beautiful women with "impossible hair" (that is, hair that is long, luxurious, and full of unnatural body), with feathers, in various stages of undress (wearing fur and hides, mainly), and with an animal as her object of focus (wolves, mainly, but sometimes owls, which are viewed as omens of bad luck and death to some tribes). The women's features, however, are always Caucasian. In a course I teach on American Indian women, I show slides of paintings of Indian Maiden Art, and students always comment that the subjects look like white women with brown skin and heavy eye make-up.

Some Native women strategize in order to obtain lighter skin coloring, presumably to distance themselves from blacks or from their own African American blood. At a powwow outside of Lawton, Oklahoma, about ten years ago an elderly Muscogee woman asked me to retrieve her umbrella from her truck's cab, saying, "Get me my umbrella, Hon, otherwise I'll be lookin' like a nigger by supper." Worrying about the same thing over a hundred years ago, students at the Cherokee Female Seminary were never without their parasols and wide-brimmed hats (see chapter 7).

On the other hand, many multi-heritage Indians may be comparatively dark in color but nevertheless lay in the sun to darken their skin in order to be accepted by their own people. Despite her Native appearance (to most non-Natives, at least), Mary Brave Bird recalled that in her youth she "waited for the summer, for the prairie sun, the Badlands sun, to tan me and make me into a real skin."

Some Native females have felt justifiably confused about what they do look like to other people. When Leslie Marmon Silko was a girl, tourists visiting Laguna wanted pictures of her friends and not of her, because she did not look Native enough. Ironically, years later she was detained at the U.S.-Mexico border because in the eyes of the border patrol she appeared dark like some Mexicans.